## EARLY CHILDHOOD EDUCATION SERIES

**Leslie R. Williams, Editor    Millie Almy, Senior Advisor**

ADVISORY BOARD: Barbara T. Bowman, Harriet K. Cuffaro, Stephanie Feeney, Doris Pronin Fromberg, Celia Genishi, Stacie G. Goffin, Dominic F. Gullo, Alice Sterling Honig, Elizabeth Jones, Gwen Morgan, David Weikart

# The Early Childhood Curriculum

## CURRENT FINDINGS IN THEORY AND PRACTICE

*THIRD EDITION*

## Edited by Carol Seefeldt

Teachers College Press
Teachers College, Columbia University
New York and London

Published by Teachers College Press, 1234 Amsterdam Avenue, New York, NY 10027

*Library of Congress Cataloging-in-Publication Data*

The early childhood curriculum : current findings in theory and practice / edited by Carol Seefeldt. — 3rd ed.
    p.    cm. — (Early childhood education series)
  Includes bibliographical references and index.
  ISBN 0-8077-3781-X (pbk. : alk. paper)
  1. Early childhood education—United States—Curricula.  2. Early childhood education—United States—Curricula—Research.
  I. Seefeldt, Carol.  II. Series: Early childhood education series (Teachers College Press)
  LB1139.4.E17  1999
  372.19'0973—dc21                      99-12138

ISBN 0-8077-3781-X (paper)

Printed on acid-free paper
Manufactured in the United States of America

06 05 04 03 02 01 00 99    8 7 6 5 4 3 2 1

# Contents

98614

# Preface

"EXACTLY WHAT is it that you teach young children? What do you want them to learn?" Historically, early childhood educators, embracing nativists' theories of learning, maintained that they teach children in developmentally appropriate ways. What they taught was never fully articulated or specified.

Today, the continuing pressures on all of education to fully prepare children for the role of citizen intensifies the need to respond to the questions of what it is we teach and what content young children are learning. Reinforcing the need to be able to specify the content of the early childhood curriculum are the intensified calls for sweeping curriculum reforms and concerns that the curriculum be inclusive and provide for the diversity of children found in today's early childhood programs.

The third edition of this text, *The Early Childhood Curriculum: Current Findings in Theory and Practice,* has been designed as a resource for early childhood educators to answer the questions of what it is they teach and what children learn in an early childhood program. The text offers graduate students and decision makers in early childhood education an overview of the various theories, research bases, and practices in curriculum content areas in early childhood education. New chapters on inclusion and the multicultural world of the early childhood classroom address current issues.

In Chapter 1, Leslie R. Williams describes how society's attitudes and views of the nature of children have always influenced the curriculum. The social forces that led to varying views of children, and thus curricula, are described. The idea of the curriculum being inseparable from the whole child provides the basis for this chapter.

"But they're only playing!" Uninformed of the power of play as an educational tool, many view play as a waste of time and call for a return to teaching basic academic skills during the period of early childhood. Early childhood educators, however, know play is the major vehicle for learning, as Doris Pronin Fromberg demonstrates in Chapter 2.

Celia Genishi and Rebekah Fassler, in Chapter 3, describe the research, theory, and issues in language learning in early childhood classrooms. They discuss the role of adults in encouraging children's talk and language interactions and review issues in the field revolving around these interactions. The chapter includes a discussion on how teachers enable children to develop communicative competence, as well as the research on their choices and on curricula that build on children's oral communicative abilities.

Questions of when and how to teach beginning reading are among the most controversial topics in early childhood education. In Chapter 4, Linda B. Gambrell and Susan Anders Mazzoni examine how young children develop as readers. They focus on the concept of emergent literacy for the insights it provides about young children's reading and writing development. The chapter concludes with an overview of what current theory and research suggest young children need to know in order to develop into successful readers.

Chapter 5, by Patricia F. Campbell, examines recent research that can inform curriculum development in mathematics. Research on creating problem-solving environments, the role of the teacher, and the clustering of mathematics instruction around themes as opposed to isolated topics is included.

Christopher E. Landry and George E. Forman, in Chapter 6, aim to help educators determine useful procedures to facilitate scientific thinking in young children. As a context for this educational research, they also present the cognitive development research that has established the goals for much of early science education.

The breadth and multidisciplinary nature of the social studies have led to lack of clarity and goals for social studies education. Richard K. Jantz and I, in Chapter 7, review some of the controversy surrounding the social studies in early childhood education and present current thinking and research on what the social studies should consist of in early childhood classrooms.

Cherie K. Stellaccio and Marie McCarthy, in Chapter 8, present research in early childhood music education, providing an overview of the nature of musical performance, perception, and the factors that influence children's developmental music aptitude.

Chapter 9 is based on the premise that the visual arts are not only inherently of interest to young children but critical in the early childhood curriculum. In this chapter I offer teachers theory and research to support the inclusion of art in the curriculum. Beginning with an overview and critique of the theories of child art, the chapter concludes with implications for teaching art.

Chapter 10, by Lourdes Diaz Soto, explores the complexity of the historical context of multicultural America and the possibility of an early childhood critical multicultural curriculum with border crossings. Salient theoretical paradigms capable of informing the field of early education are included, and a review of how literature is organized around issues of multiculturalism is given.

The history of early childhood special education, a relatively new field, is described in Chapter 11, by Joan Lieber, Ilene Schwartz, Susan Sandall, Eva Horn, and Ruth Ashworth Wolery. They describe recent changes in the field and how special education services are delivered to young children with disabilities. Challenges for professionals in inclusive programs and the current state of curricular practices are presented.

The early childhood curriculum, however, is an integrated curriculum. The concluding chapter, by Rebecca S. New, revisits the two-pronged definition of an integrated curriculum, expanding upon common understandings of both "the whole child" and "the whole story" in a way that links them to their cultural and ideological underpinnings.

The increased number of young children being cared for and educated in settings other than their homes is accompanied by more and more questions about what constitutes appropriate curriculum. Together, the chapters in this third edition of *The Early Childhood Curriculum: Current Findings in Theory and Practice* offer early childhood educators and researchers a foundation on which to answer these questions. Not only will they be able to answer the difficult question, What do you teach young children?—but they will be able to design an integrated, inclusive curriculum as well.

## ACKNOWLEDGMENTS

The significant contribution this book makes to early childhood education is the result of the expertise, energies, and time of many. First, the contributions of the authors of each of the chapters must be recognized. Each an expert in a specific area of curriculum content, the authors gave freely of their time and knowledge to write a chapter specifically for this work.

The editors at Teachers College Press are acknowledged, especially Susan Liddicoat, whose dedication to quality is always present in her guidance, careful thought, and conceptual and precise editing. Ron Galbraith, who originally acquired this text and offered support and encouragement, is remembered. I also thank Karen Osborne and Lyn Grossman.

Finally, the ideation and conceptual insights of Eugene Seefeldt must be acknowledged. Without his thoughtful insights and ideation, the third edition of this text would not have occurred.

CHAPTER 1

# Determining the Early Childhood Curriculum: The Evolution of Goals and Strategies Through Consonance and Controversy

## LESLIE R. WILLIAMS

THE WORD *curriculum* evokes many images in the minds of teachers, administrators, and parents. For most early educators prepared in European and American traditions, though, *curriculum* has a single powerful association—the image of "the whole child." Consideration of what that phrase means to those who work with young children (children from birth to age 8) and how it came to have so particular a connotation reveals some of the distinctive characteristics of early education and explains what for other educators may be considered the idiosyncratic nature of the field's curriculum literature. In early childhood education, the curriculum and the whole child tend to be seen as inseparable.

Most early educators understand "the whole child" to mean the child's complete integration of intellectual (cognitive), emotional, social, and physical capabilities. Learning in any one of these domains must necessarily involve all the others. Effective teaching, as a consequence, must draw upon those inner connections, with recognition of the distinctive ways in which young children create or take in and utilize knowledge of the world around them.

The task of determining the early childhood curriculum, therefore, hinges to a certain extent on discovering the nature of children. What young children learn is at least partially dependent upon how they learn. As this concept has evolved, how children learn has also increasingly come to be seen in relation to a *context,* a broad social and cultural base for children's emerging knowledge, skills, feelings, and attitudes. Experience has taught early educators that young children thrive on acknowledgment and use of their unique capacities for learning and that they show themselves to be capable of strong performance in all areas of accomplishment when taught as unitary, integrated beings.

This chapter explores the origins and practices of early childhood curriculum in what are currently its most widespread forms in the United States. The story told here reveals perceptions shifting over time regarding characterizations of young children's most essential natures; valued goals and expected forms of development and learning; projections of the roles teachers, materials, and peers play in that development and learning; and understandings of the act of "teaching" itself when applied to work with young children. Tensions that have periodically arisen within the field have usually stemmed from lack of consonance among two or more of these elements in competing early childhood curricular systems. Consideration of historical and current controversies, therefore, can highlight the points at which early educators make implicit or explicit decisions to determine the general content and form of the curriculum they intend to enact.

## EARLY BEGINNINGS

The idea of educating the whole child reflects a rich tradition of comprehensiveness that has characterized early education from its beginnings. This tradition arose as a response both to social conditions adversely affecting the lives of young children and to the moral, spiritual, idealistic, pragmatic, and eventually scientific (or "modern") streams of thought flowing through Western society over the past 200 years. At the current juncture, scientific responses to curriculum formulation are being challenged by increasing awareness of the influence of culture on children's development and learning and by the "postmodern" critique of the notion of development itself that may lead to still other iterations of early childhood curriculum.

Historian Philippe Ariès (1962) suggests that before the romantic period, children who reached the age of 6 or 7 years were viewed as miniature adults and thus were expected to learn in the same entirely language-based and formal mode used in adult education. The only classical distinctions made by both Plato (427–347 B.C.) and Aristotle (384–322 B.C.) were that before approximately the age of 7, young children's exposure to material such as mythic tales should be carefully censored to provide only the strictest training of character as a proper foundation for learning, and that incorporation of physical exercise into the educational plan be considered essential in providing the healthy body needed to support a healthy mind. In a vein somewhat similar to early character training, preparation of young scholars in medieval Europe was expected to be grounded in spiritual disciplines, so that the developing mind would reflect the order of the Creation or divine intent. While these provisos implied the integration of the faculties of human learning, translating that assumption into curricula was not seen except in sporadic instances—for example, in the seventeenth century, Luther's incorporation of vocational instruction into courses of study and Comenius's use of pictures as concrete referents to vocabulary studied (Braun & Edwards, 1972; Comenius, 1896/1910; Weber, 1984). By and large, it appears that the teaching of young children proceeded through "telling," on the assumption that knowledge could be directly transmitted from teacher to child, that learning occurred through children's recognition of eternal truths or their memorization of what had been passed on, and that skills were acquired through practice.

## Rousseau and the Natural Child

A clear demarcation in the image of the child came with the popularization of the work of Jean-Jacques Rousseau (1712–1788). In his educational treatise *Emile* (1762/1969), Rousseau departed from the view of children as being like adults and presented them as moving through a succession of stages, each of which had its own internal order and coherence (Gutek, 1972). Equally important was Rousseau's insistence that children learned not through the abstractions of the written word but through direct interaction with the natural physical environment. He took the extreme position that only the natural world provided guidance in this interactive process and that society corrupted children, tarnishing their innate nobility of spirit. He recommended that children be raised in situations where contact with nature could be frequent and prolonged, where children could play without social restraint until reaching the age of reason (approximately puberty). At that time, formal studies could commence without danger of distortion of the true nature of the child (Rousseau, 1762/1969). Now the conception of the role of the teacher changed from that of a transmitter passing on knowledge to that of a protector and shield who would deflect corrupting societal influences, thus enabling the inborn sequence of a child's development to unfold. The implied teaching strategy was a somewhat distanced, observational stance, coupled with occasional conversational tutorials focusing on understandings a child was acquiring through interaction with the natural world.

While Rousseau's main interest was in reforming society's total conception of education and he did not focus specifically on young children, his work is important to understanding the inner structures of most current forms of early childhood curricula because he anticipated several of the themes that characterize work in the field to this day. His awareness of the emergence of developmental stages and stage-related learning has already been mentioned. In addition, his presentation of learning as an interactive, sensorially based process and his recognition of play as a medium for learning were powerful intimations of the directions to be taken in future curriculum design.

Like all issues of import in education, however, conceptions of the roles of play and processes in learning, and their relationship to the idea of teaching the whole child, have evolved over time. Ensuing changes have been responsive to broad social patterns, needs, and priorities. In every era, new program designs and curricular formulations have revealed both unique and cumulative perceptions of the role of each of these in suiting curriculum content and teaching strategies to the distinctive characteristics of young children. Tracing the path of that evolution can contribute to our understanding of the fundamental questions behind curriculum research in early childhood education today.

Returning, therefore, to the predecessors of modern practice, we see that from the mid-eighteenth century onward, there was a clear line of development in the image of the whole child. Emphases on interactive processes and play became more and more apparent in the fabric of early childhood education, as each innovator passed insights to a new generation of persons serving, nurturing, and educating the young child.

## Pestalozzi and the Observant Child

Rousseau's work deeply influenced the thinking of Johann Pestalozzi (1746–1827), an Italian-Swiss schoolteacher who founded one of the first European schools to acknowledge children's developmental characteristics. Pestalozzi was convinced of the profound effect of social environment on children. When his novel *How Gertrude Teaches Her Children* (1801/1915) was first published in 1801, he was promulgating the then-revolutionary notion of an intimate teaching connection between parents and their children. He assumed that children were the pliant recipients of parental instruction and were in danger of corruption by society if that teaching was not of the highest moral character.

The curriculum "Papa" Pestalozzi designed for his children equated parental guidance and strong morality with the work ethic. The result was a high-intensity work training program that prepared children to face a rapidly changing economy. Manual dexterity was stressed as a survival skill in the newly emerging Industrial Revolution (Gutek, 1968).

The structure behind Pestalozzi's program was even more unconventional for its day than was its outward form. Pestalozzi saw the purpose of his work as the development of children's moral, physical, and intellectual powers. While the first two were fostered through the approach described above, intellectual growth was stimulated through *Anschauung*, a perceptual-ideational process through which concepts or clear ideas were formed. *Anschauung* involved three levels of operation. Most immediately, it represented the reception in the mind of direct sensory impressions from interaction with the external environment. One step removed from that was the formation of ideas by combining sense impressions with attention, or mental concentration, and arriving at concepts by association. At the third level of operation, mental ideas would appear without a concrete referent. *Anschauung* was developed in children through guided observation and representation of the natural world. Practice in recording the numbers and forms inherent in objects and the language associated with them ("naming," or classification) led to refinement of mental capacity and its application in the physical and moral realms. Thus the whole person was educated and became a competent and coping human being (Gutek, 1968).

A fascinating part of this system was Pestalozzi's use of older, more competent children as tutors of younger ones. Faced with large numbers of students and limited financial resources, he himself taught a group of child tutors to guide younger children in exercises of collecting, drawing, and talking about (classifying), as well as doing mathematical analyses of, objects from the natural environment—procedures he described at several points in his writings (Green, 1912). One might argue that in doing so, Pestalozzi was one of the first educators to introduce variation in teaching strategy into the foundations of early childhood professional practice.

In a review of teaching strategies or approaches used to teach young children, Lay-Dopyera and Dopyera (1992) point out that certain modes of teaching have come to be so associated with particular theoretical orientations regarding child development and learning that practitioners holding those views may not be aware of them as distinctive, and thus do not question either their use or their efficacy. In spite of this tendency, researchers over the past several decades have identified and studied specific strategies, among them promotion of positive teacher–child relationships, use of classroom management procedures, teacher–child dialogue strategies (including giving descriptive feedback; providing reinforcement for desired behaviors; coaching, prompting, and giving suggestions; and modeling), and strategies for group lessons (such as direct instruction, deductive lessons with advanced organizers, inductive lessons for concept attainment, cooperative learning, modeling lessons, problem discussion lessons, "wonderful idea" lessons, and play–debrief–replay lessons).

In Pestalozzi's work, there was originally much emphasis on the traditional technique of *direct instruction,* whereby curriculum content was presented in verbal and written form, commonly followed by student recitation. Here, Lay-Dopyera and Dopyera note, "the student's role is to learn the right response," while the teacher's role is to "tell the pupils whether they are right or wrong and to carefully arrange the presentation so that they will be right most of the time" (p. 29).

As Pestalozzi's class grew in size, however, and as he continued to refine his pedagogy over time, he introduced new elements into his strategies. Analysis of his descriptions suggests that he *modeled* his "object lessons," that is, he consciously enacted the procedures of observation that he wanted the children to imitate, a technique that in recent times has been shown to be powerful in inducing desired behaviors (Bandura, 1973, cited in Lay-Dopyera & Dopyera, 1992; Bandura & Walters, 1963).

It may also be inferred from his several articulations of *Anschauung* that Pestalozzi used an early form of *deductive lessons with advance organizers.* In this strategy, children are first provided with a general description of the features being sought (Ausubel, 1963, 1968, cited in Lay-Dopyera & Dopyera, 1992), as in Pestalozzi's "language, form, and number," and then encouraged to examine objects for those features, moving from the simple to the more complex applications of the concept (Schwadener & Lawton, 1978, cited in Lay-Dopyera & Dopyera, 1992).

Clearly foundational to all of these strategic efforts, though, was Pestalozzi's establishment of an emotional climate that promoted a loving trust between himself and his students (Gutek, 1968). In doing this, he anticipated the importance of the *positive teacher–child relationships* much later investigated by Thompson (1944, cited by Lay-Dopyera & Dopyera, 1992) and further examined by Tzelepis, Giblin, and Agronow (1983) and Shipman (1976; both studies cited by Lay-Dopyera & Dopyera, 1992), among others. Repeatedly, such studies have shown relationships between positive teacher regard and children's improved or heightened performance. Pestalozzi appears to have known the power of such relationships, and his work in this sphere set a much-emulated precedent for the curriculum designers who followed him. Without question, it made a profound impression on Friedrich Froebel and the several generations of early childhood educators who subsequently promoted Froebel's work.

## Froebel and the Child as Divine Reflection

Friedrich Froebel (1782–1852) studied with Pestalozzi; but he, designing a curriculum in 1837, 50 years after Pestalozzi's first work, found his teacher's vision of the child inadequate to capture the spirit of the new age. He molded and changed that vision to encompass "self-actualization" as a legitimate goal of early childhood education. Young children, said Froebel, arrive on this earth with an impressive repertoire of inborn knowledge and skills. The role of the teacher was to bring these capabilities to fruition by making children consciously aware of and able to use all that they know.

Froebel created a curriculum that was fascinating both in its complexity and in its inherent appeal to the children of his day. It consisted of a carefully sequenced set of manipulative materials known as the Gifts, complemented by an equally carefully sequenced set of handwork projects called the Occupations. The Gifts and Occupations together were designed to illustrate fundamental mathematical principles that Froebel believed were part of the creative human spirit and that echoed essential workings of the cosmos, or the mind of God (Froebel, 1826/1887).

Froebel is generally considered the founder of early childhood education not only because he was the first to design a curriculum specifically for young children (Pestalozzi's work encompassed the range from early childhood through adolescence) but also because he introduced play as a major medium for instruction. For the first time, children "played" in school, that is, used manipulatives specially designed to teach concepts and skills. Formal games, music, art, and outdoor activities (such as gardening and care of pets) were integrated into the daily program to supplement the use of the Gifts and the Occupations.

Froebel's notion of "play" was substantially different from modern conceptions. He saw play as a teacher-directed process, largely imitative in nature and revolving around predetermined content. But he also understood play to be a form of "creative self-activity," expressing children's emerging capabilities and reflecting their particular way of learning (Froebel, 1826/1887).

Froebel's work turned the attention of educators to the importance of specially designed teaching materials in promoting particular kinds of learning in young children. Additionally, while continuing to emphasize a central role for the teacher as a verbal mediator of children's activity, Froebel, like Pestalozzi, shifted attention away from direct instruction to several types of *teacher–child dialogue strategies*. Children did follow teacher direction in use of the materials, and they often modeled on the teacher's manipulations of the Gifts and Occupations. Teachers were expected, however, to maintain a flow of classroom talk with children that included such dimensions as *coaching, prompting,* and *giving suggestions,* as well as *asking questions,* all in the context of group activity. In recent years, the importance of the role of the teacher as a key player in classroom talk has been reaffirmed in the work of such researchers as Almy, Monighan, Scales, and Van Hoorn (1984) and Katz and Chard (1989; both studies cited in Lay-Dopyera & Dopyera, 1992). While work over the past several decades in this area has most commonly focused on the effects of dialogic strategies on the work of underachieving or "disadvantaged" children (as in Christie, 1982; Feitelson & Ross, 1973; Rosen, 1974; and Smilansky, 1968; all cited in Lay-Dopyera & Dopyera, 1992), a more recent review influenced by the research of Lev Vygotsky (Bodrova & Leong, 1996) has pointed to the effectiveness of such uses of language as a tool for the development of all children.

Other teaching strategies prominent in Froebel's curriculum were similar to those used by Pestalozzi—*modeling,* as previously noted, and *deductive lessons with advance organizers.* Teachers were expected to be warm and accepting and to develop strong, caring bonds with the children they taught. This emphasis on *the teacher–child relationship* continued to be a major characteristic of early childhood curriculum through the 1960s, and it has remained a feature to the present day.

## FIRST HALF OF THE TWENTIETH CENTURY

Froebel's mystical formulation dominated curriculum design in early childhood education for 50 years. In the 1890s, however, a new generation of persons concerned with the well-being of young children and their families began to challenge the view of the child contained in the Froebelian kindergarten curriculum.

### Dewey and Progressive Education

While not rejecting the picture of children as innately creative beings, the Progressive followers of John Dewey reached backward in time to reclaim some of Pestalozzi's understanding of learning through direct experience with the natural world, and forward into the new century to envision children as builders of a new social order—a democratic society. Progressive educators found the highly defined and teacher-directed Froebelian curriculum to be too removed from the challenges and problems of daily living. Instead, they suggested, a curriculum for young children should be designed to meet the circumstances children faced as members of a group living in a modern world (Dewey, 1944/1966).

Children were thus seen as social beings, and the curriculum became a flexible grouping of activities to promote social problem-solving processes largely within the realm of social studies. Examples of such activities were joint efforts in the preparation of food for lunch or small-group work on representation in the classroom of a familiar community institution such as the local grocery store. Through such activities, children were expected to develop a sense of mutual responsibility and an understanding of at least some of the workings of the society in which they lived (Dewey, 1902).

New conceptions of play and the use of process in teaching and learning were emerging. The nature of children as learners was being seen in relation to experience (Dewey, 1938/1963). This meant connection with real-life activities that tended to integrate subject areas and require coordination of socioemotional, psychomotor, and cognitive responses from children. Such responses frequently took the form of sociodramatic play, in which the children reenacted what they had observed or directly experienced, often adding new dimensions to the scene in ways that revealed the processes behind their growing understanding.

Not surprisingly with this change in basic curriculum orientation, new teaching strategies began to be developed that were consonant with the aims for children's development and learning. Of particular interest was use of various forms of *cooperative learning.* Because the children were working on activities that tended to carry on over several days or even weeks, the development and maintenance of the work needed several children to be engaged with it at one time; and children and teachers together needed to identify cooperative roles and enable each other to carry them out. At later points in early childhood curriculum development, the cooperative strategies begun in the Progressive context were extended further by educators interested in fostering the social integration of young children with special needs into "general" education classrooms (K. A. Miller, 1989, cited in Lay-Dopyera & Dopyera, 1992) or in providing opportunities for comparison and contrast of ideas as part of the exercise of emerging cognitive capabilities in young children (Kohlberg & Lickona, 1987, cited in Lay-Dopyera & Dopyera, 1992).

An equally prominent strategy was incorporation of *problem discussion lessons.* Using as a point of focus social problems that arose in the process of classroom activities, teachers and children together would identify the issues, discuss their ramifications, and pose possible solutions (Cuffaro, 1995). As noted by Lay-Dopyera and Dopyera (1992), "the goal is not to teach the 'right' or 'best' answer but to develop children's awareness of the need for solutions and to develop a repertoire of viable possibilities in problem situations" (p. 32). These discussions would often lead to new curriculum ideas that could be jointly developed by both teachers and children.

## Montessori and Education for Social Competence

As the Progressive movement was gathering momentum in the United States, Maria Montessori in Italy was transforming her observations of the nature of the whole child into another process-oriented curriculum. Like Dewey, Montessori was keenly aware of societal demands on children. Instead of looking at the functioning of children in groups, however, she focused on the promotion of social competence in individuals. She saw children as very sensitive to sensorial stimulation, "capable of sustaining mental concentration when genuinely interested in their work," loving cleanliness and order, "preferring work to play and didactic materials to toys, and having a deep sense of personal dignity" (Standing, 1962, pp. 40–43). Consequently, she designed her curriculum to foster independence in self-care and individual responsibility for one's own learning. Children worked individually or with self-chosen companions, practicing skills on specially made, self-corrective manipulative materials that provided immediate feedback on their accomplishment.

Montessori had a deep understanding of learning as process. Her curriculum was organized around several "periods" in the child's development, each of which had its particular requirements for interaction with the environment. Assuming a continuum between refinement of the senses and broader intellectual functioning, she devised procedures and didactic materials that were responsive to children's evolving learning characteristics. During the period of the "absorbent mind" (birth to age 6), and most especially in the substage of greatest sensitivity and receptivity (3 to 6 years), she engaged the children in exercises of "practical life" and sense training. Practical life work emphasized cleanliness, self-care, and care and maintenance of the learning environment. Work in sense training promoted fine powers of sensory discrimination and developed readiness for the writing, reading, and other academic learnings that followed in the primary grades (Montessori, 1912/1964).

All of the exercises were process-oriented. While the didactic materials were designed to achieve specific outcomes (such as the ability to order cylinders from largest to smallest in height), they were also made to encourage the repetition of tasks, which in Montessori's view typically precedes and follows mastery in young children. Thus, while specific accomplishment was important, how children achieved mastery and continuing opportunity to demonstrate mastery were seen to be even more significant to their emerging competence.

Not only were Montessori's curricular aims and understandings of the essential nature of children a departure from conceptualizations among Progressive educators, but her teaching strategies also posed interesting differences. Having built upon a tradition of interaction with materials as the activity leading intellectual development, she offered a view of the adult in the classroom as a "directress" rather than a teacher in the conventional sense of that term. Adults were to observe children's behavior and to facilitate children's choices of increasingly complex materials as the children demonstrated their acquisition of the requisite skills for each one. Montessori did not believe one should praise children for their accomplishments, but she did anticipate the strategy of *giving descriptive feedback* by noting exactly what children had accomplished with the materials when children called adults' attention to what they had done. Unlike the later work done in investigation of this strategy (Anker, Foster, McLane, Sokel, & Weissbourd, 1974; Hess & Shipman, 1965; both cited in Lay-Dopyera & Dopyera, 1992), however, Montessori used language sparingly to amplify the interactions with materials, rather than as a vehicle for elaborating concept development. Her concentrated use of child observation as a basis for curriculum refinement, on the other hand, did parallel a strategy that was gaining strength in the Child Study Movement in the United States.

## The Child Development Perspective

Simultaneously with Dewey's and Montessori's separate efforts, the American Child Study Movement, under the leadership of G. Stanley Hall (1844–1924), was starting to influence early childhood practice. Observations of children's behavior in a variety of contexts began yielding powerful data that, in turn, were causing curriculum makers to rethink what were appropriate learning experiences for young children (Kessen, 1965; Weber, 1984). The complexity of "the whole child" was beginning to reveal itself and to require increasingly sensitive applications of integrated approaches to teaching and learning.

As the century advanced, the conception of the child as a social being was expanding to include an accounting of the individual child's physical and psychological growth patterns. From the 1920s through the 1950s, the attention of early educators focused successively on children's social functioning, physical development and maturational milestones, emotional health, and, finally, underlying cognitive skills that signaled stage-appropriate mental functioning. Drawing on the work of Gesell and Ilg,

Erikson, and Piaget, among others, early childhood educators in the late 1950s generally espoused what came to be known as the "child development" point of view (Braun & Edwards, 1972; Weber, 1984).

Notable during this 30–year period was the work of such finely tuned educators as Susan Isaacs in Britain and Harriet Johnson, Caroline Pratt, and Lucy Sprague Mitchell in the United States. By mid-century, the names of Lawrence Frank, Daniel Prescott, Arthur Jersild, and James L. Hymes had been added to the list (Weber, 1984). While these early childhood advocates each had a distinct point of view, they all emphasized the centrality of process, and play as an expression of process, in the growth, development, and education of young children. Teaching strategies utilized by early educators during this period continued in the vein of those previously described.

## THIRTY YEARS OF GROWTH: 1950-1980

As understanding of the processes of children's learning became more refined through extended child observation, curriculum content was increasingly linked with the everyday occurrences of children's lives. This was so partly because of the continuing influence of Dewey's thinking on classroom practice and partly because there was new theoretical support for the power of such content from two giants in the field of child development, Erik Erikson (1902–1994) and Jean Piaget (1896–1980). Mentioned above in the context of changing emphases in early childhood education, the work of these two researchers requires particular attention because of the depth and breadth of their influence on curriculum design to the present day.

### Erikson and Development Through Conflict Resolution

As a young teacher raised in Europe, Erik Erikson came under the tutelage of Anna Freud, the daughter of the founder of the psychodynamic school of psychology, Sigmund Freud. Prepared by her for work in child therapy, he soon became intrigued by the interactions he discerned between the course of psychosexual development in young children as described in classic psychodynamic literature and the sociocultural milieu in which children were being raised.

Erikson accepted the point of departure of psychodynamic thought— that the essential nature of human beings is instinctual and manifests itself in the realm of feeling and emotion. Cognition arises from unfulfilled desire, as a secondary characteristic of human nature. He understood socioemotional development as proceeding through the resolution of a series of conflicts, each of which addresses a fundamental issue of the human psyche. Proceeding from trust versus mistrust, to autonomy versus shame, to initiative versus guilt, and beyond through all eight distinctive "ages of man," children (and adults) strive to achieve integration and maintain balance in the context of the particular demands their society places upon them (Erikson, 1950/1963).

Young children, said Erikson, most commonly work through their current conflicts by reconstructing them in symbolic play. For curriculum developers influenced by Erikson's formulation, play centering on day-to-day events and familiar objects became a critical element in early childhood programs. It provided an arena for children's coming to terms with their existential dilemmas and encouraged cognition through channeling of childhood fantasy.

## Piaget and the Child's Construction of Knowledge

Piaget's theory of intellectual development gave a different but equally potent justification for including play in the early childhood curriculum. Piaget concluded that the essential nature of human beings was their power to construct knowledge through adaptation to the environment. From birth, children engage in the reciprocal acts of "assimilation" and "accommodation" in order to form, extend, and expand the structures of their minds. In assimilation, children match information, concepts, and skills arising from interaction with the environment and with previously formed mental structures. Accommodation, on the other hand, requires that the structures be modified in order to make sense of the new information or concepts, or to represent new skills (Piaget & Inhelder, 1969).

These complementary processes are fueled by children's direct activity, said Piaget. Play especially exercises the assimilation process, using action and frequently language as proving grounds for newly acquired ideas. As children proceed through the four periods of intellectual development (sensorimotor, preoperational, concrete operational, and formal operational) described by Piaget, play assumes a variety of forms; and within any one period, it can have multiple functions. Sensorimotor play, for example, generally revolves around practicing physical skills acquired through use of the five senses. However, it can also be used as a medium for establishing social relationships. During the preoperational period, play might be used symbolically or constructively to solidify physical knowledge of one's surroundings, to practice solving problems in the adult world, or to create a microsociety in which to try out new capabilities or to refine social interactions (Piaget, 1962).

## Implications for Curriculum

Early childhood program designers who accepted Erikson's and Piaget's descriptions of child development found that they could interpret the work of the two theorists according to their own instructional leanings. Erikson and Piaget themselves did not transform their theories into specifications for classroom practice. Curriculum makers, therefore, were free to draw implications leading to a variety of approaches to addressing the socioemotional and cognitive characteristics of young children. The one common feature of these approaches was that abundant malleable and manipulable materials and ample time for the children to interact directly with them were seen as vital spurs to the children's continued cognitive development.

By the early 1960s, therefore, the concept of teaching the whole child through a process orientation and incorporating play experiences into the curriculum was well established. Many "child development" programs reflected a psychodynamic (Freudian, Eriksonian) or, less frequently, a Piagetian point of view that stressed the interconnection of experiences and the roles of emotion, cognition, and maturation in the promotion of learning. Other programs remained more closely aligned to the earlier Deweyan point of view or to the "readiness" rationale stemming from child study. In spite of the variety of theoretical underpinnings, however, classroom practice tended to have common characteristics.

Typically, early childhood classrooms were arranged into "interest centers" such as the block corner, library, art area, family or sociodramatic play corner, and sand/water areas. Daily schedules incorporated both child-initiated and teacher-directed work periods. The areas of the room were stocked with a range of malleable and manipulable materials used, according to the orientation of the program, to promote social interaction, skill/concept development, or a combination of the two. The curriculum was derived from teachers' observations of the children's interests and developmental needs, from the possibilities presented by the learning materials themselves, and from awareness of the school content that would follow in the first grade. Again, the teaching strategies used were those that have been previously described.

## Head Start

At this time (approximately 1959–1963) the federal government intervened in early childhood education in ways that altered the course of curriculum development for the next 15 years. Distressed by descriptions of the depressed physical and intellectual condition of the nation's grow-ing number of children living in poverty, the United States Office of Child Development (now the Administration for Children, Youth and Families) initiated a new federally funded early childhood program—Project Head Start.

Head Start originally espoused the child development tradition in its early learning centers. The educational program was designed around a flexible schedule of child-initiated play and group-learning experiences, which were generally aimed at connecting the three domains of learning. The purpose of the program was to enable each child to develop as fully as possible all facets of his or her "being," while being prepared for the social, emotional, cognitive, linguistic, and physical demands of the first grade.

The public school expected that children would come to the first grade with a firm command not only of social behavior that would enable them to work effectively in a classroom, but also of premath, prereading, and other "readiness" skills. The very name "Head Start" implied such a preparation. The public school's conception of curriculum at that time was, generally speaking, not developmental in nature. It was focused in-stead on the acquisition of specific content (the facts or substance of math, science, language, literature, and so forth). If children came to the first grade for some reason not ready (in the sense of not having had initial exposure to that content, or not having acquired particular "learning how to learn" skills that met the school's expectations), they were considered to be "disadvantaged."

Head Start's mission was to ensure that children would not fail. Con-sequently, there were new initiatives among Head Start curriculum mak-ers. Strongly influenced by learning theorists and analysts of school con-tent, some of the curriculum developers in experimental projects turned away from the child development approach to return to direct instruction in a variety of readiness skills, inclusion of a focus on prereading and pre-math content, and utilization of a high proportion of teacher direction in each day's work.

In some of the innovative curriculum models, the interest centers characterizing the early childhood classroom disappeared. They were re-placed by high-intensity, small-group interactions; by practice with work-book exercises; or by other forms of focus on behavioral sequences geared to the acquisition of skills and attitudes related to upcoming school expe-riences (Evans, 1975). Teaching strategies subsequently shifted from a more generalized concern with the teacher–child relationship to articula-tion of *classroom management* procedures and techniques largely derived from behavioral theories of learning.

Lay-Dopyera and Dopyera (1992) describe classroom management as "teacher behavior aimed at keeping children engaged appropriately and reducing the likelihood of [children's] behavior that requires the teacher to give children negative feedback" (p. 21). Studies in the effectiveness of teachers using such strategies in work with young children have focused on the need for clarity in setting expectations for children's behavior, explicit orientation of the children to the classroom (including attention to routines such as toileting and eating), arrangement of classroom space to facilitate particular activities and protect personal possessions, provision of specific feedback about children's performance, and mobility of the teacher in the classrooms that enables redirection of the children's behavior whenever seen as necessary (Anderson, Evertson, & Emmer, 1979; Brophy & Evertson, 1976; Tzelepis et al., 1983; all cited in Lay-Dopyera & Dopyera, 1992).

Another strategy prominent in these programs was use of *behavioral reinforcement*. Here the focus lay on identifying desired behaviors in children (including goals for learning) and providing positive consequences for their demonstration. Teachers introduced to behavioral theory (Bijou & Baer, 1978; Skinner, 1974; both cited in Lay-Dopyera & Dopyera, 1992) became conscious of the power of social gestures of approval (such as smiles, handshakes, or positive comment) and material tokens of approval (such as stickers, food, or the opportunity to play with certain toys) and learned to use these to increase the incidence of performance of desired behaviors among the children.

In other new curriculum models that made up Head Start's "planned variations," the familiar interest centers remained in the classroom but were used in new ways to promote school-related skills and attitudes, and behavioral teaching strategies similar to those described above were commonly used. Some of the planned variations did, however, return to problem-solving strategies previously popularized in Progressive classrooms or developed strategies that elicited the engagement of particular kinds of cognitive processes, such as use of *inductive lessons for concept attainment* or "*wonderful idea*" lessons. In the former, strategies developed by Bruner, Goodnow, and Austin (1956) that focused on comparison and contrast of exemplars and nonexemplars of a concept were used to expand and elaborate the children's funds of knowledge and conceptual skills. In the latter, work done by Eleanor Duckworth (1972, as reported by Meek, 1991) was used in introduction of activities to young children that caused them to wonder and question what they were observing. Their cognitive engagement was then furthered through eliciting comments from them and through subsequent building of more and more differentiated conceptual systems as the children learned from each other's observations. Whatever the case, children who entered the programs were observed or assessed to see what their needs were—that is, where they were lacking skills—and learning experiences were designed to develop those skills. While there were some notable exceptions in program design, many of the recommended learning activities encouraged use of materials commonly found in public school kindergartens and first grades, such as felt circles, squares, and triangles to teach shapes, and monthly calendars to teach passage of time.

## Curriculum Research

Between 1967 and 1973, in response to some of the trends in Head Start, curriculum research in early childhood education in general also began to take a particular turn. Instead of focusing so heavily on defining and understanding the essential nature of the child as a learner, psychologists and early childhood educators began to explore which program designs would yield the greatest gains in the children's performance on standardized IQ and readiness tests. Some studies indicated that children did equally well in demonstration or experimental programs that were radically different from one another, provided that certain parameters such as parent involvement and consistent teacher planning were present (Weikart, 1969). Other studies indicated that academically based programs that made strong use of direct instruction did result in higher scores on standardized tests (L. Miller & Dyer, 1975), but that these scores were not generally maintained beyond third grade without follow-up intervention in the public school (Gray, Ramsey, & Klaus, 1982; L. Miller & Dyer, 1975).

The results of that wave of research raised a number of interesting questions. What were the factors that accounted for some measure of success with some children but not with others in the same classroom? Which programs would be best for children with particular sets of characteristics (Smith & Bissell, 1970)? What were the contextual variables (such as focus on the children's direct experiences and incorporation of culturally derived content into the curriculum) that might account for heightened performance in given situations (Juarez & Associates, 1982)? These and other concerns surfaced throughout the 1970s, refocusing attention on the complexity of the whole child and the many dimensions involved in teaching young children.

## DEBATES AT THE END OF THE CENTURY

In the two decades spanning the beginning of the 1980s to the end of the 1990s, several new curriculum development movements appeared. These movements heightened a sense of controversy that had become sub-merged during the era of heavy federal funding for early childhood pro-grams stressing IQ gains and attention to school-related achievement. Many early educators began to voice concern about what they took to be a loss of focus on children's developmental patterns and urged recog-nition and reestablishment of child development theory as foundational for early childhood curriculum. Others felt that child development theory was an insufficient or even erroneous base for early childhood curriculum development. The resulting debates have had several different points of focus and have led directly to present-day generation of new variations in early childhood curriculum. The first wave of "new" debate, however, actually returned the attention of early educators to perennial issues in the field—namely, the proper curriculum content and teaching strategies for kindergarten programs.

## The All-Day Kindergarten Movement

The most recent iteration of the kindergarten debate arose in response to a growing nationwide initiative to provide all-day kindergartens in public schools. Unlike the Head Start program, full-day kindergartens would be designed to address the needs of all children attending public school, re-gardless of socioeconomic status. While promotion of a longer kinder-garten day has been fueled by a variety of political, social, economic, and educational rationales, the net result has been a reassessment of the needs and responses of 5–year-olds in such extended programs.

Particularly prominent in this movement has been renewed interest in the teaching of traditional school skills and subject areas in kindergar-ten programs. This interest has in fact sparked lively exchanges between those who feel that formal, academic skills such as beginning reading and mathematical computation should be taught in kindergarten, and those who feel that acquisition of academic skills is not a "developmentally ap-propriate" goal for kindergartners.

The former group believes that school skills and subjects should be presented as soon as possible to young children so that academic achieve-ment can be accelerated. This point of view assumes that young children learn in fundamentally the same ways that older children do and that the key to their eventual proficiency in the use of basic skills and acquisition of subject matter is "time on task." The latter group, on the other hand, argues that more important than promoting facility with use of symbols and accumulation of facts is developing young children's underlying thinking processes—the foundations for problem solving and critical thinking that can be applied later to traditional academic learning. The advocates for providing these "foundations" point out that the elements of all the subject and skill areas can be integrated into learning activities designed to both respond to and promote young children's direct engagement with the world around them. Because of children's developmental characteristics, this group argues, children can best grasp such content when it is highlighted in common events of interest and when the material is presented in ways that draw upon children's social, emotional, and psychomotor as well as cognitive responses. Incorporation of play into early childhood programs, the developmentalists maintain, should not be abandoned in favor of increased direct instruction, because play serves the function of relating skills and subject matter or content to the children's particular ways of knowing.

The debate between the two opposing camps had become so pronounced by the mid-1980s that the National Association for the Education of Young Children (NAEYC, the largest professional association of early childhood educators in the United States) decided in 1986 that it should produce a policy paper defining its position on the issue. The NAEYC statement (Bredekamp, 1987), commonly known as the DAP (developmentally appropriate practice) guidelines, rapidly became a major rallying point for the developmentalists. At the same time, it sparked a new debate.

## Recognizing Diversity

The new debate centered on what was meant by "appropriateness" and by "development" in the NAEYC statement advocating developmentally appropriate practice. In part, the new conversation had been framed by work already underway in the area of multicultural early childhood practice. During the early 1980s a multicultural stream of early childhood curriculum development had begun to make its presence felt. Linked with earlier movements addressing intergroup relationships and promoting ethnic studies, as well as with needs and controversies highlighted in bilingual educational settings, initial designs for multicultural early childhood curricula had appeared by 1979 through a federal funding initiative of the Administration for Children, Youth and Families (ACYF, Head Start Strategy for Spanish-Speaking Children). Within a short period of time, the four curricula originally funded by ACYF had been published (Cox, Macauley, & Ramirez, 1982; Hanes, Flores, Rosario, & Weikart, 1979; Williams, De Gaetano, Harrington, & Sutherland, 1985; Zamora, 1985); and these were joined by work done under other auspices (Chud & Fahlman, 1985; Kendall, 1983/1996; King, Chipman, & Cruz-Janzen, 1994; Ramsey, 1987; Ramsey, Vold, & Williams, 1989; York, 1991). By the 1990s, the concept of multicultural education had broadened to working with issues of diversity in all of its forms (De Gaetano, Williams, & Volk, 1998; Miller-Lachmann & Taylor, 1995; Ramsey, 1998)—that is, not only issues of culture, language, race, gender, class, and sexual orientation, but also issues of inclusion of young children with special educational needs in general early childhood classrooms, and issues of environmentalism and consumerism. All of this work heightened the awareness of many early childhood educators regarding the effects of culture on human development and learning, and of the role of culturally and individually shaped values on the processes of curriculum development and implementation.

Increasing attention to multiculturalism thus called into question the meaning of "appropriate" as the concept was being used in DAP. What was appropriate practice in one culture might not be appropriate in another (Mallory & New, 1994). Moreover, the previously widely accepted descriptions of child development were seen in a new light as they began to be examined through the lenses of cultural influences on children's development and learning. Rather than a background to children's emerging development, culture was beginning to be viewed by some psychologists and early educators as a foreground that leads to development. Intersecting with these visions was renewed focus on the work of a Russian psychologist whose research was embedded in the Marxist tradition of understanding human development as an artifact of society.

## Vygotsky and the Social Construction of Knowledge

Due to a number of political and historical circumstances, the work of Lev Vygotsky (1896–1934) was not disseminated widely in Russia or in the rest of the world during the first half of the twentieth century. By the early 1960s, however, there was enough interest in it in the United States to support translation of some of his writings into English (Vygotsky, 1962/1986). Interpretation of Vygotsky's findings has subsequently taken different forms in Russia and the United States, due to fundamental differences in the orientations of psychological studies and visions of the aims of education in the two countries. In the United States, several major features of the work have become salient and are beginning to affect the theory and practice of early childhood education (Bodrova & Leong, 1996; Lee, 1992a, 1992b).

Although Vygotsky's theory of development resembles behaviorism in the sense that he saw the external environment, specifically society or culture, as the stimulus for development, he is considered a constructivist in the way he theorized about the nature of human knowledge (Lee, 1992a). Unlike Piaget and others who saw human development as pro-

ceeding in stages through the emergence of an internal schedule of maturation within the individual child in interaction with the physical and
social environment, Vygotsky understood development to proceed without stages and through a social (rather than individual) process. Learning
is mediated through the social phenomenon of language, and learning
leads development instead of the other way around (Vygotsky, 1962/
1986). Knowledge is thus understood to be a social construction, deeply
embedded in the historical and cultural contexts of people's lives.

Especially influential in this process of learning and knowledge construction is the role of adults (teachers) and more capable peers, who
through language and other social communication systems can move
children from what they are able to do and understand on their own to
a higher level of performance. Vygotsky called this psychological "space"
in which influence can occur the "zone of proximal development" (now
commonly referred to as the "ZPD").

In recent years, broad implications have been drawn from Vygotsky's
research to early childhood curriculum development and implementation. Highlighted among these are the importance of social contexts (especially the contexts of family and community) as sources of learning
and development, and the role of language in development (Bodrova &
Leong, 1996; Williams, 1991). Strategies such as use of the ZPD and "leading activities" that involve language growth and expansion for children
of different ages, and especially the use of play to foster development, are
recommended parts of Vygotskian-influenced early childhood curricula
(Bodrova & Leong, 1996). These considerations, as well as the convergence of concern about cultural appropriateness in early childhood teaching practice, gave further impetus to the controversy surrounding DAP.

## Toward Reconceptualization of the Field

Keeping apace with the multicultural movement and the introduction
of Vygotskian theory, a group of early childhood theorists, researchers,
and practitioners has established new lines of curriculum inquiry from
critical, postmodern, poststructural, and feminist perspectives (Cannella,
1997; Kessler, 1990; Kessler & Swadener, 1992; Mallory & New, 1994).
Known as the "early childhood reconceptualists," this group has begun
to raise issues of continued disenfranchisement of some populations from
the early childhood educational systems, continued inequity in distribution of resources, and continued lack of recognition of the role values
play in curriculum development and enactment.

In the mid-1990s, responding to critiques from this and other groups
as well as to its own internal processes, NAEYC reassessed its position state-

ment and issued a revision (Bredekamp & Copple, 1997) incorporating greater attention to the role of families and culture in children's development and highlighting the role of the teacher as decision maker and curriculum developer. The revision did retain the idea of "appropriate" versus "inappropriate" practices, however, and debate has continued regarding that formulation.

## CONCLUSION

What appears to be a central motif in the ongoing conversation regarding early childhood curriculum is the notion that children's knowledge is not only individually but socially constructed. For that reason, culture and belief systems also play a role in what and how children learn and must further expand the notion of the whole child. Knowledge in these areas is acquired largely through the children's observation of their society and playful imitation of the expectations and ways of life that they see around them, and their processing of these through language.

Thus, the image of the whole child and arguments for the roles of process and play in promoting development and learning remain vital today; and the themes that have characterized early childhood program formulations continue to reveal themselves in curriculum research. Opposing ideas introduced in some periods of innovation and exploration have served to sharpen the distinctive viewpoint—that the young child should be approached as an integrated being—permeating the field. The chapters that follow explore that viewpoint both within subject areas and across the themes traced in our brief history. The fundamental curriculum questions and the approaches to their possible resolution provided by each author suggest directions for future early childhood curriculum development.

## REFERENCES

Almy, M., Monighan, P., Scales, B., & Van Hoorn, J. (1984). Recent research on play: The teacher's perspective. In L. G. Katz (Ed.), *Current topics in early childhood education* (Vol. 5, pp. 1–25). Norwood, NJ: Ablex.

Anderson, L., Evertson, C., & Emmer, E. (1979). *Dimensions in classroom management derived from recent research.* Austin: Texas University Research and Development Center for Teacher Education. (ERIC Document Reproduction Service No. ED 175 860)

Anker, D., Foster, J., McLane, J., Sokel, J., & Weissbourd, B. (1974). Teaching children as they play. *Young Children, 29,* 203–213.

Ariès, P. (1962). *Centuries of childhood* (R. Balkick, Trans.). New York: Knopf.

Ausubel, D. P. (1963). *The psychology of meaningful verbal learning.* New York: Grune & Stratton.

Ausubel, D. R. (1968). *Educational psychology: A cognitive view.* New York: Holt, Rinehart & Winston.

Bandura, A. (1973). *Aggression: A social learning analysis.* Englewood Cliffs, NJ: Prentice-Hall.

Bandura, A., & Walters, R. H. (1963). *Social learning and personality development.* New York: Holt, Rinehart & Winston.

Bijou, S. W., & Baer, D. M. (1978). *Behavior analysis of child development.* Englewood Cliffs, NJ: Prentice-Hall.

Bodrova, E., & Leong, D. J. (1996). *Tools of the mind: The Vygotskian approach to early childhood education.* Englewood Cliffs, NJ: Merrill.

Braun, S., & Edwards, E. (1972). *History and theory of early childhood education.* Worthington, OH: Jones.

Bredekamp, S. (Ed.). (1987). *Developmentally appropriate practice in early childhood programs serving children from birth through age 8* (rev. ed.). Washington, DC: National Association for the Education of Young Children.

Bredekamp, S., & Copple, C. (1997). *Developmentally appropriate practice in early childhood programs* (rev. ed.). Washington, D.C.: National Association for the Education of Young Children.

Brophy, J. E., & Evertson, C. M. (1976). Learning from teaching. *A developmental perspective.* Boston: Allyn & Bacon.

Bruner, J. S., Goodnow, J. J., & Austin, G. A. (1956). *A study in thinking.* New York: Wiley.

Cannella, G. S. (1997). *Deconstructing early childhood education: Social justice and revolution.* New York: Lang.

Christie, J. F. (1982). Sociodramatic play training. *Young Children, 37,* 25–32.

Chud, G., & Fahlman, R. (1985). *Early childhood education for a multicultural society: A handbook for educators.* Vancouver: Western Education Development Group, The University of British Columbia.

Comenius, J. A. (1910). *The great didactic* (M. W. Keating, Trans.). New York: Russell & Russell. (Original translation 1896).

Cox, B. G., Macauley, J., & Ramirez, M. (1982). *Nuevas fronteras/new frontiers.* New York: Pergamon.

Cuffaro, H. K. (1995). *Experimenting with the world: John Dewey and the early childhood classroom.* New York: Teachers College Press.

De Gaetano, Y., Williams, L. R., & Volk, D. (1998). *Kaleidoscope: A multicultural approach for the primary school classroom.* Columbus, OH: Merrill/Prentice-Hall.

Dewey, J. (1902). *The child and the curriculum.* Chicago: University of Chicago Press.

Dewey, J. (1963). *Experience and education.* New York: Macmillan. (Original work published 1938)

Dewey, J. (1966). *Democracy and education.* New York: Free Press. (Original work published 1944)

Duckworth, E. (1972). The having of wonderful ideas. *Harvard Educational Review, 42,* 217–231,

Erikson, E. (1963). *Childhood and society.* New York: Norton. (Original work published 1950)

Evans, E. (1975). *Contemporary influences in early childhood education* (2nd ed.). New York: Holt, Rinehart & Winston.

Feitelson, D., & Ross, G. S. (1973). The neglected factor—Play. *Human Development, 16,* 202–223.

Froebel, F. (1887). *The education of man* (W. Hailman, Trans.). New York: Appleton. (Original work published 1826)

Gray, S. W., Ramsey, B. K., & Klaus, R. A. (1982). *From 3 to 20: The early training project.* Baltimore: University Park Press.

Green, J. A. (1912). *Pestalozzi's educational writings.* London: Longman.

Gutek, G. L. (1968). *Pestalozzi and education.* New York: Random House.

Gutek, G. L. (1972). *A history of the Western educational experience.* New York: Random House.

Hanes, M. L., Flores, M. I., Rosario, J., & Weikart, D. (1979). *Un marco abierto: An open framework for educators.* Ypsilanti, MI: High/Scope.

Hess, R. O., & Shipman, V. C. (1965). Early experience and the socialization of cognitive modes in children. *Child Development, 36,* 869–886.

Juarez & Associates. (1982). *An evaluation of the Head Start bilingual bicultural curriculum development project* (Contract No. HEW 105–7–1048). Washington, DC: Head Start Bureau, Administration for Children, Youth and Families, Department of Health and Human Services.

Katz, L., & Chard, S. (1989). *Engaging children's minds: The project approach.* Norwood, NJ: Ablex.

Kendall, F. E. (1996). *Diversity in the classroom: A multicultural approach to the education of young children.* New York: Teachers College Press. (Original work published 1983)

Kessen, W. (1965). *The child.* New York: Wiley.

Kessler, S. (1990, April). *Early childhood education as caring.* Paper presented at the annual meeting of the American Educational Research Association, Boston.

Kessler, S., & Swadener, B. B. (1992). *Reconceptualizing the early childhood curriculum: Beginning the dialogue.* New York: Teachers College Press.

King, E. W., Chipman, M., & Cruz-Janzen, M. (1994). *Educating young children in a diverse society.* Boston: Allyn & Bacon.

Kohlberg, L., & Lickona, T. (1987). Moral discussion and the class meeting. In R. DeVries with L. Kohlberg (Eds.), *Constructivist early education: Overview and comparison with other programs* (pp. 143–181). Washington, DC: National Association for the Education of Young Children.

Lay-Dopyera, M., & Dopyera, J. (1992). Strategies for teaching. In C. Seefeldt (Ed.), *The early childhood curriculum: A review of current research* (2nd ed., pp. 16–41). New York: Teachers College Press.

Lee, P. C. (1992a). Constructivism. In L. R. Williams & D. P. Fromberg (Eds.), *The encyclopedia of early childhood education* (pp. 206–207). New York: Garland.

Lee, P. C. (1992b). Vygotsky, Lev Semenovich. In L. R. Williams & D. P. Fromberg (Eds.), *The encyclopedia of early childhood education* (p. 203). New York: Garland.

Mallory, B. L., & New, R. S. (Eds.). (1994). *Diversity and developmentally appropriate practice: Challenges for early childhood education.* New York: Teachers College Press.

Meek, A. (1991). On thinking about teaching; A conversation with Eleanor Duckworth. *Educational Leadership, 48*(6), 30–34.

Miller, K. A. (1989). Enhancing early childhood mainstreaming through cooperative learning: A brief literature review. *Child Study Journal, 19,* 285–294.

Miller, L., & Dyer, J. L. (1975). Four preschool programs: Their dimensions and effects. *Monographs of the Society for Research in Child Development, 40*(5–6, Serial No. 162). Chicago: University of Chicago Press.

Miller-Lachmann, L., & Taylor, L. S. (1995). *Schools for all: Educating children in a diverse society.* Albany, NY: Delmar.

Montessori, M. (1964). *The Montessori method.* New York: Schocken. (Original work published 1912).

Pestalozzi, J. H. (1915). *How Gertrude teaches her children* (L. E. Holland & F. C. Turner, Trans.). Syracuse, NY: Bardeen. (Original work published 1801)

Piaget, J. (1962). *Play, dreams and imitation in childhood* (H. Weaver, Trans.). New York: Norton.

Piaget, J., & Inhelder, B. (1969). *The psychology of the child* (C. Gattegno & F. M. Hodgson, Trans.). New York: Basic Books.

Ramsey, P. G. (1987). *Teaching and learning in a diverse world: Multicultural education for young children.* New York: Teachers College Press.

Ramsey, P. G. (1998). *Teaching and learning in a diverse world: Multicultural education for young children* (2nd. ed.). New York: Teachers College Press.

Ramsey, P. G., Vold, E. B., & Williams, L. R. (1989). *Multicultural education: A source book.* New York: Garland.

Rosen, C. (1974). The effects of sociodramatic play on problem-solving behavior among culturally disadvantaged preschool children. *Child Development, 45,* 920–927.

Rousseau, J.-J. (1969). *Emile or on education* (A. Bloom, Trans.). New York: Basic Books. (Original work published 1762).

Schwadener, E., & Lawton, J. T. (1978). *The effects of two types of advance organizer presentations on preschool children's classifications, relations, and transfer task performance.* Madison: University of Wisconsin Center on Cognitive Learning. (ERIC Document Reproduction Service No. ED 152 413)

Shipman, V. (1976). *Notable early characteristics of high and low achieving Black low-SES children* (Progress Report 76–21). Princeton, NJ: Educational Testing Service.

Skinner, B. F. (1974). *About behaviorism.* New York: Knopf.

Smilansky, S. (1968). *The effects of sociodramatic play on disadvantaged preschool children.* New York: Wiley.

Smith, M. S., & Bissell, J. S. (1970). Report analysis: The impact of Headstart. *Harvard Educational Review, 40*(1), 51–104.

Standing, E. M. (1962). *Maria Montessori: Her life and work.* New York: Mentor Omega Books.

Thompson, C. G. (1944). The social and emotional development of preschool children under two types of educational programs. *Psychological monographs, 56* (5, Whole No. 2M).

Tzelepis, A., Giblin, P. T., & Agronow, S. J. (1983). Effects of adult caregivers' behaviors on the activities, social interactions, and investments of nascent preschool day-care groups. *Journal of Applied Developmental Psychology, 4,* 201–216.

Vygotsky, L. V. (1986). *Thought and language.* Cambridge, MA: MIT Press. (Original work published 1962)

Weber, E. (1984). *Ideas influencing early childhood education: A theoretical analysis.* New York: Teachers College Press.

Weikart, D. (1969, March). *A comparative study of three preschool curricula.* Paper presented at the biennial meeting of the Society for Research in Child Development, Santa Monica, CA.

Williams, L. R. (1991). Curriculum making in two voices: Dilemmas of inclusion in early childhood education. *Early Childhood Research Quarterly, 6*(3), 303–311.

Williams, L. R., De Gaetano, Y., Harrington, C. C., & Sutherland, I. R. (1985). ALERTA: *A multicultural bilingual approach to teaching young children.* Menlo Park, CA: Addison-Wesley.

York, S. (1991). *Roots and wings: Affirming culture in early childhood programs.* St. Paul, MN: Redleaf.

Zamora, G. (1985). *Nuevo amanecer/new dawn.* Lincolnwood, IL: National Textbook Co.

CHAPTER 2

# A Review of Research on Play

## Doris Pronin Fromberg

WHY WOULD we want children to play in early childhood classes? How would we provide worthwhile conditions? In exploring ways to answer these questions, the synthesis of research in this chapter focuses on the dynamics of sociodramatic interaction that are integral to understanding related aspects of development and education.

### DEFINING PLAY

*Play* functions as both a verb and a noun. Rather than a category, property, or stage of behavior, play is a *relative* activity that manifests shifting functions in different settings. Perhaps because play is relative behavior, scholars have studied it from the differing perspectives of historians, philosophers, linguists, anthropologists, educators, and psychologists. Scholars and researchers have considered the child as solitary, playing with objects or imagination, as well as a social player with one or more peers or adults. They have considered the immediate contexts in which play occurs, the content, the interaction of context and content, the cultural environment, and the player's experience, and they have differentiated play from exploration, dividing social play into structured games-with-rules and sports, as contrasted with the evolving forms of sociodramatic play.

   The focus of this chapter is on current theories of play, except where contrast may serve to highlight an issue. To begin, I propose a definition of play that might serve as a foil to parry with the various theoretical perspectives. Young children's play is

> Symbolic, in that it represents reality with an "as if" or "what if" attitude
>
> Meaningful, in that it connects or relates experiences
>
> Active, in that children are doing things
>
> Pleasurable, even when children are engaged seriously in activity
>
> Voluntary and intrinsically motivated, whether the motive is curiosity, mastery, affiliation, or something else
>
> Rule-governed, whether implicitly or explicitly expressed
>
> Episodic, characterized by emerging and shifting goals that children develop spontaneously and flexibly.

Dewey (1933) suggested that play "emphasizes" activity rather than "outcomes" (p. 285). However, he cautioned that when there is no outcome play can "degenerate into fooling, and work into drudgery. . . . To be playful and serious at the same time is possible, and it defines the ideal mental condition" (p. 286). His work suggests the following continuum: fooling–play–work–drudgery. For example, work may come to feel like play in certain circumstances, such as the experiences of "functional autonomy" (Allport, 1958) and "flow" (Csikszentmihalyi, 1988), when the worker is "unaware of time passing [with work being] satisfying and focused enough in the present to transcend the moment" (Fromberg, 1997, p. 191).

The content of play is influenced by children's experiences (text) and also by the context in which they find themselves. Context may include the physical environment, time, other children or adults, and cultural sanctions and expectations. The contexts of two broad theoretical perspectives on play are discussed below.

## THEORIZING ABOUT PLAY

The psychological and the cultural theoretical positions emphasize different ways of looking at the same intrinsically motivated activity.

### Psychological Perspectives

Jean Piaget, a psychologist, epistemologist, and biologist, saw children as taking an active role in forming their play symbols. Building on the object play of solitary children, he proposed that play can be "pure assimilation" but that it is the "predominance" of assimilation over accommodation that defines an activity as play (1962). In emphasizing assimilation, he saw play as a state of imbalance.

**Present-Time Behavior with a Past or Future Orientation.** Piaget (1962) suggested that children's play "distorts" reality to fit the child's current level of understanding and focuses on past experiences "to transform reality" (1966, pp. 111).

In contrast, Vygotsky (1978) suggested that children at play act "against immediate impulse" by subordinating themselves to rules. There is a paradox in Vygotsky's dialectic between pleasure in being "emancipated from situational constraints" while acting spontaneously, and subordinating oneself to the rules of play as the "path to maximal pleasure in play" (p. 99). In this way, children at play exercise their greatest self-control and behave "in advance of development" (p. 129). Vygotsky contended that "play creates a zone of proximal development" (p. 102) that also is a context for instruction that is oriented toward the future development of children.

If a major benefit of play for Vygotsky was the creation of a precursor of development, the major benefit of play for others was its creative, "combinatorial" (Bruner, Jolly, & Sylva, 1976, p. 153; Sutton-Smith, 1979, p. 315), and "generative" aspect (Bruner & Sherwood, 1976, p. 277). For Piaget, it would be the ongoing consolidation by children of their experiences, a process that leads toward construction of internal representations of the world, and a transition between egocentric thought and the development of reciprocity. Vygotsky (1976) saw play as a bridge ("pivot") that joins objects and actions with their representation in thought. Until children can separate the thought from the object or action, they must have something to act as a "pivot" in the form of a meaningful substitute, for example, "a stick denoting a horse" (p. 546).

It is interesting to consider how the process of making connections and substitutions occurs. Piaget (1962, 1976) suggested the dynamic of "cognitive conflict" similar to the concept of "cognitive dissonance" (Festinger, 1957). There is an element of novelty or surprise caused by the discrepancy between what one expects and what one finds, a contrast that stimulates fresh perceptions. The contrast and movement between familiar and strange stimulate perception; cognitive conflict represents one of the powerful conditions for learning that teachers can use.

**Wish-Fulfillment and Mastery.** Investigators have agreed that children use play to represent wish-fulfillment. Vygotsky (1976) suggested that play reflects "generalized affects" rather than "isolated wishes" and that the "union of affect and perception" is characteristic of early childhood (pp. 540, 545). There is also general agreement that play helps children to feel in control and to experience a sense of mastery. Thus children come to understand the limits of their own power to control and predict the environment (Corsaro, 1990). Recent researchers in the development of children's "theory of mind" also have pointed to the significance of learning about predictability and control in the development of awareness of one's own thoughts as well as those of others, and noted the isomorphism between children's developing theory of mind and pretend play (Astington, 1993; Bartsch & Wellman, 1995; Garvey, 1993; Leslie, 1995).

Other commentators have seen play as a way in which children attempt to cope with their environment and find refuge (Gaynard, 1998), as well as a way to "reconcile" themselves to varied levels of success and influence (Opie & Opie, 1976). Children also control the intensity of play activity, as in "play fighting" (Aldis, 1975, p. 180). These views parallel the idea that children have a need to feel competent and capable of influencing their world (White, 1959).

## Cultural Perspectives

The cultural viewpoints emphasize the contextual and *relative* aspects of play. Some investigators have contended that what may be play in one time and place may be ritual or religious, frivolous, or technical behavior elsewhere (Roopnarine, Johnson, & Hooper, 1994; Slaughter & Dombrowski, 1989). The cultural context also determines who may, or is likely to, engage in various kinds of play (Geertz, 1976; Whiting, Edwards, et al., 1988).

**Play as a Categorization Frame.** Some commentators have identified the concept of a play frame, background, or context. Our culture teaches us what to expect and how to categorize reality and pretend play (Bateson, 1976, 1979). In this way, play is progress in the "evolution of communication" and "metacommunication" (Bateson, 1976, pp. 121, 125). Bateson suggested that children demonstrate by their behavior that they can categorize play and not-play as they enter into and step outside the framework of play situations.

Studies of North African immigrant families in Israel found that parents taught their preschool children to categorize objects, kinship structures, and myths in unique ways (Janiv, 1976) that appeared to influence their play (Smilansky, 1968). In a longitudinal study in the United States,

Heath (1983) found that North Carolina urban middle-class Black and White children arrived at school with similar backgrounds, whereas the play and language use of rural working-class Black and White children differed from one another and from the middle-class children. The rural Black children brought to school strengths such as creative narratives, rich metaphors, humor, and fluid alternative uses of time and space. Teachers typically did not appreciate these strengths until the intermediate grades, by which time many children had become alienated and discouraged. The rural working-class White children tended to receive approval at home for single "correct" behaviors and the use of playthings in a single correct way. This limited approach served them in the school's primary grades but did not serve them as they encountered the need to make connections in the intermediate grades. Understanding children's category systems and the emphases of their early play experiences suggests the need to appreciate, rather than rank, differences.

The metacommunication that takes place in social play makes it possible for children to pretend together as they accept or reject each other's play premises, plans, and suggestions. Still another way to consider the fruitful notion of metacommunication in play is to consider that representation takes place every time children play with objects or events as "pivots" that bridge the gap between real and make-believe, or when they collaborate with others to "map" a play territory together. In this respect, play seemed to lead development (Leslie, 1995; Nelson et al., 1986). This is evident when the surface structures of children's play reveal their deeper propositional structures (Garvey, 1979; Johnson-Laird, 1995). Some researchers would concur, finding that 2-year-olds appear to understand, cooperate in, and contribute to joint pretend play earlier, and to engage in play with longer themes, when at home with older siblings (Farver & Wimbarti, 1995).

**Play Contexts.**  Situational context makes a difference in children's play competence. Familiar and private settings appear to facilitate more creative and competent play (Aureli & Coecchia, 1996; J. Dunn, 1988; Howes, Droege, & Matheson, 1994; Ramsey & Lasquade, 1996). In a "strange situation, the range and diversity of play became considerably restricted and the tempo was reduced. Nothing happened to the structural variables" (Fein, 1985, p. 26).

These findings suggest that we might expect children to behave in *relation* to contexts and constraints. The physical and verbal aspects of sociodramatic play offer opportunities to observe children's "theory of mind" through their capacity to represent the real as well as the imaginary, the real as imagined, and to "represent mental representations" (Lillard, 1993, p. 349).

## TRANSFORMATIONAL DYNAMICS OF PLAY

Looking at play with a psychological as well as a cultural emphasis suggests that children *integrate* both the shared symbols of social players and the personal, representational aspects of play, while interacting within cultural and situational contexts. The content of children's sociodramatic play, therefore, is intrinsically multicultural in nature.

Several theoretical perspectives address the issues of how children's sociodramatic pretend play functions. There is some isomorphism among script theory, narrative structures, theory of mind, and complexity theory that can help us to appreciate the nonlinearity in representational social play.

### Script Theory

Script theory takes the position that children develop sociodramatic play content out of the event knowledge that they acquire in daily life within their distinct cultural contexts (Bretherton, 1984; Mandler, 1992; Schank & Abelson, 1977). In this sense, scripts predispose perception in play and in understanding narratives (Bower, Black, & Turner, 1994). Event knowledge might include such routines as food acquisition, preparation, and consumption; relations between adults and children in culturally defined situations; and experiences and responsibilities for participating in family or community events.

Young children amass experiences that they then play out together within a combined process of shared predictability and collaborative novelty in a temporal sequence (e.g., events at a health clinic or food-gathering event) and within particular, culturally defined spaces (e.g., playing "farming" alongside a field in which mothers engage in farming [Whiting & Edwards et al., 1988], making faces behind the teacher's back in a classroom [Corsaro, 1990], or engaging in enriched play within home spaces [Squibb & King, 1996]). Such play scripts serve as evidence of the recursive relation between the shared cultural understandings of young children and their capacity to interactively plan, share, enact, elaborate, and further develop thematic content.

Script theory investigators propose that shared-event schemata serve as figurative, sequential frameworks (Bretherton, 1984). Other researchers have observed that a story narrative "grammar" and parallel problem-solving capacity undergird children's pretend play (Ariel, 1992; Eckler & Weininger, 1989; Harris & Kavanaugh, 1993).

Script theory embodies a kind of syntactic structure and context for sociodramatic play. Scripts contain a finite set of figurative structures that can generate an infinite set of combinations, a grammar for play. While children understand the signals of play such as voice change, posture, gestures, or facial expression, they seem to follow certain organizational rules that are more or less complex. Their play explicitly represents their implicit understanding of the "script."

### Integration of Social, Cognitive, and Affective

Within the play context, there is an interaction of affective, social, and cognitive aspects of play that change in relation to the communication content or text. Piaget (1965) made the point that when children build rules together as they play, they become more independent and increase their ability to see points of view other than their own, the process of *decentering* from oneself and one's immediate environment. We might see the ongoing social feedback in sociodramatic play as a kind of coaching system that helps children decenter. For example, a study of the natural play of preschoolers found that they ask for feedback from one another by various conventional statements, such as "OK?" "See?" "Right?" and "Don't we?" as they seek confirmation, information, compliance, argument, and attention (Chafel, 1984). As they play, they are able to move outside the play frame for brief negotiations about how to keep the play going and then maintain pretense during the play. They proceed "with the least possible acknowledgment of the playframe" (Giffin, 1974, p. 88). As they do so, their play events manifest a greater number of more expansive and extended scripts (Nelson & Seidman, 1984). Thus, the isomorphic imagery shared within the social/cultural context becomes part of the child's individual/personal perspective. Discussion of these dynamics follows.

### Complexity Theory and the Power of Oscillating Contrasts

The negotiations of social play in particular appear to involve an oscillating process between what you expect in somebody else's behavior and what you find. This oscillation stimulates the decentration that characterizes development in cognition, socialization, and play. Contrasts, cognitive dissonance, the imbalance in transitional experiences, negotiations, pivots, and scaffolding are among the dynamic processes that characterize sociodramatic play. These processes are transformational in nature and function as if they were "phase transitions" between different states of experience (Robertson & Combs, 1995; Waldrop, 1992). As phase transitions, these processes reflect an *oscillating balance* between freedom and control, one state and another, reality and make-believe, a kind of dynamic fulcrum that fluctutates between the metacommunication and representation that take place between emplotment and enactment. The study of play, therefore, is the study of relational rather than skeletal phenomena; it is a nonlinear, dynamic system. Play, cultural systems, narrative systems, and theory of mind systems represent nonlinear dynamics.

As such, nonlinear naturalistic settings—however inconvenient to a researcher's schedule—offer considerable promise as locations for research. The most fruitful questions to pursue within this framework would include those that might shed light on how young children's phase transitions function. It is intriguing to witness the functioning of these oscillating fulcrums. Investigation of children's play might illuminate references to script theory's dynamic processes, such as "image-schemas" (Mandler, 1992), "flags" (Harris & Kavanaugh, 1993), manipulable "multiple mental models" (Johnson-Laird, 1995; Perner, 1991), "decouplers" (Leslie, 1995), "desire-belief psychology" (Bartsch & Wellman, 1995; Repacholi & Gopnik, 1997), "cognitive templates" (Whyte & Owens, 1989), "affective representational templates" (Fein, 1985), "perceptual models" (Fromberg, 1995; McLuhan, 1963), "cognitive seeds" (Lucariello & Rifkin, 1986), or "ludic infrastructures" (Sutton-Smith, 1971).

## Theory of Mind

It is apparent that sociodramatic play is a form in which implicit meaning may be evident in explicit forms. Researchers who pursue a study of "theory of mind" also have noticed that pretend play looks as if young players understand that they are playing; that other players have thoughts, feelings, and intentions; and that it is possible to interpret and predict others' behaviors. Studies vary in their queries about if/then, as-if/if-then, and sometimes convoluted verbal formats to try to understand what young children understand about others' desires, beliefs, false beliefs, and deception. They also disagree about the age (between 2 and 4 years) of children's explicit self-awareness of themselves as players and thinkers, and their awareness of others as conscious thinkers. In sum, the authors of studies and their reviewers disagree about theoretical, developmental, and methodological issues.

The value of these studies, neverthless, lies in their quest for a clearer understanding of the dynamics of young children's development of meanings; such an understanding promises to offer insights into the processes of pretend play as well as cognitive development. Perhaps it will be possible for early childhood teacher-researchers to become play astronomers who might glimpse the "oscillating fulcrum" in sociodramatic play activities.

## THE RELATIONSHIP OF PLAY AND DEVELOPMENT

Depending on one's theoretical position, one sees play as extending cognitive, literacy, and social learning, or as reinforcing what children already have learned. Children extend their imagination and improve associative fluency, or they lack the capacity for imagining what is not or has not been present. If one agrees that intervention in play can improve ·children's learning and imagination, then one would create a different environment for children than if one disagrees.

Researchers also have wondered whether play, or "improved" play, could change the course of development. Therefore they have engaged in studies that attempt to find out if modeling, or otherwise stimulating children to be more playful, could influence social competence, creativity, cognitive development, and literacy development. Although children's sociodramatic play simultaneously involves these dimensions in integrated ways, the sections that follow discuss these attempts by following along the more or less separate strands of research pathways. Therefore, as we look at the sequence of play development, it makes sense to expect trends with variations rather than fixed results.

### Social Development

There is consensus that sociodramatic play influences social competence. In general, social and moral development take place as young children interact with others. The social negotiations of pretend play are a particularly potent and influential realm of experience. Researchers have found that "social behavior was more mature [and reciprocal] in pretend play than in nonpretend activities" (Connolly, Doyle, & Reznick, 1988, pp. 311–312). Others concurred (Barnes & Vangelisti, 1995; de Lorimer, Doyle, & Tessier, 1995), finding that children maintained stability and consistency through sharing meanings (Meckley, 1994).

Some studies supported the notion that toddlers play for a longer time and with greater complexity when their parents play with them, model play behaviors, and verbally appreciate children's play (Haight & Miller, 1992; Landry, Garner, Swank, & Baldwin, 1996; Youngblade & Dunn, 1995). An adult presence with toddlers from varied backgrounds (Eckerman & Didow, 1989) and preschoolers from low-income families stimulated more complex play and language (Smilansky, 1968). Other studies found that young children's play and language are more advanced with older children or older siblings than with peers, regardless of socio-economic or national background (Brownell, 1990; Farver & Wimbarti, 1995; Howes, with Unger & Matheson, 1992). Pellegrini (1984a) found otherwise—that the presence of other preschoolers provided more opportunity for cognitive conflicts—and wondered whether his middle-class children were less likely than the low-income population to express disagreement with an adult.

Fein (1985) and Reynolds and Jones (1997) identified and studied "master players," defined as children who engage in extended social pretend play, characterized by fluidity, flexibility, risk taking, and affective relationships. More competent and more cooperative, less argumentative players were also the object of peer acceptance (Pellegrini, 1988; Trawick-Smith, 1994) and positive teacher assessment of sociability and school adjustment (Ladd & Price, 1987). More secure children also spent more time in pretend play, which might have contributed to their autonomy as organizers and planners (Fagot, 1997), particularly when sensitive teachers were nearby (Howes, 1997). A related finding was that children who received more child-care changes, often associated with more stressed families, manifested less competent play (Howes & Stewart, 1987). If they might meet, in dialogue, the more psychological or more sociocultural investigators cited above might all agree that there is a significant interaction between the child's developmental capacity and the play's social context.

Children engage in pretend play at about 18 months of age, by representing an as-if model of reality, a phase that precedes coordinated social pretend play in the third year (Perner, 1991). Other researchers reported a progression in children's play from solitary and beginning joint play (2-year-olds), to more relatedness and talk (2½-year-olds), and then to reciprocal role playing (3-year-olds) (Miller & Garvey, 1984; see also Parten, 1971). Language development through scaffolding (Eckerman & Didow, 1989) paralleled and had a recursive relationship with decontextualized play and social cognition in these studies (Shore, 1990).

It is possible, however, that more sophisticated thinking may require solitary play (Eddowes, 1991; Rubin & Howe, 1986). For example, there was consensus among researchers that although children become increasingly competent and complex in their sociodramatic play through 5 years of age, such play declines among 6-year-olds, perhaps because of schooling and the internalization of imagination (Cole & LaVoie, 1985; Voss, 1987). Between 5 and 7 years of age, the nature of children's concern shifted from actions within the pretense to purposes of the actions (Forbes & Yablick, 1984).

## Imagination

There is controversy surrounding the body of research that deals with the influence of play on children's creativity. Feitelson and Ross (1973) hypothesized that thematic play influences children's creativity and that it does not develop automatically but through modeling. They found more combinatorial play on post-tests after kindergarten children received tutoring and encouragement in the use of combinatorial play and unstructured props. Related studies supported their findings (Dansky, 1986; Freyberg, 1973). Divergent players seemed to be more willing to try alternatives, when compared with children who had played with convergent materials that suggested a narrower range of options or had observed play with either type of material. Convergent materials seemed to constrain the activities of the children. Researchers have cautioned that the effects were short-term and recommended longitudinal study.

Fein (1985) saw "pretense as an orientation in which the immediate environment is deliberately treated in a divergent manner" (p. 21). Eisner (1990) pointed to the shared representational power and significance of art and play. Pellegrini (1992) found a relationship between flexible rough-and-tumble players and their social problem-solving flexibility. These views point to the importance of studying play as related to associative fluency and creativity.

Observations of young children in their natural group settings suggested that pairs or trios of children are most effective in stimulating each other's imagination (Bruner, 1980) and that children working within the group itself might have helped to reduce aggressive behavior (Farver, 1996). Thus such studies support the paradigm that children who are stimulated to play more imaginatively show improved ability to make new connections.

Critics have challenged the validity of methods used in the body of associative fluency and play research, raising questions of unconscious experimenter bias or whether play had occurred (Smith & Whitney, 1987). Their challenges have extended an ongoing dialogue within this paradigm (Dansky, 1985; L. Dunn & Herwig, 1992). The volleying of studies is likely to continue.

## Cognitive Development

There is a general consensus, with some methodological reservations, that the integration of cognitive and socioemotional development during play supports cognitive development.

**Sociocultural Contexts.** Smilansky's position, like that of others (Rogoff, 1990; Scales, Almy, Nicolopoulou, & Ervin-Tripp, 1991), leans toward the notion that the contents of sociodramatic play and cognitive development depend on cultural and contextual factors. Thus different environmental experiences, available resources, and historical and cultural expectations affect children's perceptions, practices, preferences, and achievements in distinct ways.

Smilansky (1968) suggested that young children need adult intervention in their play. She observed that less advanced sociodramatic play co-varied with academic failure and a disadvantaged background. When teachers intervened to stimulate the sociodramatic play of low-income preschool children in their classrooms, children became more flexible planners, used language more elaborately and expansively, sustained play for longer periods, and improved their use of pretense. Teachers attempted to vary the intervention on the basis of the different skills with which individual children came to school.

Contrary findings are reported by Eifermann (1971). Eifermann, based on a study of 14,000 elementary school children, found that a similar population of 6- to 8-year-olds displayed more, not less, social symbolic play than the low-income children about whom Smilansky wrote, and proposed that low-income children may develop symbolic play at a later age.

Levenstein (1992), however, hypothesized that play skills need to be taught and that mothers of children from low-income families could learn to assist their toddlers in improving play skills. She posited that children's play is related to problem solving, academic skills, classroom attitudes, and IQ; she found and replicated significant increases in the children's IQ's.

Believing that opportunities to play could influence cognitive development, Golomb (1979) and Golomb, Gowing, and Friedman (1982) created a strategy to stimulate the conservation of quantity among preschoolers who were pretested and post-tested in a clinical Piagetian manner. They concluded that pretend play facilitated the acquisition of conservation of quantity. They suggested that their subjects used intuitive and unreflective reversibility, which they proposed is a spontaneous precursor to genuine reversibility of operational thought.

A related study concerning 3-year-olds' early moral development within the family included story stems (problem narratives) with doll play and props in both laboratory and home settings (Buchsbaum & Emde, 1990). The researchers found the children, at younger ages than Piagetian researchers might predict, capable of offering coherent and "alternative prosocial choices in a moral dilemma . . . when the task is altered so as to be accessible to younger children both in terms of its affective significance and the mode of required response" (p. 150). They related their research to script theory as a representational form that derives its content and power from contextual factors.

**Resources as Contexts.** Toddlers who used objects and toys alone and with others increasingly developed the capacity to pretend substitutions with less prototypical objects or with more than one symbolic transformation in ways that were more diverse and complex (Fein, 1975). Others confirmed these findings (Copple, Cocking, & Matthews, 1984).

After studying the symbolic play of toddlers, one team of researchers concluded that play can be enhanced or depressed by contextual variation when adults model play behavior at home or in a study setting (Bretherton, O'Connell, Shore, & Bates, 1984). Another investigator concluded, after modeling, that the social pretend play of toddlers both reflects and contributes to decentration; Fenson (1984) proposed that children progress in turn through the processes of decentering, decontextualization, and integration. Development, from this perspective, proceeds from a focus on the self toward active, other-directed acts. The indicators of decontextualization are symbolic transformation, substitutions, and inventive acts, as children become less dependent on prototypical representation. An increasing ability to combine individual action sequences into multi-scheme combinations characterizes integration, with an increased predominance of speech with age. There was no gender effect on language, but Fenson found more integrative play among girls; another researcher found that girls used more explanations and boys more self-referential statements (B. Black, 1992). There also was confirmation that children who use low-specificity toys engage in more interactive play and maintain a shared social script more continuously than children who use high-specificity props (McGhee, Etheridge, & Berg, 1984; McLoyd, 1983)

**Personal Developmental Contexts.** The study of individual differences provides another contribution to understanding the dynamics of play. Researchers have identified "patterners" (i.e., object-oriented) and "dramatists" (i.e., symbol-oriented) (Gardner, 1982); they and others (Taylor & Carlson, 1997) have interpreted each style to be a reflection of underlying "mental structures" and personality, a valid route toward general symbolic competence. These styles appear to parallel Adler's (1923) introvert–extrovert categories.

J. L. Singer (1973) reported findings concerning a related difference—individuals who displayed a profile of high or low fantasy in their play. Others supported his findings (Connolly & Doyle, 1984; Moran,

Sawyers, Fu, & Milgram, 1984). J. L. Singer and D. Singer (1979) found that high-imagination children reported greater contact with parents who modeled or provided specific opportunities for fantasy play. High-imagination children manifested a capacity to wait quietly for a longer period of time, reporting fantasy play as they did so. They also scored higher in imaginative storytelling, made more analogic kinds of statements, and were more persevering than low-fantasy children. Schwartzman (1984) cautioned us to be careful about labeling children as "nonimaginative, noncreative, nonconceptual" (p. 58) rather than stylistically different.

**Gender.** Teacher awareness of gender patterns in choices of themes (MacNaughton, 1995) and play centers (e.g., older preschoolers choosing same-sex children for play [Urberg & Kaplan, 1989]) is important for educational equity. Moreover, access to the traditionally male domain of blocks, with which young children can develop their visual-spatial skills, was found to be related significantly to mathematical learning (Maccoby & Jacklin, 1974).

During play, researchers have found that girls asserted themselves by balancing their own perspectives with those of others (Sheldon, 1992) and engaged in longer episodes of shared pretense, suggesting that they might value the mutual interaction while boys' goals were to gain "acceptance of their own suggestions" (G. Black, 1989, p. 390). In a related finding, boys initiated more play topics to which more girls responded, and girls engaged in "more sophisticated, constructive play [when playing with blocks] with boys" (Pellegrini & Perlmutter, 1989, p. 295). In a similar vein, boys' play was dramatically different from the predominantly housekeeping play of girls, even when thematic content varied (Dodge & Frost, 1986). Researchers have identified boys' play as more fluent and girls' play as more flexible, original, and elaborative (Gonen, Uzmen, Akcin, & Ozdemir, 1993).

Other investigators have found that boys engaged in more active play, rough-and-tumble play, games with rules, and games involving spatial relations (Paley, 1984; Pellegrini, 1987). Within rough-and-tumble play, the children may perceive themselves to be collaborative rather than confrontational, regardless of adult conclusions.

## Literacy Development

There is a distinctive body of applied research concerning classroom provision of alternative sociodramatic play themes (e.g., bank, office, post office, restaurant, veterinary office, hospital, pet shop) that include literacy materials as play props and their influence on children's increased use of language literacy skills (Christie, 1991; Morrow, 1997; O'Brien & Bi, 1995) and emergent numeracy (Cook, 1996). Cazden (1971) reported that, while the quantity of oral language was plentiful during classroom housekeeping corner play, the syntax and content were repetitious rather than elaborative and expansive. Other researchers have found that children use more varied and extensive language when teachers provide materials for varied themes (Dodge & Frost, 1986; Levy, Schaefer, & Phelps, 1986). These studies documented a powerfully recursive relationship between play and literacy development within the classroom context of thematic learning centers. In effect, play provides a collaborative medium in which children may practice literacy skills, mutually develop scripts based on event knowledge, provide mutual scaffolding, and further expand and extend literacy use. Studies tend to support the notion that play as the locus of children's power can prevail when the teacher models and extends rather than directs.

In addition to looking at how language and play coincide developmentally, researchers have suggested that children enjoy playing with language because it makes them feel in control (Freud, 1916/1960; Kirschenblatt-Gimblett, 1979). They have observed play such as sounds or words repeated for their own sake as well as in riddles, jokes, and metaphors. Thus, just as pretend play may suggest "the hallmark of an emerging artistic and literary ability" (Bretherton, 1988, p. 211), playing with language may have poetic as well as metalinguistic functions.

There also are intervention studies concerning how play influences the recall of stories. Investigators found that children's story comprehension improved after training in thematic fantasy play. Interventions that facilitated the ability to retell stories included role playing, rather than adult-led discussion (Pellegrini & Galda, 1982); peer-directed play (Pellegrini, 1984b); engaging in imaginative play actions themselves, rather than through puppets (Marbach & Yawkey, 1980); repeated opportunities to play out stories in small groups (Williamson & Silvern, 1991); and an effective combination of fantasy, verbalization, and conflict (Pellegrini, 1985). The investigators implied that the metacommunication children used in order to maintain the play frame made it possible for the children to move between their own role and their peers' role interpretations, supporting Vygotsky's notion of play as leading development (Galda, Pellegrini, & Cox, 1989).

Throughout studies that considered the relation of young children's play and their literacy development, there flowed a strong current that carries the message: Social pretend play involves the development of scripts that evolve collaboratively. The negotiation processes provide a scaffolding similar to that of an editor and author. These images suggest that young children's increasing oral language skills are the foundations upon which they build their skills as writers, learning how to communicate with an audience and what voices to use.

## IMPLICATIONS FOR CURRICULUM DEVELOPMENT

The research on play indicates that it is an important part of the lives of young children. Play has lymphatic, in the sense of pervasive and interconnected, implications for their education. While there has been a scant body of research (Wing, 1995) directly dealing with the impact of teacher attitudes toward play, Torrance (1962) reported that teachers perceive creative children as more of a problem than garden-variety achievers. We expect that the spontaneous nature of play will be a burden to teachers with this attitude. Teachers need to be joyful and playful, open to accepting the unexpected connection or alternative with good humor.

### Ways of Encouraging Play

Teachers can encourage play by modeling, planning with children, and playing with language.

**Modeling.** Teachers could model play behavior that stimulates development through challenge. This would mean attracting children to play by providing a variety of options with which they can feel comfortable and in which they perceive a chance for success, thereby creating an oscillating balance. Part of the teacher's task is to vary the level of structure of props and themes for different children in order to facilitate varied perspectives, meanings, motives, and enactments. The best options are those that children can actively structure and for which there may be more than one possible outcome. Thus the teacher would help children extend rather than merely replay and repeat experiences (Tizard, 1977).

Inasmuch as children come to school with different experiences, providing materials and opportunities will yield different outcomes. Therefore, teachers could actively bring children into play activities in varied ways, sometimes by taking roles, creating contrasts, or entering a play frame with an extendable model or dramatized suggestion.

Interage play as well as peer play helps children to learn as they see attainable models. In a sense, playmates are natural examples of new figures highlighted against familiar backgrounds. Therefore teachers could try to help children who tend to be isolates to move into parallel and collaborative play with other children. For isolates as well as others, mixed-age play may assist the development of more complex and extended play forms.

Modeling also takes place when a teacher asks questions that suggest a variety of possible responses. Such questions and situations that suggest more than one way to proceed are likely to encourage an openness to various problem solutions. If there is only one material or method, children receive the message that independent thinking is unwelcome. An array of possibilities, however, might encourage play.

**Planning with Children.** Children need enough time to play out their themes. Paley (1984) found that some of her kindergarten children needed extended amounts of time to engage in sociodramatic play before they could focus on artwork at a table. There is evidence that 30 minutes provides a minimum amount of time within which young children might develop a sociodramatic play theme (Christie, Johnsen, & Peckover, 1988). Beyond minimal time, there is need for one or more long blocks of time during the school day.

Thematic learning centers with 4- to 8-week shifts in content focus are important provisions for children's play throughout the primary grades as well as in kindergartens and preschools. Children also need the time and opportunity to explore new materials and situations as well as to play. In order to strike a balance, teachers need to infuse novelty, variety, and fresh challenges. In order to foster continuity with children's meanings, teachers effectively pace the *contrasts* between the strange and the familiar, so that children are able to perceive a new figure when it is contrasted clearly against a known background. To the extent that children construct their learning in self-directed ways, they acquire increasingly realistic expectations about the future and a sense of confidence and control.

Some children need time to be alone in the unique fantasy world of classrooms. Therefore, teachers can organize space for privacy, as well as for participation with others, in order for children to create their own structures and pace.

In these ways, teachers can create classroom cultures that define and tolerate different levels and types of play; they can focus in a comfortable way on the game-playing process rather than on only the outcome. When teachers find children creating opportunities to play at unplanned times or in unexpected places, it is likely that the children need more time to play or might feel overwhelmed by adult expectations.

**Playing with Language.** In addition to modeling and planning with children for the use of materials, time, and space, teachers can encourage children to play with words through legitimizing peer interaction and providing child-controlled literacy materials.

Teachers can improve story comprehension with small groups by playfully questioning and asking children to interpret and imagine what might happen in stories, tell the stories, and then role play. Practice improves this process: A teacher who plays a larger early role as an exemplar can later reduce her or his participation. Paley (1984) reported harnessing rough-and-tumble and superhero play with which she felt uncomfortable by asking children to "save" their ideas for use in a collaborative language experience setting.

## Power of Play

This is a time when extreme views are pressing on early childhood education. There is a push in one direction toward limiting the function of public schools to the three Rs and stating facts, crisply advanced. There is advocacy from the opposite direction for a folklorist tradition in early childhood education, vaguely propounded.

We need a more valid basis for developing curriculum than decision making that is based solely on what children can learn, or what certain factions want them to learn, or what tradition has dictated. We need to consider what is worth learning.

There is abundant evidence, accruing at meteoric rates, indicating the power of play as a developmental lymphatic system. In the course of early childhood development, play seems to be a cauldron in which, at different times and in different contexts, various proportions of cultural, social, cognitive, linguistic, creative, aesthetic, and emotional ingredients blend.

We might playfully entertain the notion that play serves to merge the hypothetical functions of the right and left hemispheres of the brain. In this way, normal children manage to maintain a balance in their experience as human beings. The implications of current interest in imagery and metacognition can be considered as part of the concern for children to have "thinking skills."

Imagery processes interacting with metacognitive processes serve problem solving. *Imagery* is the creative aspect of experience and the capacity of human beings to make connections. For young children, it is an early form of symbolic representation in such activities as sociodramatic play and personal analogy. There has been conjecture that the right hemisphere of the brain, dealing with metaphoric and aesthetic ways of knowing the world, can be developed and strengthened by experiences that are rich in imagery. *Metacognition* is the development of self-awareness about one's own thinking. It takes place in a gradual process as we have experiences, get feedback from our environments, and experience cognitive dissonance. There has been conjecture that improved metacognition can strengthen and develop the functions of the brain's left hemisphere, dealing with logical ways of knowing the world. Working jointly, the processes of imagery and metacognition function in the service of problem solving.

To attempt to "teach" young children these integrative skills separate from direct, concrete experiences is akin to trying to learn to ride a bicycle with a stationary exercycle. To use linear workbooks for these nonlinear functions that develop naturally with healthy play is to be irrelevant if not downright abusive.

For young children, play is a way to strengthen worthwhile, meaningful learning and cooperation with others rather than merely acquiring facts alone. Play may well be the ultimate relativist integrator of development. As an ethical issue, the role of play as part of early education touches on many dimensions of development and can affect the sheer joy of living fully. The transformational potential of play in itself is a potent lever for making new connections in a rapidly changing world.

Thus, teachers of young children have an ethical responsibility to create situations that can help to improve the conditions of learning and life in schools. We need to intervene in indirect and playful ways to the extent of our own potential capacities for professionalism and playfulness.

## REFERENCES

Aldis, D. (1975). *Playfighting.* New York: Academic Press.

Allport, G. W. (1958). The functional autonomy of motives. In C. L. Stacy & M. F. DeMartino (Eds.), *Understanding human motives* (pp. 68–81). Cleveland: Howard Allen.

Ariel, S. (1992). Semiotic analysis of children's play: A method for investigating social development. *Merrill-Palmer Quarterly, 38*(1), 119–138.

Astington, J. W. (1993). *The child's discovery of the mind.* Cambridge, MA: Harvard University Press.

Aureli, T., & Coecchia, N. (1996). Day care experience and free play behavior in preschool children. *Journal of Applied Developmental Psychology, 17*, 1–17.

Barnes, M. K., & Vangelisti, A. L. (1995). Speaking in a double-voice: Role-making as influence in preschoolers' fantasy play situations. *Research on Language and Social Interaction, 28*(4), 351–389.

Bartsch, K., & Wellman, H. M. (1995). *Children talk about the mind.* New York: Oxford University Press.

Bateson, G. (1976). A theory of play and fantasy. In J. S. Bruner, A. Jolly, & K. Sylva (Eds.), *Play—Its role in development and evolution* (pp. 119–129). New York: Basic Books.

Bateson, G. (1979). *Mind and nature.* New York: Dutton.

Black, B. (1992). Negotiating social pretend play: Communication differences related to social status and sex. *Merrill-Palmer Quarterly, 38*(2), 212–232.

Black, G. (1989). Interactive pretense: Social and symbolic skills in preschool play groups. *Merrill-Palmer Quarterly, 35*(4), 379–397.

Bower, G. H., Black, J. B., & Turner, T. J. (1994). Scripts in memory for text. In R. B. Ruddell, M. R. Ruddell, & H. Singer (Eds.), *Theoretical models and processes of reading* (pp. 538–581). Newark, DE: International Reading Association.

Bretherton, I. (Ed.). (1984). *Symbolic play: The development of social understanding.* New York: Academic Press.

Bretherton, I. (1988). Reality and fantasy in make-believe play. In D. Bergen (Ed.), *Play: A medium for learning and development* (pp. 209–211). Portsmouth, NH: Heinemann.

Bretherton, I., O'Connell, B., Shore, C., & Bates, E. (1984). The effect of contextual variation on symbolic play development from 20 to 28 months. In I. Bretherton (Ed.), *Symbolic play: The development of social understanding* (pp. 271–298). New York: Academic Press.

Brownell, C. A. (1990). Peer social skills in toddlers: Competencies and constraints illustrated by same-age and mixed-age interaction. *Child Development, 61,* 838–848.

Bruner, J. S. (1980). *Under five in Britain.* Ypsilanti, MI: High/Scope.

Bruner, J. S., Jolly, A., & Sylva, K. (Eds.). (1976). *Play—Its role in development and evolution.* New York: Basic Books.

Bruner, J. S., & Sherwood, V. (1976). Peekaboo and the learning of rule structures. In J. S. Bruner, A. Jolly, & K. Sylva (Eds.), *Play—Its role in development and evolution* (pp. 276–285). New York: Basic Books.

Buchsbaum, H. K., & Emde, R. N. (1990). Play narratives in 36-month-old children. *The Psychoanalytic Study of the Child, 45,* 129–155.

Cazden, C. (1971). Language programs for young children: Notes from England and Wales. In C. S. Lavatelli (Ed.), *Language training in early childhood education* (pp. 119–153). Urbana: University of Illinois Press.

Chafel, J. A. (1984). "Call the police, okay?" Social comparison by young children during play in preschool. *Early Child Development and Care, 14,* 201–216.

Christie, J. F. (Ed.). (1991). *Play and early literacy development.* Albany: State University of New York Press.

Christie, J. F., Johnsen, E. P., & Peckover, R. B. (1988). The effects of play period duration on children's play patterns. *Journal of Research in Childhood Education, 3*(2), 123–131.

Cole, D., & LaVoie, J. C. (1985). Fantasy play and related cognitive development in 2– to 6–year-olds. *Developmental Psychology, 21*(2), 233–240.

Connolly, J. A., & Doyle, A. (1984). Relation of social fantasy play to social competence in preschoolers. *Developmental Psychology, 20,* 797–806.

Connolly, J. A., Doyle, A., & Reznick, E. (1988). Social pretend play and social interaction in preschoolers. *Journal of Applied Developmental Psychology, 9,* 301–313.

Cook, D. (1996). Mathematical sense making and role playing in the nursery. *Early Child Development and Care, 121,* 56–66.

Copple, C. C., Cocking, R. R., & Matthews, W. S. (1984). Objects, symbols, and substitutions: The nature of the cognitive activity during symbolic play. In T. D. Yawkey & A. D. Pellegrini (Eds.), *Child's play: Developmental and applied* (pp. 105–123). Hillsdale, NJ: Erlbaum.

Corsaro, W. A. (1990). The underlife of the nursery school: Young children's social representations of adult rules. In G. Duveen & B. Lloyd (Eds.), *Social representations and the development of knowledge* (pp. 11–26). New York: Cambridge University Press.

Csikszentmihalyi, M. (1988). Introduction: The flow of experience and its significance for human psychology; The future of flow. In M. Csikszentmihalyi & I. S. Csikszentmihalyi (Eds.), *Optimal experience: Psychological studies of flow consciousness* (pp. 3–14, 15–35, 364–483). New York: Cambridge University Press.

Dansky, J. L. (1985). Questioning "A Paradigm Questioned": A commentary on Simon and Smith. *Merrill-Palmer Quarterly, 31,* 279–284.

Dansky, J. L. (1986). Play and creativity in young children. In K. Blanchard, W. W. Anderson, G. E. Chick, & E. P. Johnsen (Eds.), *The many faces of play* (pp. 69–79). Champaign, IL: Human Kinetics.

de Lorimer, S., Doyle, A., & Tessier, O. (1995). Social coordination during pretend play: Comparisons with nonpretend play and effects on expressive content. *Merrill-Palmer Quarterly, 41*(4), 497–512.

Dewey, J. (1933). *How we think.* Boston: Heath.

Dodge, M. K., & Frost, J. L. (1986). Children's dramatic play: Influence of thematic and nonthematic settings. *Childhood Education, 62,* 166–170.

Dunn, J. (1988). *The beginnings of social understanding.* Cambridge, MA: Harvard University Press.

Dunn, L., & Herwig, J. E. (1992). Play behavior and convergent and divergent thinking skills of young children attending full-day preschool. *Child Study Journal, 22*(1), 23–38.

Eckerman, C. P., & Didow, S. M. (1989). Toddlers' social coordinations: Changing responses to another's invitation to play. *Developmental Psychology, 25*(5), 794–804.

Eckler, J. A., & Weininger, O. (1989). Structural parallels between pretend play and narratives. *Developmental Psychology, 25*(5), 736–743.

Eddowes, A. E. (1991, Fall). The benefits of solitary play. *Dimensions,* pp. 31–34.

Eifermann, R. K. (1971). Social play in childhood. In R. E. Herron & B. Sutton-Smith (Eds.), *Child's play* (pp. 270–297). New York: Wiley.

Eisner, E. W. (1990). The role of art and play in children's cognitive development. In E. Klugman & S. Smilansky (Eds.), *Children's play and learning: Perspectives and policy implications* (pp. 43–56). New York: Teachers College Press.

Fagot, B. I. (1997). Attachment, parenting, and peer interactions of toddler children. *Developmental Psychology, 33*(3), 489–499.

Farver, J. (1996). Aggressive behavior in preschoolers' social networks. *Early Childhood Research Quarterly, 11*(3), 333–350.

Farver, J. M., & Wimbarti, S. (1995). Indonesian children's play with their mothers and older siblings. *Child Development, 66*(5), 1493–1503.

Fein, G. G. (1975). A transformational analysis of pretending. *Developmental Psychology, 11,* 291–296.

Fein, G. G. (1985). The affective psychology of play. In C. C. Brown & A. W. Gottfried (Eds.), *Play interactions* (pp. 19–28). Skillman, NJ: Johnson & Johnson.

Feitelson, D., & Ross, G. S. (1973). The neglected actor—Play. *Human Development, 16,* 202–223.

Fenson, L. (1984). Developmental trends for action and speech in pretend play. In I. Bretherton (Ed.), *Symbolic play: The development of social understanding* (pp. 249–270). New York: Academic Press.

Festinger, L. (1957). *Cognitive dissonance.* New York: Harper.

Forbes, D., & Yablick, G. (1984). The organization of dramatic content in children's fantasy play. In F. Kessel & A. Goncu (Eds.), *Analyzing children's play dialogues* (pp. 230–236). San Francisco: Jossey-Bass.

Freud, S. (1960). *Jokes and their relation to the unconscious* (J. Strachey, Trans.). New York: Norton. (Original work published 1916)

Freyberg, J. T. (1973). Increasing the imaginative play of urban disadvantaged children through systematic training. In J. L. Singer (Ed.), *The child's world of make-believe: Experimental studies of imaginative play* (pp. 129–154). New York: Academic Press.

Fromberg, D. P. (1995). *The full-day kindergarten: Planning and practicing a dynamic themes curriculum* (2nd ed.). New York: Teachers College Press.

Fromberg, D. P. (1997). Play issues in early childhood education. In C. Seefeldt (Ed.), *Continuing issues in early childhood education* (2nd ed., pp. 190–212). Columbus, OH: Merrill.

Galda, L., Pellegrini, A. D., & Cox, S. (1989). The short-term, longitudinal study of preshoolers' emergent literacy. *Research in the Teaching of English, 23*(3), 292–309.

Gardner, H. (1982). Art, mind, and brain: A cognitive approach to creativity. New York: Basic Books.

Garvey, C. (1993). Diversity in the conversational repertoire: The case of conflicts and social pretending. *Cognition and Instruction, 11*(3&4), 251–264.

Gaynard, L. (1989). Play as ritual in health care settings. In D. P. Fromberg & D. M. Bergen (Eds.), *Play from birth to twelve and beyond* (pp. 248–256). New York: Garland.

Geertz, C. (1976). Deep play: A description of the Balinese cockfight. In J. S. Bruner, A. Jolly, & K. Sylva (Eds.), *Play—Its role in development and evolution* (pp. 656–674). New York: Basic Books.

Giffin, H. (1984). The coordination of meaning in the creation of a shared make-believe reality. In I. Bretherton (Ed.), *Symbolic play: The development of social understanding* (pp. 73–100). New York: Academic Press.

Golomb, C. (1979). Pretense play: A cognitive perspective. In N. R. Smith & M. B. Franklin (Eds.), *Symbolic functioning in childhood* (pp. 101–116). Hillsdale, NJ: Erlbaum.

Golomb, C., Gowing, E. D. G., & Friedman, L. (1982). Play and cognition: Studies of pretense play and conservation of quantity. *Journal of Experimental Child Psychology, 33*, 257–279.

Gonen, M., Uzmen, S., Akcin, N., & Ozdemir, N. (1993). Creative thinking at 5–6 years old [*sic*] kindergarten children. *Building bridges: International collaboration in the 1990s.* Warwick, UK: Warwick University International Early Years Conference Proc. [ERIC Document Reproduction Service No. PS023789 ED392 516]

Haight, W., & Miller, P. J. (1992). The development of everyday pretend play: A longitudinal study of mothers' participation. *Merrill-Palmer Quarterly, 38*(3), 331–349.

Harris, P. L., & Kavanaugh, R. D. (1993). Young children's understanding of pretense. *Monographs of the Society for Research in Child Development, Serial No. 231, 58*(1).

Heath, S. B. (1983). *Ways with words: Language, life, and work in communities and classrooms.* New York: Cambridge University Press.

Howes, C. (1997). Teacher sensitivity, children's attachment and play with peers. *Early Education and Development, 8*(1), 41–49.

Howes, C., Droege, K., & Matheson, C. C. (1994). Play and communicative processes within long- and short-term friendship dyads. *Journal of Social and Personal Relationships, 11*, 401–410.

Howes, C., & Stewart, P. (1987). Child's play with adults, toys, and peers: An examination of family and child-care influences. *Developmental Psychology, 23*(3), 423–430.

Howes, C., with Unger, O., & Matheson, C. C. (1992). *The collaborative construction of pretend: Social pretend play function.* Albany: State University of New York Press.

Janiv, N. N. (1976, April). *Kedmah.* Paper presented at the bicentennial conference on early childhood education, Coral Gables, FL.

Johnson-Laird, P. N. (1995). Mental models and probabilistic thinking. In J. Mehler & S. Franck (Eds.), *COGNITION on cognition* (pp. 171–191). Cambridge, MA: MIT Press.

Kirschenblatt-Gimblett, B. (1979). Speech play and the verbal art. In B. Sutton-Smith (Ed.), *Play and learning* (pp. 219–238). New York: Gardner.

Ladd, G. W., & Price, J. M. (1987). Predicting children's social and school adjustment following the transition from preschool to kindergarten. *Child Development, 58*, 1168–1189.

Landry, S. H., Garner, P. W., Swank, P. R., & Baldwin, C. D. (1996). Effects of maternal scaffolding during joint toy play with preterm and full-term infants. *Merrill-Palmer Quarterly, 42*(2), 177–199.

Leslie, A. M. (1995). Pretending and believing: Issues in the theory of ToMM. In J. Mehler & S. Franck (Eds.), *COGNITION on cognition* (pp. 193–220). Cambridge, MA: MIT Press.

Levenstein, P. (1992). Mother–child home program (toy demonstrators). In L. R. Williams & D. P. Fromberg (Eds.), *The encyclopedia of early childhood education* (pp. 481–482). New York: Garland.

Levy, A. K., Schaefer, L., & Phelps, P. C. (1986). Increased preschool effectiveness:

Enhancing the language abilities of 3- and 4-year-old children through planned sociodramatic play. *Early Childhood Research Quarterly, 1,* 133–140.

Lillard, A. S. (1993). Pretend play skills and the child's theory of mind. *Child Development, 64,* 348–371.

Lucariello, J., & Rifkin, A. (1986). Event representation as the basis for categorical knowledge. In K. Nelson et al., *Event knowledge: Structure and function in development* (pp. 189–203). Hillsdale, NJ: Erlbaum.

Maccoby, E. E., & Jacklin, C. T. (1974). *The psychology of sex differences.* Stanford, CA: Stanford University Press.

MacNaughton, G. (1995). *The power of Mum! Gender and power at play.* Watson, Australia: Australia Early Education Association.

Mandler, J. M. (1992). How to build a baby: II. Conceptual primitives. *Psychological Review, 99*(4), 587–604.

Marbach, E. S., & Yawkey, T. D. (1980). The effect of imaginative play actions on language development in five-year-old children. *Psychology in the Schools, 17,* 257–263.

McGhee, P. E., Etheridge, L., & Berg, N. A. (1984). Effect of toy structure on preschool children's pretend play. *Journal of Catholic Education, 144,* 209–217.

McLoyd, V. (1983). The effects of the structure of play objects on the pretend play of low-income preschool children. *Child Development, 54,* 626–635.

McLuhan, M. (1963). We need a new picture of knowledge. In A. Frazier (Ed.), *New insights and the curriculum* (pp. 57–70). Washington, DC: Association for Supervision and Curriculum Development.

Meckley, A. (1994). Shared knowledge of play events in young children's social play construction. *Communication and Cognition, 27*(3), 287–300.

Miller, P., & Garvey, D. (1984). Mother–baby role play: Its origins in social support. In I. Bretherton (Ed.), *Symbolic play: The development of social understanding* (pp. 101–131). New York: Academic Press.

Moran, J. D., II, Sawyers, J. K., Fu, V. R., & Milgram, R. M. (1984). Predicting imaginative play in preschool children. *Gifted Child Quarterly, 28,* 92–94.

Morrow, L. M. (1997). *Literacy development in the early years* (3rd ed.). Boston: Allyn & Bacon.

Nelson, K., & Seidman, S. (1984). Playing with scripts. In I. Bretherton (Ed.), *Symbolic play: The development of social understanding* (pp. 45–71). New York: Academic Press.

Nelson, K., et al. (1986). *Event knowledge: Structure and function in development.* Hillsdale, NJ: Erlbaum.

O'Brien, M., & Bi, X. (1995). Language learning in context: Teacher and toddler speech in three classroom play areas. *Topics in Early Childhood Special Education, 15*(2), 148–163.

Opie, I., & Opie, P. (1976). Street games: Counting-out and chasing. In J. S. Bruner, A. Jolly, & K. Sylva (Eds.), *Play—Its role in development and evolution* (pp. 394–412). New York: Basic Books.

Paley, V. G. (1984). *Boys and girls: Superheroes in the doll corner.* Chicago: University of Chicago Press.

Parten, M. (1971). Social play among preschool children. In R. E. Herron & B. Sutton-Smith (Eds.), *Child's Play* (pp. 83–95). New York: John Wiley.

Pellegrini, A. D. (1984a). The social cognitive ecology of preschool classrooms: Contextual relations revisited. *International Journal of Behavioral Development, 7,* 321–332.

Pellegrini, A. D. (1984b). Identifying causal elements in the thematic-fantasy play paradigm. *American Educational Research Journal, 21,* 691–701.

Pellegrini, A. D. (1985). The relations between symbolic play and literate behavior: A review and critique of the empirical literature. *Review of Educational Research, 55,* 171–121.

Pellegrini, A. D. (1987). Rough-and-tumble play: Developmental and educational significance. *Educational Psychologist, 22,* 23–43.

Pellegrini, A. D. (1988). Elementary-school children's rough-and-tumble play and social competence. *Developmental Psychology, 24*(6), 802–806.

Pellegrini, A. D. (1992). Rough-and-tumble play and social problem solving flexibility. *Creativity Research Journal, 5*(1), 12–26.

Pellegrini, A. D., & Galda, L. (1982). The effects of thematic-fantasy play training on the development of children's story comprehension. *American Educational Research Journal, 19,* 443–452.

Pellegrini, A. D., & Perlmutter, J. C. (1989). Classroom effects on children's play. *Developmental Psychology, 25*(2), 289–296.

Perner, J. (1991). *Understanding and the representational mind.* Cambridge, MA: MIT Press.

Piaget, J. (1962). *Play, dreams, and imitation in childhood* (C. Gattegno & M. F. Hodgson, Trans.). New York: Norton.

Piaget, J. (1965). *The moral judgment of the child* (M. Gabain, Trans.). New York: Free Press.

Piaget, J. (1966). Response to Brian Sutton-Smith. *Psychological Review, 73,* 111–112.

Piaget, J. (1976). *The grasp of consciousness.* Cambridge, MA: Harvard University Press.

Ramsey, P. G., & Lasquade, C. (1996). Preschool children's entry attempts. *Journal of Applied Developmental Psychology, 17,* 135–150.

Repacholi, B. M., & Gopnik, A. (1997). Early reasoning about desires: Evidence from 14- and 18-month olds. *Developmental Psychology, 33*(1), 12–21.

Reynolds, G., & Jones, E. (1997). *Master players.* New York: Teachers College Press.

Robertson, R., & Combs, A. (1995). *Chaos theory in psychology and the life sciences.* Mahwah, NJ: Erlbaum.

Rogoff, B. (1990). *Apprenticeship in thinking: Cognitive development in social context.* New York: Oxford University Press.

Roopnarine, J. L., Johnson, J. E., & Hooper, F. H. (Eds.). (1994). *Children's play in diverse cultures.* New York: State University of New York Press.

Rubin, K. H., & Howe, N. (1986). Social play and perspective taking. In G. G. Fein & M. Rivkin (Eds.), *The young child at play* (pp. 113–125). Washington, DC: National Association for the Education of Young Children.

Scales, B., Almy, M., Nicolopoulou, A., & Ervin-Tripp, S. (Eds.). (1991). *Play and the social context of development.* New York: Teachers College Press.

Schank, R., & Abelson, R. (1977). *Scripts, plans, goals and understanding: An inquiry into human knowledge.* Hillsdale, NJ: Erlbaum.

Schwartzman, H. B. (1984). Imaginative play: Deficit or difference? In T. D. Yaw-key & A. D. Pellegrini (Eds.), *Child's play: Developmental and applied* (pp. 49–62). Hillsdale, NJ: Erlbaum.

Sheldon, A. (1992). Conflict talk: Sociolinguistic challenges to self-assertion and how young girls meet them. *Merrill-Palmer Quarterly, 38*(1), 95–117.

Shore, C. (1990). Combinatorial play, conceptual development, and early multi-word speech. *Developmental Psychology, 22*(2), 184–190.

Singer, J. L. (Ed.). (1973). *The child's world of make-believe: Experimental studies of imaginative play.* New York: Academic Press.

Singer, J. L., & Singer, D. (1979). The values of imagination. In B. Sutton-Smith (Ed.), *Play and learning* (pp. 195–218). New York: Gardner.

Slaughter, V. T., & Dombrowski, J. (1989). Cultural continuities and discontinuities: Impact on social and pretend play. In M. N. Bloch & A. D. Pellegrini (Eds.), *The ecological context of children's play* (pp. 282–310). Norwood, NJ: Ablex.

Smilansky, S. (1968). *The effects of sociodramatic play on disadvantaged preschool children.* New York: Wiley.

Smith, I. (1991). Preschool children "play" out their grief. *Death Studies, 15,* 169–176.

Smith, P. K., & Whitney, S. (1987). Play and associative fluency: Experimenter effects may be responsible for previous positive findings. *Developmental Psychology, 23*(1), 49–53.

Squibb, B., & King, J. (1996). Play in home spaces in family child care. *Child and Youth Care Forum, 25*(3), 195–205.

Sutton-Smith, B. (1971). A syntax for play and games. In R. E. Herron & B. Sutton-Smith (Eds.), *Child's play* (pp. 298–371). New York: Wiley.

Sutton-Smith, B. (Ed.) (1979). *Play and learning.* New York: Gardner.

Taylor, M., & Carlson, S. M. (1997). The relation between individual differences in fantasy and theory of mind. *Child Development, 68*(3), 436–455.

Tizard, B. (1977). The child's way of learning. In B. Tizard & D. Harvey (Eds.), *The biology of play* (pp. 199–208). Philadelphia: Lippincott.

Torrance, E. P. (1962). *Guiding creative talent.* Englewood Cliffs, NJ: Prentice-Hall.

Trawick-Smith, J. (1994). *Interactions in the classroom.* New York: Merrill.

Urberg, K. A., & Kaplan, M. G. (1989). An observational study of race-, age-, and sex-heterogeneous interaction in preschoolers. *Journal of Applied Developmental Psychology, 10*(3), 299–311.

Voss, H-G. (1987). An empirical study of exploration-play sequences in early childhood. In D. Gorlitz & J. F. Wohlwill (Eds.), *Curiosity, imagination, and play* (pp. 152–179). Hillsdale, NJ: Erlbaum.

Vygotsky, L. S. (1976). Play and its role in the mental development of the child. In J. S. Bruner, A. Jolly, & K. Sylva (Eds.), *Play—Its role in development and evolution* (pp. 537–554). New York: Basic Books.

Vygotsky, L. S. (1978). *Mind in society: The development of higher psychological processes* (M. Cole, V. John-Steiner, S. Scribner, & E. Souberman, Eds.). Cambridge, MA: Harvard University Press.

Waldrop, M. M. (1992). *Complexity: The emerging science at the edge of order and chaos.* New York: Simon & Schuster.

White, R. W. (1959). Motivation reconsidered: The concept of competence. *Psychological Review, 65,* 297–333.

Whiting, B. B., Edwards, C. P., et al. (1988). *Children of different worlds: The formation of social behavior.* Cambridge, MA: Harvard University Press.

Whyte, J., & Owens, A. (1989). Language and symbolic play: Some findings from a study of autistic children. *Irish Journal of Psychology, 10*(2), 317–332.

Williamson, P. A., & Silvern, S. B. (1991). Thematic-fantasy play and story comprehension. In J. F. Christie (Ed.), *Play and early literacy development* (pp. 69–90). Albany: State University of New York Press.

Wing, L. A. (1995). Play is not the work of the child: Young children's perceptions of work and play. *Early Childhood Research Quarterly, 10*(2), 223–247.

Youngblade, L. J., & Dunn, J. (1995). Individual differences in young children's pretend play with mother and sibling: Links to relationships and undestanding of other people's feeling and beliefs. *Child Development, 66,* 1472–1492.

CHAPTER 3

# Oral Language in the Early Childhood Classroom: Building on Diverse Foundations

## CELIA GENISHI
## REBEKAH FASSLER

FROM THEIR earliest days, children are participants in the world around them. Oral language, the focus of this chapter, offers them access to a number of communities in that world. This is especially noticeable in classroom communities where increasing numbers of young children are learning in a language they do not speak at home. Like the children in this example (drawn from Fassler, 1995), they use language, gestures, and the people around them as resources in their attempts to participate in the events of school:

> Children are being introduced to drawing life-sized portraits on brown paper. Mrs. Barker, the teacher, has traced Ogusan's body outline, and is calling upon children individually to color in details of features and clothing. Jerry, whose home language is Chinese, uses Chinese and English to weave a web of relationships among his peers. In this whole-group situation he has trouble getting Mrs. Barker's attention so that he can take a turn at coloring part of the portrait. "Do you get a turn?" Ogusan (a Turkish speaker) asks Jerry. Jerry answers plaintively, "I can't get a turn," and Daniel (an Albanian speaker) chimes in:
>
> DANIEL: No, you don't get a chance?
> JERRY: I like this (raises hand). Teacher not pick me.
> OGUSAN: Raise your hand like this (raises his).
> JERRY: I like this (raises hand).

DANIEL: And the teacher don't give you?
JERRY: No.

Moments later, when Mrs. Barker asks, "Who did not get a chance?" Daniel points out Jerry's raised hand, "Mrs. Barker, him!" She looks up, finally notices Jerry's hand, and invites him to come forward, "Jerry, Jerry, do one shoe." (p. 174)

Jerry and his friends know something about the ways words, sentences, and ideas are constructed through language. And they demonstrate that, like most children, they must learn how to convey meanings in particular ways—in North America usually in English—to negotiate the world of school. Jerry is aware that there are languages other than the one he uses at home. He is a member of a Chinese-speaking community at the same time that he is entering the English-speaking world and the overlapping community of the literate.

How do children learn a first language? What is known about how Jerry, Ogusan, and Daniel became the speakers and learners that they are? How large a role has the adult played to encourage talk and interaction? What issues in the field of early childhood education are reflected in such interaction and influence the kind of curriculum children will experience? This chapter addresses these questions by focusing on the following topics related to the processes of language acquisition: the historical context of language in early childhood education; the nature of language and its acquisition; developing communicative competence in the classroom—issues and choices; and curricula that build on children's oral communicative abilities.

## THE HISTORICAL CONTEXT

In the last 30 years, language has been a special issue in early childhood education in the United States. The social programs and movements of the 1960s and 1970s, including Head Start and the women's movement, affected public expectations for preschool and primary education. People looked to compensatory programs such as Head Start as forces for social and economic reform. A variety of social groups, including ethnic minorities, participated in changing the structure and look of early education, especially at the preschool level. Parents became an integral part of administrative groups for Head Start and sometimes for day care centers and schools.

Because the dialect or language of minority group children is often different from that of middle-class children, traditional views of language in schools have been challenged since the 1960s. Twenty-five or more years ago most people assumed that there was one kind of English with which teachers needed to be concerned: standard (newscasters' or textbook) English. When educators or researchers wrote about varieties or different dialects of English, they often wrote about them as if dialects were inappropriate and incorrect. For example, in a report of pioneering research about the language of elementary school children, Loban (1963) stated in his summary of findings: "For Negro subjects with southern background, using appropriately the verb *to be* proves to be 12 times as troublesome as for northern Caucasian or Negro subjects" (p. 85).

Later, in the 1960s, linguists such as Labov (1970) demonstrated that speakers of vernacular dialects of English, including what many call black English, use forms of the verb *to be* in ways that are consistently different from standard English forms. These different uses are not "troublesome" within the Black English-speaking community. Smitherman (1994) provided the example of *be* or *bees* to indicate continuous action, as in "Every time we see him, he be dressed like that" (p. 7). Speakers of Black English, which Smitherman refers to as AAE (African American English), also omit *is* or *are*, especially in contractions, as in "What up?" instead of "What's up?"

By 1985 a number of books had been written about Black English (Burling, 1973; Labov, 1972). Many authors emphasized the fact that *everyone* uses a dialect and that the term *dialect* is neutral, not negative. Educators' understanding of variation in language grew, so that they no longer assumed that standard English was the only acceptable dialect for classroom settings. When the federal Bilingual Education Act of 1968 marked the recognition that a growing number of U.S. students spoke a language other than English, the horizons of language education expanded even further. Broadened views of language led educators to reconsider their goals for young children's learning at the same time that parents and practitioners called for "culturally relevant" education. Taking into account the culture and previous experiences of children led to the creation of some innovative programs and curricula. These included the frequent use of languages other than English, for example, the Rough Rock Navajo and the Tucson (Spanish) Language Experience models (John & Horner, 1971), or the incorporation of Black English features into materials for the teaching of reading (Simpkins, Simpkins, & Holt, 1977).

By the 1980s, policy makers and the public wondered about the effectiveness of compensatory programs, even though some studies (for example, Schweinhart & Weikart, 1980) showed the long-term benefits of Head Start. As a group, minority children still achieve less well in school than majority or mainstream children. Educators and researchers continue to ask why this happens. They study children's home and school environments as they try to discover what kinds of experiences and curricula might improve learning and teaching for all groups. So in recent decades the educator's domain of concern extends beyond the classroom to the home.

In the late 1990s language is still a primary issue in the field. Classrooms in which the majority of children are second-language learners and come from many different language backgrounds have become the rule rather than an exception in many urban areas. More and more teachers are seeking strategies to encourage full participation of children from all language backgrounds in the academic and social life of the classroom. The paucity of native English speakers as language models in these settings highlights the importance of research that examines how young non-native English speakers might support and enhance each other's learning (Fassler, 1995, 1998).

At the same time, there has been much discussion of the need for "developmentally appropriate" practices that are respectful of the child's culture (Bredekamp, 1987; Bredekamp & Copple, 1997) and for curricula that acknowledge the diversity of young children and their families (De Gaetano, Williams, & Volk, 1998; Gregory, 1997). How aspects of language learning fit within appropriate ways of educating children is a subject of debate, revolving around topics such as "dialect differences," "multiculturalism," and "developmentally appropriate" curricula. Each topic reflects persistent concerns of educators and parents, and each will be discussed below in the section on "Developing Communicative Competence in the Classroom: Issues and Choices."

In linguistics and language acquisition, researchers have expanded their areas of study in tandem with educators. Linguists now focus on functions of language across different situations, along with rules related to its forms. Researchers discuss the growth of communication, not just language, and the boundary between spoken and written uses of language is blurred. Further, the processes of acquisition that they study are those of working-class and minority, not just middle-class, children. The findings of researchers whose work is most pertinent to early childhood language education are discussed in the next section.

## LANGUAGE AND THE PROCESSES OF ACQUISITION

We take for granted our ability to make language do what we need it to do. In or out of the classroom, language gives our thoughts substance. As we talk to ourselves, language helps us to remember, plan, understand what happens to us, and formulate ideas. Language is part of the individual's uniquely human way of knowing, feeling, being. As we use language with others, it shapes our identities and social lives. The way our own language sounds to listeners leads them to make judgments about where we are from, what our occupation is, how friendly or clever we are.

We easily see what language does, and we can see this without having to describe what it is. Understanding what language is, how it is structured, and how it works is the task of linguists who describe language in terms of components. These are summarized below to show just how impressive—for adult and child—the feat of learning a language is.

Each language component is made up of parts and the rules that enable speakers to combine those parts. *Phonology* refers to the sounds of a language. English speakers easily produce the sounds of English, and without knowing the word *ruddle*, will know that it sounds like a possible English word, whereas *fwoodr* does not. English speakers also know the *morphology* of their language, or the rules for how morphemes are combined to form words. (Words like *happy, look,* or *jump* or parts of words like *-ing* or *un-* are morphemes.)

The way we combine morphemes in an utterance or sentence is known as *syntax.* We know that in this sentence, "Carla is jumping," the morphemes are arranged in a way that makes sense to English speakers. We say *Carla* before *is* and *is* before *jumping.* We would not ordinarily say "Jumping is Carla" or "Carla jumping is," although we could say "Is Carla jumping?" and change the meaning of the sentence. We are no longer telling; we are asking. Linguists would describe the change from a declarative ("Carla is jumping") to a question ("Is Carla jumping?") in terms of the syntactic rules the speaker knows about forming questions. One of these rules for question formation has to do with saying *is* before *Carla.*

Finally, *pragmatics* relates not to combining morphemes within sentences but to combining sentences with other sentences. Here linguists are concerned with rules for carrying on conversations, for using language in human interaction. Because rules of usage are different for different groups (e.g., New Yorkers may find appropriate something that Coloradans think is offensive), pragmatic rules are slippery. They include rules about what kind of answer may follow a question in order to be judged polite or appropriate in a particular situation. For example, saying a simple, "Yes," after someone asks, "Do you know how to get to 14th Street?" is not appropriate, whereas following the "Yes" with directions to 14th Street is.

In summary, we know a great many rules, rules for combining

sounds into morphemes, morphemes into words, words into sentences, sentences into conversations. The wonder is that no one explicitly teaches us these rules. Yet like kindergartners Jerry, Ogusan, and Daniel, we apply them without being aware of them. We know them in an unconscious way and that knowledge—sometimes called *linguistic competence*—enables us able to use language as we need to.

Most people easily go through life without defining the components of language or reflecting on the marvels of the human mind that enable people to learn and use language. They have no need to study it or understand how an individual learns it. Why should early childhood educators understand what language is and how it comes to be? One reason is that language acquisition is a major part of human development. In fact, when it comes to oral language, children have experienced a rich and spontaneous "curriculum" since birth. Understanding what they know and how they come to know it can aid the teacher in planning activities and teaching strategies that build on children's ways of learning. Another reason to know about this aspect of development is that language is at the center of school learning. Almost every area of the curriculum entails language in the teaching/learning process. Third, as noted earlier, increasing numbers of children enter early childhood settings with a language other than English. Knowing that children acquire a first language so well at an early age helps teachers see that children are healthy learners, regardless of what language they use. How do children come to know the language they bring with them to the classroom?

## Learning Language Through Interaction

The process of learning language is enormously complicated. Thus theories that explain how children acquire it cannot be simple. For example, according to a strict *innatist* theory, a person's genes are the sole source of language and communicative development; a child born with no physical handicaps should learn language. Unfortunately, researchers know that this is not the case. A child whose physical needs are met but lacks any opportunity for social interaction does not become a language user (Curtiss, 1977). At the other extreme, a strict *behaviorist* theory grounds communicative development only in the environment—what is outside the learner. From this point of view, children learn what they hear around them through imitation, repetition, and reinforcement. Children do imitate what they hear, and they learn the language of those around them; but they also say things they have never heard before, such as "goed" or "footses" or "Why you putted it there?" They use these forms even when no one reinforces or encourages them to do so. These forms—what adults would call mistakes—suggest that a full explanation of how children acquire language must include children's ability to think and formulate rules for themselves.

Current theories about language acquisition are neither strictly innatist nor behaviorist. Most child language specialists believe that acquiring language depends on interaction between nature and nurture, between genes and the environment. Human beings are biologically prepared to use language in ways that no other organism is. What is with a person at birth, however, must be cultivated by an environment consisting of other people, objects, and actions, the essentials of interaction and bases of development. The theoretical approach of many researchers of children's communication is, therefore, termed *interactionist* and *constructivist* (Piaget & Inhelder, 1969; Vygotsky, 1978). The process of acquisition is based on the interaction of inborn abilities to formulate rules, act physically upon the environment, and seek social interaction. The child constructs, through her or his own activity and thinking in varied social situations, knowledge about how language works.

## Early Language or Early Communication?

In the 1960s and early 1970s, child language researchers focused on the development of *language,* primarily the syntactic rules of child speakers. What words did they say first? How did children combine their first two words? Were the combinations similar to adult forms? By the mid-1970s researchers had taken a step back, toward infancy, to investigate the foundations of language. Researchers broadened their focus to study the growth of *communicative competence,* a person's ability to speak and act appropriately in different social situations. This competence depends on many kinds of knowledge: knowledge of linguistic rules (the speaker's linguistic competence) as well as of social rules for appropriate verbal and nonverbal behavior. Young children are in the process of learning these complicated rules for communicating, which develop in a broad range of contexts.

To document ways in which communication develops, Stern (1977) watched mothers and children, between birth and age 6 months, "dance" with each other. From the first weeks of life, each partner accommodated the other; the child's smile was followed by the mother's smile, for example. These early behaviors are elementary, but researchers believe they underlie more complex interaction in the future. During and after the first 6 months of life, infants communicate in nonverbal ways, and they also vocalize—or coo and babble—using sounds that will eventually be combined into adultlike words. Sometime after the first birthday, most children begin to verbalize. They use words like *juice, car,* or *up* to refer to their concrete world. As they become competent communicators, the dance between caregivers and themselves continues as each child expands his or her role in interaction to coordinate words with previously learned nonverbal behaviors and actions.

Nelson (1973) studied early words by documenting the first 50 words of 18 one- to two-year-olds. She found that most of these words were nouns like *sock, key,* and *shoe,* which named things that were common in the child's environment, movable and handled by the children themselves. These objects were the basis for children's actions; first words were grounded in sensory and physical activity. More recently Nelson has investigated early words as part of the broader process of children's conceptual development (Nelson, 1985, 1986). She sees as critical the ordinary and repeated experiences of infants' lives. What the child comes to know and remember is an *event* or whole episode of an activity such as feeding or bathing. Over time this event is mentally represented and broken down or analyzed into component parts. These are eventually labeled, but only after many occurrences of the event. Thus the child's actions, experience, and cognitive abilities to represent, remember, and analyze all contribute to the making of a young language user.

Although Nelson provides insights into how children learn words as a by-product of sensory and physical experiences, other researchers (Barrett, 1982; Clark, 1983) propose alternatives to Nelson's approach. According to these researchers, children may first name common objects in their environment, but to acquire the full meaning of a word, they may need to go through an unconscious analysis of its features. They note features that are functional (how is a shoe used?) and perceptual (what is its shape, size, texture, and so on?). At first, children may refer only to their shoes as shoes; then they may focus on noticeable features, for example, the shoe's shape. For a short while they may call both shoes and house slippers "shoes," but over time they are finally able to identify the features that set shoes apart from boots and slippers. At this point, children have acquired the bundle of features and concepts that define the word. Along the way, the young child, intent on communicating about what is new to him, makes the most of what he already knows to make sense of experience (Wong Fillmore, 1976).

Beyond the stage of using one word at a time, most children continue to expand their vocabularies with an impressive effortlessness and speed. G. A. Miller and Gildea (1987) point out that the average number of words learned a day as children acquire their first language is about 10, a number that suggests a large number of "events" and experiences from which to draw new concepts and words. (See Genishi [1988b] for further discussion of word learning.) In addition, researchers have found that varied experiences are critical not only at the early childhood level. Snow, Barnes, Chandler, Goodman, and Hemphill (1991) indicate that second-through sixth-graders who make progress in literacy learning in the classroom had teachers who stressed vocabulary learning *in context*, that is, in all content areas. They used diverse materials, such as maps, trade books, comic books, and encyclopedias, and experience-broadening activities such as field trips. Thus the need for experience as a source of verbal knowledge extends well beyond the early childhood years.

## Combining Words: The Development of Syntax

Linguists and psychologists interested in child language in the 1960s focused not on the acquisition of words but on rules of syntax, which guide the ways we combine words to form grammatical utterances. Pioneers in this search included Brown and his collaborators (Brown, Cazden, & Bellugi, 1969; W. Miller & Ervin, 1964). These and other psycholinguists recorded and studied thousands of utterances to discover the rules children unconsciously use to combine their first words in conversations. An example is this conversation between Karen, 19 months old, and her father, who is watching television and attending to both his daughter and an adult visitor:

> KAREN: Mommy tape. Mommy tape. Mommy tape. Mommy tape. Mommy tape.
> FATHER: Invisible mending tape ("translating" for other adult).
> ADULT: Oh!
> FATHER: You can have *this* much (shows with his thumb and index finger how long the piece can be).
> KAREN: Daddy knee (pointing toward his face). (Genishi & Dyson, 1984, p. 46)

The rules underlying Karen's two-word utterances are part of her early grammar; over a period of years she will construct a number of grammars, not just one. Note that by using a simple rule for combining a noun with another noun ("Mommy tape"), Karen has managed to start a conversation about tape. She refers to the mending tape as her mother's; later she cryptically calls Daddy's face his "knee," perhaps making a joke. In another conversation, she may apply a rule to combine noun and verb, as in "Daddy sleep." In a few weeks or months she might say "Mommy's tape" and "Daddy's knee," and eventually she might add *-ed* to all verbs to form a past tense, as in *walked, goed,* or *hided,* probably even to verbs that have irregular past forms *(went, hid).* These constructions are especially informative when they occur consistently, since they reveal what the child's own rules are. Well before kindergarten age, then, children's speech reflects their knowledge of basic syntactic rules.

In addition to noting spontaneous child utterances—such as "two feets," "Bubba eating," or "Gram goed"—researchers have tested children's rules experimentally. Berko (1958) created an ingenious test for tapping children's knowledge of specific rules for combining morphemes, or parts of words, to form other words. Berko used nonsense words, such as *wug, gling,* and *spow,* to see whether children aged 4 to 7 years could look at a picture related to the word and then form an appropriate new word. A child might respond that a picture of more than one *wug* (drawn like a cartoon animal) was a picture of *wugs.* Or the experimenter might show a picture of a man doing something he called *spowing* to see if the child could say that the man *spowed* yesterday. Berko concluded that children who were able to produce such forms as plural, progressive tense, and past tense with nonsense words also knew rules for producing these forms with ordinary English words. Along with their spontaneous "mistakes" *(goed, hided)* in conversation, children's responses on the Berko test prove that children learn language by means other than strict imitation of adult forms. Instead they unconsciously construct and apply the rules of their developing grammars.

Researchers in the 1970s shifted their focus from syntax to meaning, or semantics. Their question became: What do children's early word combinations mean? One syntactic structure could have more than one meaning; for example, "Mommy juice" could mean "Mommy's juice," or "Mommy, give me juice," and so on. Brown believed a satisfactory explanation of possible meanings was based on a "rich interpretation." According to this view, young speakers are able to convey a variety of basic meanings and relationships (Brown, 1973). "Mommy juice" might express the relationship technically called possession or agent (the "doer") + object (what "receives" the action). At other times children use language to convey the meaning of nomination (naming things, as in "this doggie") or of nonexistence (remarking on the disappearance of a person or object, as in "allgone car"). Those meanings will continue to be the foundation of what speakers say throughout the language acquisition process. The utterances and rules underlying them eventually become much more elaborate, but behind the technical terms describing any utterance, Brown believes there is always an active, thinking, meaning-seeking, and meaning-creating child.

## Contexts for the Development of Communicative Competence

We know that most children learn to communicate in a first language. We know, too, that children learning the same language differ in the rate at which they learn language but follow the same general sequence as they learn linguistic forms. A particular 2-year-old may be able to say more than her 3-year-old sister did at age 2, but in the course of development, both will utter one word before two, simple sentences before complex sentences. What in the child's environment is absolutely necessary for this learning to take place? Researchers are far from knowing the answer. This section presents examples of interaction in different contexts to illustrate the range of situations that successfully support communicative development.

> ADULT: Bo-o-at. Puppy dog. What's a dog say, Robert? What's a dog say, huh?
> CHILD: [Babbles]
> ADULT: Hey, Chrissy, what's a dog say? What's a dog say? Arf, arf, arf!
> CHILD: [Screams happily]
> ADULT: No-o-se. No-o-se. Where's Chrissy nose? Um hmmmm. Bird. Bird. Can you flap your wings like a bird? Like this. That's what birds do. They fly. They go wheee!
> CHILD: [Noises]
> ADULT: The birds. Whatcha got, Brian? Whatcha got? Uh boo! (Genishi & Dyson, 1984, p. 65)

This conversation was overheard in the infant room of a day-care center, where the caregiver shared a picture book with three children. Her talk has many of the characteristics, which adults may find cute or silly, of "baby talk," or adult-talk-to-children (ATC). Researchers have been interested in this way of adjusting one's speech for young children because they suspect that it provides a simplified model for child language learners (Schachter & Strage, 1982). Some of the features of ATC are

1. Short utterances
2. Lots of repetition
3. Vowel lengthening (as in no-o-se)
4. Exaggerated intonation (extreme ups and downs)
5. Lots of questions

Much of the research that describes ATC has been done with middle-class standard English–speaking mothers and children. And many middle-class families, whatever their race or ethnicity, engage in conversations similar to the one above. One of its features is that the adult often asks questions to which she already knows the answer. After the child responds, non-verbally or verbally, the adult encouragingly asks another question. Researchers have called this and other gamelike exchanges a *routine* or *format* (Bruner, 1983) and have found that in some homes, the routine changes over time.

For many middle-class adults, routines are a staple of adult–child interaction both at home and in school. Heath (1983b) has pointed out that not every child has engaged in this kind of talk and that adults who are not middle-class may judge this talk to be pointless. A grandmother in a working-class Black community had this to say about her grandson Teegie's learning and talking: "He gotta learn to know 'bout dis world, can't nobody tell 'im. . . . Gotta watch hisself by watchin' other folks. Ain't no use me tellin' im: Learn dis, learn dat. What's dis? What's dat?" (Heath, 1983b, p. 84). Teegie's grandmother captures the child-rearing values and life circumstances of her own community when she emphasizes Teegie's ability to figure things out on his own. As she implies, children in other communities may hear instead frequent lessonlike routines in which adults often ask, "What's this? What's that?"

The communicative ways of White working-class families also vary from a middle-class "standard," as Heath (1983b), P. Miller (1982) in South Baltimore, and Tizard and Hughes (1984) in the United Kingdom have vividly documented. And in more geographically remote Papua New Guinea, Schieffelin (1979) found that adults do not use "baby talk" features in their speech and believe that any parent should be discouraged from using them so that their children can learn language normally. Thus different communities have their own beliefs about language socialization processes: how adults should talk to children and how children learn to talk. As Heath puts it, they all have their own "ways with words." No one "way" is superior to another, and families everywhere raise children who learn the complex social and linguistic rules of their community.

To summarize briefly the major points of this section:

1. Language is an enormously complex system through which people construct and convey meaning. Its main components are *semantics* (the system of meanings), *phonology* (the sound system), *syntax* (the rules for combining morphemes in sentences), and *pragmatics* (the rules underlying conversations).
2. Imitation is not the key to acquiring language. The active, thinking,

meaning-seeking, and meaning-constructing child, in interaction with people and things, gradually figures out for herself or himself the intricacies of language and communication.

3. All normal children develop communicative competence within their own communities. Different communities' ways of talking and communicating may vary widely, and researchers are just beginning to study these ways in communities that are not middle-class. Thus we cannot make judgments about what social contexts are "better" than others or what specific features in the contexts are essential for children's communicative development to occur.

## DEVELOPING COMMUNICATIVE COMPETENCE IN THE CLASSROOM: ISSUES AND CHOICES

It is crucial to respect the out-of-school social contexts in which children learn their families' ways of communicating, but not everyone agrees on how to act upon that respect. How educators value a child's dialect or language and how they teach about language in early childhood settings depend largely on each educator's values and personal understandings of a curriculum that is responsive to a wide range of children. Embedded in the construction of such a curriculum are some overlapping topics, including *multiculturalism, dialect differences,* and *developmentally appropriate practice.* These topics may become controversial issues primarily when children in the same setting have diverse social and linguistic backgrounds or when these backgrounds differ from the teacher's or school's. In this section issues most closely related to language education are considered as a prelude to a look at examples of classroom practices.

### Multiculturalism and Language Choice

Questions have been raised about *whose* culture, language, or dialect should dominate in both classrooms and other institutions. Some answers to the questions are presented here in the context of a broad vision of multicultural education, whose advocates work toward "awareness of, respect for, and enjoyment of the diversity of our society and world" (Ramsey, Vold, & Williams, 1989, p. ix). In this view multicultural education is not restricted to minority-group children and aims toward equity for all members of society (see also Derman-Sparks & the ABC Task Force, 1989; Goodwin, 1997). This definition provides no facile prescriptions for educators who wish to bring multiculturalism to life in the classroom, but it does provide space for *choices* that educators can make, for example, regarding dialect or language use.

**Dialects and "Success" in School.** Research consistently shows that children who are academically successful in school, especially in language arts and reading, come from homes where the ways of interacting are similar to those of the school; or they come from homes in which parents or adults share the school's values and goals (Durkin, 1982; Heath, 1983b). Put another way, children whose out-of-school experiences have *not* provided them with a "hidden curriculum"—including the school's ways with words—may have difficulty with academic tasks.

What should schools do to make the "hidden curriculum" visible to all children? In terms of language, many would say that one of the school's obligations is to "teach" children the forms and content of "school talk," or standard English. Unfortunately, no one has demonstrated that a second dialect can be taught, at least in direct, lessonlike ways. Few studies look carefully at changes in dialect use in individual speakers over time, and long-term evaluations of instructional methods are also lacking (but see Stockman [1984] for a study of acquisition of Black English). Past attempts to teach standard English forms in highly structured ways have not succeeded, whereas teachers' acceptance and encouragement of children's own language forms have led to greater learning (Cullinan, Jaggar, & Strickland, 1974; Piestrup, 1973; Rentel & Kennedy, 1972).

**Different Languages and the Match Between Home and School.** Teachers in early childhood settings and statisticians both note that the number of children in the United States speaking languages other than English at home is increasing significantly. The number of non–English speaking children is highest in urban areas. For example, in New York City at least 17% of all children enrolled from kindergarten to grade 12 are termed "limited English proficient," an increase of 7% since 1988. Of this segment, the two largest language groups are Spanish speakers (67.5%) and Chinese speakers (9.3%). Officials have identified a total of 145 different language groups from 197 different countries of origin (New York City Board of Education, 1996–97).

Questions about appropriate programs for these children are enormously complex and, as with dialect issues, revolve around choices that are not only linguistic but also social and political (Valdes, 1997). As the twentieth century ends, a few states in the United States have approved "English only" as their official language, and legal immigrants are fearful of losing benefits they have had in the past. Thus political reactions to linguistic and cultural differences can have significant consequences.

Regardless of political climate, researchers agree on two points: (1) Learning two or more languages in early childhood is in itself not harmful or "confusing"; in fact it may be beneficial to cognitive development (Hakuta & Diaz, 1984); and (2) learning a second language, like learning the first, occurs over a period of time, sometimes years (Genesee, 1994; Wong Fillmore, 1991). A third point is more controversial. Based on a limited number of studies, researchers support the maintenance of the home language while learners develop a second language. That is, they say *adding* a second language to a simultaneously growing foundation in the first language strengthens learning in general (Cummins, 1994). Thus a transitional program that employs children's home language for only a short period of time, for example, a year, may be ineffective for most second-language learners.

Regarding choices among curricula, parents and teachers vary. Some would like the home language maintained in school as a way of supporting the children's culture, so that Spanish-speaking children would use Spanish for part of the day at school. But often parents are more concerned with their children's learning English than maintaining their home language (Wong Fillmore, 1991). In many parts of the United States, alternatives to exclusively English-speaking classrooms are lacking. Particularly at the prekindergarten level, there are few programs and curricula that are widely available and even fewer that have been both explicitly described and carefully evaluated (see Soto, 1991). The current consensus regarding appropriate curricula, even with older learners, is that explicit teaching about the *forms* of English is not useful; being able to *use* English, as well as hear it in comprehensible ways, is critical (Krashen, 1985).

In keeping with this emphasis on language use, classroom teachers Fournier, Steen, Lansdowne, and Pastenes and teacher educator Hudelson (1992) describe a second-grade Spanish–English bilingual classroom that emphasizes the use of both languages in every part of the curriculum. They do not claim to be typical of other bilingual classrooms, but they present their own rationale for a language-rich, "whole-language," teacher-evaluated program. Also, they present enough detail in their presentation to aid others in developing their own curricula for children of diverse backgrounds, not just bilinguals.

## What Is Multiculturally and Developmentally Appropriate?

For purposes of this chapter, a program that is both multicultural and developmentally appropriate *takes into account the nature of each learner.* In this kind of program, teachers are trusted to know the children as indi-

viduals in contexts, with particular social, cultural, and linguistic histories. Which curriculum a child experiences is not determined by the score
on a "readiness test," and the curricular activities are not dictated by a
publisher or textbook. Published materials may play a role, but teachers'
judgments, guided by children's responses and actions, are primary. This
broad, child-oriented notion of developmental appropriateness has been
a familiar one to early childhood teachers for many years. Descriptions
and elaborations of appropriate curriculum within today's context are becoming available (this volume is an example; see also DeGaetano et al.,
1997; Harris, 1991).

At the same time, educators legitimately ask whether there can be
a *single* developmentally appropriate approach that meets all children's
needs. Speaking from an African American perspective, Delpit (1988)
presents an eloquent argument in favor of carefully considering approaches that narrow rather than broaden children's options. For example, according to some definitions, programs that are referred to as
"child-centered," "whole language," or "process-oriented" include little
direct teaching of skills (including letter–sound correspondences) to children. Yet direct teaching is what many African-American parents expect
and want. From Delpit's point of view, waiting for children who lack such
skills to "discover" them on their own is a failure to teach. Other educators make related points (Schickedanz, 1989; Throne, 1994), especially
regarding the futility of advocating a single theoretical or pedagogical position. They conclude that most children need a combination of approaches that include teaching specific information and skills, along with
time for the holistic activities that lead to discovery and understanding.
Using a musical analogy, Delpit (1988) highlights the need for teachers to
combine approaches and "to coach those [student] voices to produce
notes that will be heard clearly in the larger society" (p. 296). Access
to the larger society—to its social and economic opportunities—is what
virtually every family wants for its children. The characteristics of classrooms that may enhance this access are considered next.

## LANGUAGE IN THE CLASSROOM

Language in the classroom takes on many forms. In some classrooms it's
inaudible as children sit quietly filling in worksheets, which contain little
written language. In others it's both audible and visible as children interact through talk and print as if they are participating in a language "bath"
(Dyson & Genishi, 1993; Lindfors, 1987). Still other settings are audibly
distinctive, as children and sometimes teachers use languages other than

English. And a single classroom or setting can vary in the course of a day: It can incorporate talk-filled times and periods of silence, as well as teacher-directed lessons. This section contains descriptions of classroom research and practice that work toward combining children's needs for specific information and spontaneous expression, toward expanding their communicative competence, and toward being both multicultural and developmentally appropriate.

## The Importance of Story

The use of story, whether told by adults or created through the dramatic play of children, is essential to the communication of human experience. It is also an important link among members of the same family, across families and generations, across communities and different cultures, and across oral and written modes of language. Teacher-researchers have been particularly thought-provoking as they have documented children's and their own stories. Vivian Paley, for example, has told numerous stories-within-stories, often focusing on individual children such as Reeny, the title character of a recent book, *The Girl with the Brown Crayon* (Paley, 1997). Paley tells of Reeny's and other children's fascination with particular published stories by Leo Lionni while she links the stories with and reveals her own struggle with questions of school and society: How do children respond—in and out of the context of stories—to those who are "different" from themselves? Do children benefit from racially integrated education? How do parents answer such a question? How does she herself address it, after decades in the classroom? One of the strengths of storytelling is that it allows for multiple plots and endings. Like other storytellers, Paley formulates not solutions, but possibilities, within the context of life in early childhood classrooms (see also Dyson & Genishi, 1994; Paley, 1979, 1981, 1995).

**Stories and Their Variation.** Educators often assume that children who have had stories told or read to them are likely to join the community of the literate with ease, since stories told should be bridges to stories read. But this assumption rests on shared definitions of story, which do not always exist (Cazden, 1988; Heath, 1983a). Karen Gallas (1992), a first/second-grade teacher-researcher, has also illustrated the variation that children introduce when they create stories. For instance, when Gallas decided to modify sharing time in her classroom, she asked children to volunteer to participate, rather than asking everyone to take a turn. Jiana, a girl who remained silent for a period of time, eventually volunteered, although she had few material things to show or share. After a class trip to the zoo, however, Jiana chose to tell a fictitious story about petting a gorilla. Gallas told her that this was a time for "true stories," an action she regretted. She later allowed Jiana to share her story, which continued over time and evolved into a new genre of story, one that grew and incorporated Jiana's classmates as main characters. The lesson for Gallas was profound, especially because she had wondered at the beginning of the school year if Jiana should be referred for special education. Gallas's flexibility allowed for a new child-developed definition of story. Accomplishments such as Jiana's are reminders that stories are like other culturally derived phenomena; there is nothing inherently "better" about one style of storytelling over another, just as there is nothing inherently better about one language or dialect over another.

**Story as Drama: Playing Roles.** "In play a child behaves beyond his average age, above his daily behavior; in play it is as though he were a head taller than himself" (Vygotsky, 1978, p. 102). Child-watchers know that when children engage in pretend or dramatic play, they take on characteristics of people who behave and speak differently from themselves. Children can display what they are learning in novel ways. In their self-contained English-as-a-second-language classroom, these four children dramatize a familiar tale, incorporating vocabulary previously introduced by the teacher: Penny (Cantonese speaker), Oleg (Russian), Daniel (Albanian), and Ogusan (Turkish) sit at their table, reenacting the story again and again, changing roles and adding stage directions:

> PENNY: You pigs. You three pigs.
> OGUSAN: I'm second 'cause I'm gonna, I'm gonna build strong house.
> OLEG: He's the third little, the third little. He's the third house.
> DANIEL: No. I wanna be the big bad wolf (Penny becomes the third little pig).
> PENNY: My house not broke. I have strong house—strong house.
> OGUSAN: (to Daniel, the wolf) You can't blow. Get a something.
> DANIEL: I got an idea. I'll get a lad (ladder). Ow! (pretending to land in the hot soup). (Fassler, 1995, pp. 102–103)

For the final enactment that day, Penny becomes the first girl in the class to claim the wolf role, asserting, "I'm gonna be the wolf!" and the boys eagerly prompt her through the part (pp. 102–103). Children in this class clearly weave teacher-presented vocabulary, such as *second, third, strong,* and *ladder,* into their dramatic play. Like children learning a first language, these children construct in their second language their own understandings of its many rules. Errors are naturally a part of this interactive process.

The dramatic play setting, enjoyable and usually free from adult intervention, truly encourages talk that is "a head taller" than the ordinary. It can also push children to take others' points of view, as they create scripts for their characters (Nelson & Gruendel, 1979). Representing through play talk the way others think or present themselves can enrich children linguistically and cognitively, whether they are bilingual or monolingual (Reynolds & Jones, 1997; Van Hoorn, Nourot, Scales, & Alward, 1993). Thus opportunities for dramatic play, so often limited to preschools and kindergartens, would also benefit children in the primary grades, as the next example demonstrates.

Ms. Raney, a second-grade teacher, has her children act out different roles as they read the play "The Bremen Town Musicians" together:

> DOG: Good morning.
> DONKEY: Good morning. Where is your—where's your Mastah?
> DOG: I'm running away from her.
> DONKEY: That's funnah. I'm runnin' away from mine. For many years it's been nothing but work, work, work. Now that I'm old and tired, he wants to get rid of me. . . . Where are you going? (Genishi & Dyson, 1984, p. 201)

To teach children about their own language, Ms. Raney audiotapes her children in different speaking situations, so that they can hear themselves sound casual in some and more formal in others—as Ms. Raney says, more "how they talk on TV." Alex, as the donkey, talks in TV talk, though at another time he described a picture in this way: "Dat cah right dere goin' to hit da cub [curb] 'n dat cah right dere goin' ta hit da ho'se'n dat cah right dere goin' to hit da do-ug [dog]" (Genishi & Dyson, 1984, p. 201). When playing the donkey, Alex uses some features of the sound system of standard English, pronouncing crisply and carefully (*going,* instead of *goin'*), whereas in the second example, he uses many features of his own community's dialect, African American vernacular or Black English. Ms. Raney has her children both dramatize plays in standard English and speak in their own dialect in less formal situations. Without the use of repetitious language drills, she acts on a belief that children should grow in their communicative competence, by adding standard English to their repertoires while they develop as speakers, writers, and readers.

The many facets of story, then, provide showcases for children's abilities in language at the same time that they present teachers with opportunities for judicious intervention. The intervention may be direct, as when a first-grader struggles with the spelling of a word in her story that she wants to "get right," or it may be more subtle, as when a teacher urges a child to try the home corner one day during choice time. Teachers can assess aspects of language use, such as fluency, in oral storytelling, complexity of speech, extent of bilingualism, or imaginativeness in dramatic play by careful watching and listening. These aspects of oral language are not often measured by standardized tests but are important to teachers who aim to extend children's communicative competence. (See Genishi & Borrego Brainard [1995] for further discussion of assessment.)

## Talking Across the Curriculum

Much of what is accessible to young children is embedded in the talk of stories, although not all learners are drawn to literary or fictional stories. Thus offering opportunities to talk about experiences related to social studies, the arts, science, or math is also important. A child's drawing easily leads to a discussion of its content or a conversation about the child's name, which she or he has written or asked a teacher to write. Science, too, when taught with children's ways of learning in mind, is another area that is enhanced through talk (see Gallas, 1995).

Dyson (1993) describes how Louise, a primary grade teacher, capitalizes on children's talk when she asks her class how to find an answer to Brett's science-related question, "Where does space begin and end?"

> MOLLIE: Ask a scientist.
> JAMEEL: Read a book or think about it.
> JULIAN: Go in a space rocket.
> LOUISE: Maybe we should do some empirical research.
> BERTO: Yeah, but Louise doesn't know very much about going into a space rocket and going up to space either.

Louise has to agree with Berto's evaluation. What she has done, she says, is "pretty much what Jameel suggested." She has gone to the school library and gotten three space books. But she is not happy with them. The copyright dates are in the 1960s.

> LOUISE: Let me tell you something, folks. In 1960, I was in high school. They've learned a lot about space since I was in high school.
> BRAD: We weren't even born.
> SHAWNDA: Usually people who graduated then, they be dead by now.

The notion of the copyright dates is fascinating to the children, and for the remainder of the year, one child or another will remind Louise to check the date when she reads to them. (p. 36)

In Louise's class, questions that originate in one "subject area" easily blend with others, expanding the content of discussions and influencing thinking and talk over time.

Almost every activity presents an opportunity for talk when teachers nurture it. The computer, the object of scrutiny and controversy in some early childhood programs, is a machine that could be socially isolating and impersonal. But like many other things, it can also prompt talk. In the following example, first-graders are using a computer program to create designs on their screens:

FLORA:  Help him. He doesn't know how to do it.
MARGARET:  (to Juan) Want me to help you?
JUAN:  Yeah.
MARGARET:  OK. First, press that one down (demonstrates. Juan presses the key while Margaret presses another.) There.
JUAN:  I can do it.
MARGARET:  OK, and you keep pushing that one (goes back to her own computer, but quickly checks Juan's again). Now you need to make your plus (a cross-like shape), so you go up here and you do that, and go here, like that (she touches the screen as she traces a cross). If you need help, just ask me, OK? (Genishi, 1988a, p. 187)

Computer activity among first-graders and younger children can be talk-generating and cooperative (Genishi, 1988a; Genishi, McCollum, & Strand, 1985). The easily viewed computer screen can lead to children's learning from and helping each other.

## CONCLUSIONS

Everything in this chapter acts in praise of children's enormous accomplishments as communicators in varied settings. Returning to the questions about Daniel's, Jerry's, and Ogusan's talk at the beginning of the chapter, we now know that like all children, the three have become speakers and learners through a complex process over time. With the human gift for learning language in interaction with people and objects, they have figured out huge numbers of rules related to the phonology, syntax, semantics, and pragmatics of their home language and are on a path toward learning the rules of English, a second language. As active, thinking children, they have been at the core of the learning process. We know, too, that the language adults hear in school settings represents tiny bits of any child's linguistic and communicative competence. If a child's communicative development could be viewed like a kaleidoscope that is constantly moving, individual teachers would see only a few of the intricate patterns that make up the whole of children's communicative histories.

The classroom or center is only one setting in which that history evolves. So much more of it has been embedded in children's own communities, where the events and conversations of everyday life have a seamless look and feel. For some children, the seamlessness of the years outside of school ends abruptly when they enter a setting where adults talk and behave differently from their parents or friends. Unless there are opportunities to learn "school talk," in partnership with supportive others, a center or school may become an uncomfortable and difficult place for the child.

Teachers ease the transition to school when they nurture talk with these characteristics across the curriculum:

1. Talk between adults and children and between children serves a variety of purposes or functions. That is, language is used to inform, tell stories, question, pretend, have fun, discuss, plan, and so on.
2. Since talk flows when people have something to talk about or tell each other, teachers provide for and engage the children in activities and experiences that are the focus of talk.
3. Conversations are comfortable for both child and teacher. Talk is fluent because the communicators are absorbed in getting their messages across, and their conversations are meaning-oriented, not form-oriented.

Though the language forms—and sometimes the language—that a child uses may not always match the teacher's, the communicative purposes of the two can match. In developmentally appropriate settings, educators choose collaboratively with parents the range of purposes to be included, depending on their values and their views of language and learning.

The teacher plays a critical role in deciding whether oral language is inaudible or provides a "language bath" for children throughout the day. Before children read and write with ease, talk is the adult's versatile and ready tool for finding out what children know, what their individual social histories are, which adult meanings elude them, and how they view their experiences. In the complex processes of teaching and learning, talk makes visible some of children's thinking. Thus teachers draw on their own knowledge of development, language, and human communities as they try to see what children see, with the goal of helping them experience and know more.

## REFERENCES

Barrett, M. D. (1982). Distinguishing between prototypes: The early acquisition of the meaning of object names. In S. Kuczaj II (Ed.), *Language development: Vol. 1. Syntax and semantics* (pp. 313–334). Hillside, NJ: Erlbaum.

Berko, J. (1958). The child's learning of English morphology. *Word, 14,* 150–177.

Bredekamp, S. (Ed.). (1987). *Developmentally appropriate practice in early childhood programs serving children from birth through age 8* (rev. ed.). Washington, DC: National Association for the Education of Young Children.

Bredekamp, S., & Copple, C. (1997). *Developmentally appropriate practice in early childhood programs* (rev. ed.). Washington, DC: National Association for the Education of Young Children.

Brown, R. (1973). *A first language: The early stages.* Cambridge, MA: Harvard University Press.

Brown, R., Cazden, C., & Bellugi, U. (1969). The child's grammar from I to III. In J. P. Hill (Ed.), *Minnesota symposium on child psychology* (Vol. 2, pp. 28–73). Minneapolis: University of Minnesota Press.

Bruner, J. S. (1983). *Child's talk.* New York: Norton.

Burling, R. (1973). *English in Black and White.* New York: Holt, Rinehart & Winston.

Cazden, C. B. (1988). *Classroom discourse: The language of teaching and learning.* Portsmouth, NH: Heinemann.

Clark, E. V. (1983). Meanings and concepts. In P. H. Mussen (Ed.), *Handbook of child psychology* (4th ed., Vol. 3, pp. 787–840). New York: Wiley.

Cullinan, B. E., Jaggar, A. M., & Strickland, D. (1974). Language expansion for Black children in the primary grades: A research report. *Young Children, 29*(1), 98–112.

Cummins, J. (1994). Knowledge, power, and identity in teaching English as a second language. In F. Genesee (Ed.), *Educating second language children: The whole child, the whole curriculum, the whole community* (pp. 33–58). New York: Cambridge University Press.

Curtiss, S. (1977). *Genie: A psycholinguistic study of a modern-day "Wild-Child."* New York: Academic Press.

De Gaetano, Y., Williams, L. R., & Volk, D. (1998). *Kaleidoscope: A multicultural approach for the primary school classroom.* Upper Saddle River, NJ: Prentice-Hall.

Delpit, L. D. (1988). The silenced dialogue: Power and pedagogy in educating other people's children. *Harvard Educational Review, 58,* 280–298.

Derman-Sparks, L., & the ABC Task Force. (1989). *Anti-bias curriculum: Tools for empowering young children.* Washington, DC: National Association for the Education of Young Children.

Durkin, D. (1982). *A study of poor Black children who are successful readers* (Reading Education Report No. 33, No. ED 216 334). Urbana, IL: Center for the Study of Reading.

Dyson, A. Haas (1993). *Social worlds of children learning to write in an urban primary school.* New York: Teachers College Press.

Dyson, A. Haas, & Genishi, C. (1993). Visions of children as language users: Language and language education in early childhood. In B. Spodek (Ed.), *Handbook of research on the education of young children* (pp. 122–136). New York: Macmillan.

Dyson, A. Haas, & Genishi, C. (Eds.). (1994). *The need for story: Cultural diversity in classroom and community.* Urbana, IL: National Council of Teachers of English.

Fassler, R. Z. (1995). Room for talk: The use of English in a self-contained multi-language English as a second language kindergarten. Doctoral dissertation, Teachers College, Columbia University. *Dissertation Abstracts International, 56–71,* 2554A.

Fassler, R. (1998). "Let's do it again!" Peer collaboration in picture book reading in an ESL kindergarten. *Language Arts, 75*(3), 202–210.

Fournier, J., Lansdowne, B., Pastenes, Z., Steen, P., & Hudelson, S. (1992). Learning with, about, and from children: Life in a bilingual second grade. In C. Genishi (Ed.), *Ways of assessing children and curriculum: Stories of early childhood practice* (pp. 126–162). New York: Teachers College Press.

Gallas, K. (1992). When the children take the chair: A study of sharing time in a primary classroom . . . *Language Arts, 69*(3), 172–182.

Gallas, K. (1995). *Talking their way into science: Hearing children's questions and theories, responding with curricula.* New York: Teachers College Press.

Genesee, F. (Ed.). (1994). *Educating second language children: The whole child, the whole curriculum, the whole community.* New York: Cambridge University Press.

Genishi, C. (1988a). Kindergartners and computers: A case study of six children. *Elementary School Journal, 89,* 185–202.

Genishi, C. (1988b). Research in review: Children's language: Learning words from experience. *Young Children, 44*(1), 16–23.

Genishi, C., & Borrego Brainard, M. (1995). Assessment of bilingual children: A dilemma seeking solutions. In E. E. Garcia & B. McLaughlin, with B. Spodek & O. N. Saracho (Eds.), *Meeting the challenge of linguistic and cultural diversity in early childhood education: Yearbook in early childhood education, Vol. 6* (pp. 49–63). New York: Teachers College Press.

Genishi, C., & Dyson, A. Haas (1984). *Language assessment in the early years.* Norwood, NJ: Ablex.

Genishi, C., McCollum, P., & Strand, E. (1985). Research currents: The interactional richness of children's computer use. *Language Arts, 62,* 526–532.

Goodwin, A. L. (Ed.). (1997). *Assessment for equity and inclusion: Embracing all our children.* New York: Routledge.

Gregory, E. (Ed.). (1997). *One child, many worlds: Early learning in multicultural communities.* New York: Teachers College Press.

Hakuta, K., & Diaz, R. (1984). The relationship between bilingualism and cognitive ability: A critical discussion and some new longitudinal data. In K. E. Nelson (Ed.), *Children's language* (Vol. 5, pp. 319–344). Hillsdale, NJ: Erlbaum.

Harris, V. J. (1991). Research in review: Multicultural curriculum: African American children's literature. *Young Children, 46*(2), 37–44.

Heath, S. B. (1983a). Research currents: A lot of talk about nothing. *Language Arts, 60,* 999–1007.

Heath, S. B. (1983b). *Ways with words: Language, life, and work in communities and classrooms.* New York: Cambridge University Press.

John, V., & Horner, V. (1971). *Early childhood bilingual education.* New York: Modern Language Association.

Krashen, S. (1985). *The input hypothesis: Issues and implications.* London: Longman.

Labov, W. (1970). The logic of nonstandard English. In F. Williams (Ed.), *Language and poverty* (pp. 153–189). Chicago: Markham.

Labov, W. (1972). *Language in the inner city: Studies in the Black English vernacular.* Philadelphia: University of Pennsylvania.

Lindfors, J. W. (1987). *Children's language and learning* (rev. ed.). Englewood Cliffs. NJ: Prentice-Hall.

Loban, W. D. (1963). *The language of elementary school children.* Urbana, IL: National Council of Teachers of English.

Miller, G. A., & Gildea, P. M. (1987, September). How children learn words. *Scientific American,* pp. 94–99.

Miller, P. (1982). *Amy, Wendy, and Beth.* Austin: University of Texas Press.

Miller, W., & Ervin, S. M. (1964). The development of grammar in child language. In U. Bellugi & R. Brown (Eds.), The acquisition of language. *Monographs of the Society for Research in Child Development, 29,* 9–34 (1, Serial No. 92).

Nelson, K. (1973). Structure and strategy in learning to talk. *Monographs of the Society for Research in Child Development, 38* (1–2, Serial No. 149).

Nelson, K. (1985). *Making sense: The acquisition of shared meaning.* New York: Academic Press.

Nelson, K. (Ed.). (1986). *Event knowledge: Structure and function in development.* New York: Academic Press.

Nelson, K., & Gruendel, J. M. (1979). At morning it's lunchtime: A scriptal view of children's dialogues. *Discourse Processes, 2,* 73–94.

New York City Board of Education. (1996–97). *Bilingual Education Student Information Survey.* Office of Bilingual Education, Division of Management Information Services, New York.

Paley, V. (1979). *White teacher.* Cambridge, MA.: Harvard University Press.

Paley, V. (1981). *Wally's stories.* Cambridge. MA: Harvard University Press.

Paley, V. (1995). *Kwanzaa and me: A teacher's story.* Cambridge, MA: Harvard University Press.

Paley, V. (1997). *The girl with the brown crayon.* Cambridge, MA: Harvard University Press.

Piaget, J., & Inhelder, B. (1969). *The psychology of the child.* New York: Basic Books.

Piestrup. A. (1973). *Black dialect interference and accommodation of reading instruction in first grade.* Berkeley: University of California, Language-Behavior Research Laboratory.

Ramsey, P. G., Vold, E. B., & Williams, L. R. (Eds.). (1989). *Multicultural education: A source book.* New York: Garland.

Rentel, V., & Kennedy, J. (1972). Effects of pattern drill on the phonology, syntax, and reading achievement of rural Appalachian children. *American Educational Research Journal, 9,* 87–100.

Reynolds, G., & Jones, E. (1997). *Master players.* New York: Teachers College Press.

Schachter, F. F., & Strage, A. A. (1982). Adult's talk and children's language development. In S. G. Moore & C. R. Cooper (Eds.), *The young child: Review of research* (Vol. 3, pp. 79–96). Washington, DC: National Association for the Education of Young Children.

Schickedanz, J. A. (1989). The place of specific skills in preschool and kindergarten. In D. S. Strickland & L. M. Morrow (Eds.), *Emerging literacy: Young children learn to read and write* (pp. 96–106). Newark, DE: International Reading Association.

Schieffelin, B. B. (1979). Getting it together: An ethnographic approach to the study of the development of communicative competence. In E. Ochs & B. B. Schieffelin (Eds.), *Developmental pragmatics* (pp. 73–108). New York: Academic Press.

Schweinhart, L. J., & Weikart, D. P. (1980). Young children grow up: Effects of the Perry Preschool Program on youths through age 15. *Monographs of the High/Scope Educational Research Foundation (7).* Ypsilanti, MI: High/Scope.

Simpkins, G., Simpkins, C., & Holt, G. (1977). *Bridge: A cross-culture reading program.* Boston: Houghton Mifflin.

Smitherman, G. (1994). *Black talk: Words and phrases from the hood to the amen corner.* New York: Houghton Mifflin.

Snow, C. E., Barnes, W. S., Chandler, J., Goodman, I. F., & Hemphill, L. (1991). *Unfulfilled expectations: Home and school influences on literacy.* Cambridge, MA: Harvard University Press.

Soto, L. D. (1991). Research in review: Understanding bilingual/bicultural young children. *Young Children, 46*(2), 30–36.

Stern, D. (1977). *The first relationship: Infant and mother.* Cambridge, MA: Harvard University Press.

Stockman, I. (1984). *A developmental study of Black English* (Phase 1, Final Report). Washington, DC: Center for Applied Linguistics. (ERIC Document Reproduction Service No. 245555)

Throne, J. (1994). Living with the pendulum: The complex world of teaching. *Harvard Educational Review, 64,* 195–208.

Tizard, B., & Hughes, M. (1984). *Young children learning.* Cambridge, MA: Harvard University Press.

Valdes, G. (1997). Dual-language immersion programs: A cautionary note concerning the education of language-minority students. *Harvard Educational Review, 67*(3), 391–429.

Van Hoorn, J. L., Nourot, P., Scales, B., & Alward, K. (1993). *Play at the center of the curriculum.* Upper Saddle River, NJ: Prentice-Hall.

Vygotsky, L. S. (1978). *Mind in society.* Cambridge, MA: Harvard University Press.

Wong Fillmore, L. (1976). *The second time around: Cognitive and social strategies in second language acquisition* (Pts. 1 & 2). Unpublished doctoral dissertation. Stanford University, Stanford, CA. *Dissertation Abstracts International, 37–10,* 6443A.

Wong Fillmore, L. (1991). Language and cultural issues in early education. In S. L. Kagan (Ed.), *The care and education of America's young children: Obstacles and opportunities* (Part I, 90th Yearbook of the National Society for the Study of Education, pp. 30–49). Chicago: National Society for the Study of Education.

CHAPTER 4

# Emergent Literacy: What Research Reveals About Learning to Read

## Linda B. Gambrell
## Susan Anders Mazzoni

THE QUESTIONS of when and how to teach beginning reading are among the most controversial topics in early childhood education. One of the reasons for the continuing controversy is that we all care so deeply about helping our children become successful in developing the literacy skills that provide the foundation for education and the ideals of a democratic society (Adams, 1990).

While definitions of reading vary, most of them acknowledge the common elements of print, language, and comprehension. There is a general consensus in the research community that reading is a *constructive* and *interactive* process. That is, reading is viewed as a meaning-making process that involves not only the reader but also the text and the contextual setting in which reading is taking place (Gambrell, 1996; Guthrie, 1996; Vygotsky, 1978). The constructive-interactive view also posits that reading is a cognitive process and that different instructional practices as well as assessment techniques are necessary in order to tap the multitude of factors involved in reading.

In this chapter we examine how young children develop as readers. First, we focus on the concept of emergent literacy for the insights it provides about young children's reading and writing development. We then move to a review of the theory and research on home and school factors associated with learning to read. Next, we provide an overview of what current theory and research suggest young children need to know in order to develop into successful readers. We conclude with a review of several studies that focus on the characteristics of effective literacy instruction. Throughout the chapter we emphasize research that explores how children develop literacy knowledge, motivation, and behaviors.

## THE EMERGENT LITERACY PERSPECTIVE

Over the past 10 years, a new view of early literacy development has emerged that has had a profound impact on how we think about beginning reading instruction. Prior to the 1960s, researchers believed that young children would benefit from reading instruction only when a certain level of cognitive, social, emotional, and physical maturity had been attained. This perspective, known as "reading readiness," suggested that reading instruction should be withheld until the child had either "naturally" matured to a mental age of 6½ years (Morphett & Washburne, 1931) or had acquired the skills necessary to pass a reading readiness test. The reading readiness view of learning was based on the belief that certain specific skills (e.g., auditory discrimination, left-to-right eye progression, large motor skills) had to be attained before a child would be able to profit from reading instruction.

Since the 1960s, there has been a gradual shift away from the reading readiness perspective toward a view of literacy as an emerging set of knowledge and skills that have their beginnings in very young children. For almost all children, learning to read and write begins very early in life. Even as infants, children have experiences with written language as parents read them books and engage them in playing with alphabet blocks. At 2 or 3 years of age, many children can identify signs, labels, and logos that are a part of their environment (Teale & Sulzby, 1987).

As researchers began to observe and report the literacy activities of preschool children, they found that young children engage in a wide range of emergent literacy behaviors, such as listening to stories, discussing stories, making up stories, scribbling "letters" to family and friends, writing their names, and creating invented printlike signs (Clay, 1977, 1979). Today there is general consensus in the research community that literacy learning is a process that begins at birth, when babies begin to experiment with oral language (Clay, 1977; Hiebert, 1981).

Prior to formal reading instruction, young children interact with others in their homes and communities and experience the forms, functions, conventions, and values of reading, writing, speaking, and listening. Research by Clay (1979) has documented that, as a result of their interactions with others, young children develop logical, though unconventional, strategies about writing and comprehending the written word as well as important competencies that contribute to literacy development—such as understanding that print communicates meaning and that there is a difference between print and drawing, understanding the difference between "words" and "letters," and understanding how to handle books. This view, known as the "emergent literacy" perspective (Teale & Sulzby, 1988), views young children as continuously "in the process of becoming literate" (p. 197), as opposed to viewing children as "ready" to learn to read at a given point in time. The emergent years continue until the child is independently reading and writing at a conventional level (L. M. McGee & Purcell-Gates, 1997).

Since research supports the premise that children develop knowledge and values about literacy prior to formal schooling, the emergent perspective also suggests that children are best benefited by providing classroom reading experiences that build on their understandings about literacy in order to help them gradually develop more conventional reading and writing practices (Purcell-Gates, 1994, 1996). Moreover, contrary to the reading readiness perspective, there is mounting evidence to suggest that children benefit from reading instruction prior to the first grade (Blatchford, 1987; Teale & Sulzby, 1987), regardless of ethnic, gender, and socioeconomic differences (Hansen & Farrell, 1995). In fact, research has shown that many of the reading readiness skills can be acquired *while* learning to read (Ehri, 1979).

The emergent literacy perspective reflects the view that literacy is a continuum that begins at birth and continues throughout life. This perspective also acknowledges that reading and writing develop concurrently and interrelatedly in young children (Teale & Sulzby, 1987). Researchers have identified clear developmental patterns that emerge when children endeavor to read and write. In the emergent literacy perspective, these attempts should be recognized as valuable approximations toward more conventional reading and writing practices.

Sulzby (1985), who studied hundreds of preschool children reading storybooks, described five stages of children's emergent reading of favorite storybooks. During the first stage, children as young as 2 or 3 may begin "reading" by pointing to pictures and naming them without weaving a story around the pictures. In the next three stages, children still attend to pictures but also tell oral stories that sound mostly conversational. Children's oral intonation eventually sounds as if they are reading; using picture prompts, they tell stories that are complete and sound as if they are written. The final stage of emergent storybook reading involves the child's attempting to attend to print.

In young children, the development of reading and writing are closely linked. For example, Harste (1989) showed that writing improved children's reading skills and decoding skills. According to Teale and Sulzby (1988), "children do not first learn to read and then learn to write" (p. 3); therefore, it seems appropriate that we speak of literacy development, not of reading readiness or of prereading. It is important that educators recognize and build on the close and complementary relationship between reading and writing in the literacy experiences that we provide for young children.

## FACTORS ASSOCIATED WITH LEARNING TO READ SUCCESSFULLY

Clearly, learning to read is a complex process. Researchers have examined a range of factors to determine if there are relationships between learning to read and family literacy practices such as storybook reading, exposure to environmental print, and home–school connections. Likewise, research has focused on a range of classroom factors to determine if there are relationships between learning to read and classroom-based literacy practices such as the social and motivational context of the classroom, teacher storybook reading, and shared reading experiences.

### Family Literacy Practices

Researchers are becoming increasingly aware of how young children's social environment mediates literacy learning. Many researchers (e.g., Bronfenbrenner, 1977, 1979; Gee, 1992; Rogoff, 1990; Vygotsky, 1978, 1987) have drawn on social-constructivist perspectives, which posit that learners construct knowledge as a result of interaction with others within sociocultural contexts. Some emergent literacy research grounded in the social-constructivist perspective has attempted to determine family literacy practices that contribute to emergent literacy knowledge (Heath, 1983; Purcell-Gates, 1996). Other ressearchers have investigated how differences in children's knowledge about print affect their interpretation of the instruction received during schooling (Dyson, 1984; Heath, 1983; Purcell-Gates & Dahl, 1991), as well as how the social context of the classroom community affects learning (Purcell-Gates & Dahl, 1991).

**Storybook Reading.** The single most important literacy activity for building the knowledge and skills that are eventually required for reading is having an adult or adults who read aloud to the child on a continuing basis (Anderson, Hiebert, Scott, & Wilkinson, 1985). It appears that children make the most growth when the materials that are read aloud are slightly above the child's vocabulary and syntax level (Chomsky, 1972).

Some researchers assert that it is the interactive nature of the storybook reading that makes the most substantial contribution to literacy development (Adams, 1990; Teale, 1984; Wigfield & Asher, 1984). Parents or other adults support and nurture children's literacy development during read-aloud experiences when they build on the child's comments about the text; pose challenging questions; suggest alternative interpretations; encourage personal reactions; draw attention to letters, words, and illustrations; and engage in extended discussions about the text.

Interestingly, recent research by Bus (1994) demonstrated that a young child's interest in storybook reading with a parent appears to relate primarily to the intimate, shared time with a parent as opposed to reading the book itself. In summary, there is evidence to suggest that children who read early have books readily accessible to them (Applebee, Langer, & Mullis, 1988; Morrow, 1983; Sticht & McDonald, 1989) and have parents who read to them often (Adams, 1990; Durkin, 1966; Sulzby & Teale, 1991).

There is much to be gained from reading and discussing books with children. Clay (1979) and Smith (1988) propose that the read-aloud experience helps children learn about the features of written language. Children learn that written language is different from oral language, that print generates meaning, and that printed words on a page have sounds. According to Mason (1983), children who are read to by an adult develop metacognitive knowledge about how to approach reading tasks. Metacognition, one's own awareness about how learning takes place in particular settings, is clearly associated with literacy development (Flavell, 1976; Mason, 1983).

The behaviors of the adult during read-aloud experiences have been found to be associated with literacy development. These specific parent/adult behaviors include questioning, scaffolding dialogue and responses, positive feedback, offering extended information, clarifying information, restating information, directing discussion, sharing personal reactions, and relating concepts to life experiences. Flood (1977) described the reading styles of parents during read-aloud sessions with prekindergarten children. He found that the following parent behaviors were among the best predictors of children's success on readiness scores: (1) number of preparatory questions asked by the parent, (2) number of poststory evaluative questions asked by the parent, and (3) positive reinforcement offered by the parent.

Heath's (1980) research revealed that interactive language behaviors that occur during read-aloud experiences change over time as children get older. Parents initially expect very young children to interrupt stories, and the parents accept dialogue and questioning from the children during the story-reading event. By the age of 3, Heath observed, the child is expected to listen to the story and learn information from it, as in traditional school settings. The adult begins to question the child after a reading to determine content understanding and recall. Sulzby and Teale (1991), in their study of the storybook reading behaviors of eight families, found similar changes over time in the interactive patterns between parents and children.

Though a plethora of home literacy events have been found to occur in lower-socioeconomic-status (SES) communities, research has documented that children from these communities generally score lower on literacy measures than children from middle-income communities (Kaestle, Damon-Moore, Stedman, Tinsley, & Trollinger, 1991). One hypothesis to explain this difference is that adults from the middle-income "mainstream" spend more time reading aloud to children (Adams, 1990; Heath, 1983), though it is important to note that variation in family literacy practices may be great within a single community (Heath, 1983).

In summary, research on read-aloud experiences, also referred to as interactive reading and shared reading, has documented its positive effect on children's interest in reading (Cullinan, 1992; Huck, 1992), familiarity with book language (Anderson et al., 1985), awareness of story structure (Morrow & Weinstein, 1982), verbal expression and vocabulary (Purcell-Gates, 1988; Wells, 1985; Whitehurst & Lonigan, 1998), and story comprehension (Morrow & Weinstein, 1982; Wells, 1986). Consequently, many current intervention programs for young children incorporate an emphasis on interactive storybook reading (Fox, 1990; Meyerhoff & White, 1986; Morrow & O'Connor, 1995) as well as increased access to books (Gambrell, Almasi, Xie, & Heland, 1995), both of which have resulted in positive gains in children's literacy growth.

**Environmental Print Experiences.** Research has identified a variety of literacy events in homes across a range of SES communities that afford opportunities for children to learn about print. For example, reading and writing experiences in low-SES homes have been found to include demonstrations of reading texts on containers, flyers, coupons, advertisements, and movie or TV notices; writing grocery lists; signing names; participation in story and Bible-study experiences; and written communication with social services (Purcell-Gates, 1996; D. Taylor & Dorsey-Gaines, 1988; Teale & Sulzby, 1988). The frequency of literacy activities and the degree of children's participation in literacy events in the home have been shown to relate to young children's reading motivation (Baker, Serpell, & Sonnenschein, 1995; Lomax, 1976; Morrow, 1983; Rowe, 1991) and knowledge about the function of print and the alphabetic principle, though different practices appear to be related to different types of knowledge (Purcell-Gates, 1996). Some researchers argue that the presence of environmental print in a literate society such as ours helps to ensure children's understanding about the forms and functions of print (Goodman & Goodman, 1979); however, recent research suggests that if parents and their children do not view print as useful within their own cultural communities, environmental print may contribute little to emergent literacy knowledge (Purcell-Gates, 1994).

**Home–School Connections.** As described earlier, research has shown that children experience literacy differently as a result of their home cultures. However, it is important that educators focus on what students can do and draw upon these strengths in order to address student's needs. Swap (1993) argued that some parent involvement programs assume a "deficit" model, that is, non-mainstream-culture families are "deficient" and are in need of remediation regarding how they can fit the practices in schools. On the other hand, an "anti-deficit" model is grounded in the view that children will benefit from experiences and instruction that draw upon their home and community life. If we believe in the associative capacity of human cognition, then a range of home and community experiences can be viewed as relevant and meaningful for classroom literacy instruction.

Recently, research has begun to focus on home–school connections, or lack of home–school connections, and their effects on children's learning. One of the most influential studies that shed light on the influence of home–school connections on children was conducted by Heath (1983), who found that cultural mismatches between parent–child and teacher–child linguistic interactions affected children's performance in school. Similarly, Au (1980) found that Hawaiian children performed better when reading lessons incorporated "talk story" as opposed to the traditional lesson format (teacher asks a question/students respond/teacher evaluates). Research has demonstrated that the home and community, as well as preschool literacy experiences, can shape children's literacy knowledge and such knowledge may impede or facilitate learning in school (Dahl & Freppon, 1995; McGill-Franzen & Lanford, 1994; Neuman & Roskos, 1997; Purcell-Gates & Dahl, 1991; Sonnenschein et al., 1996; D. Taylor & Dorsey-Gaines, 1988).

## Classroom-Based Literacy Practices

**The Social Context of Classroom Literacy Experiences.** A number of researchers have investigated the classroom social environment and its effects on literacy learning. One reason that children read and write involves an intrinsic desire to interact with others (Wigfield, 1994). Socially supportive classroom environments, where children are encouraged to discuss and share reading and writing with peers, have been found to enhance the literacy motivation of first- (Gambrell, 1993), second- (Morrow & Rand, 1994), and third-graders (Ng, Guthrie, McCann, Van-Meter, & Alao, 1996). Other studies have shown that collaboration promotes achievement and higher-level cognition (Morrow & Smith, 1990). These studies support the notion that learning is enhanced when the classroom environment reflects a community of literacy learners (Brown, 1994) and when children and their parents are invited to "join the literacy club" (Smith, 1988).

Research also suggests that teachers can encourage collaborative interaction among peers by asking fewer questions or by using nonquestioning techniques, such as rephrasing or restating children's comments (Orsolini & Pontecorvo, 1992). However, none of the studies reviewed suggested that children benefit from collaborative discussions about text when teachers remove themselves completely from the discussion process. K. G. McGee (1992) reported that first-graders who participated in peer-led discussions (with the teacher present) and who were asked a single teacher-posed interpretive question tended to provide many more interpretive responses than the peer-led group that was not asked the teacher-posed question. Wiseman, Many, and Altieri (1992) found that teacher-guided discussion that focused third-graders' attention on thinking and talking about aesthetic and literary responses was a more effective instructional context for enriching students' experiences of a literary work than non-teacher-guided discussion. Even though social approaches to learning are supported by a consistent and compelling research base, some researchers have suggested that students should not work collaboratively all the time because they need to learn how to work within other classroom contexts as well (Johnson, Johnson, Holebec, & Roy, 1984).

## The Motivational Context of Classroom Literacy Experiences.

One important long-term goal of beginning reading instruction is to foster an intrinsic desire to read. Effective readers must possess both the skill and the will to read (Anderson et al., 1985; Borkowski, Carr, Rellinger, & Pressley, 1990; Gambrell, 1996; Paris & Oka, 1986), yet there is evidence to suggest that as grade level increases, children tend to have less positive attitudes toward reading (McKenna, Kear, & Ellsworth, 1995). It is important to note that children who are motivated and who spend more time reading are better readers (Anderson, Wilson, & Fielding, 1988; Morrow,

1992; B. M. Taylor, Frye, & Maruyama, 1990). Supporting and nurturing reading motivation and achievement are crucial to improving educational prospects for children who find learning to read difficult (Allington, 1986, 1991; Smith-Burke, 1989).

Motivation is a broad construct in the affective domain that encompasses an individual's set of beliefs, values, and goals that guide their actions (Wigfield & Karpathian, 1991). How can teachers create an environment in which students will be motivated to read? Research suggests that classroom cultures that foster reading motivation at the first-, second-, and third-grade levels are characterized by environments that promote challenge, choice, and collaboration (Gambrell, 1996; Gambrell & Morrow, 1995; Morrow, 1992; Turner, 1995).

**Opportunities for Challenge.** Recent theories emphasize that self-perceived competence or capability beliefs are strongly tied to motivation (Ford, 1992; McCombs, 1989). In other words, children's beliefs about how well they can read will influence whether they approach or avoid reading tasks. The important question, then, is how we can provide a motivating instructional context that supports children in developing positive capability beliefs with respect to their reading ability. According to Bandura (1986), the single greatest predictor of self-perceived competence and task engagement is success.

Recent literacy motivation studies have revealed important insights about the kind of success that is needed to foster self-perceived competence in learners (Spaulding, 1992; Turner, 1992). These studies suggest that children's capability beliefs are enhanced when they are successful at *challenging* learning tasks. Challenging tasks are those tasks that are appropriate for the learner, in that they are not too easy, nor are they too difficult. When a learning task is too easy, children become uninterested and do not feel personal accomplishment when they successfully complete the task. On the other hand, if the task is too difficult, children become frustrated and "turned off," and they often give up on completing the task. Furthermore, there is evidence to suggest that repeated exposure to failure tends to generate increasingly negative attitudes, self-concepts, and expectations about reading (Johnston & Winograd, 1985), all of which are associated with low motivation (Gambrell, Palmer, Codling, & Mazzoni, 1996). When young readers try yet do not succeed in learning to read, they often become unmotivated and inactive because their previous efforts have not produced positive results, and they expect the same pattern of effort and failure to occur in later attempts. They may attribute their failure to uncontrollable factors such as luck or teacher skill and consequently cease trying to learn. Johnston and Winograd (1985) proposed the term *passive failure* to describe poor readers who disassociate effort with outcome, credit success to uncontrollable forces, and attribute failure to lack of ability. The result of passive failure is that poor readers often do not develop motivational patterns, and their lack of effort then contributes to a cycle of failure.

In further support of the contention that affective factors are related to reading achievement, McKenna and colleagues (1995) found a strong positive relationship between children's recreational attitudes toward reading and reading achievement in a study of children in grades 1 through 6 across the United States. The authors stated that their findings suggested that "a reader's history of success or frustration plays a central role in shaping attitude" (p. 936). Thus it is critical that teachers assess students' strengths and needs so that appropriate and challenging literacy experiences can be provided that afford growth in achievement as well as foster feelings of competence and capability (also see Vygotsky's [1978] notion of the "zone of proximal development").

**Opportunities for Choice.** In motivational theory and research, the role of choice in general and reading motivation in particular is well recognized (Spaulding, 1992). Studies of first- and third-graders have found that when children told researchers about both narrative and information books they "most enjoyed" reading, more than 80% responded that they had self-selected the books from the classroom libraries (Gambrell, 1995; Gambrell et al., 1995; Palmer, Codling, & Gambrell, 1994). Only 10% of the children in these studies talked about books or stories that had been assigned by the teacher. Researchers have documented that task engagement and motivation increase when students are provided with opportunities to make choices about their learning (Deci & Ryan, 1985; Turner, 1995). In addition, findings from a number of studies suggest a strong correlation between choice and the development of intrinsic motivation (Paris & Oka, 1986; Rodin, Rennert, & Solomon, 1980; Turner, 1992).

A number of studies during the past decade have also provided support for the notion that when children have environments that are book-rich, the motivation to read is high (Elley, 1992; Gambrell, 1993; Lundberg & Linnakyla, 1993; Morrow, 1992; Purcell-Gates, McIntyre, & Freppon, 1995), although there is evidence to suggest that a book-rich classroom environment is not sufficient for the development of highly motivated readers (Ingham, 1981).

**Opportunities for Collaboration.** Recent conceptualizations of motivation have been developed that reflect the important role of collaboration in motivation to learn (McCombs, 1989; Oldfather, 1993). Current

theories of motivation recognize that learning is facilitated by social interactions among peers (McCombs, 1989), and they acknowledge the social
nature of literacy learning (Brandt, 1990; Oldfather, 1993). The opportunity to socially interact with others has been shown to foster both reading
motivation and reading development (Almasi & Gambrell, 1994; Gambrell, 1995, 1996; Guthrie, Schafer, Wang, & Afflerbach, 1993; Mullis,
Campbell, & Farstrup, 1993; Slavin, 1990). For these reasons, collaboration is viewed as a critical dimension of the motivating instructional context as well.

**Storybook Reading in the Early Childhood Classroom.** Several
studies using experimental designs have investigated the effects of storybook reading as a regular classroom practice on children's achievement
in various aspects of literacy development. In these investigations, the
children in the experimental classrooms who were read to daily over long
periods of time scored significantly better on measures of vocabulary,
comprehension, and decoding ability than children in the control groups
who were not read to by an adult (Bus, Ijzendoorn, & Pellegrini, 1995;
Dickinson & Smith, 1994; Elley, 1989; Feitelson, Goldstein, Iraqi, &
Share, 1993).

In studies carried out in school settings where children participated
with their teacher and/or peers in some part of the storybook-reading
experience, their comprehension and sense of story structure improved
in comparison to children in a control group. The storybook-reading experiences involved activities implemented *prior* to story reading, *during*
story reading, and *after* story reading. Activities implemented prior to
story reading included previewing the story through discussion, prediction, and setting a purpose for listening prior to the story's being read.
Activities implemented during the story reading focused on issues related
to the story that were spontaneously discussed at appropriate times. Activities implemented after the reading included discussing predictions,
discussing purposes set, role-playing stories, retelling stories, and reconstructing stories through pictures. These activities provided children with
opportunities to relate various parts of the story to each other and to
integrate story information (Morrow, 1985).

**Shared Reading in the Early Childhood Classroom.** Because research has shown benefits of at-home "lap reading" (see McCracken &
McCracken [1972] for a description of "lap reading"), many teachers use
oversized texts, called "Big Books," for in-class read-alouds so that young
children can experience the intimacy of at-home lap reading and can be
exposed to the print and pictures as the teacher reads aloud. As the Big

Books are read aloud, the teachers model the directionality of print, voice-to-print match, and the concept of a word by pointing to the words as they read to the children (McCracken & McCracken, 1986; Slaughter, 1983).

## BECOMING A SUCCESSFUL READER: WHAT YOUNG CHILDREN NEED TO KNOW

Becoming a successful reader means orchestrating many areas of awareness, mastering specific skills, and acquiring both decoding and comprehension strategies. Children need to understand that reading is first and foremost a meaning-getting process, and they must also have adequate and accurate concepts about what print is and what words are. Children also need to learn to decode well and be able to move from letters to sounds to real words and, ultimately, to comprehend the meaning of the text they read. This section provides an overview of the several factors that are associated with becoming a successful reader: phonological awareness, alphabetic understanding, phonics instruction, and reading as a meaning-getting process.

### Phonological Awareness

Research on what young children need to know about sounds in spoken words in order to be successful readers highlights the importance of learning letters and their sounds together. Research by Ohnmacht (1969) revealed that teaching children to recognize letters of the alphabet produced little benefit unless the children were also taught the sounds the letters represent. Likewise, it appears that training in recognizing sounds in spoken words has little effect on reading unless children are also taught the printed letters that represent their spoken counterparts (Bradley & Bryant, 1983).

Recent research has supported the important role of phonological awareness in learning to read (Adams, 1990; Ayres, 1995; Cornwall, 1992; Mann, 1993). Phonological awareness is the ability to hear and manipulate the constituent sounds of words. The term *phonological awareness* is inclusive in that it refers to all sizes of sound units, such as phonemes, syllables, and words, while the term *phonemic awareness* refers only to the phoneme level, the smallest unit of sound (e.g., the sound represented by the letter *p* in the word *pink*). Current research suggests that phonological awareness "is a hallmark characteristic of good readers while its absence is a consistent characteristic of poor readers" (Smith, Simmons, & Kameenui, 1995).

Evidence is mounting to suggest a cause-effect as well as a reciprocal relationship between phonological awareness and reading development (Adams, 1990; Seymour & Evans, 1994; Spector, 1995). It is not difficult to understand how phonological awareness is related to reading ability. A child who either does not consciously realize that words are made of sounds or who is unable to hear or manipulate sounds in words will most likely have difficulty linking letters to sounds or sounds to letters. The tasks associated with assessing phonological awareness that have been shown to predict reading performance include comparing and contrasting rhyming words, blending, syllable-splitting, phonemic segmentation, and deleting or adding phonemes to create new words (see Adams [1990] for a complete description of these tasks).

Intervention studies have demonstrated that a variety of phono-logical-training activities can enhance reading achievement. There is evidence to suggest that a combination of phonemic-awareness training along with letter–sound associations enhances reading development (Ball & Blachman, 1991; Byrne & Fielding-Barnsley, 1989). For example, phonemic-segmentation training, whereby kindergartners were asked to repeat sounds, move concrete objects to represent sounds, and connect letters to the sounds, improved kindergartners' reading and spelling skills more than phonics instruction alone (Ball & Blachman, 1991). In a recent study by Ayres (1995), direct instruction in phonological awareness was more effective than indirect instruction, and direct instruction was most effective when provided during the second half of the kindergarten year. Furthermore, Cunningham (1990) found that when a metacognitive stra-tegic component of instruction was integrated with phonemic-awareness and letter–sound training, there were greater gains in kindergartners' and first-graders' reading achievement than when instruction did not include the strategic component.

Our knowledge about phonological awareness, assessment, and in-struction is far from complete. One concern that research has not ad-dressed is whether children are differentially affected by instruction that teaches phonemic awareness by focusing on segmenting phonemes only versus instruction that is embedded within more meaningful, functional contexts (L. M. McGee & Purcell-Gates, 1997).

## Alphabetic Understanding

The term *alphabetic understanding* refers to the knowledge that letters rep-resent sounds and that whole words have a structure consisting of individual sounds and patterns of groups of sounds. Research conducted in the 1960s provided evidence to suggest that the best predictor of beginning reading achievement was a child's knowledge of letter names (Bond & Dykstra, 1967; Chall, 1967). This finding is particularly interesting in light of Ehri's (1989) finding that some children enter kindergarten knowing very few letters of the alphabet. Subsequent research on the significance of letter-name knowledge as a predictor of reading success has clarified the role of alphabetic understanding in learning to read. It appears that children's ability simply to recognize and name the letters in the alphabet is not as important as their ease and fluency in doing so (Adams, 1990).

A number of reasons have been hypothesized regarding why letter-naming speed and accuracy may be advantageous in learning to read. One hypothesis is that those children who are able to rapidly and accurately name letters have a deeper and more thorough knowledge of letters and are therefore better able to focus on patterns within words. On the other hand, children who cannot rapidly and accurately name letters appear to spend greater cognitive energy on letter discrimination. Also, because letter names are closely related to sounds, those children who are able to name letters quickly will be better able to associate letters with sounds.

## Phonics Instruction

The term *letter–sound correspondence* refers to the ability to link discrete phonemes (sounds) and individual letters or patterns of letters (symbols). Phonics instruction stresses the sound–symbol relationships. In the early stages of reading and writing development, children demonstrate their awareness of letter–sound correspondence in a variety of ways. For example, in early attempts to write children use the letter names they hear in the words, such as *ppl* for people, or *kot* for coat (Harste, Burke, & Woodward, 1982). The invented spellings of young children appear to be attempts at mapping the sound system rather than a means for identifying words. In early attempts at reading children often "sound-out" the initial letter or letters in a word they are attempting to read, for example, they will voice the sound of *d* in the word *dog* or the *t* in the word *top*. While many children spontaneously begin to incorporate knowledge of letter–sound correspondence in their early reading and writing, there is converging evidence that a combination of phonemic awareness and training in letter–sound correspondence facilitates reading as well as spelling development (Adams, 1990; Ball & Blachman, 1991; Mann, 1993; Snowling, 1991).

According to Adams (1990), the fundamental purpose of phonics instruction is to develop the students' ability to read connected text fluently. The relationship between phonics and reading connected text is an important one. Phonics can help children read more fluently while, at the same time, reading connected text for enjoyment and information may serve to reinforce students' learning of phonics.

## Reading as a Meaning-Getting Process

While research clearly indicates that the most significant factor underlying fluent word reading is the ability to recognize letters, spelling patterns, and whole words easily and automatically, it is equally important to keep in mind that the ultimate goal of all reading is comprehension. As children engage in reading text, they interpret the meaning by gathering new information as they proceed through the text. This information is interpreted in light of prior knowledge and experiences (Anderson, 1977; Bowey, 1984). As reading proceeds, the reader forms judgments about the meaning of the text based on prior knowledge, but as new information is acquired from the text, the reader reevaluates the meaning of the text. Clearly, comprehension is interactive in nature and depends as much on the readers' knowledge as it does on the information revealed in the text (Mason, 1984).

Since the 1980s there has been an increasing interest in expanding children's repertoire of comprehension skills. In the late 1980s the National Assessment of Educational Progress (Applebee et al., 1988) revealed that reading instruction needed to emphasize the higher-level thinking skills and strategies that provide the foundation for interpretive and reasoning abilities. Although interest in expanding instruction in comprehension processes has increased, very few studies have examined the effects of such instruction on young readers (Block, 1993).

Block (1993) conducted a study with elementary-aged children, including grades 2 and 3, that focused on instruction designed to increase students' strategic knowledge and comprehension. Some of the comprehension strategies that were taught to the children included clarifying ideas, summarizing, making inferences, interpreting, evaluating, problem solving, and creative thinking. In this study, students were randomly assigned, by classrooms, to experimental or control conditions. In the comprehension-strategy-instruction group, students received lessons twice weekly for 32 weeks. The lessons consisted of two parts: (1) teacher explanation and modeling of a thinking and reading comprehension strategy (e.g., decoding an unknown word, predicting) using written strategy application guides, and (2) student selection of literature and application of the previously taught cognitive strategy. In the control group students received traditional instruction that did not emphasize strategy instruction. The results revealed that the comprehension-strategy-instruction group outperformed the control group on the reading comprehension, vocabulary, and total battery sections of the Iowa Text of Basic Skills. In addition, students in the comprehension-strategy-instruction group also outperformed control students in the ability to transfer cognitive strategies to out-of-school applications and on measure of self-esteem and critical and creative thinking.

A qualitative case study was conducted by Baumann and Ivey (1997) to explore what second-grade students learned about reading, writing, and literature in a program of strategy instruction integrated within a literature-based classroom environment. During this year-long study, Baumann was the full-time classroom teacher and Ivey was a participant–observer in the classroom. Data sources included personal journals kept by both investigators, individual student interviews and interviews with parents and caregivers, videotapes of regular classroom literacy activities, artifacts of students' reading and writing, assessments of students' literacy learning, and the teacher's daily plan book. A content analysis of the data sources revealed that students grew in overall reading performance and came to view reading as a natural component of the school experience. The students demonstrated high levels of engagement with books; developed skill in word identification, fluency, and comprehension; and grew in written-composition abilities. This qualitative study provides support for the efficacy of teaching students reading and language arts strategies. Bauman and Ivey (1997) suggest

> that there is a bidirectional, mutually reinforcing relationship between the presence of a literature environment and contextualized strategy instruction. The immersion in literature and the embedded strategy instruction created a kind of symbiotic, synergistic relationship in which each program characteristic contributed to and fed off the other. In other words, the rich literature enhanced students' reading and writing fluency, and their developing literacy abilities promoted their literary knowledge and appreciation. (p. 272)

## WHAT RESEARCH REVEALS ABOUT EFFECTIVE READING INSTRUCTION IN THE PRIMARY GRADES

In general, studies of effective teaching have focused on issues of classroom management and pedagogy without regard to the content being covered (Dunkin & Biddle, 1974). Recently, reading researchers have begun to study effective literacy instruction in primary grade classrooms (Pressley, Rankin, & Yokoi, 1996; Wharton-McDonald, Pressley, & Mistretta, 1996). This research is grounded in the view that insights about how to teach beginning reading should come from careful study of effective teaching.

In a study of exemplary kindergarten, first-, and second-grade teachers, Pressley and colleagues (1996) asked reading supervisors around the United States to identify their very best teachers. Each of the nominated teachers was then asked to list 10 practices the teacher believed were "essential in her or his literacy instruction." The questionnaire stressed that the teacher's list should include only practices that actually occurred in her or his classroom. Responses were received from 113 of the 135 nominated teachers.

The 300 practices the teachers cited in responding to the questionnaire were categorized, and a second questionnaire was developed to specifically assess reading and writing instruction. For the second questionnaire, 86 out of 113 teachers responded (76% response rate). The questionnaire survey revealed that outstanding primary-level teachers provided literacy instruction with the following characteristics:

1. *There is a literate environment.* The classroom environment includes in-class libraries; displays of student work; chart stories/poems; posting of word lists; and listening, reading, and writing centers.
2. *Outstanding children's literature is read.* The reading of outstanding children's literature is central in the curriculum, through the use of Big Books, chart poems, and stories, as well as picture, patterned, and predictable storybooks.
3. *Students read aloud to others.* Students read aloud to the teacher and to peers, especially from stories they have written themselves.
4. *Students read along with the teacher.* There are many opportunities for students to participate in experiences such as reading along with the teacher, echo and choral reading, shared reading, daily silent reading, rereading of familiar books and stories, and reading homework (e.g., sending books home to be read with family members).
5. *Students engage in writing.* Students write stories and write in journals. They respond in writing to pictures, wordless picture books, and stories read in class. Student writing occurs in planning, drafting, and revising cycles, often culminating in a student-authored book or story.
6. *Literacy instruction is integrated across the curriculum.* Reading instruction also incorporates extension activities and experiences that relate to other areas of the curriculum.
7. *Many skills are taught.* The skills taught include those that are prerequi-

site to reading (e.g., auditory and visual discrimination, attending and listening skills), concepts of print, letters and their sounds, the alphabetic principle, decoding strategies and phonics, vocabulary and sight vocabulary, spelling, text elements (e.g., cause-effect relationships, main ideas), comprehension strategies (e.g., prediction, visualization), and critical thinking skills (e.g., brainstorming, categorization).

8. *There is a home–school connection.* There are regular communications to students' families about literacy progress and how the school and family can work together to foster literacy learning in the home.

The findings from this questionnaire/survey study are consistent with an observational study conducted by Wharton-McDonald and colleagues (1996) in nine first-grade classrooms. The three strongest teachers in this study were observed to do almost everything reported by the exemplary teachers in the Pressley and colleagues (1996) questionnaire study. When the outcomes of the two studies are combined, there is clear support for the conclusion that outstanding primary-level literacy classrooms are characterized by intense, sustained literacy experiences and are filled with high-quality reading, writing, and skills instruction.

## SUMMARY

Learning to read is an extremely complex process, largely because it is the result of a number of contextual forces (Pressley, in press). It goes without saying, however, that parents and teachers are the most important variables in this complex constellation of forces. It is also clear that there are sound theoretical principles and suggestions that can be drawn from the research to provide direction for parents and teachers about effective strategies and techniques that can be used to foster literacy growth in emergent literacy learners.

## REFERENCES

Adams, M. J. (1990). *Beginning to read: Thinking and learning about print.* London: MIT Press.

Allington, R. L. (1986). Policy constraints and effective compensatory reading instruction: A review. In J. Hoffman (Ed.), *Effective teaching of reading: Research and practice* (pp. 261–289). Newark, DE: International Reading Association.

Allington, R. L. (1991). The legacy of "Slow it down and make it concrete." In J. Zutell & S. McCormick (Eds.), *Learner factors/teacher factors: Issues in literacy research and instruction: Fortieth yearbook of the National Reading Conference* (pp. 19–29). Chicago: National Reading Conference.

Almasi, J. F., & Gambrell, L. B. (1994). Sociocognitive conflicts in peer-led and teacher-led discussions of literature (Research Report No. 12). Athens, GA: Universities of Maryland and Georgia, National Reading Research Center.

Anderson, R. C. (1977). The notion of schemata and the educational enterprise. In R. C. Anderson, R. J. Spiro, & A. Montague (Eds.), *Schooling and the acquisition of knowledge* (pp. 415–431). Hillsdale, NJ: Erlbaum.

Anderson, R. C., Hiebert, E. H., Scott, J. A., & Wilkinson, I.A.G. (1985). *Becoming a nation of readers.* Champaign: University of Illinois, Center for the Study of Reading.

Anderson, R. C., Wilson, P. T., & Fielding, L. G. (1988). Growth in reading and how children spend their time outside of school. *Reading Research Quarterly, 23*(3), 285–303.

Applebee, A. N., Langer, J. A., & Mullis, M. (1988). *Who reads best? Factors related to reading achievement in grades 3,7, and 11.* Princeton, NJ: Educational Testing Service.

Au, K. H. (1980). Participation structures in a reading lesson with Hawaiian children: Analysis of a culturally appropriate instructional event. *Anthropology and Education Quarterly, 11,* 91–115.

Ayres, L. R. (1995). The efficacy of three training conditions on phonological awareness of kindergarten children and the longitudinal effect of each on later reading acquisition. *Reading Research Quarterly, 30*(4), 604–606.

Baker, L., Serpell, R., & Sonnenschein, S. (1995). Opportunities for literacy learning in the homes of urban preschoolers. In L. M. Morrow (Ed.), *Literacy connections in families, schools, and communities* (pp. 236–252). Newark, DE: International Reading Association.

Ball, E. W., & Blachman, B. A. (1991). Does phoneme awareness training in kindergarten make a difference in early word recognition and developmental spelling? *Reading Research Quarterly, 24*(1), 49–66.

Bandura, A. (1986). *Social foundations of thought and action: A social cognitive theory.* Englewood Cliffs, NJ: Prentice-Hall.

Baumann, J. F., & Ivey, G. (1997). Delicate balances: Striving for curricular and instructional equilibrium in a second-grade, literature/strategy-based classroom. *Reading Research Quarterly, 32*(3), 244–275.

Blatchford, P. (1987). Associations between pre-school reading-related skills and later reading achievement. *British Educational Research Journal, 13*(1), 15–23.

Block, C. C. (1993). Strategy instruction in a literature-based reading program. *The Elementary School Journal, 94*(2), 139–151.

Bond, G. L., & Dykstra, R. (1967). The cooperative research program in first-grade reading instruction. *Reading Reasearch Quarterly, 2,* 5–142.

Borkowski, J. G., Carr, M., Rellinger, E., & Pressley, M. (1990). Self-regulated strategy use: Interdependence of metacognition, attributions, and self-esteem. In B. F. Jones & L. Idol (Eds.), *Dimensions of thinking: Review of research* (pp. 2–60). Hillsdale, NJ: Erlbaum.

Bowey, J. A. (1984). The interaction of strategy and context in children's oral reading performance. *Journal of Psycholinguistic Research, 13*(2), 99–117.

Bradley, L., & Bryant, P. E. (1983). Categorizing sounds and learning to read—A causal connection. *Nature, 301,* 419–421.

Brandt, D. (1990). *Literacy as involvement: The acts of writers, readers, and text.* Carbondale: Southern Illinois University Press.

Bronfenbrenner, U. (1977). Toward an experimental ecology of human development. *American Psychologist, 32,* 513–531.

Bronfenbrenner, U. (1979). *The ecology of human development.* Cambridge, MA: Harvard University Press.

Brown, A. (1994). The advancement of learning. *Educational Researcher, 28*(8), 4–12.

Bus, A. G. (1994). The role of social context in emergent literacy. In E. M. Assink (Ed.), *Literacy acquisition and social context* (pp. 9–24). New York: Harvester Wheatsheaf.

Bus, A. G., Ijzendoorn, M. H., & Pellegrini, A. D. (1995). Joint book reading makes for success in learning to read: A meta-analysis on intergenerational transmission of literacy. *Review of Educational Research, 65,* 1–21.

Byrne, B., & Fielding-Barnsley, R. (1989). Phonemic awareness and letter knowledge in the child's acquisition of the alphabetic principle. *Journal of Educational Psychology, 81,* 313–321.

Chall, J. S. (1967). *Learning to read: The great debate.* New York: McGraw-Hill.

Chomsky, C. (1972). Stages in language development and reading exposure. *Harvard Educational Review, 42,* 1–33.

Clay, M. M. (1977). *Reading: The patterning of complex behavior.* Exeter, NH: Heinemann.

Clay, M. M. (1979). *Reading: The patterning of complex behavior.* (2nd ed.). Exeter, NH: Heinemann.

Cornwall, A. (1992). The relationship of phonological awareness, rapid naming and verbal memory to severe reading and spelling disability. *Journal of Learning Disabilities, 25*(8), 532–538.

Cullinan, B. E. (1992). *Invitations to read: More children's literature in the reading program.* Newark, DE: International Reading Association.

Cunningham, A. (1990). Explicit vs. implicit instruction in phonemic awareness. *Journal of Experimental Child Psychology, 50,* 429–444.

Dahl, K., & Freppon, P. (1995). A comparison of inner-city children's interpretations of reading and writing instruction in the early grades in skills-based and whole language classrooms. *Reading Research Quarterly, 30,* 50–74.

Deci, E., & Ryan, R. (1985). *Intrinsic motivation and self-determination in human behavior.* New York: Plenum.

Dickinson, D. K., & Smith, M. W. (1994). Long-term effects of preschool teachers' book readings on low income children's vocabulary and story comprehension. *Reading Research Quarterly, 29*(2), 104–122.

Dunkin, M. J., & Biddle, B. J. (1974). *The study of teaching.* New York: Holt, Rinehart & Winston.

Durkin, D. (1966). *Children who read early.* New York: Teachers College Press.

Dyson, A. H. (1984). Emerging literacy in school contexts: Toward defining the gap between school curriculum and child mind. *Written Communication, 1,* 5–53.

Ehri, L. C. (1979). Linguistic insight: Threshold of reading acquisition. In T. G. Waller & G. E. MacKinnan (Eds.), *Reading research: Advances in theory and practice* (Vol. 1, pp. 63–111). New York: Academic Press.

Ehri, L. C. (1989). Movement into word-reading and spelling: How spelling contributes to reading. In J. M. Mason (Ed.), *Reading and writing connections* (pp. 65–81). Boston: Allyn & Bacon.

Elley, W. B. (1989). Vocabulary acquisition from listening to stories. *Reading Research Quarterly, 24,* 174–187.

Elley, W. B. (1992). *How in the world do students read?* Hamburg, Germany: International Association for the Evaluation of Educational Achievement.

Fietelson, D., Goldstein, Z., Iraqi, J., & Share, D. L. (1993). Effects of listening to story reading on aspects of literacy acquisition in a diagnostic situation. *Reading Research Quarterly, 28,* 71–79.

Flavell, J. H. (1976). Metacognitive aspects of problem solving. In L. B. Resnick (Ed.), *The nature of intelligence* (pp. 176–193). Hillsdale, NJ: Erlbaum.

Flood, J. (1977). Parental styles in reading episodes with young children. *The Reading Teacher, 30,* 864–867.

Ford, M. E. (1992). *Motivating humans.* Newbery Park, CA: Sage.

Fox, B. J. (1990). Teaching reading in the 1990s: The strengthened focus on accountability. *Journal of Reading, 33*(5), 336–339.

Gambrell, L. B. (1993). *The impact of* RUNNING START *on the reading motivation and behavior of first-grade children* (Research Report). College Park: University of Maryland, National Reading Research Center.

Gambrell, L. B. (1995). Motivation matters. In W. M. Linek & E. G. Sturtevant (Eds.), *Generations of literacy: Seventeenth yearbook of the College Reading Association* (pp. 2–24). East Texas, TX: College Reading Association.

Gambrell, L. B. (1996). Creating classroom cultures that foster reading motivation. Distinguished Educator Series. *The Reading Teacher, 50,* 14–25.

Gambrell, L. B., Almasi, J. F., Xie, Q., & Heland, V. (1995). Helping first-graders get a running start in reading. In L. Morrow (Ed.), *Family literacy: Connections in schools and communities* (pp. 143–154). Newark, DE: International Reading Association.

Gambrell, L. B., & Morrow, L. M. (1995). Creating motivating contexts for literacy learning. In L. Baker, P. Afflerbach, & D. Reinking (Eds.), *Developing engaged readers in home and school communities* (pp. 115–136). Mahwah, NJ: Erlbaum.

Gambrell, L. B., Palmer, B. M., Codling, R. M., & Mazzoni, S. A. (1996). Assessing motivation to read. *The Reading Teacher, 49,* 2–19.

Gee, J. P. (1992). *The social mind: Language, ideology, and social practice.* New York: Bergin & Garvey.

Goodman, K. S., & Goodman, Y. (1979). Learning to read is natural. In L. B. Resnick & P. Weaver (Eds.), *Theory and practice of early reading* (Vol. 1, pp. 137–154). Hillsdale, NJ: Earlbaum.

Guthrie, J. T. (1996). Educational contexts for engagement in literacy. *The Reading Teacher, 49*(6), 432–443.

Guthrie, J. T., Schafer, W., Wang, Y., & Afflerbach, P. (1993). *Influences of instruction on amount of reading: An empirical exploration of social, cognitive, and instructional indicators* (Reading Research Report No. 3). Athens, GA: National Reading Research Center, Universities of Georgia and Maryland College Park.

Hansen, R. A., & Farrell, D. (1995). The long-term effects on high school seniors of learning to read in kindergarten. *Reading Research Quarterly, 30*(4), 908–933.

Harste, J. C.(1989). The basalization of American reading instruction: One researcher responds. *Theory into Practice, 28,* 265–273.

Harste, J. C., Burke, C. L., & Woodward, V. A. (1982). Children's language and world: Initial encounters with print. In J. A. Langer & M. T. Smith-Burke (Eds.), *Reader meets author/bridging the gap* (pp. 105–131). Newark, DE: International Reading Association.

Heath, S. B. (1980). The functions and uses of literacy. *Journal of Communication, 30*(1), 123–133.

Heath, S. B. (1983). *Ways with words: Language, life, and work in communities and classrooms.* Cambridge, UK: Cambridge University Press.

Hiebert, E. H. (1981). Developmental patterns and interrelationship of pre-school children's print awareness. *Reading Research Quarterly, 16,* 236–260.

Huck, C. S. (1992). Books for emergent readers. In C. E. Cullinan (Ed.), *Invitations to read: More children's literature in the reading program* (pp. 2–13). Newark, DE: International Reading Association.

Ingham, J. (1981). *Books and reading development.* London: Heinemann.

Johnson, D. W., Johnson, R. T., Holebec, E. J., & Roy, P. (1984). Circles of learning: Cooperation in the classroom. Washington, DC: Association for Supervision and Curriculum Development.

Johnston, P. H., & Winograd, P. N. (1985). Passive failure in reading. *Journal of Reading Behavior, 17*(4), 279–301.

Kaestle, C. F., Damon-Moore, H., Stedman, L. C., Tinsley, K., & Trollinger, Jr., W. V. (1991). *Literacy in the United States.* New Haven, CT: Yale University Press.

Lomax, C. (1976). Interest in books and stories at nursery school. *Educational Research, 19,* 100–112.

Lundberg, I., & Linnakyla, P. (1993). *Teaching reading around the world.* Hamburg, Germany: International Association for the Evaluation of Educational Achievement.

Mann, V. A. (1993). Phoneme awareness and future reading ability. *Journal of Learning Disabilities, 26*(4), 259–269.

Mason, J. M. (1983, March). *Acquisition of knowledge about reading in the preschool period: An update and extension.* Paper presented at the Convention of the Society of Research in Child Development, Detroit.

Mason, J. (1984). A schema-theoretic view of the reading process as a basis for comprehension instruction. In G. G. Duffy, L. R. Roehler, & J. Mason (Eds.), *Comprehension instruction: Perspectives and suggestions* (pp. 26–38). New York: Longman.

McCombs, B. L. (1989). Self-regulated learning and academic achievement: A phenomenological view. In B. J. Zimmerman & D. H. Schunk (Eds.), *Self-regulated learning and academic achievement: Theory, research, and practice* (pp. 51–82). New York: Springer-Verlag.

McCracken, M., & McCracken J. (1972). *Reading is the only tiger's tail.* San Rafael, CA: Lewsing.

McCracken, R. A., & McCracken, M. J. (1986). *Stories, songs, and poetry to teach reading and writing.* Chicago: American Library Association.

McGee, K. G. (1992). An exploration of meaning construction in first graders' grand conversations. In C. K. Kinzer & D. J. Leu (Eds.), *Literacy research, theory, and practice: Views from many perspectives,* 41st Yearbook of the National Reading Conference. Chicago, IL: National Reading Conference.

McGee, L. M., & Purcell-Gates, V. (1997). So what's going on in research on emergent literacy? *Reading Research Quarterly, 32*(3), 310–318.

McGill-Franzen, A., & Lanford, C. (1994). Exposing the edge of the preschool curriculum: Teachers' talk about text and children's literacy understandings. *Language Arts, 71,* 264–273.

McKenna, M. C., Kear, D. J., & Ellsworth, R. A. (1995). Children's attitudes toward reading: A national survey. *Reading Research Quarterly, 30*(4), 934–956.

Meyerhoff, M. K., & White, B. L. (1986). New parents as teachers. *Educational Leadership, 44*(3), 42–46.

Morphett, M. V., & Washburne, C. (1931). When should children begin to read? *Elementary School Journal, 31,* 496–508.

Morrow, L. M. (1983). Home and school correlates of early interest in literature. *Journal of Educational Research, 76,* 221–230.

Morrow, L. M. (1985). *Promoting voluntary reading in school and home.* Bloomington, IN: Phi Delta Kappa Educational Foundation.

Morrow, L. M. (1992). The impact of a literature-based program on literacy achievement, use of literature, and attitudes of children from minority backgrounds. *Reading Research Quarterly, 27,* 250–275.

Morrow, L. M., & O'Connor, E. (1995). Literacy partnerships for change with "at risk" kindergartners. In R. Allington & B. Walmsley (Eds.), *No quick fix: Rethinking literacy programs in America's elementary schools* (pp. 97–115). New York: Guilford.

Morrow, L. M., & Rand, M. K. (1994, Spring). *Physical and social contexts for motivating reading and writing: The WRAP program* (Instructional Resource No. 5). Athens, GA: National Reading Research Center, Universities of Georgia and Maryland College Park.

Morrow, L. M., & Smith, J. K. (1990). The effects of group size on interactive storybook reading. *Reading Research Quarterly, 25*(3), 213–231.

Morrow, L. M., & Weinstein, C. S. (1982). Increasing children's use of literature through programs and physical design changes. *Elementary School Journal, 83,* 131–137.

Mullis, I., Campbell, J., & Farstrup, A. (1993). NAEP reading report card for the nation and the states. Washington, DC: National Center for Education Statistics.

Neuman, S. B., & Roskos, K. (1997). Literacy knowledge in practice: Contexts of participation for young writers and readers. *Reading Research Quarterly, 32*(1), 10–32.

Ng, M. M., Guthrie, J. T., McCann, A. D., VanMeter, P. V., & Alao, S. (1996, Summer). *How do classroom characteristics influence intrinsic motivation for literacy?* (Reading Research Report No. 56). Athens, GA: National Reading Research Center, Universities of Georgia and Maryland College Park.

Ohnmacht, D.C. (1969, April). *The effects of letter knowledge on achievement in reading in the first grade.* Paper presented at the annual meeting of the American Educational Research Association, Los Angeles. Reviewed in Ehri, L. (1983). Summary of Dorothy C. Ohnmacht's study: The effects of letter knowledge on achievement in reading in the first grade. In L. M. Gentile, M. L. Kamil, & J. S. Blanchard (Eds.), *Reading research revisited* (pp. 141–142). Columbus, OH: Merrill.

Oldfather, P. (1993). What students say about motivating experiences in a whole language classroom. *The Reading Teacher, 46,* 672–681.

Orsolini, M., & Pontecorvo, C. (1992). Children's talk in classroom discussions. *Cognition and Instruction, 9*(2), 113–136.

Palmer, B. M., Codling, R. M., & Gambrell, L. B. (1994). In their own words: What elementary children have to say about motivation to read. *The Reading Teacher, 48,* 176–179.

Paris, S., & Oka, E. R. (1986). Children's reading strategies, metacognition, and motivation. *Developmental Review, 6,* 25–56.

Pressley, M. C. (in press). *Reading instruction that works: The case for balanced teaching.* New York: Guilford.

Pressley, M. C., Rankin, J., & Yokoi, Y. (1996). A survey of instructional practices of primary teachers nominated as effective in promoting literacy. *Elementary School Journal, 96*(4), 363–384.

Purcell-Gates, V. (1988). Lexical and syntactic knowledge of written narrative held by well-read-to kindergartners and second graders. *Research in the Teaching of English, 22,* 128–160.

Purcell-Gates, V. (1994). Nonliterate homes and emergent literacy. In D. F. Lancy (Ed.), *Children's emergent literacy: From research to practice* (pp. 41–51). Westport, CT: Praeger.

Purcell-Gates, V. (1996). Stories, coupons, and the *TV Guide:* Relationships between home literacy experiences and emergent literacy knowledge. *Reading Research Quarterly, 31*(4), 406–428.

Purcell-Gates, V., & Dahl, K. (1991). Low-SES children's success and failure at early literacy learning in skills-based classrooms. *Journal of Reading Behavior, 23,* 1–34.

Purcell-Gates, V., McIntyre, E., & Freppon, P. (1995). Learning written storybook language in school: A comparison of low-SES children in skills-based and whole language classrooms. *American Educational Research Journal, 32,* 659–685.

Rodin, J., Rennert, K., & Solomon, S. (1980). Intrinsic motivation for control: Fact or fiction. In A. Baum, J. E. Singer, & S. Valios (Eds.), *Advances in environmental psychology II* (pp. 177–186). Hillsdale, NJ: Erlbaum.

Rogoff, B. (1990). *Apprenticeship in thinking.* New York: Oxford University Press.

Rowe, K. J. (1991). The influence of reading activity at home on students' attitudes toward reading, classroom attentiveness and reading achievement. An application of structural equation modelling. *British Journal of Educational Psychology, 61,* 19–35.

Seymour, P. H. K., & Evans, H. M. (1994). Levels of phonological awareness and learning to read. *Reading and Writing, 6,* 221–250.

Slaughter, J. P. (1983). Big Books for little kids: Another fad or a new approach for teaching beginning reading? *The Reading Teacher, 36,* 758–763.

Slavin, R. E. (1990). *Cooperative learning: Theory, research, and practice.* Englewood Cliffs, NJ: Prentice-Hall.

Smith, F. (1988). *Joining the literacy club: Further essays into education.* Portsmouth, NH: Heinemann.

Smith-Burke, T. M. (1989). Political and economic dimensions of literacy: Challeges for the 1990s. In S. McCormick & J. Zutell (Eds.), *Cognitive and social perspectives for literacy research and instruction* (pp. 1–18). Chicago: National Reading Conference.

Snowling, M. (1991). Words, nonwords, phonological processes: Some comments on Gathercole, Willis, Emslie, and Baddeley. *Applied Linguistics, 12*(3), 369–373.

Sonnenschein, S., Baker, L., Serpell, R., Scher, D., Fernandez-Fein, S., & Munsterman, K. A. (1996, Winter). *Strands of emergent literacy and their antecedents in the home: Urban preschoolers' early literacy development* (Reading Research Report No. 48). Athens, GA: National Reading Research Center, Universities of Maryland and Georgia.

Spaulding, C. L. (1992). The motivation to read and write. In J. W. Irwin & M. A. Doyle (Eds.), *Reading/writing connections: Learning from research* (pp. 177–201). Newark, DE: International Reading Association.

Spector, J. (1995). Phonemic awareness training: Application of principles of direct instruction. *Reading and Writing Quarterly, 11,* 37–51.

Sticht, T. G., & McDonald, B. A. (1989). *Making the nation smarter: The intergenerational transfer of cognitive ability.* San Diego, CA: Applied Behavioral and Cognitive Sciences.

Sulzby, E. (1985). Children's emergent reading of favorite storybooks: A developmental study. *Reading Research Quarterly, 20,* 458–481.

Sulzby, E., & Teale, W. (1991). Emergent literacy. In R. Barr, M. L. Kamil, P. Mosenthal, & P. D. Pearson (Eds.), *Handbook of Reading Research* (Vol. 2, pp. 727–758). White Plains, NY: Longman.

Swap, S. (1993). *Developing home–school partnerships.* New York: Teachers College Press.

Taylor, B. M., Frye, B. J., & Maruyama, G. M. (1990). Time spent reading and reading growth. *American Educational Research Journal, 27,* 351–362.

Taylor, D., & Dorsey-Gaines, C. (1988). *Growing up literate.* Portsmouth, NH: Heinemann.

Teale, W. (1984). Reading to young children: Its significance for literacy development. In H. Goelman, A. Oberg, & F. Smith (Eds.), *Awakening to literacy* (pp. 110–121). Exeter, NH: Heinemann Educational Books.

Teale, W., & Sulzby, E. (1987). Literacy acquisition in early childhood. In D. Wagner (Ed.), *The future of literacy in a changing world* (Vol. I, pp. 120–129). New York: Pergamon.

Teale, W., & Sulzby, E. (1988). *Emergent literacy: Writing and reading.* Norwood, NJ: Ablex.

Turner, J. C. (1992, April). *Identifying motivation for literacy in first grade: An observational study.* Paper presented at the annual meeting of the American Educational Research Association, San Francisco.

Turner, J. C. (1995). The influence of classroom contexts on young children's motivation for literacy. *Reading Research Quarterly, 30*(3), 410–441.

Vygotsky, L. S. (1978). *Mind in society. The development of higher psychological processes.* Cambridge, MA: Harvard University Press.

Vygotsky, L. S. (1987). Speech and thinking. In R. Rieber & A. Carton (Eds.), & N. Minick (Tr.), *The collected works of L. S. Vygotsky* (Vol. 1, pp. 39–285). New York: Plenum.

Wells, G. (1986). *The meaning makers: Children learning language and using language to learn.* Portsmouth, NH: Heinemann.

Wharton-McDonald, R., Pressley, M., & Mis†retta, J. (1996). *Outstanding literary instruction in first grade: Teaching practices and student achievement.* Albany, NY: National Reading Research Center.

Whitehurst, G. J., & Lonigan, C. J. (1998). Child development and emergent literacy. *Child Development, 69,* 848–873.

Wigfield, A. (1994, April). *Dimensions of children's motivations for reading: An intitial study.* Paper presented at the annual meeting of the American Educational Research Association, New Orleans.

Wigfield, A., & Asher, S. R. (1984). Social and motivational influences on reading. In P. D. Pearson, R. Barr, M. L. Kamil, & P. Mosenthal (Eds)., *Handbook of research on reading* (pp. 423–452). New York: Longman.

Wigfield, A., & Karpathian, M. (1991). Who am I and what can I do? Children's self-concepts and motivation in motivational theory and research. *Educational Psychologist, 26*(3,4), 233–261.

Wiseman, D. L., Many, J. E., & Altieri, J. (1992). Enabling complex aesthetic responses: An examination of three literary discussion approaches. In C. K. Kinzer & D. J. Leu (Eds.), *Literary research, theory, and practice: Views from many perspectives, 41st Yearbook of the National Reading Conference* (pp. 283–290). Chicago, IL: National Reading Conference.

CHAPTER 5

# Fostering Each Child's Understanding of Mathematics

## Patricia F. Campbell

EXAMINATION OF early childhood mathematics curricula since the mid-1970s reveals a shift from viewing mathematics as a set of skills and procedures, to defining problem solving as "the focus of school mathematics" (National Council of Teachers of Mathematics [NCTM], 1980, p. 1), to characterizing mathematics as the "science of pattern and order" (National Research Council, 1989, p. 31). In recent curricula, mathematics is viewed as a way of thinking about quantity, relationships, and patterns through modeling, symbolism, inference, analysis, and abstraction. Problem solving in mathematics is no longer limited to end-of-the-unit word problems. Rather, preschool and primary-aged children are challenged to make sense of the mathematics in problem situations that arise in their direct experience, to make sense of symbolic mathematics as recordings of meaningful conceptual relationships, and to make sense of observable characteristics leading to generalizable geometric properties and mathematical patterns. This does not mean that computation, traditional word problems, and numerical algorithms are no longer important. It does mean that assumptions about the teaching and learning of early childhood mathematics have changed substantially since the 1970s.

Reports guiding curriculum reform in mathematics education (e.g., Commission on Standards for School Mathematics, 1989; Commission on Teaching Standards for School Mathematics, 1991; National Research Council, 1989) were informed by a substantial body of research developed over the past 15 years about how children learn mathematics, particularly about how children come to understand number and quantitative relations. The major assumption underlying the current reform in mathematics education is the perception that students should understand mathematics (Hiebert & Carpenter, 1992). While this idea is not uniformly accepted by the public at large, it is one of the most widely held tenets in the mathematics education community.

This chapter examines recent research that may inform curriculum development in early childhood mathematics. Theoretical perspectives for defining an appropriate mathematics curriculum are considered first. Second, because knowledge about children's thinking can provide a framework for defining curriculum (Carpenter, 1988), interpretations of research on children's mathematical thinking are presented. The chapter then reviews instructional issues that must be addressed when creating learning environments, drawing from current research projects that consider classroom discourse, teacher questioning, and instructional decision making.

## THEORETICAL PERSPECTIVES ON TEACHING AND LEARNING MATHEMATICS

In 1989, two documents were published that presented a vision of the mathematics curriculum as a broad range of content, encompassing a variety of applied and abstract contexts, with deliberate connections being drawn between mathematical ideas (Commission on Standards for School Mathematics, 1989; National Research Council, 1989). Furthermore, this perspective called for instruction wherein children communicated and reasoned about their interpretation of the mathematics. There are those who promote an opposing view of school mathematics, interpreting algorithmic procedures as the foundation of school mathematics, with demonstration and practice framing instruction because skill mastery is a presumed prerequisite for conceptual knowledge. Yet, within the mathematics education community, there seem to be four themes regarding the nature of mathematics and mathematical knowledge:

1. Mathematics is a growing, dynamic discipline.
2. Students actively construct mathematical knowledge.
3. Understanding in mathematics comes from perceiving relationships either between or within mathematical ideas.
4. Knowledge may be fostered through social interaction.

## Mathematics—A Dynamic Discipline

"Knowledge is not a basket of facts" (Anderson, 1984, p. 5), and mathematics is not simply a static network of terms, rules, and procedures that are conveyed by teachers and absorbed by students for recall upon demand. Mathematics is the active science of defining relationships in the search for order and pattern in the world around us (National Research Council, 1989). Defining relationships implies that a mathematical topic or situation is perceived as a component of, or connected to, a "big idea" (Campbell & Johnson, 1995). In early childhood education, a critical aspect of curriculum development is to select and define those big ideas, for it is through the process of constructing meaning for the big ideas that children come to understand mathematics. Over time, as children apply their existing understandings to new mathematical experiences and problems, children not only learn new content, their "individual knowledge of an existing portion of mathematics" grows (Dossey, 1992, p. 44).

The challenge in early childhood mathematics education is "to use children's intial understandings to proactively support their *continued* mathematical development" (Campbell, 1997, p. 106). That is, in early childhood mathematics, the content of the curriculum and the instructional approach must challenge without frustration so that children will build "progressively more advanced understandings and simultaneously perceive mathematics as 'making sense'" (p. 106). This means that children must be engaged in instructional activity that causes them to explore, examine, quantify, order, relate, invent, use, represent, verify, interpret, justify, and communicate (Commission on Standards for School Mathematics, 1989). It also means that the underlying goal is for children to construct understandings that are consistent with established standards for mathematics. Mathematics curricula and instruction must emphasize the power and potential of mathematics, the interrelatedness of mathematical ideas, and the development of quantitative reasoning, as well as each child's individual understandings and confidence to undertake such investigation (Romberg & Tufte, 1987).

## Construction of Knowledge

This perception of mathematics and of a mathematics curriculum does not coincide with instruction wherein bits of information that compose a network of established rules and procedures are transmitted to children (via either textbooks, worksheets, or teacher demonstration). One current theoretical perspective is that students actively construct mathematical knowledge; they do not absorb mathematics or receive it. The basic tenet is that knowledge is constructed by actively processing and relating new information or experiences to what was already known or by connecting ideas that were previously understood but isolated from each other (Noddings, 1990). Thus learning is more than simply accumulating bits of information. Learning means new insights in the way that one thinks about something. However, these insights are interpreted from within; they are not meaningless responses in a manner previously prescribed by an authority figure (cf. Baroody, 1987). This perspective, generally termed *constructivism*, is rooted in the writings of Piaget. While there are philosophical and epistemological distinctions in the implications drawn by constructivist theorists (e.g., von Glasersfeld, 1991), the perspective that knowledge is actively constructed rather than passively received has had critical implications for mathematics education.

In their studies of mathematical knowledge, researchers distinguish between conceptual knowledge and procedural knowledge. Conceptual knowledge refers to the knowledge of relationships. Mathematical concepts—that is, principles and constraints that define or characterize ideas and experiences—are relationships; yet these concepts can be related or integrated with other concepts. Children develop conceptual knowledge when they construct relationships between pieces of information. Procedural knowledge entails (1) the written symbols that are used to represent mathematical ideas and (2) the rules and procedures that are used when solving mathematics problems. These procedures should entail strategies that foster the solution of problems while preserving or enriching the constructed meaning of mathematical concepts. Thus procedural knowledge should have a conceptual base and generally has a symbolic referent (Gelman & Greeno, 1989; Hiebert & Lefevre, 1986).

## Mathematics Instruction

As noted by Pierie and Kieren (1992), there is "no 'constructivist teaching model' out there waiting to be implemented" (p. 506). However, because the constructivist view of mathematics learning raises implications for instruction, there have been numerous studies to investigate primary mathematics instruction based on a constructivist model. These studies generally apply one of two instructional approaches, each of which relies on research-based knowledge of the development of children's learning of mathematics but differs in what it defines to be the optimal learning environment.

One approach uses visible representations (manipulative materials, diagrams, and/or symbols) to characterize the desired mathematical relationship or concept in a form that is felt to be more meaningful or accessible to the child. The critical points of the instruction revolve around making connections between the varying representations (e.g., between objects and numerals) as a means of clarifying the mathematical concept (Fuson & Briars, 1990; Hiebert & Wearne, 1992; Resnick, 1983a, 1983b). The level of direction provided by the teacher regarding manipulation of the symbolic or concrete referents varies in these studies, but it is often quite directive during the initial lessons. A question raised regarding this instructional approach is what meaning is attached to these visible representations by the child (Baroody, 1989; Cobb et al., 1991). The issue is as follows: The teacher or adult readily identifies the intended mathematical structure within the referent. But is that referent meaningful to the child? Does the child interpret the same mathematical structure perceived by the adult, some variant of that structure, or no structure at all (Nesher, 1989)? Further, if a teacher directly instructs or demonstrates a procedure, either symbolically or with manipulatives, does that limit the probability that the child will reason and make sense of the activity? Might the child simply attempt to mimic the teacher's actions (Cobb, 1988)? Questions regarding children's mathematical sense making are addressed later in the chapter in terms of children's use of place-value manipulatives.

Another approach being studied also involves the use of manipulatives but limits teachers' direct instruction. This approach uses cognitive-based research as a means of identifying mathematical activities wherein children are engaged in solving problems that are challenging but conceptually attainable (Campbell & White, 1997; Carpenter, Fennema, Peterson, Chiang, & Loef, 1989; Carpenter, Franke, Jacobs, Fennema, & Empson, 1998; Cobb et al., 1991; Fuson, Wearne, et al., 1997; Wood & Sellers, 1997). These activities may also be intended to provoke the child to relate existing understandings, to construct new knowledge, or to develop strategies or procedures. Because circumstantially based knowledge may be applied by a child when solving problems based in a context that is familiar to that child (Leinhardt, 1988), these instructional activities may evolve from experiences common and familiar to the children. In this approach, the teacher does not demand a particular procedure or expect the children to use their materials in a prescribed manner; no strategy is valued more than another. Children are given the opportunity to solve the problems; frequently strategies are constructed within the social construct of the classroom as children share their ideas and invented strategies. This approach is not simply discovery learning. Rather, the teacher must pose tasks that may stimulate appropriate conceptual reorganizations in the students. This then requires the teacher to understand the expected developmental sequence of mathematical understandings, as well as the current levels of mathematical understandings held by the children. Further, teachers must maintain standards for what is mathematically correct, generalizable, and efficient, raising questions to promote each child's mathematical growth without devaluing any child's current level of understanding (Campbell, 1997).

Researchers in mathematics education also differ regarding the use of manipulative materials within this approach. While some researchers (e.g., Cobb et al., 1991; Fennema, Carpenter, & Peterson, 1989; Fuson, Wearne, et al., 1997) use manipulatives, they do so after first considering the degree to which that referent might foster each child's own thinking and the potential for that referent to assist the children in communicating their meaning to each other and to the teacher (Fischbein, 1987). However, Kamii (1990; Kamii & Joseph, 1988) opposes the use of manipulatives such as bundles of counting sticks, saying that young children neither abstract concepts from concrete referents nor internalize concepts from the external, physical environment.

## Social Interaction and the Learning of Mathematics

Social-cognitive and social-constructivist theories posit the importance of student interaction in the mathematics classroom (Cobb, Yackel, & Wood, 1992). When children share their interpretations or conjectures, offer verification or explain their reasoning, question each other, and, if necessary, expand upon or justify their perceptions, there is an increased likelihood that they will correct, interpret, and reorganize their own thinking (Ball, 1993; Lampert, 1990; Resnick, 1988). Cobb and his colleagues (1991) hypothesize that classrooms that foster this type of social interaction permit the children and the teacher to "mutually construct taken-to-be-shared mathematical interpretations and understandings" (p. 6). A number of research studies have investigated the teaching and learning of mathematics within classrooms that seek to employ these social settings, noting higher levels of perfomance, particularly in mathematical problem solving (e.g., Campbell & Rowan, 1995; Carpenter et al., 1989; Cobb et al., 1991; Hiebert & Wearne, 1993; Wood & Sellers, 1997).

A common characteristic of the social interaction in many of these classrooms is the sharing of approaches or strategies by the children without a labeling or a judgment of "correct" or "incorrect" by the teacher. This does not mean that all answers are interpreted as being correct. Learning will not be fostered if teachers accept all responses without further interaction simply because the answer is an expression of a child's understanding. Rather, through questioning and through individual, group, or class interaction with the teacher, the children determine and justify the mathematical validity of answers. Teacher and student questioning may cause a child to address a misconception or to experience dissonance and to subsequently modify his or her thinking. At other times, even though questioning may not cause a child's understanding to change to reflect adult society's perception of mathematics, the child's thinking will become more explict to the teacher. Then the teacher must reflect on what kinds of problems or experiences might be necessary to further stimulate that child's mathematical growth (Campbell & Johnson, 1995). In any case, however, the climate in which the questioning and interaction take place must enhance children's trust and willingness to talk about mathematics and support their confidence to investigate further problems.

## CHILDREN'S MATHEMATICAL THINKING

### Developing Number Sense

"The major objective of elementary school mathematics should be to develop number sense" (National Research Council, 1989, p. 46). This recommendation identifies a critical distinction between traditional mathematics programs for young children and a mathematics curriculum that supports and fosters children's understanding. Number sense refers to a child's "intuition about numbers, their magnitudes, their effects in operations, and their relationships to real quantities and phenomena" (Van de Walle, 1998, p. 4). The NCTM *Curriculum and Evaluation Standards for School Mathematics* (Commission on Standards for School Mathematics, 1989) notes that children who have number sense understand the meaning of number as they are able to define many different relationships among numbers. In addition to recognizing the relative size of numbers and the effect of operating on numbers, these children define their own referents for use in measuring common objects and events. Number sense is a flexible way of thinking about numbers, and it presupposes a child's belief that mathematics should and does make sense (Carpenter, 1989; Resnick, 1989; Silver, 1989). Because it entails flexible thinking about numerical situations, it is presumed that number sense advances problem solving, supports children's construction of more enriched understandings, and perpetuates its own development.

According to a cognitivist perspective, if a child has a concept of a number, then the child has constructed a meaning for that number in terms of its relationship to other numbers. For example, 5 is

2 and 3
1 more than 4
A lot less than 30
Only a little less than 7
As many fingers as are on one hand
With 5 more, 10 altogether

An early childhood curriculum that fosters the development of number sense permits children to understand number as more than the product of counting.

**Early Constructs of Quantity.** The next section of this chapter addresses research regarding the development of meaningful counting, from rote counting to place-value numeration concepts. But first, consider the development of a concept of number. Through experiences in the home, young children develop primitive notions of quantity. As children begin to solve problems in their environment involving quantity, they begin to construct meaning for number (Fuson, 1989; Gelman & Meck, 1986, 1992; Saxe, Guberman, & Gearhart, 1987). Steffe and his colleagues (Steffe, Cobb, & von Glasersfeld, 1988) have investigated the types of entities or settings for which children display increasingly sophisticated meanings for number. They note that initially children count collections of objects and learn to construct sets of a given size but require physical objects to which they attach their numerical words. With growth, children begin to quantify the motions they create (pointing to locations, putting up fingers). Eventually, children abstract counting. When a child abstracts counting, the child's construction of meaning for a number (e.g., 5) is independent of the presence of concrete objects or motor activity. To a child who is an abstract counter, number refers not only to any set, image, or action that contains or depicts that many items but also to the sequence bounded by that number (e.g., 1, 2, 3, 4, 5). Thus abstract counters can count the act of counting. For example, in the problem, *Marissa has 7 stickers. How many more stickers does she need to have 11 stickers?* an abstract counter may respond, "8, 9, 10, 11. . . . She needs 4 more stickers."

**Part–Whole Constructions.** A number may be associated with a set of objects. However, that set can also be separated into subsets, and each of those subsets also has a referent number. This critical partitioning relationship within number is generally termed part–part–whole. Resnick (1983a) noted the importance of this construction, stating:

> Probably the major conceptual achievement of the early school years is the interpretation of numbers in terms of part and whole relationships. With the application of a Part–Whole schema to quantity, it becomes possible for children to think about numbers as compositions of other numbers. This enrichment of number understanding permits forms of mathematical problem solving and interpretation that are not available to younger children. (p. 114)

With a part–whole construction, children may relate the concepts of number, addition, and subtraction (Baroody, Ginsburg, & Waxman, 1983; Campbell & Johnson, 1995); reach the most advanced problem-solving level for addition and subtraction problems (Riley, Greeno, & Heller, 1983); and support the conceptual adjustments involved when learning place value (Resnick, 1983a). Fischer (1990) noted that a kindergarten mathematics curriculum based on a part–part–whole approach fostered children's development of number concepts and facilitated their construction of strategies to solve addition and subtraction word problems, even though addition and subtraction applications were not taught.

## Counting and Numeration

**Early Counting.** The ability to find out *how many* is a powerful tool that children use as they begin to model and solve problems. Researchers offer differing perspectives regarding the meaning and growth of counting. Some researchers contend that children first learn a rote sequence of number words without reference to the objects being counted and then make the transition to coordinating each number word in the sequence with an object in a set to determine the cardinality of the set (Baroody, 1993; Frye, Braisby, Lowe, Maroudas, & Nicholls, 1989; Fuson, 1989, 1992; Sophian, 1992; Wynn, 1990). These researchers do not presume that initial "attempt[s] to carry out counting activity" (Fuson, 1989, p. 398) indicate a manifestation of implicit counting principles. Others suggest that even very young children have some implicit principled understanding of counting because they respond to the presence of quantity in their environment (Gelman & Greeno, 1989; Gelman & Meck, 1986, 1992; Strauss & Curtis, 1984). Despite differences in defining an initial principled knowledge of counting, it is generally accepted that explicit knowledge of counting is a prerequisite for increasing, decreasing, and comparing quantities (Greeno, Riley, & Gelman, 1984). In most instances, the ability to count rationally enables children to solve simple word problems.

Gelman and Gallistel (1978) define five principles of counting:

1. *Stable order*—Counting names are used in a stable order.
2. *One–one correspondence*—Every object is assigned one and only one unique counting name.
3. *Cardinality*—The last counting name identifies the number in the set.
4. *Order irrelevance*—Objects may be counted in any order and a change in the order does not affect the total.
5. *Abstraction*—Any set, or collection, of objects may be counted.

Gelman and Meck (1986) posit that the first three principles represent a developmental sequence in learning how to count. Fuson (1992) characterizes five levels of qualitative change in children's use of number words within a counting task. For example, initially children must begin their counting sequence with the words, "1, 2, 3, . . ." As their understanding of number matures, they are able to begin a count with a number other than 1.

**Numeration.** Children initially use number words to represent *unitary* conceptual structures, where each number word refers to a single item in a collection of objects (Fuson, 1990; see also Fuson, Smith, et al., 1997; Fuson, Wearne, et al., 1997). For example, a child counting a set of 26 blocks will count "1, 2, 3, . . . 24, 25, 26" and will interpret the number word "twenty-six" as referring to the total collection of 26 single objects. This interpretation of number does not reflect an understanding of our base-ten number system but does allow a child to operate with numbers larger than ten. A more sophisticated structure for multidigit numbers is constructed by children when they "disembed" groups of 10 objects from the total collection, recognizing that an item may simultaneously be assigned to a group (1 of 10 objects) and to the collection (1 of 26 objects) (Steffe et al., 1988). When children disembed, they have begun "to construct *multiunit* conceptual structures in which the meanings or referents of the number words are collections of entities" (Fuson, 1990, p. 273). For example, a child who disembeds understands that 43 is composed of 40 or 4 tens (groups of 10 objects) and 3 single objects. When children learn to recite the decades in sequence (e.g., 10, 20, 30, 40), they initially interpret each decade as a grouping of ten. Thus, in the example above, a child focuses on the objects in the groups and has a count of 40 so far, with 3 more loose objects. This sequential count of the tens or decades becomes linked to the groups of ten and, in time, the children may count the groups as *units of ten* (e.g., "1 ten, 2 tens, 3 tens, 4 tens" or "1, 2, 3, 4, . . . 4 tens"). These units of ten are initially separate from any remaining *units of one*, but eventually the units of ten and the units of one are integrated. Then the child has great flexibility both for counting and problem solving as interpretations of 43 rapidly shift from 43 separate objects (1, 2, 3, . . . , 43 *ones*), to 4 groups of ten objects each (10, 20, 30, 40 *ones*) and 3 more objects (3 *ones*), to 4 groups of ten objects (1, 2, 3, 4 *tens*, so that's 40) and another set of 3 more objects (3 *ones*), to knowing that 4 tens and 3 ones is *43* (Fuson, Wearne, et al., 1997). Understanding multiunit structures is the foundation for developing place value concepts.

The complexity of interpreting multidigit numbers is influenced by language (Fuson & Kwon, 1992; Yang & Cobb, 1995). The English system of number words does not support the conceptual components of multiunit numbers. There are irregularities in the English system that make it difficult to count and to identify the tens and ones structure in two-digit numbers. For example, as children learn the counting word sequence, there is consistency in counting *within* decades (e.g., 1, 2, 3, . . . 7, 8, 9; 21, 22, 23, . . . 27, 28, 29), but children have difficulty bridging *across* decades (e.g., 21, 22, . . . 28, 29, ??). In terms of supporting conceptual structures, 26 is named "twenty-six" in the English language. The named value representation for 26 in several Asian languages (e.g., Chinese, Japanese, Korean), is "two ten six," making explicit the idea that the number is composed of 2 units of ten and 6 units of one. In English the link between the number word for numbers between 10 and 20 and the conceptual structure of the number is even less transparent. For example, in the number word "thirteen" there is little support for children's construction of 13 as 1 unit of ten and 3 units of ones. In a comparison of the children who spoke English or an Asian language, Fuson and Kwon (1992) reported that speakers of the Asian languages seemed to construct multiunit conceptual structures for two-digit numbers earlier than the English-speaking cohort. The Asian languages, which emphasize the conceptual structure of numbers, were found to influence children's understanding of multiunits. Essentially, the string of English counting words implies a unitary meaning for numbers and does not encourage children to think of number with the more sophisticated construction of multiunits.

The transition from counting by ones to counting by tens, hundreds, and so on is necessary in order for children to develop effective problem-solving strategies and meaning for place value. Successful manipulation of symbols within computation problems does not imply this transition. Children may compute accurately without understanding (Kamii & Joseph, 1988). Several tasks have been developed to assess children's understanding of number and numeration. For example, Kamii (1989) describes a digit correspondence task where a child is shown the numeral

16 and asked to construct a set with sixteen chips. Then the child is asked which part of the set is represented by each of the digits in the numeral, first focusing on the 6, then on the 1. Children who do not understand place value often correctly respond that the 6 represents six chips in the set, but they assign only one chip, rather than ten chips, to the numeral 1, the tens digit. This response indicates that the multidigit number is perceived of as a series of concatenated single digits and the relative position of the digits is not significant. As a result of this assessment, Kamii (1989) posits that direct instruction with traditional addition and subtraction algorithms, where columns of number are treated as single units and operated on from right to left, inhibits children's understanding.

**Place-Value Instruction.** There is continuing discussion (Baroody, 1990; Fuson, 1990) as to whether children should first establish a firm understanding of base-ten numbers with place-value concepts before investigating multidigit addition and subtraction procedures. Some researchers feel that the learning of place-value concepts and multidigit procedures should be integrated (Fuson, Smith, & Lo Cicero, 1997). Hiebert and Wearne (1996) noted the interrelationship of place-value understandings and use of multidigit procedures for addition and subtraction. However, their study did not clarify whether procedural strategies developed after or concurrent with place-value understandings.

Whether multidigit addition and subtraction are taught after or concurrent with place value, understanding how children make the transition from unitary to multiunit conceptual structures has direct implications for instruction. For example, Fuson and Briars (1990) reported a series of studies in which first- and second-grade teachers used base-10 blocks (see Figure 5.1) to support children's construction of multiunit conceptual structures and an understanding of place value concepts. This structured teaching/learning setting was characterized by the study of advanced counting strategies for adding and subtracting sums to 18 followed by work with groupings of ten. Children were then taught how to link actions on the base-10 blocks with written procedures for adding and subtracting multidigit numbers; trading ten-for-one was always ordered from right to left. The use of base-ten blocks seemed to support the construction of multiunits for second-graders and above-average first-graders. Average and below-average first-graders maintained a unitary counting sequence, but they did not construct multiunit conceptual structures. When problem-solving instruction is carefully designed to promote classroom discourse and to facilitate the link between children's emerging interpretations of multidigit numbers, their actions on concrete models,

**Figure 5.1.** Base-ten blocks.

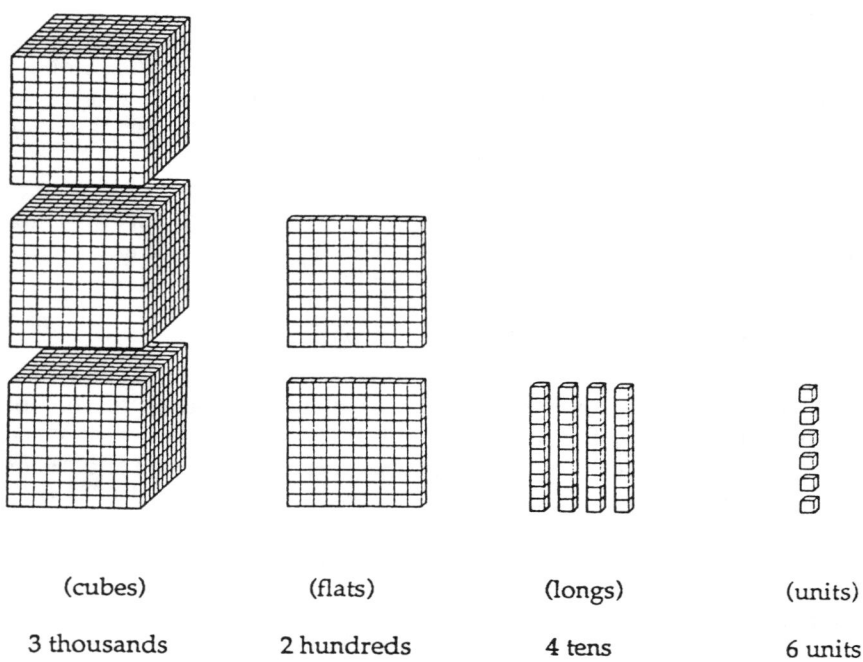

|                |               |              |              |
|:--------------:|:-------------:|:------------:|:------------:|
| (cubes)        | (flats)       | (longs)      | (units)      |
| 3 thousands    | 2 hundreds    | 4 tens       | 6 units      |

3,246

and symbolic representations, children's understanding of place value and multidigit addition and subtraction increases (Hiebert &Wearne, 1993).

In general, the use of concrete models to help facilitate young children's mathematical thinking has been accepted as an appropriate teaching strategy. However, the use of manipulatives, such as base-ten blocks or Unifix cubes, to help children make the transition from constructing unitary to multiunit conceptual structures raises two specific issues (Baroody, 1989; Kamii, 1989).

First, if manipulatives are used in instruction, there is a caution about what children are actually learning from them. Ross (1989) suggests that

concrete embodiments have their limitations and may be successfully ma-
nipulated without meaning. A manipulative can be treated as a symbol
system. Children may learn the rules and procedures associated with a
given manipulative material without ever establishing the link between
that manipulative and the concept it is to embody. For example, the relationship of ten-for-one already exists in base-ten blocks where 1 ten is a
rod of 10 units and 1 hundred is a flat of 10 tens. With the blocks, children
can practice trading 10 units for 1 ten and 10 tens for 1 hundred. They
can successfully group a set of 26 units and trade the grouped units for 2
tens. However, when asked to count the resulting collection of 2 tens and
6 ones, a young child who has not mentally constructed ten as a unit will
proceed to count the entire collection by ones or count the first ten as a
unit and then continue counting by ones, "10, 11, 12, 13, . . . 26." A child
who has mentally constructed ten as a unit will count "10, 20, 21, 22, 23,
24, 25, 26." Unless young children are asked to communicate their thinking, it is not clear what they understand about a task involving concrete
models or what mathematical concept they have constructed.

The second issue regarding manipulatives is the question of rele-
vance. Kamii (1989) asserts that requiring children to physically construct
sets of ten with manipulatives is not helpful because construction of multiple groupings can only be an intellectual activity; she holds that place
value cannot be perceived from concrete materials.

Young children need to engage in a variety of counting tasks where
quantity is partitioned into parts and the parts are subsequently related
to the whole quantity. In kindergarten and first grade, children may investigate how many ways a set of objects (e.g., 9 chips) may be separated
into two or more parts (e.g., three sets of 3 chips; 5 chips and 4 more
chips). In first and second grade, this partitioning supports place-value
construction as children understand, for example, 34 as 3 sets of ten and
4 more. This flexibility with numbers is evident when a child who solves
a problem such as 27 + 35 states: "20 plus 30 is 50 . . . 7 more is 57
. . . and 5 more, . . . 58, 59, 60, 61, 62." This solution strategy clearly
demonstrates a mature understanding of number. The power of the part–
whole construct for number is its flexibility. In a curriculum that encourages the flexible use of the part–whole construct, addition and subtraction
problems are open to many solution strategies, limited only by the numerical insights of the child. For example, another child may solve this
same problem by counting: "35, . . . [+10] 45, . . . [+10] 55, . . . [+7],
56, 57, 58, 59, 60, 61, 62."

Both of these solution strategies are examples of informal algorithms
or invented strategies that children may construct, building on their
understanding of multidigit numbers and their ability to coordinate the

counting of tens and ones. Informal strategies are invented both individually and collectively as children use manipulatives to model quantity and numerical relationships and as children use counting strategies. Frequently, children's invented strategies seem to be an application of place-value knowledge. There is growing evidence that when arithmetic concepts and procedures are approached as problem solving, children's invented strategies foster number sense and understanding of multidigit addition and subtraction (Carpenter et al., 1998). However, it is critical that teachers hold children's informal algorithms to mathematical standards for what is mathematically correct, generalizable, and efficient. Further, teachers and curriculum developers cannot presume that every response that a child offers will be correct, complete, or easily interpreted, just because the child can explain and justify his or her strategy (Campbell, 1997).

## Development of Problem-Solving Abilities

During the past 15 years, studies on children's thinking have yielded a well-developed body of research defining addition and subtraction word problems as well as the strategies young children use to solve those problems (Briars & Larkin, 1984; Carpenter & Moser, 1983, 1984; Carpenter, Moser, & Romberg, 1982; Riley et al., 1983). Addition and subtraction problems have been classified according to the action or relationship of the quantities in the word problem (Carpenter & Moser, 1983; Riley et al., 1983). The relative difficulty of these problems is determined by children's solution strategies.

Research indicates that prior to formal instruction, children can successfully solve simple word problems by directly modeling the action in the problem with concrete objects and then counting the objects. Young children then develop more advanced strategies for solving problems, moving from modeling, to advanced counting strategies, to use of derived facts, to the recall of number facts. Even young children who generally use direct modeling to solve problems may use derived facts or recall strategies occasionally, depending on the problem type and the size of the numbers involved. For example, consider this problem: *Anna had some balloons. She gave 7 of them to her best friend. Now Anna has 5 balloons left. How many balloons did Anna have to start with?* Children who use a derived fact to solve this problem may recognize that $7 = \underline{5} + \underline{2}$ and thus $5 + \underline{5} = 10$ and $10 + \underline{2} = \underline{12}$, the solution. Children become more flexible in their choice of solution strategy as a result of changes in their conceptual knowledge (Carpenter, 1985).

Young children's successful problem-solving abilities are well documented. However, children's problem-solving experiences in traditional classrooms are limited (Stigler, Fuson, Ham, & Kim, 1986). In most programs children are restricted to simple word problems where two sets are joined or some amount is removed from a set. Because these types of problems do not challenge children's thinking, particularly in terms of the solution strategies required to solve them, the current early childhood curriculum can be considered impoverished. Children should be given a variety of word problems to solve. Further, the implication of this research for curriculum development is clear: "It is not necessary to defer instruction on word problems until computational skills have been mastered" (Romberg & Carpenter, 1986, p. 855).

The decision about what problems to consider should be determined by the teacher's knowledge of the relative difficulty of the problem types and knowledge of individual children's solution strategies. The critical curriculum issue is not whether the problem can be classified as addition or subtraction. For example, consider the following problem: *Keisha saved 6 pennies. How many more pennies does she need to save to have 10 pennies altogether?* This type of problem has traditionally been referred to as a missing addend problem. This problem, once determined by some to be too difficult for first-grade children, can be solved by subtracting 6 from 10. This subtractive solution strategy requires an explicit understanding of the part–whole relationship. However, first-grade children are very successful at solving this problem using an appropriate additive solution strategy (e.g., 6, . . . 7, 8, 9, 10, . . . 4 pennies) (Briars & Larkin, 1984; Carpenter & Moser, 1984; De Corte & Verschaffel, 1987; Riley et al., 1983). Solving the symbolic missing addend problem, $6 + \underline{\phantom{xx}} = 10$, without the support of a problem context is a difficult task for young children. The experience of solving meaningful word problems that can be represented by a missing addend sentence should not be confused with having children solve symbolic computation problems with missing addends. These are two distinct tasks that require different knowledge.

Young children also can solve simple multiplication (grouping) and division (partitioning) word problems by direct modeling (Kouba, 1989). Indeed, even kindergarten-aged children can solve multiplicative problems if concrete materials are present and if the actions or relationships described in the problems can be modeled by movement of counters (Carpenter, Ansell, Franke, Fennema, & Weisbeck, 1993). The development of children's solution strategies for these problems is similar to those for addition and subtraction. Direct modeling is replaced with counting strategies and eventually by derived facts and recall. Children do not suddenly advance from one strategy to the next; rather they seem to develop an increasing number of alternative approaches (Carpenter et al., 1993; Mulligan & Mitchelmore, 1997). Because young children do not view multiplication as commutative, modeling 3 sets of five is a different task from modeling 5 sets of three. As a result of this distinction, children also perceive division problems differently. In a problem such as, *Max has 12 marbles. He wants to put 4 marbles in each bag. How many bags will he need?*, children construct a set of 12 objects and then make groups of four. When all the objects have been grouped, the number of groups is counted for the solution. In a problem such as, *Max has 12 marbles and 3 bags. If he puts the same number of marbles in each bag, how many marbles are in each bag?*, children construct a set of 12 objects and then deal them out into three piles until all the objects are dealt. The number of objects in a pile is counted for the solution. Both solution strategies directly model the problem situation; therefore children's actions on the objects are different for the two problems. These problems are challenging, yet they are appropriate in the early childhood curriculum because they can be modeled meaningfully by young children and they build on children's understanding of addition and subtraction. The key is to allow the children to solve them in their own ways, as opposed to requiring assignment of a recalled multiplication fact (Clark & Kamii, 1996).

Curriculum decisions about what types of word problems to include in early childhood mathematics should be made by considering whether the problem is set in a meaningful context for children, portraying appropriate mathematical structures. Young children solve problems that go beyond simple addition and subtraction events.

## Representation

Young children understand number and can solve problems without using written symbols. Children are introduced to the use of symbols to represent mathematical concepts so they may develop meaning for written symbolic representations. The process of connecting written symbols with real-world referents, such as objects or actions on objects, develops meaning for symbols (Hiebert, 1988). The links young children have established between a symbol and its referent need to be transparent before young children can be expected to manipulate symbols as abstract quantities.

Number sentences (e.g., $a + b = \underline{\hspace{1cm}}$, $a - b = \underline{\hspace{1cm}}$) are symbolic representations used by young children to directly model the action described in problems. Number sentences are an extension of children's problem-solving abilities and reflect their solution strategies. As children become more flexible in their choice of solution strategy, they are able to use a variety of appropriate number sentences. Consider the problem:

*Casey had some pennies. She lost 5 of them. Now she has 7 pennies left. How many pennies did Casey have to start with?* First-grade children link the representation ___ $- 5 = 7$ with this problem when given a choice of several alternative number sentences (Carey, 1991). As children develop a more generalized part–whole schema, they also use $7 + 5 =$ ___ as an appropriate representation for this problem. Adding the two parts given in the problem is an explicit representation of the part–whole relationship. This is a more sophisticated representation because it does not directly translate from the problem situation. Although children can solve problems, there are differences in the number sentences used to represent them. Decisions about what representations are appropriate are determined by how young children think about a problem.

## Geometric Concepts and Spatial Sense

> Mathematics curricula at all levels must introduce more of the breadth and power of the mathematical sciences. As mathematics is more than calculation, so education in mathematics must be more than mastery of arithmetic. Geometry . . . [is] as important as numbers in achieving mathematical power. . . . To prepare students to use mathematics in the twenty-first century, today's curriculum must evoke the full spectrum of the mathematical sciences. (National Research Council, 1989, p. 43)

The traditional mathematics curriculum for young children has been dominated by the study of number and numerical relationships. One study noted that *less than 7%* of the pages in basal mathematics textbooks for kindergarten through fourth grade conveyed geometry (Fuys, Geddes, & Tischler, 1988). In the United States, there is no coherent, accepted geometry curriculum for children (Usiskin, 1987).

If mathematics is perceived as the search for order, pattern, and relationships to characterize ideas and experiences, then geometry and spatial sense should be central topics in a mathematics curriculum for young children. Through hands-on experiences with the geometric nature of their world, young children may construct geometric ideas. The traditional geometry curriculum for young children has emphasized vocabulary, focusing on verbal definitions and rules. Current research indicates that children in the upper primary grades generally do not use these "learned" definitions and rules when they solve problems involving geometry and space. Instead, they rely on the conceptual structures they have constructed from real-life experiences, both in school and at home. This reliance on informally constructed geometric concepts as opposed to verbal definitions has been noted not only for children who have incomplete recall of definitions and rules as presented in school, but also for children who can accurately restate the verbal rules and definitions (Clements & Battista, 1989, 1992).

Research indicates that young children can discern some of the properties of shapes and can readily think of two-dimensional figures in terms of paths and motions (Clements & Battista, 1989). Instruction can foster young children's geometric understandings and improve their spatial-perception abilities, but the instruction should start at a young age and provoke children to reflect on the manipulation of geometric structures and to construct concepts interpreting perceived geometric properties of figures (Clements & Battista, 1992; Del Grande, 1987). Research suggests a framework for developing curriculum and instruction in geometry (van Hiele, 1986). For example, young children should manipulate concrete geometric shapes and consider geometric forms in real-world settings. This reliance on visual interpretation is hypothesized as a mechanism for fostering the child's construction of definitions and recognition of geometric relationships (Fuys et al., 1988).

Although calls for change are clear, incorporation of geometry and spatial sense in school mathematics remains an important yet prodigious charge. With that challenge in mind, some researchers have begun to develop curriculum units to support geometric knowledge and spatial sense (e. g., Clements, Battista, Sarama, Swaminathan, & McMillen, 1997).

## CREATING PROBLEM-SOLVING ENVIRONMENTS

### The Role of the Teacher

The early childhood mathematics curriculum is influenced by teachers' instructional decisions. Decisions should be based on what is known about the development of children's thinking and the thinking evidenced by individual children in the classroom. Mathematics instruction facilitates a child's construction of knowledge when a teacher knows what a child understands about a concept and how that concept develops. Teachers' knowledge of their children's problem-solving skills is related to student learning (Carpenter et al., 1989; Fennema, Franke, Carpenter, & Carey, 1993). The assessment of problem-solving skills need not be accomplished in a formal task; it can occur during instruction. When teachers observe children's approaches to problems, when they listen to children's explanations, when they challenge children to clarify their thinking, and when they evaluate the level of sophistication inherent in children's individual solutions, teachers are assessing. Assessing children's thinking is a continuing process and an important part of effective instruction. Appropriate assessment and instructional tasks can be determined as a result of teachers' questioning, listening to, and observing children. This type of ongoing instruction/assessment provides a natural context for children to do and to communicate mathematics. Communication in classrooms serves two purposes: (1) It fosters children's development of patterns of verbal communication as they talk about mathematics, and (2) it allows teachers to learn about their children's thinking. When teachers ask questions, they focus children's attention on a particular aspect of a task or they convey expectations. Instructional tasks and classroom discourse affect how children perceive a task, how they process information, and what relationships they construct. When children have increased opportunities to reflect and to explain their thinking, increased achievement results (Hiebert & Wearne, 1993).

## Learning Contexts

Curriculum focusing on mathematical ideas and problem solving needs resources for realistic, engaging problems. The best resources are the experiences of the children, either planned experiences occurring in the school setting or experiences from outside the classroom that are common to all the children. The critical issue is to conceive of problems that are meaningful to *each* child and are part of *every* child's environment. Then the mathematics classroom may be a place "where ideas are accepted, where suggestions are investigated, and where meaningful problems are solved" (Campbell & Langrall, 1993, p. 110). For this to occur, preschool and primary classrooms must be places where each child's thinking is valued, where the involvement of each child is expected, where sufficient time is permitted for investigations, and where questioning and listening are the norm (Campbell & Langrall, 1993). When this occurs, the classroom becomes a powerful force in a young child's life. It is the place where "knowledge is continuously recreated, recycled and shared" (Ladson-Billings, 1992, pp. 113–114).

## CHALLENGE FOR THE FUTURE

This is a vibrant period for mathematics education, as educators from all avenues (mathematics educators, mathematicians, practitioners, and policy makers) seek to reform and revitalize mathematics curriculum and instruction. The premise of this chapter is that these changes in mathematics education must begin in the early childhood years.

When mathematics is perceived as meaningful, understandable, and challenging, a child experiences the power of mathematics.

> Mathematics . . . provide[s] one of the few disciplines in which the growing student can, by exercising only the power inherent in his or her own mind, reach conclusions with full assurance. More than most other school subjects, mathematics offers special opportunities for children to learn the power of thought as distinct from the power of authority. This is a very important lesson to learn, an essential step in the emergence of independent thinking. (National Research Council, 1989, p. 4)

This chapter presents a review of research that may direct and guide curriculum reform to meet the challenge implied above. An early childhood mathematics "curriculum should include a broad range of content, . . . emphasize the application of mathematics, . . . be conceptually oriented, . . . actively involve children in doing mathematics, . . . [and] emphasize the development of children's mathematical thinking and reasoning abilities" (Commission on Standards for School Mathematics, 1989, pp. 18–19).

**Acknowledgment.** The work reported herein was supported by grants from the National Science Foundation to the author (ESI 94-54187 and ESI 95-54186). Any opinions, findings, and conclusions expressed in this publication are those of the author, and no endorsement from the National Science Foundation should be inferred.

## REFERENCES

Anderson, R. C. (1984). Some reflections on the acquisition of knowledge. *Educational Researcher, 13*(9), 5–10.

Ball, D. L. (1993). Halves, pieces, and twoths: Constructing and using representational contexts in teaching fractions. In T. P. Carpenter, E. Fennema, & T. A. Romberg (Eds.), *Rational numbers: An integration of research* (pp. 157–195). Hillsdale, NJ: Erlbaum.

Baroody, A. J. (1987). *Children's mathematical thinking: A developmental framework for preschool, primary, and special education teachers.* New York: Teachers College Press.

Baroody, A. J. (1989). Manipulatives don't come with guarantees. *Arithmetic Teacher, 37*(2), 4–5.

Baroody, A. J. (1990). How and when should place-value concepts and skills be taught? *Journal for Research in Mathematics Education, 21,* 281–286.

Baroody, A. J. (1993). The relationship between the order-irrelevance principle and counting skill. *Journal for Research in Mathematics Education, 24,* 415–427.

Baroody, A. J., Ginsburg, H. P., & Waxman, B. (1983). Children's use of mathematical structure. *Journal for Research in Mathematics Education, 14,* 156–168.

Briars, D. J., & Larkin, J. G. (1984). An integrated model of skills in solving elementary word problems. *Cognition and Instruction, 1,* 245–296.

Campbell, P. F. (1997). Connecting instructional practice to student thinking. *Teaching Children Mathematics, 4,* 106–110.

Campbell, P. F., & Johnson, M. J. (1995). How primary students think and learn. In I. M. Carl (Ed.), *Seventy-five years of progress: Prospects for school mathematics* (pp. 21–42). Reston, VA: National Council of Teachers of Mathematics.

Campbell, P. F., & Langrall, C. (1993). Making equity a reality in classrooms. *Arithmetic Teacher, 41*(2), 110–113.

Campbell, P. F., & Rowan, T. E. (1995). *Project IMPACT: Increasing the mathematical power of all children and teachers* (1989–1994 Final Report; Phase One Implementation). College Park, MD: University of Maryland, Center for Mathematics Education.

Campbell, P. F., & White, D. Y. (1997). Project IMPACT: Influencing and supporting teacher change in predominantly minority schools. In E. Fennema & B. S. Nelson (Eds.), *Mathematics teachers in transition* (pp. 309–355). Mahwah, NJ: Erlbaum.

Carey, D. (1991). Number sentences: Linking addition and subtraction word problems and symbols. *Journal for Research in Mathematics Education, 22,* 265–280.

Carpenter, T. P. (1985). Learning to add and subtract: An exercise in problem solving. In E. A. Silver (Ed.), *Teaching and learning mathematical problem solving: Multiple research perspectives* (pp. 17–40). Hillsdale, NJ: Erlbaum.

Carpenter, T. P. (1988). Teaching as problem solving. In R. I. Charles & E. A. Silver (Eds.), *The teaching and assessing of mathematical problem solving* (pp. 187–202). Reston, VA: Erlbaum/National Council of Teachers of Mathematics.

Carpenter, T. P. (1989). Number sense and other nonsense. In J. T. Sowder & B. P. Schappelle (Eds.), *Establishing foundations for research on number sense and related topics: Report of a conference* (pp. 89–91). San Diego, CA: Center for Research in Mathematics and Science Education, San Diego State University.

Carpenter, T. P., Ansell, E., Franke, M. L., Fennema, E., & Weisbeck, L. (1993). Models of problem solving: A study of kindergarten children's problem-solving processes. *Journal for Research in Mathematics Education, 24,* 428–441.

Carpenter, T. P., Fennema, E., Peterson, P. L., Chiang, C-P., & Loef, M. (1989). Using knowledge of children's mathematical thinking in classroom teaching: An experimental study. *American Educational Research Journal, 26,* 499–531.

Carpenter, T. P., Franke, M. L., Jacobs, V. R., Fennema, E., & Empson, S. B. (1998). A longitudinal study of invention and understanding in children's multidigit addition and subtraction. *Journal for Research in Mathematics Education, 29,* 3–20.

Carpenter, T. P., & Moser, J. M. (1983). The acquisition of addition and subtraction concepts. In R. Lesh & M. Landau (Eds.), *Acquisition of mathematics: Concepts and processes* (pp. 7–44). New York: Academic Press.

Carpenter, T. P., & Moser, J. M. (1984). The acquisition of addition and subtraction concepts in grades one through three. *Journal for Research in Mathematics Education, 15,* 179–202.

Carpenter, T. P., Moser, J. M., & Romberg, T. A. (Eds.). (1982). *Addition and subtraction: A cognitive perspective.* Hillsdale, NJ: Erlbaum.

Clark, F. B., & Kamii, C. (1996). Identification of multiplicative thinking in children in grades 1–5. *Journal for Research in Mathematics Education, 27,* 41–51.

Clements, D. H., & Battista, M. T. (1989). Learning of geometric concepts in a Logo environment. *Journal for Research in Mathematics Education, 20,* 450–467.

Clements, D. H., & Battista, M. T. (1992). Geometry and spatial reasoning. In D. A. Grouws (Ed.), *Handbook on research on mathematics teaching and learning* (pp. 420–464). New York: Macmillan.

Clements, D. H., Battista, M. T., Sarama, J., Swaminathan, S., & McMillen, S. (1997). Students' development of length concepts in a Logo-based unit on geometric paths. *Journal for Research in Mathematics Education, 28,* 70–95.

Cobb, P. (1988). The tension between theories of learning and instruction in mathematics education. *Educational Psychologist, 23,* 87–103.

Cobb, P., Wood, T., Yackel, E., Nicholls, J., Wheatley, G., Trigatti, B., & Perlwitz, M. (1991). Assessment of a problem-centered mathematics project. *Journal for Research in Mathematics Education, 22,* 3–29.

Cobb, P., Yackel, E., & Wood, T. (1992). A constructivist alternative to the representational view of mind in mathematics education. *Journal for Research in Mathematics Education, 23,* 2–33.

Commission on Standards for School Mathematics. (1989). *Curriculum and evaluation standards for school mathematics.* Reston, VA: National Council of Teachers of Mathematics.

Commission on Teaching Standards for School Mathematics. (1991). *Professional standards for teaching mathematics.* Reston, VA: National Council of Teachers of Mathematics.

De Corte, E., & Verschaffel, L. (1987). The effect of semantic structure on first graders' strategies for solving addition and subtraction word problems. *Journal for Research in Mathematics Education, 18,* 363–381.

Del Grande, J. (1987). Spatial perception and primary geometry. In M. M. Lindquist (Ed.), *Learning and teaching geometry, K–12* (pp. 126–135). Reston, VA: National Council of Teachers of Mathematics.

Dossey, J. A. (1992). The nature of mathematics: Its role and its influence. In D. A. Grouws (Ed.), *Handbook on research on mathematics teaching and learning* (pp. 39–48). New York: Macmillan.

Fennema, E., Carpenter, T. P., & Peterson, P. L. (1989). Learning mathematics with understanding: Cognitively guided instruction. In J. Brophy (Ed.), *Advances in research on teaching* (Vol. 1, pp. 195–219). Greenwich, CT: JAI Press.

Fennema, E., Franke, M. L., Carpenter, T. P., & Carey, D. A. (1993). Using children's mathematical knowledge in instruction. *American Educational Research Journal, 30,* 555–583.

Fischbein, E. (1987). *Instruction in science and mathematics: An educational approach.* Dordrecht, The Netherlands: D. Reidel.

Fischer, F. E. (1990). A part–part–whole curriculum for teaching number in the kindergarten. *Journal for Research in Mathematics Education, 21,* 207–215.

Frye, D., Braisby, N., Lowe, J., Maroudas, C., & Nicholls, J. (1989). Young children's understanding of counting and cardinality. *Child Development, 60,* 1158–1171.

Fuson, K. C. (1989). *Children's counting and concepts of number.* New York: Springer-Verlag.

Fuson, K. C. (1990). Issues in place-value and multidigit addition and subtraction learning and teaching. *Journal for Research in Mathematics Education, 21,* 273–280.

Fuson, K. C. (1992). Research on whole number addition and subtraction. In D. A. Grouws (Ed.), *Handbook on research on mathematics teaching and learning* (pp. 243–275). New York: Macmillan.

Fuson, K., & Briars, D. J. (1990). Using a base-ten blocks learning/teaching approach for first and second-grade place value and multidigit addition and subtraction. *Journal for Research in Mathematics Education, 21,* 180–206.

Fuson, K. C., & Kwon, Y. (1992). Learning addition and subtraction: Effects of number words and other cultural tools. In J. Bideaud, C. Meljac, & J. P. Fischer (Eds.), *Pathways to number* (pp. 283–302). Hillsdale, NJ: Erlbaum.

Fuson, K. C., Smith, S. T., & Lo Cicero, A. M. (1997). Supporting first graders' ten-structured thinking in urban classrooms. *Journal for Research in Mathematics Education, 28,* 738–766.

Fuson, K. C., Wearne, D., Hiebert, J. C., Murray, H. G., Human, P. G., Olivier, A. I., Carpenter, T. P., & Fenneman, E. (1997). Children's conceptual structures for multidigit numbers and methods of multidigit addition and subtraction. *Journal for Research in Mathematics Education, 28,* 130–162.

Fuys, D., Geddes, D., & Tischler, R. (1988). The van Hiele model of thinking in geometry among adolescents. *Journal for Research in Mathematics Education* (Monograph No. 3). Reston, VA: National Council of Teachers of Mathematics.

Gelman, R., & Gallistel, C. R. (1978). *The child's understanding of number.* Cambridge, MA: Harvard University Press.

Gelman, R., & Greeno, J. G. (1989). On the nature of competence: Principles for understanding in a domain. In L. B. Resnick (Ed.), *Knowing, learning and instruction: Essays in honor of Robert Glaser* (pp. 125–186). Hillsdale, NJ: Erlbaum.

Gelman, R., & Meck, E. (1986). The notion of principle: The case of counting. In J. Hiebert (Ed.), *Conceptual and procedural knowledge: The case of mathematics* (pp. 29–57). Hillsdale, NJ: Erlbaum.

Gelman, R., & Meck, E. (1992). Early principles aid early but not later conceptions of number. In J. Bideaud, C. Meljac, & J. P. Fischer (Eds.), *Pathways to number* (pp. 171–189). Hillsdale, NJ: Erlbaum.

Greeno, J. G., Riley, M. S., & Gelman, R. (1984). Conceptual competence and children's counting. *Cognitive Psychology, 16,* 94–143.

Hiebert, J. (1988). A theory of developing competence with written mathematical symbols. *Educational Studies in Mathematics, 19,* 333–355.

Hiebert, J., & Carpenter, T. P. (1992). Learning and teaching with understanding.

In D. A. Grouws (Ed.), *Handbook on research on mathematics teaching and learning* (pp. 65–97). New York: Macmillan.

Hiebert, J., & Lefevre, P. (1986). Conceptual and procedural knowledge in mathematics: An introductory analysis. In J. Hiebert (Ed.), *Conceptual and procedural knowledge: The case of mathematics* (pp. 1–27). Hillsdale, NJ: Erlbaum.

Hiebert, J., & Wearne, D. (1992). Links between teaching and learning place value with understanding in first grade. *Journal for Research in Mathematics Education, 23,* 98–122.

Hiebert, J., & Wearne, D. (1993). Instructional tasks, classroom discourse, and students' learning in second-grade arithmetic. *American Educational Research Journal, 30,* 393–425.

Hiebert, J., & Wearne, D. (1996). Instruction, understanding, and skill in multidigit addition and subtraction. *Cognition and Instruction, 14,* 251–283.

Kamii, C. (1989). *Young children continue to reinvent arithmetic—2nd grade.* New York: Teachers College Press.

Kamii, C. (1990). Constructivism and beginning arithmetic (K–2). In T. J. Cooney & C. R. Hirsch (Eds.), *Teaching and learning mathematics in the 1990s* (pp. 22–30). Reston, VA: National Council of Teachers of Mathematics.

Kamii, C., & Joseph, L. (1988). Teaching place value and double-column addition. *Arithmetic Teacher, 35*(6), 48–52.

Kouba, V. (1989). Children's solution strategies for equivalent set multiplication and division word problems. *Journal for Research in Mathematics Education, 20,* 147–158.

Ladson-Billings, G. (1992). Culturally relevant teaching: The key to making multicultural education work. In C. A. Grant (Ed.), *Research and multicultural education: From the margins to the mainstream* (pp. 106–121). Bristol, PA: Falmer.

Lampert, M. (1990). When the problem is not the question and the solution is not the answer: Mathematical knowing and teaching. *American Educational Research Journal, 27,* 29–63.

Leinhardt, G. (1988). Getting to know: Tracing students' mathematical knowledge from intuition to competence. *Educational Psychologist, 23,* 119–144.

Mulligan, J. T., & Mitchelmore, M. C. (1997). Young children's intuitive models of multiplication and division. *Journal for Research in Mathematics Education, 28,* 309–330.

National Council of Teachers of Mathematics (NCTM). (1980). *An agenda for action: Recommendations for school mathematics of the 1980s.* Reston, VA: Author.

National Research Council. (1989). *Everybody counts: A report to the nation on the future of mathematics education.* Washington, D.C.: National Academy Press.

Nesher, P. (1989). Microworlds in mathematical education: A pedagogical realism. In L. B. Resnick (Ed.), *Knowing, learning and instruction: Essays in honor of Robert Glaser* (pp. 187–215). Hillsdale, NJ: Erlbaum.

Noddings, N. (1990). Constructivism in mathematics education. In R. B. Davis, C. A. Maher, & N. Noddings (Eds.), *Constructivist views on the teaching and learning of mathematics (Journal for Research in Mathematics Education Monograph No. 4,* pp. 7–18). Reston, VA: National Council of Teachers of Mathematics.

Pierie, S., & Kieren, T. (1992). Creating constructivist environments and constructing creative mathematics. *Educational Studies in Mathematics, 23,* 505–528.

Resnick, L. B. (1983a). A developmental theory of number understanding. In H. P. Ginsburg (Ed.), *The development of mathematical thinking* (pp. 109–151). New York: Academic Press.

Resnick, L. B. (1983b). Towards a cognitive theory of instruction. In S. G. Paris, G. M. Olson, & W. H. Stevenson (Eds.), *Learning and motivation in the classroom* (pp. 5–38). Hillsdale, NJ: Erlbaum.

Resnick, L. (1988). Treating mathematics as an ill-structured discipline. In R. I. Charles & E. A. Silver (Eds.), *The teaching and assessing of mathematical problem solving* (pp. 32–60.) Reston, VA: Erlbaum/National Council of Teachers of Mathematics.

Resnick, L. B. (1989). Defining, assessing, and teaching number sense. In J. T. Sowder & B. P. Schappelle (Eds.), *Establishing foundations for research on number sense and related topics: Report of a conference* (pp. 35–39). San Diego, CA: Center for Research in Mathematics and Science Education, San Diego State University.

Riley, M. S., Greeno, J. G., & Heller, J. I. (1983). Development of children's problem-solving ability in arithmetic. In H. P. Ginsburg (Ed.), *The development of mathematical thinking* (pp. 153–200). New York: Academic Press.

Romberg, T. A., & Carpenter, T. P. (1986). Research on teaching and learning mathematics: Two disciplines of scientific inquiry. In M. C. Wittrock (Ed.), *Handbook of research on teaching* (3rd ed., pp. 850–873). New York: Macmillan.

Romberg, T. A., & Tufte, F. W. (1987). Mathematics curriculum engineering: Some suggestions from cognitive science. In T. A. Romberg & D. M. Stewart (Eds.), *The monitoring of school mathematics: Background papers: Vol. 2. Implications from psychology: Outcomes of instruction* (pp. 71–108). Madison: Wisconsin Center for Education Research, University of Wisconsin-Madison.

Ross, S. H. (1989). Part, wholes, and place value. *Arithmetic Teacher, 36*(6), 47–51.

Saxe, G. B., Guberman, S. R., & Gearhart, M. (1987). Social processes in early number development. *Monographs of the Society for Research in Child Development, 52*(2, Serial No. 216).

Silver, E. A. (1989). On making sense of number sense. In J. T. Sowder & B. P. Schappelle (Eds.), *Establishing foundations for research on number sense and related topics: Report of a conference* (pp. 92–96). San Diego, CA: Center for Research in Mathematics and Science Education, San Diego State University.

Sophian, C. (1992). Learning about numbers: Lessons for mathematics education from preschool number development. In J. Bideaud, C. Meljac, & J. P. Fischer (Eds.), *Pathways to number* (pp. 19–40). Hillsdale, NJ: Erlbaum.

Steffe, L. P., Cobb, P., & von Glasersfeld, E. (1988). *Construction of arithmetical meanings and strategies.* New York: Springer-Verlag.

Stigler, R. S., Fuson, K. C., Ham, M. , & Kim, M. S. (1986). An analysis of addition and subtraction word problems in American and Soviet elementary mathematics textbooks. *Cognition and Instruction, 3,* 153–171.

Strauss, M. S., & Curtis, L. E. (1984). Development of numerical concepts in infancy. In C. Sophian (Ed.), *Origins of cognitive skills* (pp. 131–155). Hillsdale, NJ: Erlbaum.

Usiskin, Z. (1987). Resolving the continuing dilemmas in school geometry. In M. M. Lindquist (Ed.), *Learning and teaching geometry, K–12* (pp. 17–31). Reston, VA: National Council of Teachers of Mathematics.

Van de Walle, J. A. (1998). *Elementary and middle school mathematics: Teaching developmentally* (3rd ed.). New York: Addison Wesley Longman.

van Hiele, P. M. (1986). *Structure and insight.* New York: Academic Press.

von Glasersfeld, E. (Ed.). (1991). *Radical constructivism in mathematics education.* Dordrecht, The Netherlands: Kluwer.

Wood, T., & Sellers, P. (1997). Deepening the analysis: Longitudinal assessment of a problem-centered mathematics program. *Journal for Research in Mathematics Education, 28,* 163–186.

Wynn, K. (1990). Children's understanding of counting. *Cognition, 36,* 155–193.

Yang, M. T. L., & Cobb, P. (1995). A cross-cultural investigation into the development of place-value concepts in Taiwan and the United States. *Educational Studies in Mathematics, 28,* 1–33.

CHAPTER 6

# Research on Early Science Education

## CHRISTOPHER E. LANDRY
## GEORGE E. FORMAN

YOUNG CHILDREN have a natural inclination to learn about their world, and they spend a great deal of time engaged in physical exploration of it. Mealtime alone, as any parent knows, provides seemingly endless opportunities for children to investigate the nature of solids and liquids, changes in temperature, the use of simple tools, and the behavior of objects in motion. Children engaged in such activity are engaged in science—by which we mean the process of developing explanations about how the world works—and are developing useful and quite powerful scientific theories. Such informal science learning, we will show, must be respected and understood as we consider research on the more formal learning of science that takes place in the preschool or kindergarten classroom.

Research on early science education needs to be distinguished from research on early cognitive development. Research on cognitive development helps us understand developmental constraints on learning (such as the ability to recognize anomalous events) as well as the common misconceptions children have about a certain concept (e.g., Levin, Siegler, & Druyan, 1990). Research on science education helps us determine useful procedures to facilitate scientific thinking in young children. Such studies that deal with children under 7 or 8 years of age remain relatively difficult to find. In this chapter we present what we have found in recent journals. As a context for this research, we also summarize the cognitive development research that has helped established the goals for much of early science education.

**Figure 6.1.** Diagram of scientific thinking

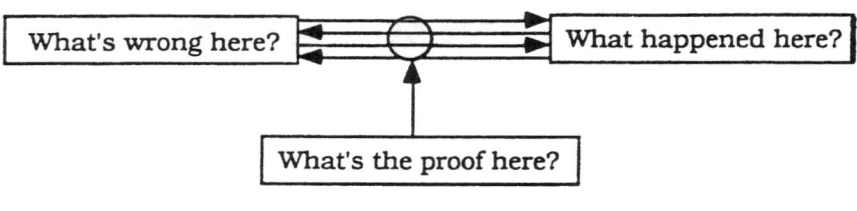

## SCIENTIFIC THINKING

Scientific thinking is a specific application of curiosity and intelligence. This form of thinking consists of the gradual understanding that certain events are anomalous and need to be explained (*What's wrong here?*); that observable data are essential to substantiate one's claims (*What happened?*); and that explanations need to meet certain criteria of logic (*What's the proof here?*). These three orientations to the world occur to children at staggered times of onset, probably in the order mentioned. The orientations can be diagrammed as a set of relations (see Figure 6.1).

The first orientation to the world represents a shift from a passive acceptance of an event to an active comparison of that event with something that was expected but did not occur. For example, the child sees a heavy object float and compares that with her expectation that this heavy object should sink. The child, through her advance to comparative thinking, has asked the first question: *What's wrong here?*

Some children may sense the anomaly but dismiss it as an isolated case. In our example, the child might think: *This* heavy object floats. The child may not relate *What happened?* to a class of events—all heavy objects float in water—but merely to the local case of one object. To proceed further, the child needs to sense that one case has implications for many cases. Furthermore, if this anomalous case is accepted, the expected case (heavy objects sink) has to be reworked.

Thinking traffics between *What's wrong?* and *What happened?* First the child tries an exact replication, just to see if the heavy object floats again (first arrow from left to right in Figure 6.1). On further inspection the child might realize that the object floats but that it pushes a bit into the water before it stabilizes. So the child reflects on the events and reinterprets her definition of *What's wrong?* (first arrow from right to left). Instead of saying, "This heavy object floats when it should sink," the child might rephrase what's wrong as "This heavy object sinks a little in the water when it should sink all the way."

This revision in turn might lead to a reworking of what happened, for example, "The object pushes against the water." The child has now moved beyond causing and into testing to see what will happen (second cycle of arrow). She makes certain things happen in order to confirm a prediction. She pushes down on the object to test its strength against her finger. This shift from causing to testing is critical to scientific thinking. This cycle among causing, interpreting, and testing is the foundation for scientific thinking and occurs in preschool-aged children (see Forman & Hill, 1984).

The step toward proof comes more slowly. At the intuitive level, proof consists mainly in making the strange familiar. Children reason by analogy. In the higher levels of science, proofs are accomplished by relating the strange to the familiar via a set of formal procedures (e.g., math) that in turn flow one to another without gaps in logical consistency. For example, the mathematical laws of falling objects, consistently applied, can account as well for the laws of orbiting satellites. For the child, proof begins as a case of analogy and consists of realizing that the event in question is actually similar to a more familiar case. For example, the child might use analogy to progress from "The heavy object is large" to "Large objects are strong; therefore strong objects can hold themselves up in water." But the proof has been inconsistently applied here, because it applies only to heavy objects that float, not to those that sink.

An arrow in Figure 6.1 connects the proof box to the traffic between the upper two boxes. This symbolizes that proof is metacognitive. That is, proof refers to thinking about thinking, in this case, the relation between hypothesis (*What's wrong?*) and facts (*What happened?*). *What's the proof* addresses the issue of how information constrains an answer to the only one possible and does not accept the same answer for opposite events (some sink, some float). As we review recent research later in the chapter, we try to assess where young children are in their understanding of proof.

While this diagram offers a useful representation of children's scientific thinking, it may be helpful to broaden our perspective somewhat and consider factors that research has identified as being critical to successful learning in the classroom. Figure 6.2 places our model in a context that reminds us that science education in school is in part a function of (1) cognitive development issues; (2) children's prior experience with and intuitive theories about science; and (3) the role of the teacher. (We could easily have added two other factors: the role of the *family* in encouraging scientific thinking and the importance of providing a rich learning *environment*—but in the interest of brevity we will focus our attention on the

**Figure 6.2.** Context of children's scientific thinking

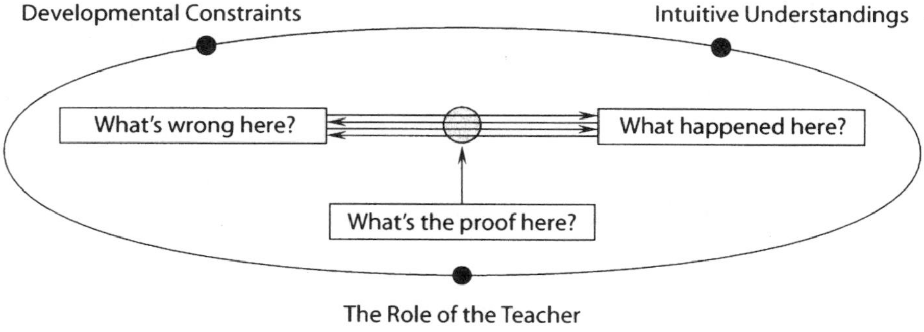

three areas illustrated in Figure 6.2.) The following sections address each of these topics in turn, within the context of recent research.

## DEVELOPMENTAL ISSUES: CHILDREN'S CONSTRUCTION OF MIND

The process of doing science requires that the child recognize when an event (this heavy object floats) conflicts with her understanding of how things work. In addition, science involves not only the construction of new knowledge, but also the construction of some means to communicate one's discoveries, to explain and defend one's ideas, and to consider the ideas and theories of others. One may know but not be able to explain. Communication necessarily requires a certain level of metacognitive processing, of stepping back and reflecting on one's own thoughts. In addition, children require a reasonably developed theory of mind before they understand the necessity to explicate their knowledge for others. These issues bring the children's concept of mind into the center of research on science education.

Research on cognition has attempted to determine when children develop an understanding of mental states and activities: belief, desire, memory, inference, and so forth. For those involved in early science education, this research can perhaps shed some light on two aspects of children's science: the child's interpretation of a physical event, and the child's ability to engage in meaningful conversation with others about that event.

Pillow (1988), in a summary of research into children's beliefs about the mental world, cites several studies showing that young children often miss helpful cues about their own cognitive processes. Six-year-olds, for example, when given instructions that could not possibly be carried out, tried to carry out the instructions instead of realizing that they had failed to comprehend the impossibility. Flavell (1988) found that while 5-year-olds showed nonverbal signs of comprehension problems, such as pauses and puzzled expressions, they did not report an awareness of their own comprehension difficulty when asked. Older children had a higher degree of awareness. Young children may not realize the significance of their fleeting feelings of uncertainty. In other words, their puzzlement does not cause them to reflect on its source.

What happens when we carry these findings over to our model of science thinking? Clearly, it becomes difficult to assume that the young child will necessarily recognize a conflict (*What's wrong here?*) between her existing knowledge structure and a physical event she observes. Cognitive conflict may not occur. If the child, for example, ignores her puzzlement upon seeing a heavy object float, and if this child does not reflect on her own prior conceptions, then the existing knowledge structure will remain unchallenged.

Having briefly dealt with knowledge of mind as it affects the child's interpretation of physical events, we now turn to knowledge of mind as it relates to communication with others. Science, for children as well as adults, is not done in a vacuum but in a social realm within which ideas are discussed, are debated, and take shape. For any meaningful give-and-take to occur, there must be agreement about the facts (*What happened?*) even if there are differences of interpretation. Konicek, King, and Teece (1990) report on the care taken by fourth-graders to distinguish "floating" from "not sinking" objects. But, as Pillow (1988) summarizes, younger children's incomplete understanding of mind often prevents them from taking the perspective of others that useful dialogue requires. Young children do not, for example, understand that a person's prior knowledge or expectations may affect that person's interpretation of a physical event. Pillow offers an example. Children see an object and are then shown an uninformative patch of that same object. Next they are asked whether someone seeing just the patch could identify the object. Most 4- and 5-year-olds incorrectly said "yes." They confused their own privileged information about the whole object with the partial information given to a new viewer. Such a failure to take the other's perspective would make it difficult for a young child to debate alternative views. Nevertheless, these early struggles at communication are the origins of social perspective-taking and collaborative problem solving. By 8 years of age these egocentric errors are rarely made.

What emerges is a picture of the young child only gradually developing an ability to decenter, to be objective enough to fruitfully compare his experience with that of his peers. We might expect that our young learner at water play would be unperturbed by the claim of a peer that a heavy object floated, but eventually perplexed if she discovered this herself. Later, perhaps at age 6 or 7, she will more readily agree with her peers that these facts present alternative views that need to be reconciled. Then she will begin to traffic freely between *What happened?* and *What's wrong?* This does *not* mean, as we show in our section on teaching strategies, that young children cannot engage in science. It does mean that the teacher, aware of these developmental constraints, will want to employ techniques that help children around them.

## INTUITIVE UNDERSTANDINGS: CHILDREN'S THEORIES ABOUT SCIENCE

Having reviewed research about children's ability to *do* science—to recognize cognitive conflict and to engage in fruitful discourse with others—we turn now to research on children's ideas *about* science. The early work in this area gave much attention to the developmental level of children. Developmental level refers to general cognitive competence, such as the ability to conserve quantity (same amount despite spatial changes) or the ability to understand class inclusion relations (some is less than all). More recently, research has taken us to specific content, such as the misconceptions children have about heat or gravity or light. In this section, we focus primarily on content-specific research.

### Principles of Constructivism

As we discussed earlier, children bring to science instruction a great deal of experience and many ideas about how things work. These ideas have been called naive theories, alternative frameworks, misconceptions, and intuitive understandings. What these terms have in common is the belief that children have constructed, through high-level thinking, their own theories about physical events. The naive theory has a sophistication of its own (see the discussion of Figure 6.1) and has been adopted (and retained) by the child because of its proven explanatory power. Thus, the teacher cannot ignore the naive theory or simply ask the child to abandon it in favor of more orthodox views. The child who is told a new explanation will often concurrently hold the misconception because it is more integrated into many other assumptions he has developed through experience in the world.

In fact, these early theories are so powerful that honors students studying college physics will fall back on them when asked to apply their knowledge to new situations, and they are widespread even among schoolteachers who teach math and science (Ginns & Watters, 1995). In the classroom, as Gardner (1991) makes clear, students may learn to provide the expected answers when tested in science, but they may never abandon the quite contradictory notions formed in early childhood. Real learning in science, then, must involve a process of conceptual change, not just the accumulation of facts. This process of reconstructing misconceptions, called constructivism, requires reconciling the intuitive theories of the young child with the expert theories developed by scientists.

Constructivism acknowledges several principles—some obvious, some less so. No one seriously assumes that the young child is a blank slate, so it is trivial to cite the tabula rasa theory as something constructivism is not. Even empiricism does not assume that 4- and 5-year-olds come to science instruction without preconceptions. But beyond this obvious principle, constructivism also posits that inference, not the raw observation of noticeable events, is the ultimate source of knowledge. Only through inference can the child organize facts into a coherent system. Furthermore, while misconceptions have a coherence that makes them resistant to mere replacement by new information from the teacher (Carey, 1986), constructivism holds, as a principle of faith, that children will be conflicted when anomalies occur and that they have innate capacities to make the inferences necessary to resolve these contradictions (Wheatley, 1991). In a constructivist classroom, teachers do not directly teach these competences but rather establish an environment that allows the children to draw on them (Duckworth, 1996). The teacher's role, which we explore in some detail later in the chapter, becomes less one of imparting information and more one of scaffolding the child's learning by (for example) increasing the likelihood of cognitive conflict, or what Gardner (1991) calls Christopherian encounters: situations in which the child must confront evidence that challenges his intuitive theories (the term honors Columbus's irrefutable proof that the earth is indeed round).

Before moving from this all-too-brief encapsulation of constructivist theory to its implications for the teacher of young children, we first (1) use evaporation to examine more closely the process of conceptual change, (2) review similar research in other content areas, and (3) discuss recent research that refines, or even challenges, the constructivist model of science education.

## Conceptual Change: Evaporation as a Case in Point

In the following example, we consider the formation and development of misconceptions. We show why these misconceptions are more than quaint, but are intuitively reasonable. This is important, because only when a teacher understands why a student's misconception is reasonable does the teacher have an entry point for effective instruction. In the service of this objective, we use one science concept, evaporation, as a case in point so that we might more fully trace the misconceptions children bring to their classwork.

Most of us have seen the surprise in a child's face when the untouched water dish, wet an hour ago, is now dry. This surprise itself comes from a rather elementary theory about liquids: (1) Liquids do not spill up, and (2) liquids do not disappear into thin air. Yet the water is gone, but the dish remains. The observation of the missing water in the presence of the empty dish violates these assumptions and leads to the first stage in Figure 6.1: *What's wrong?* From this point on, children have a variety of explanations about what happened.

Some children will cling to their theory about liquids and consider the nature of the dish. Children in the 7- to 8-year range think that the dish absorbed the water (Bar, 1989). They have some understanding of how water seeps into the ground, or into a sponge, so why not into a dish? This explanation is a first attempt to say *What happened here?* Since the children do not know that water can change from a liquid to a gas (called a phase change in science), they feel compelled to justify the *What's wrong?* question with a reworking of their assumptions about solid containers.

By the age of 9 or 10, children begin to talk about vapor, but it is a transitory concept and situationally applied. They believe that water can turn into vapor, but they still think that this vapor is contained in the clouds but does not constitute clouds (Bar, 1989). The children are comfortable with the idea of vapor because they think vapor is similar to air. They know that air is present but cannot be seen. But since they still think that vapor must be contained by something (the cloud), we can surmise that their understanding of phase change is incomplete. They understand that the water becomes vapor, but that is not the same as understanding that the water is transformed into vapor. To say that water becomes vapor is not much more than saying that water becomes invisible. The children have not tried to account for what it is about vapor that makes it invisible (drops too tiny to see). Vapor is just water that one cannot see; therefore it still has all the other properties of water (e.g., existence and weight) and so requires a container if it is to be "held" in the sky.

Figure 6.1 is again helpful in discussing children's construction and reconstruction of theory. The first *What happened?* referred to the absorbent dish; the second *What happened?* referred to the water becoming invisible and residing inside clouds. This progress is usually the result of a reworking of the *What's wrong?* question. Children try to make the dish soak up the water; it doesn't, so the first *What happened?* makes no sense. The children find it unavoidable to construct the idea of water moving because they are not willing to posit the annihilation and re-creation of matter. The theory about water moving comes when they relate the evaporation dish to a pan of boiling water. Vapor is invisible steam. In this way the children do not have to violate their belief about matter. They just add that some matter is invisible!

It is not until age 11 or 12 that children construct a coherent theory that accounts for both the invisibility and movement of water (Bar, 1989). The water vapor is made of drops that are so tiny that they cannot be seen (i.e., "They are scattered everywhere in the air"); and because they are so tiny, they can be moved by the air. Thus the phase change of water into particles accounts for the invisible movement. Likewise the particle theory explains how clouds can be made of vapor rather than containing vapor. For these older children, the proof that water vapor exists comes from their understanding that it *must* exist. Given the constraints that liquid water is heavier than air, and all other constraints, water vapor is a case of logical necessity. Similar findings come from Beveridge (1985), who extended his research to include condensation.

## Research About Other Topics

As the constructivist model of conceptual change has gained widespread acceptance, researchers have tried to determine children's misconceptions across a broad range of domains, only a few of which can be reviewed here. The reader interested in more information is referred to existing bibliographies of conceptual change research (Pfundt & Duit, 1994) or, for example, to the research base of the National Curriculum in England (Department of Education and Science, 1989), which includes children's theories about growth, evaporation and condensation, light, change in nonliving materials, sound, electricity, forces, and living things and their environment.

One of the most exhaustive and useful studies of children's theories about living things was conducted by Susan Carey (1985), who investigated the naive theories children (aged 4, 6, and 10 years) have about biology (living versus inanimate; plant versus animal; and the processes of eating, breathing, sleeping, dying, etc.). The younger children explained bodily processes in terms of social and psychological needs. For example, to the question "Why do we eat?" the young child might say, "To grow big and strong." By age 10, an "intuitive biology" emerges, with explanations similar to those of naive adults. Carey's point is that these later theories are qualitatively different from the early theories, even though they both may be incorrect: that children undergo a process of true conceptual change in which old theories are restructured and new ones emerge. This work challenges the accretion model of learning science (Lawson, 1988) that we discuss in the next section. For more work on children's ideas about ecology and matter, see Leach, Driver, Scott, and Wood-Robinson (1996).

Feher (1990) and Rice and Feher (1987) have done careful work on children's understanding of paths of light. By using the inversion of an image through a pinhole, these researchers discovered some intriguing misconceptions about light rays being "squeezed" and then "bulging out" as they pass through holes.

Galili and Bar (1997), who studied the knowledge children (ages 5 to 16) have about weight, found that young children develop their ideas based on tactile experience ("Suspended objects have no weight" is a typical misconception of young children) before becoming conservers of weight. They found that while children modify their knowledge, it was not always a complete substitution of a more advanced theory for a flawed one; depending on the situation, a young child may be both a conserver and a nonconserver.

A few of the other content areas to be studied by researchers in recent years include magnets, environmental knowledge (Palmer, 1996), forests and their inhabitants (Strommen, 1995), the concept of burning (Boudaoude, 1991), dissolving (Longden, Black, & Solomon, 1991), earthquakes, the shape of the earth (Arnold, Sage, & Worrall, 1995), and astronomy (Brewer & Samarapungavan, 1991).

In response to such work, Johnson and Gott (1996) argue that such studies may be unreliable because (1) laboratory tests make it difficult to elicit the real knowledge of children, which is imbedded in personal contexts and meaning; (2) such tests are likely to prompt instant answers instead of ones based on reflective thinking; and (3) children may misinterpret the researcher's question and the researcher may misinterpret the children's response. Chinn and Schaverien (1996) agree that children must develop trust in the researcher before they become willing to articulate shaky or partly formed ideas; their methodology emphasizes the establishment of a close working relationship between researcher and child, as does that of Maria (1997). Both these studies offer useful guidance for the would-be researcher of children's theories and answer the objections of Johnson and Gott (1996).

## Constructivism Reconsidered

The orthodoxy of constructivism is gradually being refined. Shapiro (1994) asks the practical question of why some children do not progress, even when placed in rich problem-solving environments that challenge their misconceptions. By using children's understanding of reflected light, she investigated the interaction of science learning and personality type. While this study deals with children 11 years old and older, as a research (and teaching) methodology it is well worth reading. Shapiro found that the social orientation of students contributed to their success or failure. Some children are socially acquiescent; that is, they defer to more dominant children. Others embrace the challenge of negotiating for equal status. While the socially acquiescent child does not profit from the confrontation of ideas, the socially embracing child does. Shapiro presents a needed refinement to the oversimplification that children universally have a fascination with contradiction, and she reminds us that science education involves emotional, social, and cultural issues as well as cognitive ones.

Other researchers have questioned whether conceptual change is the most accurate model of science education. Lawson (1988) interviewed elementary school children (aged 6, 9, and 11 years) to determine the extent to which they held naive misconceptions about biological concepts such as growth, circulation, and family resemblance. He found no evidence of coherent misconceptions, but rather scattered bits and pieces of knowledge (see also diSessa, 1988; Russell, Harlen, & Watt, 1989). If this is true, one would have to reason that didactic teaching could be justified, since the scattered facts would not be resistant to replacement. Lawson (1988) argues that, at least with these concepts, one should adopt an accretion theory of learning rather than a reconstruction theory. An accretion theory holds that knowledge builds in a quantitative manner as more and more facts are learned. A reconstruction theory holds that the learning comes not primarily from the acquisition of new facts, but from a reconfiguration of the system of relations among the facts.

Mintzes (1989) writes a rebuttal of Lawson by reviewing other early childhood research on naive theories of biology (Carey, 1985; Wandersee, Mintzes, & Arnaudin, 1987) but admits that the construction of a well-formed naive theory of biology may take longer than the construction of a well-formed naive theory about physical objects. He attributes this delay to the relative inaccessibility of observable events necessary to found naive theories of biology. One can also see in the case studies that Lawson (1988) provides that the youngest child was socially acquiescent. Thus the lack of a well-formed theory could be either real or simply not expressed (see Shapiro, 1989).

The possibility remains that (at least with some domains) children younger than 10 years old form loosely held analogies rather than coherent theories. For example, the rain cycle is understood as analogous to "raining up" and "raining down," without the children understanding the necessity for state changes in the water during evaporation and condensation. Does this imply that we should encourage children younger than 10 to forget their wrong analogies and to accept the more useful analogies of the teacher? Russell and colleagues (1989) argue that even if children construct loosely knit systems of attributes, they are still constructing relations; the learning child does more than accrete new facts. Thus, if we tell a child to forget a wrong fact without our understanding his loose system of relations, that wrong fact will very likely be reinvented in some other form to support his loose system of ideas.

Linder (1993) argues that the cognitive change model puts too much emphasis on displacing the child's intuitive theories. Science, he contends, is not about giving up one conception in favor of another, but of knowing when various theories (intuitive versus expert) apply. For example, a physicist using a vacuum cleaner at home might talk of it "sucking up" the dirt, even though he would not use such a framework in the laboratory. In a similar vein, Howe (1996) suggests that we modify constructivist theory by adopting a Vygotskian perspective that is less confrontational than the current model. She writes:

> In contrast to the conceptual change model, a model that accepted a Vygotskian view of the development of concepts in science would accept children's ideas as a starting point with a view toward helping them expand their knowledge, learn to use it more flexibly, apply it to more situations and, eventually, to integrate it into a system of broader, more inclusive concepts. (p. 36)

The influence of Vygotsky's sociocultural perspective would lead to a form of constructivism, Howe argues, that would rely more on discourse, allow ample time for children to reflect on and accept new ideas, and shift the focus from the solitary child to cooperative learning within a social context (Howe, 1996).

Elkind (1989), likewise, warns us not to rush 4- and 5-year olds into performing controlled experiments. Children this young do not possess the cognitive wherewithal to isolate variables or to understand the inter-action of two or more causes (see also Rudnitsky & Hunt, 1986). Elkind's warning pertains more to *What's the proof?* in Figure 6.1 than to the won-derful messing about that young children can handle when perplexed by some anomalous event. Science for these young children is quite possible, if by science one means the construction of some expectation, trying something out to confirm that expectation, and modifying the expecta-tion based on observations. This type of science can happen even in the absence of an appeal to proof or logical necessity (concrete operational thinking).

We appreciate the contributions of Linder, Howe, and Elkind as we adapt the basic constructivist approach to the specific needs and abilities of young children. After all, constructivism should not be thought of as a one-size-fits-all framework, but one that is applied in developmentally appropriate ways. Extensive work with young children in the United States (Forman & Hill, 1984) and in Reggio Emilia, Italy (Edwards, Gan-dini, & Forman, 1993), supports Howe's call for science education that (1) allows adequate time for exploration, investigation, and reflection; (2) is supported by the skillful intervention of the teacher; and (3) is car-ried out in a respectful social context in which children and teachers be-come partners in learning.

Driver, Asoko, Leach, Mortimer, and Scott (1994) raise another issue, arguing that the constructivist model of conceptual change ignores the fact that science is not merely about personal discovery based on experi-ence with physical phenomena, but is also a process of enculturation into the symbols and conventions of the scientific community. Science is not only, or even mostly, about learning from nature, but is about learning the social constructs that have been invented to explain natural phenom-ena. Since no student could possibly discover these constructs on his own, they suggest, it is as inaccurate to suggest that science knowledge is dis-covered by the learner as to suggest that it is transmitted by the teacher.

Driver and colleagues challenge the overly simplified reduction of constructivism to mere hands-on learning and move us closer to a con-structivist theory that accounts for both the process of personal discovery by the learner and the critical role of the teacher in introducing the learner to the tools and symbols of science. Becker and Varelas (1995) help us reach this goal by advocating a Vygotskian model that nicely ac-counts for the teacher's contributions. Knowledge in the Vygotskian sense is a two-way process in which the child is being empowered as an inde-pendent thinker while being inducted into the cultural practices of sci-ence (Becker & Varelas, 1995). The teacher's role is to bridge these top-down and bottom-up processes by scaffolding the child's learning; that is, by offering the socially constructed symbol systems, models, and other tools that the child needs to create his own understanding. Learning, then, is partly a process of personal discovery and partly a process of mastering the use of existing symbol systems. Their model dovetails nicely with the Vygotskian approach proposed by Howe (1996).

In summary, recent research has refined and strengthened our constructivist theory of science learning. We have moved in recent years from a simple conceptual change model, in which the child uses anomalous data to modify his existing theories, to a social constructivism model that better explains the more complicated reality of the child creating personal understanding within a broader context of socially constructed scientific symbols and methods. This revised model helps us account for the crucial role of the teacher and of peers in the learning process, and it helps us adapt the constructivist model to the developmental needs of young children.

## THE ROLE OF THE TEACHER: RESEARCH ON TEACHING EARLY SCIENCE

What is an early childhood science teacher to do? The research in this area suggests several forms of intervention, which, at times, includes no direct intervention. Duckworth (1996) makes an eloquent case for allowing students to discover and frame their own questions. The intervention, in this case, consists mainly in providing the children with a rich problem-solving environment and a teacher who reflects and records the evolution of the children's thinking. Wasserman (1988) offers a model described as play–debrief–replay. This model puts heavy emphasis on group discussion and repeated alternations among messing about, summarizing, and a higher level of messing about. As alluded to in our discussion of children's theories of mind, teachers need to monitor the communication competence of children before launching these more routinized formats of instruction.

The conceptual change model would suggest that teachers must introduce data that conflict with children's theories. But Chinn and Schaverien (1996) warn that anomalous data alone may not be enough to cause children to rework their ideas. They describe seven typical responses to conflicting data—only one of which leads to theory change. Chinn and Schaverien suggest that in order for anomalous data to be effective, the teacher must reduce the entrenchment of prior theories, introduce a plausible alternative theory, make the anomalous data credible, and encourage reflective thinking.

Beveridge (1985) used conflict inducement to study children's theories about the water cycle. Some children were asked to test water absorption using paper towels, a plastic saucer, a sponge, aluminum foil, and a metal plate. The results of these tests were meant to conflict with the students' assumption that evaporated water had been absorbed by the dish. Other children were given a lesson on steam. A mirror was placed in front of a boiling kettle and the condensation was noted.

It is interesting that these demonstrations did little to facilitate reconstruction of naive theories. Beveridge concludes that these demonstrations were ineffective because the alternative theories were resistant to change. While this borders on circular reasoning, we appreciate the intent of that conclusion. The techniques were didactic. Instead of placing the children in a situation in which they would invent their own tests (and therefore their own understanding of what the test tested), the teacher presented the test and demonstration as a given.

In contrast to the method Beveridge tested, the teacher might more profitably introduce into the learning environment materials that increase the likelihood of cognitive surprise. Unexpected events, when imbedded in the child's own process of exploration, provide rich opportunities for encouraging the flow of thinking diagrammed in Figure 6.1 (Forman & Hill, 1984). In the following sections we describe strategies that can help children become aware of their thinking (*What happened?*) and test their ideas (*What's the proof?*).

## Conversation

Our model of social constructivism has the child, not the teacher or curriculum, at its center. Therefore, Shapiro (1994) writes, the constructivist teacher must be a researcher as well, in order to understand what children are thinking about the topic at hand and how they have come to think that way. Shapiro places great emphasis on listening as both a research and teaching methodology, and she believes that successful teaching means giving great respect to the child's efforts to create understanding. Unless the teacher understands how children think about light or the water cycle, after all, she cannot help the child confront, reflect on, and rework his theories.

Driver (1995) describes what we might call the delicate dance of constructivist teaching, in which the teacher must know when to provide knowledge, when to provide experiences, and how to help the child use both to create knowledge. Like Shapiro, she argues that constructivist teaching must begin with the child's understanding, not with a predetermined curriculum. Toward this end, Maria (1997) offers a helpful case study in which she worked with a child for nearly 2 years (from age 5 to age 7) in a study of the shape of the earth, the causes of night and day, and related concepts. While Maria's goal was to observe the formation of alternate conceptions, her study is also a nice example of the artful use of conversation. What she and Shapiro have in common is the idea that the constructivist teacher of science must understand learning as a social, emotional, and cultural experience as well as a cognitive one (Shapiro, 1994).

Chinn and Schaverien (1996) describe four types of conversations that may be used both to elicit children's ideas and to assist children in the refinement of their thinking. "Coffee-table conversations," for example, are child-directed talks in which the child presents a proposed solution to a problem, much as an architect presents building plans for review. The act of placing the drawing or other construction on the table, they found, creates some emotional and cognitive distance between the child and her work, allowing the child and teacher to engage in productive review of it. Their work is recommended as a careful analysis of the power of conversation when led by a skilled teacher.

## Documentation

Our discussion of children's construction of mind raised two issues for the teacher of young children: children's ability to recognize cognitive conflict and to adopt another person's perspective well enough to exchange ideas successfully. To these, we might add a third developmental constraint: children's ability to remember. These skills develop gradually in the young child, becoming more robust over time. In the meantime, documentation of children's thinking can be an effective way to support their thinking.

Beyer (1997) describes the importance of making visible "the invisible substance of thinking." He advocates using any appropriate media—audio, video, or chalkboard—that can increase children's metacognitive reflection, or thinking about thinking. In Reggio Emilia, teachers use photographs, transcripts, audiotape, and other media to record the stages in children's thinking about a given topic. This information is not only valuable for the children, as we will discuss, but becomes an invaluable resource for the teachers, both as they plan new experiences (in Reggio, where the curriculum emerges from the work of the children, such documentation is essential) and as they share the learning process with parents, who are considered partners in the learning.

The child's construction of knowledge cannot be rushed; it requires adequate time for exploration in the environment, testing theories, and representing and discussing ideas. Extended projects that emerge from children's interests and focus their thinking on a particular topic can become powerful platforms for learning (Katz & Chard, 1996). The challenge is to help the child relate new experience with previous thinking. Four- and five-year-olds can add new meaning to a past experience but need a photograph to scaffold their memory of the past event. Photographs allow the teacher and child to discuss the past events as a narrative sequence that leads to something interesting. At the same time, when several children can look at the same series of photographs, they have a common referent for the construction of shared meaning and alternative perspectives. In addition, the very act of documenting children's thinking makes clear that their thinking is respected and valued (see, e.g., Helm, Beneke, & Steinheimer, 1998).

Photographs and videotape can be powerful tools that help children increase their reflective thinking and inference-making. The teacher is, in effect, modeling mnemonic strategies for the child. This practice, in turn, brings with it the responsibility that we, in some deliberate fashion, transfer these strategies to the child. One way to do this is to allow the children to gain experience with these media so they can eventually snap the photographs or zoom in with the video camera and decide which pictures or footage to capture for later review.

## Drawing to Learn

There is a movement at work in education to place more emphasis on how children represent science questions. It is clear from the history of science that solutions are determined, in part, by how one represents the problem. For example, one may try to improve one's chess game by drawing a sequence of boards with all the pieces in each frame or by writing out a column of letters and numbers to represent a sequence of moves piece by space. The drawings are more likely to elicit strategies about board development; the alphanumeric list is more likely to identify a weakness in overusing the queen or underusing pawns (see Forman, 1985).

For many years, Rosalind Driver (1989) asked science students to draw posters of their concepts, such as their naive theories about solids, liquids, and gases (see also Russell et al., 1989). From these early drawings children begin to ask wonderfully paradoxical questions: What's the stuff between the particles of matter? What holds the particles together in solids that is not there in liquids? This work has been done mostly with older children and has been used primarily to identify the children's

**Figure 6.3.** Simone's drawing of the rain cycle. The arrows (added to the original drawing) point to the free-fall water in the open on the left and the "pipes" for the water going up on the right.

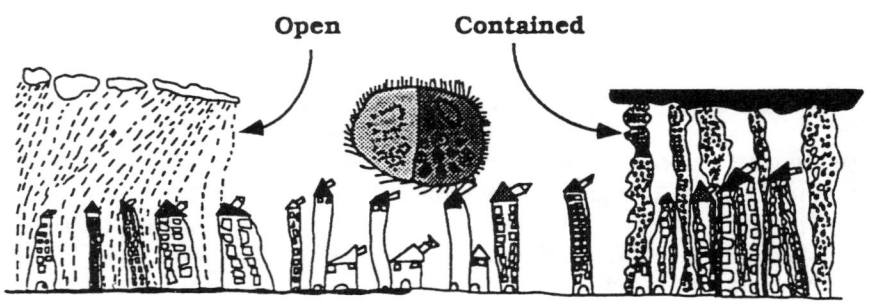

misconceptions. By extending this work, one could understand how drawing provides a source of new knowledge, not just a record of existing knowledge.

At the University of Massachusetts we have developed a graduate seminar titled Drawing to Learn. The thrust of the course is to understand the mechanism by which children, in the act of drawing their theories, gain a better understanding of their misconceptions and thereby reconstruct their misconceptions into a more sensible theory. This course refers to work by Driver (1989), Larkin and Simon (1987), and others, but for the early education years, the course gives careful attention to work that is coming from the preschools in Reggio Emilia, Italy. We can consider the example of a 5½-year-old, named Simone, who drew her understanding of the rain cycle (see Figure 6.3) and described it as follows:

> The rain falls on the houses, on the umbrellas and on the trees, then it goes on the earth, in the courtyards, then things dry up when it's sunny. Instead of continuing to go around the houses, the rain dries up, the sun heats the rain that has fallen and that's how it goes away afterwards, it goes back into the clouds and then it starts to rain again. (Cited in traveling exhibit, The Hundred Languages of Children, The Commune of Reggio Emilia, Italy)

From this description it seems that Simone has a rather complete understanding of rainfall and evaporation. But a closer look at her drawing reveals that the rain going up needs to be contained inside something like a tube (see arrow on right of Figure 6.3). These marks suggest that she is still thinking of water as liquid, and therefore this heavier-than-air substance needs to be contained in order to be transported back into the clouds.

At this point the teacher in Reggio would intervene with a comment such as this: "These marks [the tube] are very interesting, Simone. Could you tell me why you drew them?" The drawing becomes a platform for discussion among teacher and children. Drawings are frequently shared with the group, usually about four children, and the children discuss what the drawings mean. The drawings help the children develop a common referent, and this in turn helps them reconstruct their misconceptions about a science topic (see Forman, 1989). The teachers in Reggio have also used drawing to teach other concepts, such as shadows, mirror reflections, gravity on the bottom of the earth, and algorithms for making tea.

We have extended drawing to learn in the United States with other themes, such as simple machines and the crystalline growth of snow. Through careful analysis of the process of drawing, we have determined that children must make a shift from drawing how something *looks* to drawing how something *works*. This means children have to go beyond the literal stage so common around age 6 or 7, when they are overly concerned with picture realism (Gardner, 1980). Teachers and children should not confuse drawing to learn with learning to draw. These are fundamentally different enterprises.

## Collaborative Problem Solving

Educators have appreciated the power of group discussion for some time, but only recently have they begun to formalize the dynamics of collaborative problem solving. Group problem-solving research has moved beyond the realm of teaching good citizenship and into mainstream cognitive science. Through a revival of interest in Vygotsky (1978) and the reconstruction of Piaget's theory of knowledge (Doise & Mugny, 1984), basic and applied research has been forthcoming on how knowledge construction is essentially a social endeavor.

Tudge and Caruso (1988) present the implications of this research base for early childhood education. In summary, they describe the type of setups that generate quality collaborative problem solving, such as balance beams and marble rollways. They then proceed to explain just what the children do in collaborative learning that deepens their understanding. This list includes the role of cognitive conflict, the need to explicate thinking for others, and the use of inferences that go beyond what can be

**Figure 6.4.** Representation of the debate among four children on what it means to give the girls a handicap in a long-jump contest.

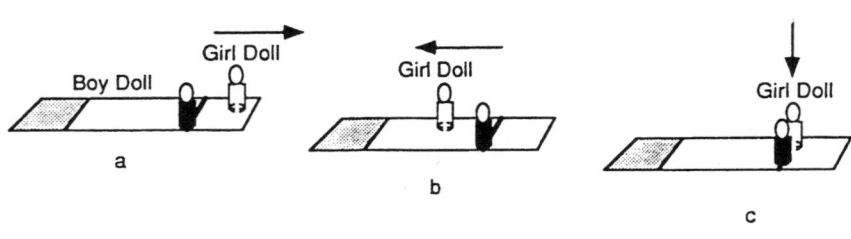

seen. These processes are more probable within social debate than when a child is working alone.

We can look again at practices in Reggio Emilia, Italy, for wonderful examples of collaborative problem solving in science. In one project, four children, ages 5½ to 6, volunteered to design an athletic event, the long jump. In the course of this project they were faced with problems of many types: rules of fairness, how to measure the long jump, how to divide the school into ability flights, and how to read the symbols on a 10-meter tape (see Forman & Gandini, 1991). Of particular interest was the following episode on how (and whether) to offer girls an advantage. This episode brings into conflict two interacting variables, speed and fatigue, as well as a challenge of sexism from the girls. The episode begins as follows:

> In order to focus the discussion of rules the teacher helps by asking the children to make a small replica of the track itself. This serves as a common referent from which the children can discuss rules of fair competition. The children have made the sand pit from a highly textured paper and the runway from a less textured paper. To facilitate the discussion the teacher provides the children with small wooden dolls that the children can move around to clarify something said.
>
> A discussion ensues about the girl and boy runners. Augusto offers his opinion that girls cannot jump as far as boys. Silvia and Stephania listen, but do not agree. Silvia says, "I told you a thousand times, woman also do sports and can do things even stronger than the Long jump."
>
> Augusto pushes his point that the girls need some sort of handicap to make the competition fair. "But, do you want more run up? Yes or no?" The girls need to start further back, so they will have more space to run before they jump, Augusto explains as he positions the girl doll further back [Figure 6.4a]. The girl doll, in the red pants, is placed several inches behind the starting line.

Stephania protests, "But if they are tired, they cannot make it, they cannot jump."

Lorenzo intervenes. He says, "Maybe I have misunderstood. She has to start further up, because she has very little strength and this way she doesn't get tired." He moves the girl doll, in red pants, in advance of the boy doll [Figure 6.4b]. Lorenzo no doubt believes that he is being fair.

Stephania takes a definite stand on this issue. "Hey no, come on. We have already decided the rule. The girls should start from the same line of departure as the boys." Silvia agrees completely with Stephania.

And with this assertion, Silvia moves the girl doll back to the start line with the boy doll [Figure 6.4c]. But for the boys the problem persists and will only be resolved toward the end of the project when they implement their rules for the actual event. (Forman & Gandini, 1991)

If we review this sequence, we can better understand the learning that takes place when children discuss issues among themselves. First, the medium of the collage layout and the dolls improve the chances that the children will share a common set of references. Young children have a tendency to use indefinite words, such as "do this" and "not that," which makes it difficult to share meanings verbally. So the tangible materials, combined with their movement and the children's gestures, make it possible for the children to focus on the debate rather than the verbal skills of making their words unambiguous.

Then, the issues themselves were wonderfully rich. Just for the moment, let's accept Augusto's premise that girls should be given an advantage. How could this be done fairly? Augusto reasons that the girls should be moved back to increase the distance from the jumping point. This is a reasonable suggestion given his premise that more distance means more speed, which in turn means longer jumps. Of course, this assumption is true only if the girls cannot reach maximum speed in the original running space. The extra running space is superfluous beyond the point of maximum speed. So, extra running space may not mean more speed.

Stephania counters Augusto with her concern about the runner getting too tired. If you move the runner back, the greater distance will make the runner more fatigued. Perhaps since this girl doll represented herself, she related more to the tired feelings than did Augusto.

But Lorenzo counters Stephania by saying the lesser distance means less fatigue, so he moves the girl doll up. Thus we see the advantage of having several children relate to the same issue. They do so in different ways, and the system of relations becomes richer for all children. More distance increases speed, which increases the jump for Augusto, but more distance increases fatigue, which decreases the jump for Stephania. Then does it follow that less distance decreases fatigue, which increases the jump, in Lorenzo's solution? Lorenzo does not consider that the effects of speed and fatigue might cancel each other out. For children to combine two relations, they need representations more formal than wooden dolls.

The problem is simply short-circuited for the moment by Stephania, who insists that there is no reason to give girls an advantage. End of sequence, but the stage has been set for a return to this problem during the actual long-jump event. The children decide that it is all right for the jumpers to begin wherever they like. The children learn to distinguish rules of fairness from strategies of choice.

## CONCLUSION

The model of science thinking in Figure 6.2 helps us develop a constructivism that accounts for the interchange among the child, her peers, and her teacher and that recognizes both developmental constraints and the importance of the child's intuitive understandings about science. This perspective leads us to a social constructionism that is child-centered while acknowledging the role of the teacher in bridging the child's discovery process and the use of socially constructed symbol systems.

The flow of thinking represented in Figure 6.1 can help us summarize what we have said so far about teaching. Teachers can enter this three-part dynamic flow in a variety of places. Class activities can be structured to increase the probability of unexpected events (*What's wrong here?*). Teachers can help children make better and better representations of what happened through drawings, diagrams, charts, lists, and observational records (*What happened here?*). Teachers can encourage children to debate and thereby reflect upon the quality of their proofs (*What's the proof here?*) and so challenge the face validity of the familiar.

Special attention should be given to the developmental level of children within each content area. Proof for young children can be a summary of the events as observed, but for older children, proofs can rely on necessary truths of deduction. For the younger child, heavy objects made of wood float; heavy objects made of metal sink. The older child will want more than an endless list of floaters and sinkers. So for older children, proof goes beyond the givens.

Scientific reasoning begins with a question. The question might be presented by the teacher, but before scientific reasoning kicks in, the children have to sense the conflict between what was expected and what was observed. We know from the diaries of Susan Isaacs, Nathan Isaacs, Jean Piaget, Frances Hawkins, and David Hawkins that children are indeed curious about a multitude of events. But these do not include all of science. Children ask about the beginning of the universe, but not about the coexistence of a star and its light. They ask about animal growth, but not about predator–prey ecosystems. They ask "Why does it rain when the sun is out?" but not "Why are the daylight hours shortening?" Questions are themselves minitheories, and a theory means that the child already has the cognitive wherewithal to relate two or more facts. But since some questions are more complicated minitheories, children cannot grasp the question itself. These questions they do not ask.

Research in early scientific thinking can inform us about why certain questions are more complex than others. This, indirectly, helps us understand why young children ask some questions and do not ask other questions. The questions that children ask can then be organized into a flexible curriculum for early science education. Research shows that an emphasis on thinking skills has an impact on achievement (Tilgner, 1990). But the implementation of basic research into science curricula continues to be a slow process. As Tilgner (1990) points out, the resistance to teaching science in the younger years is almost as common today as it was 20 years ago. We have a clearly identified need to advocate for early science education.

This advocacy should draw on research on issues that affect children's interest in and success with science, but which space has prevented us from reviewing here: research about the role of the family in promoting science learning, for example, or about why girls continue to lose interest in science in the early grades. We are also intrigued by research about children's ideas about nature, and how exposure to the natural world affects children's thinking (Nabhan & Trimble, 1994).

## REFERENCES

Arnold, P., Sage, A., & Worrall, L. (1995). Children's knowledge of the earth's shape and its gravitational field. *International Journal of Science Education, 17*(5), 635–641.

Bar, V. (1989). Children's views about the water cycle. *Science Education, 73*(4), 481–500.

Becker, J., & Varelas, M. (1995). Assisting construction: The role of the teacher in assisting the learner's construction of preexisting cultural knowledge. In L. P. Steffe & J. Gale (Eds.), *Constructivism in education* (pp. 385–400). Hillsdale, NJ: Erlbaum.

Beveridge, M. (1985). The development of young children's understanding of the process of evaporation. *British Journal of Educational Psychology, 55*, 84–90.

Boudaoude, S. B. (1991). A study of the nature of students' understanding about the concept of burning. *Journal of Research in Science Teaching, 28*, 689–704.

Carey, S. (1985). *Conceptual change in childhood*. Cambridge, MA: MIT Press.

Carey S. (1986). Cognitive science and science education. *American Psychologist, 41*(10), 1123–1130

Chinn, C. A., & Schaverien, L. (1996). Children's conversations and learning science and technology. *International Journal of Science Education, 18*(1), 105–116.

Department of Education and Science. (1989). Science in the National Curriculum. London: Department of Education and Science and the Welsh Office, Her Majesty's Services.

DiSessa, A. A. (1988). Knowledge in pieces. In G. Forman & P. Pufall (Eds.), *Constructivism in the computer age* (pp. 49–70). Hillsdale, NJ: Erlbaum.

Doise, W., & Mugny, G. (1984). *The social development of the intellect*. Oxford, UK: Pergamon.

Driver, R. (1989). Students' conceptions and the learning of science [Special issue]. *International Journal of Science Education, 11*, 481–490.

Driver, R. (1995). Constructivist approaches to science teaching. In L. P. Steffe & J. Gale (Eds.), *Constructivism in education* (pp. 234–286). Hillsdale, NJ: Erlbaum.

Driver, R., Asoko, H., Leach, J., Mortimer, E., & Scott, P. (1994). Constructing science knowledge in the classroom. *Educational Researcher, 23*, 5–12.

Duckworth, E. (1996). *"The having of wonderful ideas" and other essays on teaching and learning* (2nd ed.). New York: Teachers College Press.

Edwards, C. P., Gandini, L., & Forman, G. (Eds.). (1993). *The hundred languages of children: The Reggio Emilia approach to early childhood education*. Norwood, NJ: Ablex.

Elkind, D. (1989). Developmentally appropriate education for four year olds. *Theory into Practice, 28*(1), 47–52.

Feher, E. (1990). Interactive museum exhibits as tools for learning: Explorations with light. *International Journal of Science Education, 12*(1), 33–49.

Flavell, J. H. (1988). The development of children's knowledge about the mind: From cognitive connections to mental representations. In J. W. Astington, P. Harris, & D. Olson (Eds.), *Developmental theories of mind* (pp. 244–267). New York: Cambridge University Press.

Forman, G. (1985). The value of kinetic print in computer graphics for young children. In E. Klein (Ed.), *Children and computers* (pp. 61–75). San Francisco: Jossey-Bass.

Forman, G. (1989). Helping children ask good questions. In B. Neugebauer (Ed.), *The wonder of it: Exploring how the world works* (pp. 21–25). Redmond, WA: Exchange Press.

Forman, G., & Gandini, L. (1991). *The long jump: Using small group projects in Reggio Emilia, Italy* [160–minute VHS video]. Available from School of Education, University of Massachusetts at Amherst.

Forman, G., & Hill, F. (1984). *Constructive play: Applying Piaget in the preschool*. Menlo Park, CA: Addison-Wesley.

Galili, I., & Bar, V. (1997). Children's operational knowledge about weight. *International Journal of Science Education, 19*(3), 317–340.

Gardner, H. (1980). *Artful scribbles: The significance of children's drawings.* New York: Basic Books.

Gardner, H. (1991). *The unschooled mind: How children think and how schools should teach.* New York: Basic Books.

Ginns, I. S., & Watters, J. J. (1995). An analysis of scientific understanding of preservice elementary education students. *Journal of Research in Science Teaching, 32*(2), 205–222.

Helm, J. H., Beneke, S., & Steinheimer, K. (1998). *Windows on learning: Documenting young children's work.* New York: Teachers College Press.

Howe, A. C. (1996). Development of science concepts within a Vygotskian framework. *Science Education, 80*(1), 35–51.

Johnson, P., & Gott, R. (1996). Constructivism and evidence from children's ideas. *Science Education, 80*(5), 561–577.

Katz, L. G., & Chard, S. C. (1996). *The contribution of documentation to the quality of early childhood education.* (ERIC Document Reproduction Service No. EDO-PS-96-2)

Konicek, D., King, S., & Teece, D. (1990). Beneath the surface. *Science and Children, 27*(5), 27–28.

Larkin, J. H., & Simon, H. A. (1987). Why a diagram is (sometimes) worth a thousand words. *Cognitive Science, 19,* 65–100.

Lawson, A. (1988). The acquisition of biological knowledge during childhood: Cognitive conflict or tabula rasa? *Journal of Research in Science Teaching, 25*(3), 185–199.

Leach, J., Driver, R., Scott, P., & Wood-Robinson, C. (1996). Children's ideas about ecology 2: Ideas found in children aged 5–16 about the cycling of matter. *International Journal of Science Education, 8*(1), 19–34.

Levin, I., Siegler, R. S., & Druyan, S. (1990). Misconceptions about motion development and training effects. *Child Development, 61,* 1544–1557.

Linder, C. (1993). A challenge to conceptual change. *Science Education, 77,* 293–300.

Longden, K., Black, P., & Solomon, J. (1991). Children's interpretation of dissolving. *International Journal of Science Education, 13,* 59–68.

Maria, K. (1997). A case study of conceptual change in a young child. *The Elementary School Journal, 98*(1), 67–88.

Mintzes, J. J. (1989). The acquisition of biological knowledge during childhood: An alternative conception. *Journal of Research in Science Teaching, 2,* 823–824.

Nabhan, G. P., & Trimble, S. (1994). *The geography of childhood: Why children need wild places.* Boston: Beacon.

Palmer, D. H. (1996). Students' application of a biological concept: Factors affecting consistency. *Research in Science Education, 26*(4), 409–419.

Pfundt, H., & Duit, R. (1994). *Bibliography: Students' alternative frameworks and science education* (4th ed.). Kiel, Germany: Institute for Science Education.

Pillow, B. H. (1988). The development of children's beliefs about the mental world. *Merrill-Palmer Quarterly, 34*(1), 1–29.

Rice, K., & Feher, E. (1987). Pinholes and images: Children's conceptions of light and vision. *Science Education, 71*(4), 629–639.

Rudnitsky, A. N., & Hunt, C. R. (1986). Children's strategies for discovering cause and effect relationships. *Journal of Research in Science Teaching, 23*(5), 451.

Russell, T., Harlen, W., & Watt, D. (1989). Children's ideas about evaporation [Special issue]. *International Journal of Science Education, 11,* 566–576.

Shapiro, B. L. (1989). What children bring to light: Giving high status to learners' views and actions in science. *Science Education, 73*(6), 711–733.

Shapiro, B. L. (1994). What children bring to light: A constructivist perspective on children's learning in science. New York: Teachers College Press.

Strommen, E. (1995). Lions and tigers and bears, Oh my! Children's conceptions of forests and their inhabitants. *Journal of Research in Science Teaching, 32*(7), 683–698.

Tilgner, P. J. (1990). Avoiding science in the elementary school. *Science Education, 74*(4), 421–431.

Tudge, J., & Caruso, D. (1988, November). Cooperative problem solving in the classroom: Enhancing young children's cognitive development. *Young Children,* pp. 46–52.

Wandersee, J. H., Mintzes, J. J., & Arnaudin, M. W. (1987). Children's biology: A content analysis of conceptual development in the life sciences. In *Proceedings of the Second International Seminar on Conceptual Educational Strategies in Science and Mathematics.* Ithaca, NY: Cornell University Press.

Wasserman, S. (1988). Play–debrief–replay: An instructional model for science. *Childhood Education, 64*(4), 232–234.

Wasserman, S. (1990). *Serious Players in the primary classroom.* New York: Teachers College Press.

Wasserman, S., & George Ivany, J. W. (1996). *The new teaching elementary science: Who's afraid of spiders?* New York: Teachers College Press.

Wheatley, G. H. (1991). Constructivist perspective on science and mathematics learning. *Science Education, 75*(1), 9–21.

Vygotsky, L. S. (1978). *Mind in society: The development of higher psychological processes* (M. Cole, V. John-Steiner, S. Scribner, & E. Souberman, Eds.). Cambridge, MA: Harvard University Press.

CHAPTER 7

# Early Childhood Social Studies

RICHARD K. JANTZ
CAROL SEEFELDT

THE SEARCH for an identity for early childhood social studies is an ongoing activity. This unity quest on the part of some educators is related to the identity problems and struggles faced by the social studies profession at both the broad K-12 and the primary and elementary school levels. The National Council for the Social Studies (NCSS) is the learned society that promotes social studies education in the public schools. Although the NCSS claims sovereignty over the social studies curriculum, it is in competition with other professional groups when it comes to setting standards, establishing goals, and specifying content with disciplines such as history, geography, and economics. Thornton (1996a, 1996b), in describing the role of the NCSS in these struggles, has indicated that there are not only duplication and overlap among the various organizations in their proposals for national standards in history, geography, and social studies, but also conflicting perspectives of social studies within the NCSS.

## WHAT IS SOCIAL STUDIES?

In the early 1990s, the NCSS, without resolving the debates and controversies, began to define its mission and the nature of social studies education and to articulate its position (Barth, 1996). This resulted in the publication of *Expectations of Excellence: Curriculum Standards for Social Studies* (NCSS, 1994). These standards indicated that the focus of social studies is "designed to promote civic competence: and it is integrative" (p. 3). This integration involves knowledge, skills, and attitudes from a number of disciplines.

Part of the problem with the identity of social studies in the early grades is its relative rank in the public school curriculum. In a recent study that examined the status of social studies in Delaware, Thornton and Houser (1997) found that social studies was still perceived as a second-rank subject. There are also questions about teachers' professional interest and commitment to social studies. Jarolimek (1996) has indicated, "So much of elementary school teachers' time and effort are dedicated to teaching literacy and other basic skills that their professional interests naturally are pulled in the direction of professional organizations concerned with reading, language arts, or mathematics" (p. 104). This concern is partially addressed by the NCSS (1994) in its curriculum standards when it calls for a complete core curriculum with social studies viewed as a basic K–12 component, for "all students should have access to the full richness of the social studies curriculum" (p. 162).

Just calling for and publishing standards, however, may not be enough. There is still the need to provide leadership and promote cooperation and collaboration across the field. This may be a challenge that the NCSS is not able to meet:

> Social studies programs are today being shaped by competing constituencies who want to see the curriculum developed around what they believe to be important—whether that is one of the disciplines, i.e., history, geography, economics, civics; or social causes such as multiculturalism, diversity, ethnicity, gender; or other issues associated with the "political correctness" phenomenon. (Jarolimek, 1996, p. 109)

Even with all the concerns about the identity and nature of early childhood and elementary social studies, school systems in the early grades still have traditionally employed either a spiral- or widening-horizons approach to the curriculum—and more recently an attempt to integrate the two approaches (Ellis, 1998). The widening-horizons approach emphasizes a movement from the simple to the more complex, taking into account the developmental nature of children and a movement from self to an understanding of the global nature of the world. The spiral curriculum requires the identification of basic structures, which are revisited at increasing levels of complexity as children move through the grades. The emphasis is on in-depth coverage over time of important social science concepts.

Some teachers take a child-centered approach to the curriculum, which emphasizes self-development and appropriate practices, while other teachers stress more of a society-centered approach focusing on citizenship and democratic principles. A third common approach centers on the attainment of knowledge, including ways of knowing and focusing on key concepts from the various social science disciplines (Ellis, 1998). In reality, elements of all three of these approaches influence decisions concerning the nature of early childhood social studies.

Little has changed since 1976, when Jantz stressed the necessity for social studies teachers of young children to become decision makers centered around the knowledge, skills, and attitudes related to the social studies curriculum. He advocated that teachers be aware of the nature of the students, the nature of learning, the nature of society, and the nature of knowledge as they make choices about the social studies curriculum.

Finally, Seefeldt (1992) also called for greater cooperation and communication among various professional groups to move beyond rhetoric and to identify the fundamental role of social studies in the education of young children, but she warned decision makers of the dangers of mixing and matching the goals of early childhood education with the goals of social studies for young children:

> When the complexities of the field of social studies meet the confounding factors of early childhood education, the problems involved in specifying appropriate social studies content expand, and the question of how either field can effectively fulfill its overarching purpose—that of preparing children to become members of a democracy—remains unanswered. (p. 216)

The need for early childhood educators to become decision makers in terms of the curriculum and approaches to teaching still exists in early childhood social studies today. The question, then, for this review is: What is happening now in early childhood social studies and how is it different from what has already been reported in previous reviews? The development of key understandings from the social sciences—history and geography—by young children is still an important concern. The main focus of this chapter is on the growing knowledge of how children begin to develop historical and geographic understandings considering age-appropriateness and developmental concerns, as well as the role of national standards in both fields.

## CHANGING VIEWS OF TEACHING HISTORY

Since the 1980s, there have been a number of articles published indicating that children have a developing sense of history and that the teacher's role in this development may be changing (Egan, 1997; Levstik, 1986; Levstik & Pappas, 1992; Seefeldt, 1993; Thornton, 1990). Levstik (1986) showed how the use of narrative and students' responses were linked together in developing a sense of history. Egan (1997) advocated the use of stories to help propel students through the layers of historical understanding that develop in children. Thornton (1990) cautioned against adding more history to the curriculum but advocated the need for more research on how teachers teach and how students learn relationships among time concepts, historical understandings, and historical reasoning. Some new directions in how primary grade children develop historical understandings through the use of narrative structures were reported by Levstik and Pappas (1992). They indicated that for young children not only does the story structure have appeal, but primary grade children can also follow the sequence of events depicted. The case for teaching history to young children was made by Seefeldt (1993). She cautioned against using storytelling and myths if they were teaching misconceptions about history, advocating that they instead be used to emphasize ideas of time and change as related to continuity in human life. She stated that historical exemplars, including those in story form, need to be meaningful to the learner and connected to experiences in their lives.

## Time

Earlier reviews of early childhood social studies have indicated a strong relationship between children's cognitive development and their development of time concepts (Downey & Levstik, 1991; Jantz, 1976; Seefeldt, 1992; Wyner & Farquhar, 1991). Most of the research has centered on describing children's understanding of clock time, calendar time, and eventually psychological time. Children appear to progress from responding to time concepts, beginning to use time concepts, and finally being able to fully understand time concepts. Piaget (1971) indicated that two types of time concepts are exhibited by young children. There is intuitive time, which is "limited to successions and duration given by direct perceptions" (p. 2), and psychological time, which uses logic as a basis for the operational understanding of time. Piaget believed time to be the coordination or consideration of at least two motions. He stated, "But if time as we suggest is the operational coordination of motions themselves, then the relations between simultaneity, succession and duration must first be constructed one by one" (p. 3).

Thornton and Vukelich (1988), summarizing the research on children's development of time concepts, reported that children first become aware of personal time between 4 and 7 years of age. Children use indefinite time concepts based on linguistic patterns to differentiate the past from the present and the future. Children at this age also begin to describe daily events in a sequential pattern. Chronological time is often associated with personal time and is reflected by the cyclical nature of daily events.

> Mark, a five-year old, was asked, "How long is a day?" He replied, "It's today until you get to tomorrow!" He was then asked, "How long is that?" Mark replied, "Today is when you get up and you play and you eat lunch and you play some more and you go to school and you come home and it's nice outside and then it's night and you go to sleep and when you wake up it's tomorrow!" (Jantz, 1976, p. 96)

Finally, by about age 6 or 7, "rudimentary discriminations of clock and calendar skills begin to appear," with discrimination of clock time developed from the large units (hours) to the smaller units (minutes), and discrimination of calendar time developed from the large units (months) to the smaller units (days) (Thorton & Vukelich, 1988, p. 71).

The development of historical time requires the child to depict a person, place, artifact, or event in the past using some form of time language (Thornton & Vukelich, 1988). Thorton and Vukelich further reported that, "Many researchers believe that the development of historical time depends on the prerequisite skills of personal, calendar, and clock time" (p. 71). Downey and Levstik (1991), in a review of teaching and learning history, indicated that children do understand historical time as related to patterns and sequences in real events even though for young children these might be general and imprecise.

## History and Time

Logic would indicate that history and time are linked together; however, there is little research available to depict how these two areas are interdependent. Thornton and Vukelich (1988) identified three perspectives from researchers in the cognitive developmental perspective advocated by the British researcher Hallam (1970). In this perspective, history and time are linked with cognition. The lack of reversibility thinking in preoperational children limits their conception of history. A second, kindred perspective—supported by an American researcher, Sleeper (1975)—is related to psychosocial development. This perspective posits that a full understanding of historical time is related to formal operations and the processes of attaining adulthood. A third perspective, espoused by Spieseke (1963), relates to an organic curriculum view, which emphasizes that since time and history are interrelated, they are best taught in the context of meaningful social problems. Thornton and Vukelich (1988) advocate a position that they called developmental historical time. This perspective is based on the following points:

1. Learning time is most likely tied to the learner's current developmental structure.
2. Time understandings should be a major consideration in how historical topics are introduced.
3. Historical time concepts should be taught in conjunction with history just as clock and calendar time concepts are taught in conjunction with math.
4. Time and history are no more or less complex than algebra and trigonometry in math or the great works in literature. . . . It may be, in other words, that if the learning task is organized appropriately, then younger children can deal with more complex modes of thought than Piaget believed.
5. Consideration of historical time leads to a general point—the need for a clearer understanding of how children learn history. This is the case because time appears to be an integral component of historical reasoning. (pp. 78–80)

## Teaching History

In the learning of history, there are differences between learning dates and developing a chronological perspective (Levstik & Barton, 1997b; see also Levstik & Barton, 1997a). Dates refer to a moment in time and have little meaning for children before the age of about 10 (Barton & Levstik, 1996). This may be due in part to the lack of visual references associated with dates and in part to a lack of knowledge about the numerical basis of dates. Chronology, on the other hand, relates to the ability to order moments in time. Usually this involves visualizations or narratives that invoke a form of visualization for the particular moments. Children as young as 5 have demonstrated the capacity to order events chronologically using photographs and pictures with such broad distinctions as "long ago" and "close to now." It appears that dress and level of technology are the two primary visual clues that students use.

It should be noted, however, that visual references can also lead to misconceptions. The potential impact of images is important when considering the historical context. When teaching history using images, Rothwell (1997) reported that it is important to consider not only the historical facts but also the accuracy of images.

Since dates have little meaning for young children, "teachers have to approach dates as concepts to be developed: they have to help students associate their visual images of history with the dates that correspond to them" (Levstik & Barton, 1997b, p. 74). Although there is little or no empirical support for using timelines (Thornton & Vukelich, 1988), they are common features in classrooms and textbooks. Extending timelines into visual timelines may be one tool to help students match dates with visual images, thus using their prior knowledge of chronology to further refine their broad categories of historical time (long ago) into more distinct categories (the 1880s). Visual timelines might also help young children to begin to compare different events occurring at the same point in time, thus challenging "a particularly common aspect of children's chronological thinking, their assumption of linear historical development" (Levstik & Barton, 1997b, p. 75).

Barton and Levstik (1996) in their study of children from kindergarten through sixth grade provided an alternate to an emphasis on dates and chronology for teaching history—an emphasis on people's lived experiences. They reported:

> This research thus indicates that historical understanding can develop independently of adult temporal vocabularies and suggests that the primacy of dates and chronologies in history instruction be de-emphasized in favor of content and reasoning aimed more at helping children understand the richness and variety of people's lived experiences in different times and places. (p. 444)

Historical understanding develops in layers and is evident in the mythical, oral traditions exhibited in children's stories and storytelling from different times and places (Egan, 1989). The story structure of fairy tales tends to be binary in nature, with an emphasis on such ideas as good/bad or security/fear structured in concrete ways. Young children under the age of 8 begin to mediate these binary opposites in much the same way as they mediate "hot and cold" with "warm." Nature and culture are mediated with talking bears and rabbits. Story forms with beginnings, middles, and ultimately a finished end influence the development of one layer of historical understanding. "We can do this for children by telling them the dramatic stories of human cultures, particularly of the one of which they are a part and partial product. A potential benefit of such a history curriculum is that it introduces children to their world in a dynamic and dramatic form" (Egan, 1989, p. 290).

The power of narrative to help children understand history has been advocated by a number of researchers. McKeown and Beck (1994) stated that narrative is inherently causal and explanatory in nature; a narrative is a series of events that lead from one to the other through causes and consequences. Narrative is a familiar form even to very young learners, who have experienced it in daily interactions as well as in stories that make up the bulk of their early contact with text. (p. 21)

The linkage between history and narrative in the development of historical understandings has often been overlooked, but it can be an effective mechanism for student learning (Levstik, 1995). Narratives have a great deal of appeal for children in learning history, but students need to develop skills of critical analysis and inquiry when developing historical understanding. There are some cautions in using narratives; for example, the narrative may be too storylike, resulting in misinterpretations. Students may also focus on the linear progression of history and fail to realize that certain events were occurring simultaneously in different places at the same time. Levstick and Barton (1997b) indicate that narrative can be used with younger children but that "the relationship between narrative, history, and historical understanding is more complex than appreciation of a story well-told" (p. 92).

However, Levstik (1990) did argue that narrative can assist young children with looking at the human aspect of history, describing an approach taken by a primary grade teacher that focused on human aspects. The students, with teacher guidance, engaged in an inquiry project on why Christopher Columbus was famous. They were to consider two questions: How does the past influence the present, and how does the present influence our interpretations of the past?

These ideas were brought together through the concept of "fame." Using powerful ideas and inquiry as the focus of social studies is not new, but they can be used to help develop historical understanding and as a partial solution to the depth–breadth dilemma of the allocation of resources and time (VanSledright, 1997).

Finally, there have been some recent attempts to investigate children's thinking as it is related to the development of historical understanding. The CHATA Research Project in the United Kingdom focused on what they called second-order concepts—a cause, evidence, explanation, motive, interpretation (Ashby, Lee, & Dickinson, 1997). While the authors indicated that it was too early to form conclusions, they did find signs of progression in children's ideas about the nature of historical explanation. Children's ideas seem to progress in the following order: "Things happen because people want them to; the more agents want something, the more likely they are to achieve it; what people want has some connection with what happens, but it is not the first thing to look at to explain the outcome of actions" (p. 20).

Barton (1997), in summarizing what we know about teaching history to children, reported that the research indicates that children learn a great deal of history outside of school and this prior knowledge can be used to develop historical understanding. The source of this prior knowledge includes things children come in contact with in their everyday lives—artifacts, places, pictures, and oral traditions from their family histories. Students seem to know more about social history and have more problems with political history, particularly when it is presented in limited, text-based detail covering local, state, national, and sometimes international events in a relatively short period of time. Thornton (1997) supported the active nature of learning history: "There is growing reason to conclude that students doing history for themselves enhances both their motivation and reflect powers beyond what is ordinarily obtained from textbook-based instruction" (p. 11). Barton (1997) concluded:

> Teachers who are willing and able to engage students in active investigations, to build on what children already know and to address misconceptions, will stand a good chance of helping them to develop meaningful historical understanding. (p. 16)

## History Standards

These changing views of history and how to teach it to young children are reflected to some degree in the national standards for history (National Center for History in the Schools [hereafter NCHS], 1994). The standards were developed by the National Council for History Standards with some participation by 33 different organizations, including the Association for Supervision and Curriculum Development, the Council of State Social Studies Supervisors, and the National Council for the Social Studies. Absent were representatives from the National Association for the Education of Young Children or the Association for Childhood Education International. The standards reflect two categories: historical thinking and historical understanding. Historical thinking includes "chronological thinking . . . , historical comprehension . . . , historical analysis and interpretation . . . , historical research capabilities, [and] historical issues-analysis and decision making" (pp. 6–7). According to the standards, the historical understandings to be developed in children are "of society," including "family structures," gender roles, and relationships among individuals and groups; "the scientific quest" for efficient development; "the political sphere of activity" in the local community, state, and nation, including "the core principles and values of American democracy"; and the "human experience" as expressed in "literature, sacred writings and oral traditions, drama, art, architecture, music, and dance" (pp. 5–6).

## CHANGING VIEW OF TEACHING GEOGRAPHY

If social studies is given second-rate status in the elementary school curriculum (Thornton & Houser, 1997), then the rank of teaching geography, a key subject of social studies, is nonexistent. Just as the search for identity in the field of social studies is ongoing, so is the search for goals, objectives, and methods of teaching geography to children during the period from birth through age 8.

Even though Lucy Sprague Mitchell's influential *Young Geographers,* written in 1934, guided early childhood curriculum for decades, geography is not thought of as a core content area in the early childhood curriculum. In part, this may be due to the misinterpretation of Mitchell's ideas of children learning geography through exploration of their here-and-now world. By enlarging and enriching children's understanding of the immediate environment and their place in it, Mitchell's goal was to develop children's capabilities in terms of relationship thinking and generalizing from one experience to another. Through investigations of their immediate physical world, Mitchell postulated that children would see the relationship of one fact to another, thereby producing something different from, and adding to, the separate facts—a relationship.

Mitchell's ideas of learning through the here-and-now world were quickly embraced by the early childhood community. Unfortunately, just as quickly they became trivialized. Ignoring the geographic complexities of children's here-and-now world and the role of children as investigators of that world, teachers presented children with intellectually sterile unit topics such as Learning About Myself, Rules for Safe Living, The Shopping Center, and People Change the Earth (Jarolimek & Parker, 1993).

Geography may also be missing from the early childhood curriculum because early childhood teachers, who tend to be child-centered rather than discipline-centered, are often more concerned with developing an integrated curriculum—one that meets the social, emotional, physical, and cognitive needs of children—than with including geography in the curriculum. Teachers themselves are often ignorant of geography. As a part of their undergraduate program, they may have taken one course in the social sciences chosen from among a variety of fields—sociology, history, economics—but may never have taken a geography course. This leaves the typical early childhood teacher without a solid understanding of the geographic concepts—and even less knowledge of how concepts from the field of geography could be introduced to young children in meaningful, appropriate ways.

Aware of the void in their curriculum, the field of early childhood viewed the identification of national standards for the study of geography as positive. The identification of national standards for geography would, early childhood educators believed, provide the guidance necessary to create a sequential, conceptual, and developmentally appropriate geography curriculum for young children.

In the past inroads were made in the identification of concepts key to a given discipline. Bruner, in *Toward a Theory of Instruction* (1966) and *The Process of Education* (1960), advanced the idea that social studies, like every other discipline area, could be planned around concepts key to the discipline. With the identification of these concepts, a spiral curriculum could be implemented. The big ideas, or key concepts, could be used to coordinate the knowledge or content sequences with the cognitive stages of the learner so that at each successive stage children would be dealing with concepts they could understand, but in progressively greater complexity and depth.

Bruner's philosophy was difficult to implement. First, concepts key to geography were difficult to identify. There was lack of agreement about what these consisted of, and confusion over which were critical for young children to learn. There were other problems as well: Teachers of young children rarely had the experience necessary to translate the identified concepts into appropriate learning experiences for children.

## Standards Today

Thus it was with optimism that early childhood educators looked to the geography standards, *Geography for Life: National Standards—1994* (Geography Education Standards Project [hereafter GESP], 1994), to guide them in developing appropriate geography curricula for young children. The opening sentences of the national geography standards reflected the philosophy that children learn through questioning and exploration of their immediate environment. Both the first sentence, "Geography is for life in every sense of that expression" (GESP, 1994, p. 11), and the definition of geography as "a field of study that enables us to find answers to questions about the world around us—about where things are and how and why they got there" (GESP, 1994, p. 11), seemed congruent with early childhood philosophy and practices.

Likewise, Mitchell (1934) would have agreed with the standards' statement that the study of geography is for life, bringing together the physical and human dimensions of the study of people, places, and environments. On the other hand, Mitchell, like today's early childhood educators, would not agree with the numerous and abstract specific performance standards accompanying these valid definitions of geography.

Regrettably, the standards as now stated are of limited help to early childhood educators and may even be damaging. Instead of organizing the geography curriculum around concepts key to geography, the standards state 57 content standards (that is, what children are expected to achieve by the time they complete fourth grade) and over 60 performance standards. Embedded in each of the standards are numerous facts and concepts, negating any possibility of teachers using the standards as a guide in selecting key concepts.

"More importantly, the geography standards fail children" (Seefeldt, 1995, p. 109). Identifying meaningful concepts is but one step in the teaching/learning process. The other is knowing how to make these meaningful to young children. Created with limited knowledge of what geographic concepts children already know, the skills they possess, and which of these they could obtain with the assistance of an adult, the national geographic standards are simply overwhelming and unmanageable (Seefeldt, 1995).

The specific performance standards given for the teaching of spatial systems, physical regions, and physical systems could take over the entire early childhood curriculum. It is not that children are unable to develop initial awareness and personal knowledge of space, the physical characteristics of their world, or the physical systems of weather and seasons, but rather that preoperational children are unable to master the level of abstractness found in the standards.

## Spatial Systems

Throughout early childhood, children's awareness of spatial relationships is developing. The knowledge of object permanence and the spatial relationships between objects grows as children explore and move about their environment.

Children as young as 3 years old, without hesitation or prompting, have been found to express their understanding of spatial relationships by spontaneously drawing or building maps. Researchers have also documented young children's awareness of maps (Liben & Downs, 1993; Liben & Yekel, 1996; Trifonoff, 1995). It seems that when mapping is introduced to children in the context of their personal knowledge and understanding of maps, they can use maps quite proficiently (Marzoff &

DeLoache, 1994). Gutierrez (1993) described a primary-level field geography program in which students explored the geography and archaeology of their rural community using maps. Describing children's first-hand experiences with using maps, Maxim (1997) suggested that children's general geographic knowledge is enhanced through map-reading activities.

Even without first-hand experiences, Sowden (1996) demonstrated that preschoolers were able to interpret black-and-white aerial photographs and to solve simulated navigational programs using the photograph. Thus the first geography standard—"How to use maps and other geographic representations, tools, and technologies to acquire, process, and report information from a spatial perspective"—is achievable, at least on a preliminary, awareness level. It is doubtful, however, whether any child under the age of 7 or 8 would be able to identify and describe the basic elements of maps—"(e.g., title, legend, cardinal and intermediate directions, scale, grid, principal parallels, meridians)"—during the period of early childhood or achieve any of the other multitude of abstract, highly complex concepts of mapping, such as being able to locate major rivers, cities, or landforms on a map; to identify physical and human features along a major route on a map; or to analyze the earth's surface in terms of its spatial elements of point, line, area, and volume—all of which are called for in the geography standards.

Based on knowledge of children's ability to conceptualize and understand abstractions, it would be impossible for children under the age of 10 or so to master the abstract concepts of representation, symbolization, orientation, and direction identified in the specific performance standards of the first geography standard, The World in Spatial Terms. Before 10 or 11 years of age, children have little conceptual understanding of perspective, scale, or representation. It is not until after the development of formal thought, around age 12, that children are able to conceptualize the total relationship of a map to the objects it represents or to infer information based on those relationships (Mosenthal & Kirsch, 1990).

## Places and Regions

During the period of early childhood, children are, as Mitchell (1934) believed, very much like geographers. They dig in the sand, explore what they can do to water and how it acts on them, and question their world, asking: What is this? Why is it this way? Do sunflowers always grow here?

Naturally inquisitive about the place in which they live, young children are indeed ready to be introduced to the national geography stan-

dard of The Physical and Human Characteristics of Places. They can identify the physical characteristics of the places in which they live and learn
the names of landforms, bodies of water, soil, vegetation, weather, and
climate in their immediate environment—as called for in the geography
standards.

Mayer (1995), like Mitchell (1934), maintains that place geography
can be taught effectively—that is, if Dewey's assertion that students' experiences serve as the springboard for their learning is true. And Ely
(1994) demonstrated how young students can explore relationships, organize information, and make generalizations about the world around
them.

On the other hand, they will fail if asked to perform the specific performance standards of "using a data-retrieval chart organized by human
features of economic activity, type of housing" (GESP, 1994, p. 113); "describe physical regions by studying the physical environment at a variety
of scales and using field notes, maps, and other sources" (p. 115); or "use
graphic materials to compare the geographic characteristics of regions of
the world at similar latitudes" (p. 115).

Instruction in the geographic concepts of place and region must
match children's existing knowledge. What we introduce to children must
be achievable, yet challenging. Piaget (1971) described children's growing
awareness of the physical characteristics of the earth. Dominated by arti-
ficialism and animism, children attribute life and consciousness to the
earth, sun, moon, and stars as well as to living things (Vosniadow, 1994).
Throughout the early years, children are even confused about what constitutes life. Three-year-olds will attribute life to anything that moves.
Until about age 7 or 8, children believe cars, planes, rivers, and clouds
have life and consciousness.

Until about age 9 or 10, children also retain the belief that every
object, including natural bodies, was made for a purpose (Piaget & Inhelder, 1969). A natural object, such as the sun, a lake, or a mountain, is
made for warmth, boating, or climbing, and because it has been made for
humans, is closely allied to them.

## Physical Systems

The geography standards state that, by the fourth grade, the students
should know and understand:

1. The Physical Processes that Shape the Patterns and Earth's Surfaces
2. The Characteristics and Spatial Distribution of Ecosystems on Earth's Surfaces. (NCSS, 1994)

This includes students knowing and understanding atmosphere, lithosphere, hydrosphere, and biosphere; how patterns of location, distribution, and association of features on the earth's surfaces are shaped by physical process; and how earth–sun relations affect conditions on the earth.

As Bredekamp and Rosegrant (1995) point out, there is a cycle of learning that begins with becoming aware, proceeds to being able to explore and inquire, and culminates in using and applying what has been learned. Obviously, children during the period of early childhood will not be able to comprehend the geography standards for physical systems. How could children, who believe the moon is theirs alone, and follows them around at night (Piaget, 1951), know and understand the physical systems standards?

Children can, however, develop an awareness of the idea that the earth rotates around the sun—not by using a model, as suggested in the standards, but through their own experiences with night and day, shadows, and seasons. Mitchell, whose ideas reflected the philosophy of John Dewey, believed curriculum content stemmed directly from children's interactions with their immediate environment. Advocating building the geography curriculum on the content of children's here-and-now lives, Mitchell (1934) wrote:

> The practical tasks for each school are to study the geographic relations in the environment into which their children are born and to watch the children's behavior in their environment, to note when they first discover relations and what they are. On the basis of these findings each school will make it's own curriculum for young children. (p. 12)

Huffman (1996) illustrated how, through informal and more formal experiences with the immediate environment, young children develop knowledge and understanding of the physical systems of our earth. She found that preschool children were able to observe the weather, record their observations, and share books about weather phenomena. Children studied rain and rainbows, coaxing some into being with a prism, a garden hose, and a mirror and pan of water. They learned that the prism worked well, while their other methods did not. They observed clouds, noticing movement and shapes, and read Christina Rossetti's poem "Clouds." As Mitchell (1934) pointed out, the children Huffman studied behaved very much like geographers, not only investigating their world and learning facts but also, more importantly, relating each fact to others and forming generalizations.

## CONCLUSION

Despite current research and discussion surrounding the teaching of history and the national geography standards, early childhood educators continue, as in the past, to be responsible for the creation of the social studies curriculum. Currently, the disagreements over what should be taught to young children in the field of social studies hampers, rather than facilitates, teachers' decision making. The field, comprised of diverse constituencies, offers teachers very different and often opposing ideas about what history and geography concepts young children should learn.

Then, too, both the history and geography standards fail to address the period of early childhood before entrance into kindergarten, ignoring the fact that the majority of children under the age of 5 are enrolled in some form of school. This omission may be due to the lack of involvement of the field of early childhood in the creation of the history and geography standards. Or it may reflect that fact that the field of early childhood remains as diverse as the field of social studies.

Despite the influential early childhood associations—the National Association for the Education of Young Children and the Association for Childhood Education International—and the large government focus on programs for young children, the field of early childhood remains splintered. Diverse constituencies—the federal and state governments, local school systems, churches, businesses, charitable associations, and others—present diverse opinions and perspectives on what children should be taught when.

Nevertheless, the noninvolvement of the early childhood education field in establishing standards for history and geography education is problematic for a number of reasons. First, the early childhood curriculum is an integrated curriculum. If early childhood educators had taken part in creating the standards, then perhaps there would be greater clarity about how geography, and to a lesser extent history, could be integrated into the entire curriculum.

Perhaps because early childhood educators were not consulted, the geography standards are unobtainable by children under the age of 7 or 8. To attempt to introduce young children, who are in the preoperational and concrete stages of mental development, to these abstract ideas holds potential danger. Wyner and Farquhar (1991), in their review of early childhood social studies in the *Handbook of Research on Social Studies Teacher and Learning,* cautioned against the pressures to learn more academics earlier at the expense of developmentally appropriate practice when making decisions about the curriculum. They stated that, "Preoperational children are pushed prematurely to perform concrete mental operations" (pp. 101–141). They suggested a curriculum that produced thoughtful, active learners with an emphasis on affect and social cognition. They believe that, "Awareness of recent research on children's cognitive, affective, and social development is critical for researchers and teachers working toward the improvement of teaching and learning in early childhood social studies" (p. 109). They conclude, "Curriculum developers and teachers with knowledge of cognitive development can design appropriate social learning experiences to enable young children to begin to think about and conceptualize their life experiences" (pp. 101–141).

If mastery of abstract, complex geography concepts is expected, children's learning will be superficial at best. Next is the issue of failure. Because the geography standards are unachievable by young children, children may believe themselves failures if asked to master them. It is well known that failure leads humans to distance themselves from the situation that led to failure (Thorndike, 1913). Thus young children who fail to master the geography concepts could distance themselves from the study of geography in the future.

In the future early childhood educators and social scientists could meet together and reach agreement about what social science concepts young children should learn and how these can best be introduced to them. Using Vygotsky's (1986) theories as a guide, early childhood educators, researchers, and social scientists together could identify what children already know of specific history and geography concepts, and then what they could know and understand with the guidance of an adult.

Bruner (1966) called such a meeting in the early 1960s, beginning the process of designing meaningful social studies curricula for young children. Perhaps it is time for both fields, early childhood education and social scientists, to revisit Bruner's work. Clearly, the identification of standards in the fields of history and geography, as well as the expectations for social studies learning delineated by the NCSS, provides the foundation for continual work. With insights from Bruner's earlier work, and guidance from the philosophy of Lucy Sprague Mitchell, the next step would be to identify the standards that are achievable for children from birth through age 7 or 8, and how best to arrange for children to do so.

## REFERENCES

Ashby, R., Lee, P., & Dickinson, A. (1997). How children explain the "why" of history: The CHATA research project on teaching history. *Social Education, 61,* 17–21.

Barth, J. (1996). NCSS and the nature of social studies. In J. Davis (Ed.), *NCSS in retrospect* (Bulletin No. 92) (pp. 9–20). Washington, DC: National Council for the Social Studies.

Barton, K. (1997). History—It can be elementary: An overview of elementary students' understanding of history. *Social Education, 61,* 13–16.

Barton, K., & Levstik, L. (1996). "Back when God was around and everything": Elementary children's understanding of historical time. *American Educational Research Journal, 33,* 419–454.

Bredekamp, S., & Rosegrant, T. (1995). *Reaching potentials: Transforming early childhood curriculum and assessment* (Vol. 2). Washington, DC: National Association for the Education of Young Children.

Bruner, J. (1960). *The process of education.* Cambridge, MA: Harvard University Press.

Bruner, J. (1966). *Toward a theory of instruction.* Cambridge, MA: Harvard University Press.

Downey, M., & Levstik, L. (1991). Teaching and learning history. In J. Shaver (Ed.), *Handbook of research on social studies teaching and learning* (pp. 400–410). New York: Macmillan.

Egan, K. (1989). Layers of historical understanding. *Theory and Research in Social Education, 17,* 280–294.

Egan, K. (1997). The arts as the basics of education. *Childhood Education, 73,* 346–349.

Ellis, A. (1998). *Teaching and learning elementary social studies* (6th ed.). Boston: Allyn & Bacon.

Ely, D. (1994). The world is a colorful place. *Journal of Geography, 93*(2), 101–102.

Geography Education Standards Project (GESP). *Geography for Life: National Standards—1994.* (1994). Washington, DC: Geography Education Standards Project.

Gutierrez, E. D. (1993). Hilltop geography for young children: Creating an outdoor learning environment. *Journal of Geography, 92,* 176–179.

Hallam, R. (1970). Piaget and thinking in history. In M. Ballard (Ed.), *New movements in the study and teaching of history* (pp. 217–242). Bloomington: Indiana University Press.

Huffman, A. B. (1996). Beyond the weather chart: Weathering new experiences. *Young Children, 51*(5), 34–38.

Jantz, R. K. (1976). Social studies in early childhood education. In C. Seefeldt (Ed.), *Curriculum for the preschool-primary child: A review of the research* (pp. 82–123). Columbus, OH: Merrill.

Jarolimek, J. (1996). NCSS and elementary social studies. In J. Davis (Ed.), *NCSS in retrospect* (Bulletin No. 92) (pp. 103–110). Washington, DC: National Council for the Social Studies.

Jarolimek, J., & Parker, W. C. (1993). *Social studies in elementary education* (9th ed.). New York: Macmillan.

Levstik, L. (1986). The relationship between historical response and narrative in the classroom. *Theory and Research in Social Education, 14,* 1–15.

Levstik, L. (1990). Research directions: Mediating content through literary texts. *Language Arts, 67,* 848–853.

Levstik, L. (1995). Narrative constructions: Cultural frames for history. *Social Studies, 86,* 113–116.

Levstik, L., & Barton, K. (1997a). "Any history is someone's history": Listening to multiple voices from the past. *Social Education, 61,* 48–51.

Levstik, L., & Barton, K. (1997b). *Doing history.* Hillsdale, NJ: Erlbaum.

Levstik, L., & Pappas, C. (1992). New directions for studying historical understanding. *Theory and Research in Social Education, 20,* 369–385.

Liben, L. S., & Yekel, C. A. (1996). Preschoolers' understanding of plan and oblique maps: The role of geometric and representational correspondence. *Child Development, 67,* 780–796.

Marzoff, D. P., & DeLoache, J. S. (1994). Transfer in young children's understanding spatial representations. *Child Development, 65,* 1–16.

Maxim, G. W. (1997). Developmentally appropriate map skills instruction. *Childhood Education, 73,* 206–211.

Mayer, R. H. (1995). Inquiry into place as an introduction to world geography—Starting with ourselves. *Social Studies, 86,* 74–77.

McKeown, M., & Beck, I. (1994). Making sense of accounts of history: Why young students don't and how they might. In C. Leinhardt, I. Beck, & C. Stainton (Eds.), *Teaching and learning in history* (pp. 1–26). Hillsdale, NJ: Erlbaum.

Mitchell, L. S. (1934). *Young geographers.* New York: Bank Street College.

Mostenthal, P. B., & Kirsch, S. (1990). Understanding general reference maps. *Journal of Reading, 34*(1), 60–63.

National Center for History in the Schools (NCHS). (1994). *National standards for history grades K–4.* Los Angeles, CA: Author.

National Council for the Social Studies (NCSS). (1994). *Expectations of excellence: Curriculum standards for the social studies.* Washington DC: Author.

Piaget, J. (1951). *The child's conception of the world.* London: Routledge.

Piaget, J. (1971). *Biology and knowledge.* Chicago: University of Chicago Press.

Piaget, J., & Inhelder, B. (1969). *The psychology of the child.* New York: Basic Books.

Rothwell, J. (1997). History making and the plains Indians. *Social Education, 61,* 4–9.

Seefeldt, C. (Ed.). (1992). *The early childhood curriculum: A review of current research* (2nd ed.). New York: Teachers College Press.

Seefeldt, C. (1993). History for young children. *Theory and Research in Social Education, 21,* 143–155.

Seefeldt, C. (1995). Transforming curriculum in social studies. In S. Bredekamp & T. Rosegrant (Eds.), *Reaching potentials: Transforming early childhood curriculum and assessment* (Vol. 2) (pp. 109–123). Washington, DC: National Association for the Education of Young Children.

Sleeper, M. (1975). A developmental framework for history education in adolescence. *School Review, 84,* 91–107.

Sowden, S. (1996). Mapping abilities of four-year old children in York, England. *Journal of Geography, 95,* 107–111.

Spieseke, A. (1963). Developing a sense of time and chronology. In H. McCarpenter (Ed.), *Skill development in social studies: 33rd* yearbook. Washington, DC: National Council for the Social Studies.

Thorndike, E. L. (1913). *Educational psychology: The psychology of learning.* New York: Teachers College Press.

Thornton, S. (1990). Should we be teaching history? *Theory and Research in Social Education, 18,* 53–60.

Thornton, S. (1996a). Contested terrain: Public policy, research, and the history curriculum. *Theory and Research in Social Education, 24,* 391–415.

Thornton, S. (1996b). NCSS: The early years. In J. Davis (Ed.), *NCSS in retrospect* (Bulletin No. 92) (pp. 1–8). Washington, DC: National Council for the Social Studies.

Thornton, S. (1997). First-hand study: Teaching history for understanding. *Social Education, 61,* 11–12.

Thornton, S., & Houser, N. (1997, June). The status of elementary social studies in Delaware: A view from the field. *Resources in Education,* pp. 132–139.

Thornton, S., & Vukelich, R. (1988). Effects of children's understanding of time concepts on historical understanding. *Theory and Research in Social Education, 16,* 69–82.

Trifonoff, K. M. (1995). Going beyond location: Thematic maps in early elementary grades. *Journal of Geography, 94,* 368–374.

Van Sledright, B. (1997). Can more be less? The depth-breadth dilemma in teaching American history. *Social Education, 61,* 38–41.

Vosniadow, S. (1994). Capturing and modeling the process of conceptual change. *Learning and Instruction, 4,* 45–69.

Vygotsky, L. (1986). *Thought and language.* Cambridge, MA: MIT Press.

Wyner, N., & Farquhar, E. (1991). Cognitive, emotional, and social development: Early childhood social studies. In J. Shaver (Ed.), *Handbook of research on social studies teaching and learning* (pp. 101–146). New York: Macmillan.

CHAPTER 8

# Research in Early Childhood Music and Movement Education

CHERIE K. STELLACCIO
MARIE MCCARTHY

ALL CHILDREN, from birth, demonstrate an intuitive aptitude for thinking in tonal and rhythmic patterns (Gordon, 1990). Because intuitive aptitude for music stabilizes at about age 9 (Gordon, 1989), the early childhood years are critical to the development of the child's potential for comprehending and producing music. In a rich musical environment with appropriate guidance from adults, the young child learns to perceive, imitate, and discriminate among *rhythm* and *tonal patterns* with increasing precision (for all italicized terms, see the glossary at the end of this chapter). Thus the child begins to form concepts of *musical syntax*. In the developmental years, while assimilating music concepts into personal music-making, the child prepares for a lifetime of understanding, performing, and enjoying music "as a musician" (Gordon, 1990, p. 37).

Research in early childhood music education provides an overview of the nature of musical performance and perception and of factors that influence children's developmental music aptitude. This literature review centers on studies that have expanded knowledge of how young children perform, perceive, and create music and thus develop their natural inclination to make music.

## MUSIC PERFORMANCE

### Vocal Development and Song Acquisition

Studies in the vocal development of young children are numerous, and more is known about how children's singing voices develop than about any other topic in early childhood music education (Levinowitz, 1991). Major studies of infant vocal development have been done by Wendrich (1981), Fox (1982), and Ries (1982). Results of these observations indicate that infants (3 to 4 months of age) begin to experiment with sound; they can match *pitches* of a rather wide range (Fox, 1982); and their vocal experimentation typically has descending *melodic contours*. Aural discrimination and the vocal ability to express it are present as early as 7 months (Ries, 1982), and a high degree of musical acculturation is evident at that time (Levinowitz, 1991).

One of the most popular topics for investigation is pitch accuracy, due to its importance in tuneful singing. Goetze (1985) found that children (kindergarten through grade 3) sing more nearly at pitch level when they sing on a neutral syllable rather than with a text. But in a similar study with 4- to 5-year-olds, Levinowitz (1989) reported no difference in rhythmic accuracy but improved tonal accuracy when singing with words.

Goetze and Horii (1989) found that children sing more nearly at pitch level when they sing individually rather than in a group. This finding points to the fact that successful individual singing may precede successful group singing. In a related study, Rutkowski (1996) determined that individual/small-group singing activities did have a positive effect on the vocal development and competence of kindergarten children.

Vocal development seems to demand consistent attention to numerous skills that all contribute to the development of pitch accuracy and singing competence. For example, Davidson (1985a) found that it normally takes 4 to 5 years of singing experience for a *scale* to become a useful scheme for the child. In his opinion, "scalar knowledge may be the capstone of a whole set of subskills" (p. 26).

A number of studies confirm that development of one vocal skill, such as pitch matching, does not necessarily affect other vocal skills (e.g., pitch discrimination, vocal range, *interval* production), nor does training in pitch perception lead to improved pitch accuracy in singing (Apfelstadt, 1984; Buckton, 1983; Flowers & Dunne-Sousa, 1990; Geringer, 1983; Ramsey, 1983; Roberts & Davies, 1975). In Geringer's (1983) study of preschoolers, there appeared to be no relationship between a child's ability to echo a pitch accurately (pitch matching) and success in pitch discrimination. Flowers and Dunne-Sousa (1990) found that the ability to maintain a *tonal center* in a song and the ability to echo pitch patterns appear to be largely separate skills with 3- to 5-year-olds.

In the area of song acquisition, landmark studies have been completed, many with the advantage of being longitudinal in nature. Gardner (1983) identified a specific sequence for song acquisition. From producing undulating melodic fragments at approximately 15 months, the child progresses to intentionally produced melodic intervals (major 2nd, minor 3rd) at 18 months. By 2½ years, intervals are expanded to include 4ths and 5ths, and spontaneous song becomes a feature but as yet lacks *tonality* and rhythmic regularity. Two-year-olds also intersperse fragments of learned songs in spontaneous song, and by 3 years of age, learned songs with a developed lyrical and rhythmic structure are dominant. At age 4, children are capable of retaining *lyrics* and rhythms for learned songs, and melodic contour is mastered. Children's ability to identify the *beat* and to maintain tonality across *phrases* develops around age 5, a finding that concurs with Davidson, McKernon, and Gardner (1981), who earlier had determined that by 5 years of age the sense of tonal stability becomes well established.

Davidson (1985a) studied nine children when they were 1 to 6 years of age and concluded that "the mature performance of a song requires the use of highly sophisticated knowledge and skills that have their origin in the preschool years" (p. 25). He identified three levels of song mastery: (1) the acquisition of words and rhythmic surface of the song, (2) the mastery of melodic contour without exact pitch relationships or tonal center, and (3) stabilization of pitches and interval relationships.

In a study of children aged 5 months to 5 years, Holohan (1987) observed three qualitatively different levels of music performance. At the first level, children perform discrete music elements (e.g., a pitch, a tonal or rhythm pattern, a movement) concurrently with a music stimulus. Children proceed at the second level to perform combinations of discrete music elements, but they lack tonal and rhythmic organization or syntax. Children at this level are increasingly capable of spontaneous performance in the absence of a music stimulus. At the third level, children's spontaneous performances become more coherent and organized. They demonstrate an awareness of relationships between sounds of music in memory and those being performed in the present. Holohan's study demonstrates that spontaneous music-making is an integral and significant part of early childhood musical development (Levinowitz, 1991).

## Rhythm and Movement

The nature of children's movement to music progresses from spontaneous pleasure responses (e.g., swaying, bouncing) in infancy to complex, dancelike movements with hand gestures between 4 and 6 years of age (Gilbert, 1979, 1981; Moog, 1976a; Rainbow, 1977; Rainbow & Owen, 1979). Although young children are stimulated to move to music, their movements often are not synchronized with music in response either to a prescribed steady beat (Rainbow, 1981; Sims, 1985), specific rhythmic qualities, or overall music affect (Holohan, 1987; Sims, 1985). When synchronized rhythmic movement among young children occurs, it is likely to relate to *tempo* or a prominent beat (Metz, 1989; Sims, 1985). Music performance tasks requiring synchronization and movement activities requiring eye–hand coordination are most challenging for young and physically or mentally handicapped children (Gilbert, 1983). Speech rhythms are easiest for the youngest children, keeping a steady beat with clapping or rhythm sticks is manageable for 4-year-olds, and synchronous tasks requiring large-muscle movement are most difficult for young children (Frega, 1979; Gilbert, 1981; High, 1987; Rainbow, 1977; Rainbow & Owen, 1979). Four- and five-year-olds have difficulty with simple motor rhythmic tasks at a fast tempo (Rainbow & Owen, 1979), and simultaneous tasks such as moving and singing present a challenge to these children (Holohan, 1987; Rainbow & Owen, 1979).

Sims (1985) found that when left to their own resources under minimally structured conditions, children tend not to utilize a full range of movement categories (locomotor, axial, stationary, nonmovement). Three-year-olds are likely to remain stationary while 4- and 5-year-olds tend to utilize locomotor movement. Girls are more likely than boys to move axially. Whatever the form, young children tend to limit their movement to repetition of a few patterns. Whether such movement behavior is attributable to fascination with movement repetition (Haselbach, 1971) or limited movement repertoire (Sims, 1985) is uncertain.

Research suggests that motor, cognitive, and perceptual skills are interrelated. In a longitudinal study of children ages 5 to 8, Gilbert (1983) found a strong correlation between performance on her Motoric Music Skills Test (MMST) and Gordon's (1979) test of rhythm and tonal perception. Lewis (1986) reported that intensive movement instruction had a positive effect on primary school children's perception of dynamics and melodic direction when listening to music.

Studies by Metz (1989) and Miller (1983) provide substantive information for guiding children's movement responses to music. Metz noted that up to age 4 children are inclined to imitate their peers. However, as children mature, a social "taboo" on peer copying without invitation develops naturally, and that promotes divergence. Adult modeling combined with verbal description and suggestion is most effective in generating differentiated and synchronized movement to music. Both Metz and

Miller suggest that music be carefully selected to support children's spontaneous movement response rather than forcing conformity to "arbitrarily selected musical elements" (Metz, 1989, p. 56).

## MUSIC PERCEPTION AND COGNITION

The development of perceptual and cognitive music skills requires the ability to perceive, discriminate, and recall aspects of the performance, such as *melody,* rhythm, timbre, or instruments. Ramsey (1983) points out that, just as visual perception changes as children's cognitive structures change and develop, auditory perception may also differ with age and experience. Children appear to develop the ability to respond to various elements of music in a sequential manner (Zimmerman, 1971). It is generally accepted that pitch and harmony concepts develop later than concepts of dynamics, timbre, tempo, and duration (Greenberg, 1976). Sims (1991) makes several important points regarding preschool children's listening abilities:

- Most young children may not be ready for music-listening tasks requiring attention to more than one element at a time.
- Children can easily learn to make and label single discriminations and are receptive to learning and using language to describe music.
- Children's ability to make discriminations based on their own performance may develop earlier than their ability to make discriminations in listening situations.

### Pitch

Several researchers have shown that infants are aware of and can discriminate differences in pitches and tonal patterns (Bridger, 1961; Chang & Trehub, 1977; Summers, 1984). In a developmental sequence for melodic information processing, Dowling (1982) suggests a movement from perception of gross features, such as melodic contour, to more precise features of tonality and interval. Sergeant (cited in Simons, 1986) lists pitch-related concept development in this order: pitch, melody, tonality, and harmony.

Studies of pitch discrimination and melodic perceptual abilities with preschoolers indicate that age is a factor in the development of perceptual accuracy (Jordan-DeCarbo, 1989; Ramsey, 1983). Ramsey (1983) concluded that preschool children do perceive contour and interval aspects of melody, and that the accuracy of perceptions increases with age. Webster and Schlentrich (1982) found that recognition of pitch direction improved with age, but nearly one-third of their 3- to 5-year-old subjects could not perform this discrimination.

Children's inability to communicate understanding of concepts such as melodic direction, register, contour, and interval size may be due more to response mode than to a lack of conceptual understanding (Webster & Schlentrich, 1982). Results of numerous studies indicate that performance-based response modes are better measures of pitch discrimination than verbal response (Hair, 1977, 1982; Scott, 1977; Webster & Schlentrich, 1982). Young children frequently confuse terms associated with musical pitch and with tempo and dynamics (high/up; low/down; loud/fast; quiet/slow) (Crowther & Durkin, 1982; McMahon, 1985; Van Zee, 1976; Young, 1982). Ability to deal verbally with concepts of pitch does not necessarily develop concurrently with children's ability to perceive and understand them. Training is necessary to bridge the two disparate abilities. For example, Wassum (1980) argues that the concept of tonality is a "learned" concept and recommends consistent teaching of songs and scale-singing to develop this concept.

Scott-Kassner (1992) makes the point that children's use of, or preference for, physical or gestural responses lends credence to "theories of the existence of verbal/tactile substructures that may help children mediate their musical experience." She also writes: "Perhaps children in [preschool] categories must physically or vocally replicate the musical stimuli to get at the substructure" (p. 636).

One of the last pitch-related concepts to develop is harmony. This may be due to the child's centered perception and inability to attend to more than one element at a time. Bridges (1965) studied children in grades K–3 and found a gradual development in harmonic discrimination ability. Moog (1976b) observed preschoolers' responses to dissonance and concluded that the child is "deaf" to harmony until at least age 6. Hair (1973), on the contrary, found that the majority (83%) of first-graders could identify pairs of chords as being the same or different. Bartlett and Dowling (1982) discovered that it is easier to distinguish between melodies from harmonically distant *keys* than from harmonically similar keys. Peery's (1993) results suggest that harmonic key becomes a part of "the cognitive-cultural structure that humans use to understand music at an early age" (p. 210).

## Rhythm

In the most general sense, rhythm is the temporal structure of music. Numerous studies establish aural perception as fundamental to children's understanding of rhythmic structures and their acquisition of musical rhythmic performance and rhythm reading (Bamberger, 1980, 1982; Davidson & Colley, 1987; Hildebrandt, 1985; Lehrdahl & Jackendorff, 1983; Smith, 1989; Upitis, 1985, 1987a, 1987b, 1987c).

Extensive Piagetian-based research of the 1960s, 1970s, and early 1980s (Hargreaves & Zimmerman, 1992) and research into the relationship and interaction of rhythm knowledge and skills with other cognitive theories and models (Davidson & Colley, 1987; Demorest, 1989, 1992; Lehrdahl & Jackendoff, 1981, 1983; Upitis, 1987a) attest to age-related increases in children's perception of rhythm structures (Davidson & Colley, 1987; Gilbert, 1981; Moog, 1976b; O'Hearn, 1984; Wang & Salzberg, 1984). Several studies outline a developmental sequence in concept formation from beat to rhythm pattern to *meter* that is manifest in both rhythm perception and performance (Cox, 1977; Jones, 1976; Serafine, 1975).

Musical training appears to have a differential effect on the perception of rhythm (Demorest, 1989). Musically inexperienced listeners attend more exclusively to rhythmic qualities over tonal qualities (Davidson, 1985b; Demorest, 1989; Monahan & Carterett, 1985; Moog, 1976a), and this appears to increase with age. However, among the musically trained, sensitivity to pitch and rhythm develop proportionately (Demorest, 1992; Demorest & Serlin, 1997; Dowling, 1988). It may be that sensitivity to rhythmic information develops through informal music experiences, whereas sensitivity to pitch requires more intensive training (Demorest, 1992; Demorest & Serlin, 1997). Noting a tendency to emphasize rhythmic activities in early school experiences, researchers recommend a shift in emphasis to pitch elements as children acquire experience and maturity (Demorest, 1989, 1992; Demorest & Serlin, 1997).

Children's capacity to discriminate tempo in music appears to be fundamental to their rhythmic perception, apprehension, and performance (Sheldon, 1994). Ability to perceive tempo differences emerges early (Lawton & Johnson, 1992) and likely is more related to general developmental differences (Mills, 1985; Moog, 1976b; Petzold, 1966; Wang & Salzberg, 1984) than to either motor differences (Miller & Eargle, 1990) or music training (Geringer & Madsen, 1984; Miller & Eargle, 1990; Sheldon, 1994; Wang, 1984). Accuracy in performing a steady beat and tempo is relative to a child's innate, personal tempo and stabilizes by third grade (P. Brown, 1981; Clynes, 1982; Petzold, 1966). Research to determine whether increasing or decreasing tempi are easier to discriminate is inconclusive (Britten, 1992; Geringer & Madsen, 1984; Madsen, 1979; Madsen, Duke, & Geringer, 1986; Miller & Eargle, 1990; Sheldon, 1994; Wang, 1984; Yarbrough, 1987), but convincing evidence exists to verify that tempo perception is affected by other elements within a music composition, especially the rhythm of the melody (Davidson & Colley, 1987; Duke, 1990; Kuhn, 1987; Kuhn & Booth, 1988; Sink, 1983; Wang, 1984).

Studies investigating children's rhythm response in a variety of psychomotor contexts provide more comprehensive understanding of rhythm development. Bennett (1991) found that when given a choice of modes, children can accurately perceive and perform quite complex patterns. However, their preferred mode for executing rhythmic patterns is to sing on a neutral syllable rather than tap or write using idiosyncratic forms of notation. Studies by Davidson and Colley (1987) and by Upitis (1987a) suggest the existence of a hierarchy of rhythmic perceptual skills. Before age 5 children's perception of rhythm is dependent on rhythmic patterns of the words of a song, and they are generally unable to notate even a basic steady beat. From this point children progress rapidly. By age 7 most children can recall a rhythmic pattern without the aid of text, and they are able to notate and perform steady beat and rhythmic patterns (Davidson & Colley, 1987; Upitis, 1987c). However, Upitis notes (1987a) that children most advanced in their understanding of rhythmic relationships have had extracurricular music training.

## AFFECTIVE DEVELOPMENT

The affective dimension of children's musical development encompasses appreciations, attitudes, interests, and preferences. Scott-Kassner (1992) makes a distinction between "affect" as the emotional aspect of responding to music and "preference" as the selection of certain stimuli over others. Both affect and preference, she points out, may or may not imply valuing. For the purpose of this discussion, musical preference is regarded as an integral component of affective learning while simultaneously recognizing this distinction.

Historically, the status of music in early childhood curriculum owes much to its perceived power to influence feelings and emotions (McDonald & Simons, 1989). Kalliopuska and Ruokonen (1986) report that listening to music is similar to emotional empathy in that the listener must temporarily try to experience feelings simulated by the music, thus facilitating social interaction. In a similar vein, Saffle (1983) believes music can be a vehicle for communicating information about aesthetics from different cultures. It is important to acknowledge that the affective dimension of music learning "does not occur in a vacuum but is connected with cognitive and perceptual development" (Zimmerman, 1971, p. 210). Thus, when one considers the formation of attitudes and values in early childhood music education, it includes the development of music concepts and skills that facilitate understanding and perception of music.

Studies of affective response to music are sparse, partly due to the difficulty of investigating this area of musical response with young children. Infants are reported to have shown affective reactions to music (Michel, 1973; Moog, 1976b; Tims cited in McDonald & Simons, 1989). Nelson (1985) attempted to apply Parson's theory of aesthetic growth in the area of music with 3- to 17-year-olds and found a high correlation between the quality of aesthetic response and age. The trend in responding was from egocentric standards in the young children to more external standards in the older ones. Gardner and colleagues (Gardner, Winner, & Kircher, 1975) and Terwogt and Grinsven (1988) report that preschoolers can understand the emotional, or affective, meaning of music, while Peery (1993) argues that they have considerable ability to understand the affective meaning of music (happy, sad, angry, afraid) in ways similar to adults (p. 210).

Approaching the root problem of investigating aesthetic responsiveness with young children, McMahon (1987) tested 3- to 5-year-olds on their ability to make and justify aesthetic choices with visual, tactile, and auditory musical stimuli. She found that children could more easily verbalize their responses to objects in the tactile and visual realm than the auditory.

Studies of the development of musical preferences are numerous, and many include the early childhood years. Based on research findings of several studies, Peery (1993) identified three frequently occurring hypotheses regarding the formation of musical preferences: music training or repeated exposure to particular music, social influences, and certain qualities inherent in the music, particularly style.

The use of repetitive listening as a strategy for developing or modifying musical preference has been employed many times in research studies. Schuckert and McDonald (1968) were not able to influence preschoolers' musical preferences significantly solely by exposure to less preferred music; however, the study was limited to four sessions and children listened individually to the less preferred music while they examined such materials as puzzles. Not only is short-range exposure unsatisfactory for developing preference for a particular music, but merely exposing children to music is not sufficient in developing preferences.

A second hypothesis used in studying the formation of musical preference is rooted in social learning theory. Approval and support by adults and teachers have a positive influence on what music children select or prefer (Callihan & Cummings, 1985; Dorow, 1977; Greer, Dorow, & Hanser, 1973; Greer, Dorow, Wachhaus, & White, 1973). Greer, Dorow and Hanser (1973) concluded that children can be encouraged to listen to symphonic music over rock or "white noise" by listening with an adult who shows approval. A. Brown (1978), in comparing the effect of televised lessons to lessons taught by a teacher, also confirmed the importance of the physical presence of adults interacting with children and music in the formulation of musical preferences. Peery and Peery (1986) studied preschool children to determine the effects of positive social experience on musical preference. An experimental group received 10 months of weekly 45–minute classes. When exposed to classical music in a variety of activities and to positive reinforcement responses, experimental group children retained their enjoyment of all kinds of music, whereas, by the end of the same period, a control group had begun to show preferences for popular music.

Finally, the formation of musical preference is influenced by qualities inherent in the music, most particularly style (Peery & Peery, 1986). Preschoolers display an openness to all musical styles (Sims, 1986)—or at least have an equal preference for popular and classical styles (Greer et al., 1974; Peery & Peery, 1986; Sims, 1986). As children get older, popular music is increasingly preferred to classical music (Greer et al., 1974; LeBlanc, 1979). It is widely accepted that a trend toward a preference for rock music over nonrock music begins during the fifth year of age (Greer et al., 1974; Peery & Peery, 1986) and seems to become more established as children get older (May, 1985). Peery and Peery (1986) believe that "what you don't hear, you come to like less well" is a contributing factor to the development of stylistic bias. This bias, they suggest, can be avoided by exposing children to music appreciation training in the preschool classroom.

Children are sensitive to musical timbre from an early age, and this element of music enters into their listening preferences and responses. Michel (1973) reported that an infant can distinguish between two different timbres at age 2 or 3 months after a small number of repetitions. Fullard (1967) showed how 4-year-olds could identify instruments after instruction. Loucks (1974) found a significant increase in timbre discrimination ability with age. Scott (1977) studied the effects of timbral preference on the ability of preschoolers to classify differing pitch stimuli. Children's preference for one type of sound does not appear to interfere with their ability to classify musical pitches. Young children's sensitivity to musical timbre indicates that instruction in this element may be a useful and efficient way of approaching music listening and developing music appreciation and understanding.

Other strategies for effectively involving young children in music-listening activities and/or shaping their music preferences include use of props to act out music while listening (Callihan & Cummings, 1985). Similarly, Sims (1986) found that children are more attentive when given a hand movement activity in which to participate. She recommends that "listening experiences for young children should be characterized by active student involvement, and should be presented by the teacher with high levels of eye contact and expressiveness" (Sims, 1991, p. 7).

## MUSICAL CREATIVITY AND PLAY

Musical creativity develops under a variety of conditions and is revealed in a variety of behaviors (Webster, 1992). One body of research pertaining to creativity centers on children's musical compositions and improvisations as windows to musical thought (Bamberger, 1986; Brand & Strauss, 1997; Kratus, 1985, 1989; Levi, 1991). Another body of research more specific to the very young child investigates musical play as a factor in the development of creative thought.

Children's play is a creative venture (Vandenberg, 1980). A connection between children's play and divergent-thinking tasks is well established (Dansky & Silverman, 1973; Li, 1978). The Pillsbury studies stand as a landmark to the exploration of children's creative musical development through play. In their unhampered musical play, children of the Pillsbury Foundation School (aged 1 through 8) revealed a natural inventiveness in their chanting, singing, and instrumental exploration, from which Moorhead and Pond (1978) determined fundamental characteristics of creative musical behavior in young children. The authors reported that children used instruments to test and compare sounds as they explored wide intervals, pitch contrasts, and tone colors. In rhythmical speech phrases, chanting and singing that occur spontaneously in play activities, children demonstrated an innate musicality, especially a sense of function and form (repetition and contrast of musical idea), which is generative and continues to develop through their musical improvisations.

A small number of studies have been conducted that record the nature and properties of children's musical play. Tarnowski and Leclerc (1994) observed emerging musical behavior in the free-play of 38 children (aged 4 through 5). Children engaged primarily in spontaneous vocal and rhythmic movement behaviors to describe, act out, or express feelings about their nonmusical play activities. Of vocal behaviors, the greatest number were extemporaneous, original songs that children sang while engaged in other play activities. Other spontaneous vocal behaviors were standard songs that children had learned in more formal settings;

vocal explorations and inflections such as sounds to depict animals, machines, or human actions; rhythmic speech patterns; and chants in a singsong *sol-mi* or *sol-mi-la-sol-mi* pattern made up to express self-actions or respond to the play-acts of other children. Rhythmic movements included full body movement and moving a play object in a rhythmic way.

Observations of preschoolers' play behaviors confirm that children, in their natural settings, spontaneously engage in frequent vocal, instrumental, and movement play in a variety of forms relative to different social contexts (Moorhead & Pond, 1978; Shelley & Foley, 1979). When materials and sound sources are provided, children engage in greater numbers of spontaneous musical play behaviors than in nonmusical play settings (Littleton, 1991). It is unfortunate, then, that surveys of preschool music programs indicate that few opportunities for experimenting with musical sound are made available to children (Golden, 1990; Tarnowski & Barrett, 1992) when an environment conducive to free exploration of sound and sound construction can be readily established in preschool settings (Shelley, 1981).

Children's musical play is important to acquisition of vocal and rhythmic skills in young children (Davidson et al., 1981; Littleton, 1991), but play opportunities in which musical behaviors can evolve are often sacrificed to teacher-directed activities designed to accomplish the goals of an established curricular program (Dorman, 1990; Littleton, 1991; Shehan-Campbell, 1990). Rohwer (1997) identified several conditions that restrain creativity. They include surveillance, excessive reward systems, competition, too much teacher control, restriction of choice in activities, time limits, and "the burden of expectation" (p. 10). Similarly, Tarnowski and Leclerc (1994) investigated the effects of four adult–child interaction styles on the musical play of preschoolers. After various forms of vocal play were modeled, the children were observed in free-play time with puppets. Of 120 musical play behaviors observed, the largest number of spontaneous incidents occurred when adults watched but did not enter into the play. In three categories where adults were partners in initiating or directing children's musical play activities, the number of spontaneous play incidents was inversely proportional to the degree of adult involvement. Noting that children in the more adult-directed activities demonstrated concern for "correct" actions and sounds, Tarnowski and Leclerc (1994) concluded that, in general, adult-directed activities encourage convergent thinking and minimize capacity to engage in divergent musical explorations and constructions.

Concerned with the pervasiveness of teacher-directed learning, Pond (1981) wrote: "Unless instruction and pedagogical disciplines could be creatively related to the emergent needs that the children's discovery of sound [bring] to light, there [is] no possibility that . . . the life-giving reality of music" could be accomplished (p. 4). Pond's words remind the educator that creativity, a trait valued not only in music but in "many aspects of life" (Rohwer, 1997, p. 10), can flower in the early years from a musically rich environment in which children are encouraged to explore their creative options.

## CLOSING REMARKS

The musical impulse is strong in young children. The primary years of nurturing musical potential are the infant and early childhood years, while music aptitude is still developing. It is imperative to use the child's natural musical impulses to sing, to move, and to play with sound to build upon and respond to their musical spontaneity.

Research findings are providing vital information for sequencing early childhood music curricula in which young children develop musical perception and cognition, and acquire music skills and musical values. However, important questions are still underresearched. For example, we know that children begin to develop preferences for popular music at 5 to 6 years of age. How can we as teachers maintain their openness to musical styles, and what impact does exposure to a variety of world musics have on developing musical preferences? More needs to be known about the relationship between conceptual/cognitive development and skill development, such as why there seems to be little carryover from developing concepts of pitch to pitch accuracy in singing. Other areas in need of further research include the relationship between vocal development and social skill development; the role of language in the development of music perception; and the transition from elemental musical play to refined creative performance.

## GLOSSARY

**Beat.** The steady, underlying pulse present in most music.
**Interval.** The distance between two pitches.
**Key.** Identical with *scale;* that which determines the relationship of all pitches contained in a music composition.
**Lyrics.** The words or text of a song.
**Melody.** An organized succession of pitches.
**Melodic contour.** The shape or outline of a succession of pitches determined by tonal movement from high to low/low to high.

**Meter.** The grouping of beats in music.

**Musical syntax.** Orderly arrangement of tonal and rhythmic elements in music.

**Phrase.** A musical statement with a distinct beginning and a distinct ending, comparable to a clause in language.

**Pitch.** The "highness" or "lowness" of a musical tone as determined by the number of vibrations per second.

**Rhythm.** The organization of the duration of sound.

**Scale.** A pattern of pitches arranged in ascending and descending order as determined by a specified order of half-steps and whole steps.

**Tempo.** The speed at which musical sound progresses in time.

**Tonal center.** The central tone of a key and the first tone of a scale.

**Tonality.** The relationship of tones in a scale to the tonal center.

**Tonal pattern.** A distinctive succession of pitches that becomes a model or plan used in organizing a musical composition.

## REFERENCES

Apfelstadt, H. (1984). Effects of melodic perception instruction on pitch discrimination and vocal accuracy of kindergarten children. *Journal of Research in Music Education, 32*(1), 15–24.

Bamberger, J. (1980). Cognitive structuring in the apprehension and description of simple rhythms. *Archives de psychologie, 48,* 171–199.

Bamberger, J. (1982). Revisiting children's drawings of simple rhythms: A function of reflection-in-action. In S. Strauss (Ed.), *U-shaped behavioral growth* (pp. 191–226). New York: Academic Press.

Bamberger, J. (1986). Cognitive issues in the development of musically gifted children. In R. J. Sternberg & J. E. Davidson (Eds.), *Conceptions of giftedness* (pp. 388–413). Cambridge, UK: Cambridge University Press.

Bartlett, J. C., & Dowling, W. J. (1982). The recognition of transposed melodies: A key-distance effect in developmental perspective. *Journal of Exceptional Psychology: Human Perception and Performance, 6,* 501–515.

Bennett, P. D. (1991). Children's pattern perception, accuracy, and preference in three response modes. *Journal of Research in Music Education, 38*(4), 294–301.

Brand, E., & Strauss, S. (1997, April). *Children's mental model of their own learning: Implications for teachers.* Paper presented at a symposium on *Innovations in Music Teacher Education,* University of Oklahoma, Norman.

Bridger, W. H. (1961). Sensory habituation and discrimination in the human neonate. *American Journal of Psychiatry, 117,* 991–996.

Bridges, V. (1965). *An exploratory study of the harmonic discrimination ability of children in kindergarten through grade three in two selected schools.* Unpublished doctoral dissertation, Ohio State University, Columbus.

Britten, R. V. (1992). Perceptions in conducting: Accuracy in detecting modulated beat. *Bulletin of the Council for Research in Music Education, 113,* 1–8.

Brown, A. (1978). Effects of televised instruction on student music selection, music skills, and attitudes. *Journal of Research in Music Education, 26*(4), 445–455.

Brown, P. (1981). An inquiry into the origins of tempo behaviour—Part II: Experimental work. *Psychology of Music, 9,* 32–34.

Buckton, R. (1983). *Sing a song of six-year-olds.* Wellington, New Zealand: New Zealand Council for Educational Research.

Callihan, D. J., & Cummings, D. (1985). Expanding the music listening preferences of 3- and 4-year-olds: Fostering recognition of and responsiveness to selected works of music. In J. Boswell (Ed.), *The young child and music* (pp. 79–82). Reston, VA: Music Educators National Conference.

Chang, H. W., & Trehub, S. E. (1977). Auditory processing of relational information by young infants. *Journal of Experimental Child Psychology, 24,* 324–335.

Clynes, M. (1982). *Music, mind, and brain.* New York: Plenum.

Cox, M. O., Sr. (1977). *A descriptive analysis of the response to beat, meter and rhythm pattern by children, grades one to six.* Unpublished doctoral dissertation, University of Wisconsin, Madison.

Crowther, B., & Durkin, K. (1982). Towards an applied psycholinguistic study of musical concept development. In Proceedings of the Ninth International Seminar on Research in Music Education [Special issue]. *Psychology of Music, 10,* 82–85.

Dansky, J. L., & Silverman, I. W. (1973). Effects of play on associational fluency in preschool-aged children. *Developmental Psychology, 9,* 38–43.

Davidson, L. (1985a). Preschool children's tonal knowledge: Antecedents of scale. In J. Boswell (Ed.), *The young child and music* (pp. 25–40). Reston, VA: Music Educators National Conference.

Davidson, L. (1985b). Tonal structures of children's early songs. *Music Perception, 2,* 361–374.

Davidson, L., & Colley, B. (1987). Children's rhythmic development from age 5 to 7: Performance, notation, and reading of rhythmic patterns. In J. C. Peery, I. W. Peery, & T. W. Draper (Eds.), *Music and child development* (pp. 107–136). New York: Springer-Verlag.

Davidson, L., McKernon, P., & Gardner, H. (1981). The acquisition of song: A developmental approach. In *Documentary report of the Ann Arbor symposium: National Symposium on the Application of Psychology to the Teaching and Learning of Music* (pp. 301–317). Reston, VA: Music Educators National Conference.

Demorest, S. M. (1989). An information integration approach to modeling developmental differences in music cognition (Doctoral dissertation, University of Wisconsin, Madison). (University Microfilms No. 8923368)

Demorest, S. M. (1992). Information integration theory: An approach to the study of cognitive development in music. *Journal of Research in Music Education, 40,* 126–138.

Demorest, S. M., & Serlin, R. C. (1997). The integration of pitch and rhythm in musical judgment: Testing age-related trends in novice listeners. *Journal of Research in Music Education, 45,* 67–79.

Dorman, P. E. (1990). The importance of musical play centers for young children. *General Music Today, 3*(3), 15–17.

Dorow, L. G. (1977). The effect of teacher approval/disapproval ratios on student music selection and concert attentiveness. *Journal of Research in Music Education, 25,* 32–40.

Dowling, W. J. (1982). Melodic information processing and its development. In D. Deutsch (Ed.), *The psychology of music* (pp. 413–429). New York: Academic Press.

Dowling, W. J. (1988). Tonal structure and children's early learning of music. In J. A. Sloboda (Ed.), *Generative processes in music: The psychology of performance, improvisation, and composition* (pp. 113–128). Oxford, UK: Clarendon.

Duke, R. A. (1990). Beat and tempo in music: Differences in teachers' and students' perceptions. *Update: Applications of Research in Music Education, 9*(1), 8–12.

Flowers, P. J., & Dunne-Souse, D. (1990). Pitch-pattern accuracy, tonality, and vocal range in preschool children's singing. *Journal of Research in Music Education, 38*(2), 102–114.

Fox, D. B. (1982). *The pitch range and contour of infant vocalizations.* Unpublished doctoral dissertation, Ohio State University, Columbus.

Frega, A. L. (1979). Rhythmic tasks with three-, four-, and five-year-old children. *Bulletin of the Council for Research in Music Education, 59,* 32–34.

Fullard, W. G., Jr. (1967). Operant training of aural musical discriminations with preschool children. *Journal of Research in Music Education, 15*(3), 201–209.

Gardner, H. (1983). *Frames of mind.* New York: Basic Books.

Gardner, H., Winner, E., & Kircher, J. (1975). Children's conceptions of the arts. *Journal of Aesthetic Education, 9*(3), 60–77.

Geringer, J. M. (1983). The relationship of pitch-matching and pitch-discrimination abilities of preschool and fourth-grade students. *Journal of Research in Music Education, 31*(2), 93–99.

Geringer, J. M., & Madsen, C. K. (1984). Pitch and tempo discrimination in recorded orchestral music among musicians and non-musicians. *Journal of Research in Music Education, 32,* 195–204.

Gilbert, J. P. (1979). Assessment of motoric music skill development in young children: Test construction and evaluation procedures. *Psychology of Music, 7*(2), 3–12.

Gilbert, J. P. (1981). Motoric music skill development in young children: A longitudinal investigation. *Psychology of Music, 9*(1), 21–25.

Gilbert, J. P. (1983). A comparison of the motor music skills of nonhandicapped and learning disabled children. *Journal of Research in Music Education, 31*(2), 147–155.

Goetze, M. (1985). *Factors affecting accuracy in children's singing.* Unpublished doctoral dissertation, University of Colorado, Boulder.

Goetze, M., & Horii, Y. (1989). A comparison of the pitch accuracy of group and individual singing in young children. *Bulletin of the Council for Research in Music Education, 99,* 57–73.

Golden, K. M. (1990, March). *An examination of the uses of music in selected licensed preschools in the state of Ohio.* Paper presented at the meeting of the Music Educators National Conference, Washington, DC.

Gordon, E. (1979). *Primary measure of music audiation.* Chicago: G.I.A. Publications.

Gordon, E. E. (1989). *Learning sequences in music.* Chicago: G.I.A. Publications, Inc.

Gordon, E. E. (1990). *A music learning theory for newborn and young children.* Chicago: G.I.A. Publications.

Greenberg, M. (1976). Research in early childhood education: A survey with recommendations. *Bulletin of the Council for Research in Music Education, 45,* 1–20.

Greer, R. D., Dorow, L., & Hanser, S. (1973). Music discrimination training and the music selection behavior of nursery and primary level children. *Bulletin of the Council for Research in Music Education, 35,* 30–43.

Greer, R. D., Dorow, L. G., & Randall, A. (1974). Music listening preferences of elementary school children. *Journal of Research in Music Education, 22,* 284–291.

Greer, R. D., Dorow, L., Wachhaus, G., & White, E. R. (1973). Adult approval and students' music selection behavior. *Journal of Research in Music Education, 21,* 345–354.

Hair, H. I. (1973). The effect of training on the harmonic discrimination of first-grade children. *Journal of Research in Music Education, 21*(1), 85–90.

Hair, H. I. (1977). Discrimination of tonal direction on verbal and nonverbal tasks by first grade children. *Journal of Research in Music Education, 25*(3), 197–210.

Hair, H. I. (1982). Microcomputer tests of aural and visual directional patterns. *Psychology of Music, 10*(2), 26–31.

Hargreaves, D. J., & Zimmerman, P. F. (1992). Developmental theories of music learning. In R. Colwell (Ed.), *Handbook of Research on Music Teaching and Learning* (pp. 377–391). New York: Schirmer.

Haselbach, B. (1971). *Dance education.* London: Schott & Co.

High, L. (1987). Effects of selected rhythmic teaching strategies on beat performance skills of kindergarten children (Doctoral dissertation, University of North Carolina, Greensboro). *Dissertation Abstracts International, 43,* 420A.

Hildebrandt, C. (1985). *A developmental study of children's representations of simple rhythms.* Unpublished doctoral dissertation, University of California, Berkeley.

Holohan, J. M. (1987). Toward a theory of music syntax: Some observations of music babble in young children. In I. W. Peery, J. C. Peery, & T. W. Draper (Eds.), *Music and Child Development* (pp. 96–106). New York: Springer Verlag.

Jones, R. L. (1976). The development of the child's conception of meter in music. *Journal of Research in Music Education, 24*(3), 142–155.

Jordan-DeCarbo, J. (1989). The effect of pretraining conditions and age on pitch discrimination ability of preschool children. *Journal of Research in Music Education, 37*(2), 132–145.

Kalliopuska, M., & Ruokonen, I. (1986). Effects of music education on development of holistic empathy. *Perceptual and Motor Skills, 62,* 187–191.

Kratus, J. (1985). *Rhythm, melody, motive, and phrase characteristics of original songs by children aged five to thirteen.* Unpublished doctoral dissertation, Northwestern University, Evanston.

Kratus, J. (1989). A time analysis of the compositional processes used by children ages 7 to 11. *Journal of Research in Music Education, 12*(1), 5–20.

Kuhn, T. L. (1987). The effect of tempo, meter, and melodic complexity on the perception of tempo. In C. K. Madsen & C. A. Prickett (Eds.), *Applications of research in music behavior* (pp. 165–174). Tuscaloosa: University of Alabama Press.

Kuhn, T. L., & Booth, G. D. (1988). The effect of melodic activity, tempo change, and audible beat on tempo perception of elementary school students. *Journal of Research in Music Education, 36,* 140–155.

Lawton, J. T., & Johnson, A. (1992). Effects of advance organizer instruction on preschool children's learning of musical concepts. *Bulletin of the Council for Research in Music Education, 111,* 35–48.

LeBlanc, A. (1979). Generic style music preferences of fifth-grade students. *Journal of Research in Music Education, 27,* 255–271.

Lehrdahl, F., & Jackendoff, R. (1981). On the theory of grouping and metre. *Musical Quarterly, 67,* 470–506.

Lehrdahl, F., & Jackendoff, R. (1983). *A generative theory of tonal music.* Cambridge, MA: MIT Press.

Levi, R. (1991). *A field investigation of the composing processes used by second-grade children creating original language and music pieces.* Unpublished doctoral dissertation, Case Western Reserve University, Cleveland, OH.

Levinowitz, L. M. (1989). An investigation of preschool children's comparative capability to sing songs with and without words. *Bulletin of the Council for Research in Music Education, 100,* 14–19.

Levinowitz, L. M. (1991). Selected references on vocal development in early childhood during the 1980's. *Music in Early Childhood: A Research Journal, 1*(1), 12–17.

Lewis, B. E. (1986). *The effect of movement-based instruction on the aural perception skills of first and third-graders.* Unpublished doctoral dissertation, Indiana University, Bloomington.

Li, A. K. F. (1978). Effects of play on novel responses of preschool children. *Alberta Journal of Educational Research, 24,* 31–36.

Littleton, D. (1991). Influence of play settings on preschool children's music and play behaviors (Doctoral dissertation, University of Texas at Austin). *Dissertation Abstracts International, 52-4,* 1198A.

Louks, D. G. (1974). *The development of an instrument to measure instrumental timbre concepts of four-year-old and five-year-old children: A feasibility study.* Unpublished doctoral dissertation, Ohio State University, Columbus.

Madsen, C. K. (1979). Modulated beat discrimination among musicians and nonmusicians. *Journal of Research in Music Education, 27,* 57–67.

Madsen, C. K., Duke, R. A., & Geringer, J. M. (1986). The effect of speed alteration on tempo note selection. *Journal of Research in Music Education, 34,* 101–110.

May, W. V. (1985). Musical style preferences and aural discrimination skills of primary grade school children. *Journal of Research in Music Education, 32*(1), 7–22.

McDonald, D. T., & Simons, G. M. (1989). *Musical growth and development: Birth through six.* New York: Schirmer.

McMahon, O. (1985). Young children's perceptions of the dimensions of sound. *Bulletin of the Council for Research in Music Education, 85,* 131–139.

McMahon, O. (1987). An exploration of aesthetic awareness in preschool age children. *Bulletin of the Council for Research in Music Education, 91,* 97–102.

Metz, E. (1989). Movement as a musical response among preschool children. *Journal of Research in Music Education, 37*(1), 48–60.

Michel, P. (1973). The optimum development of musical ability in the first years of life. *Psychology of Music, 1,* 14–20.

Miller, L. (1983). Music in early childhood: Neutralistic observation of young children's musical behavior (Doctoral dissertation, University of Kansas). *Dissertation Abstracts International, 44,* 3316A.

Miller, L. K., & Eargle, A. (1990). The contributions of development versus musical training to simple tempo discrimination. *Journal of Research in Music Education, 38,* 294–301.

Mills, J. I. (1985). Some developmental aspects of aural perception. *Bulletin of the Council for Research in Music Education, 85,* 126–131.

Monahan, C. B., & Carterette, E. C. (1985). Pitch and rhythm as determinants of musical spaces. *Music Perception, 3,* 1–32.

Moog, H. (1976a). The development of musical experience in children of pre-school age. *Psychology of Music, 4*(2), 38–45.

Moog, H. (1976b). *The musical experience of the pre-school child.* London: Schott.

Moorhead, G., & Pond, D. (1978). *Music for young children.* Santa Barbara: Pillsbury Foundation for the Advancement of Music Education. (Reprinted from 1941–1951 edition).

Nelson, D. J. (1985). Trends in the aesthetic responses of children to the musical experience. *Journal of Research in Music Education, 33*(3), 193–203.

O'Hearn, R. (1984). An investigation of the response to change in music events by children in grades one, three and five. Unpublished doctoral dissertation, University of Wisconsin, Madison.

Peery, J. C. (1993). Music in early childhood education. In B. Spodek (Ed.), *Handbook of research in the education of young children* (pp. 271–244). New York: Macmillan.

Peery, J. C., & Peery, I. W. (1986). Effects of exposure to classical music on the musical preferences of preschool children. *Journal of Research in Music Education, 34*(1), 24–33.

Petzold, R. (1966). *Auditory perception of musical sounds by children in the first six grades* (Cooperative Research Project No. 1051). Madison: University of Wisconsin.

Pond, D. (1981). A composer's study of young children's innate musicality. *Bulletin of the Council for Research in Music Education, 68,* 1–12.

Rainbow, E. L. (1977). A longitudinal investigation of the rhythmic ability of preschool age children. *Bulletin of the Council for Research in Music Education, 50,* 55–61.

Rainbow, E. (1981). A final report on a three-year investigation of the rhythmic abilities of preschool aged children. *Bulletin of the Council for Research in Music Education, 66–67,* 69–73.

Rainbow, E. L., & Owen, D. (1979). A progress report on a three-year investigation of the rhythmic ability of preschool age children. *Bulletin of the Council for Research in Music Education, 59,* 84–86.

Ramsey, J. H. (1983). The effects of age, singing ability, and instrumental experiences on preschool children's melodic perception. *Journal of Research in Music Education, 31*(2), 133–145.

Ries, N. L. (1982). *An analysis of the characteristics of infant-child singing expressions.* Unpublished doctoral dissertation, Arizona State University, Tempe, AZ.

Roberts, E., & Davies, A. D. M. (1975). Poor pitch singing: Response of monotone singers to a program of remedial training. *Journal of Research in Music Education, 23*(4), 227–239.

Rohwer, D. A. (1997). The challenges of teaching and assessing creative activities. *Update, Applications of Research in Music Education, 15*(2), 8–11.

Rutkowski, J. (1996). The effectiveness of individual/small-group singing activities on kindergartners' use of singing voice and developmental music aptitude. *Journal of Research in Music Education, 44*(4), 353–368.

Saffle, M. (1983). Aesthetic education in theory and practice: A review of recent research. *Bulletin of the Council for Research in Music Education, 74,* 22–38.

Schuckert, R. F., & McDonald, R. L. (1968). An attempt to modify the musical preferences of preschool children. *Journal of Research in Music Education, 16*(1), 39–44.

Scott, C. R. (1977). *Pitch perception formation in preschool children.* Unpublished doctoral dissertation, University of Washington, Seattle.

Scott-Kassner, C. (1992). Research on music in early childhood. In R. Colwell (Ed.), *Handbook of Research on Music Teaching and Learning* (pp. 633–650). Reston, VA: Music Educators National Conference.

Serafine, M. L. (1975). *A measure of meter conservation in music based on Piaget's theory.* Unpublished doctoral dissertation, University of Florida, Tallahassee.

Shehan-Campbell, P. (1990). The significance of musical play in early childhood. *General Music Today 3*(2), 19–20.

Sheldon, D. A. (1994). Effects of tempo, musical experience, and listening modes on tempo modulation perception. *Journal of Research in Music Education, 42*(3), 190–202.

Shelley, S. (1981). Investigating the musical capabilities of young children. *Bulletin of the Council for Research in Music Education, 68,* 26–34.

Shelley, S. J., & Foley, J. R. (1979). Observing the nature of young children's musicality. *Current Issues in Music Education: Music of Young Children, 12,* 44–54.

Simons, G. (1986). Early childhood musical development: A survey of selected research. *Bulletin of the Council for Research in Music Education, 86,* 36–52.

Sims, W. (1985). Young children's creative movement to music: Categories of movement, rhythmic characteristics, and reactions to changes. *Contributions to Music Education, 12,* 42–50.

Sims, W. L. (1986). The effect of high versus low teacher affect and passive versus active student activity during music listening on preschool children's attention, piece preference, time spent listening, and piece recognition. *Journal of Research in Music Education, 34*(3), 173–191.

Sims, W. L. (1988). Movement responses of pre-school children, primary grade children, and pre-service classroom teachers to characteristics of musical phrases. *Psychology of Music, 16,* 110–127.

Sims, W. L. (1991). Research on music listening in early childhood. *Music in Early Childhood: A Research Journal, 1*(1), 5–7.

Sink, P. E. (1983). Effects of rhythmic and melodic alterations on rhythmic perception. *Journal of Research in Music Education, 31,* 101–113.

Smith, K. C. (1989). *The representation of musical rhythm by children and adults.* Unpublished doctoral dissertation, Queen's University, Kingston, Ontario.

Summers, E. K. (1984). *Categorization and conservation of melody in infants.* Unpublished doctoral dissertation, University of Washington, Seattle.

Tarnowski, S. M., & Barrett, J. R. (1992, April). *A survey of preschool music programs in Wisconsin daycare centers and preschools.* Paper presented at the meeting of the Music Educators National Conference, New Orleans.

Tarnowski, S. M. & Leclerc, J. (1994). Musical play of preschoolers and teacher–child interaction. *Update, Applications of Research in Music Education, 13*(1), 9–16.

Terwogt, M. M., & Grinsven, F. V. (1988). Recognition of emotions in music by children and adults. *Perceptual and Motor Skills, 67,* 697–698.

Upitis, R. (1985). *Children's understanding of rhythm: The relationship between development and musical training.* Unpublished doctoral dissertation, Harvard University, Cambridge, MA.

Upitis, R. (1987a). Children's understanding of rhythm: The relationship between development and musical training. *Psychomusicology, 7,* 41–60.

Upitis, R. (1987b). A child's development of musical notation through composition: A case study. *Arts and Learning Research, 5,* 102–119.

Upitis, R. (1987c). Toward a model for rhythm development. In J. C. Peery, I. W. Peery, & T. W. Draper (Eds.), *Music and child development* (pp. 54–79). New York: Springer Verlag.

Vandenberg, B. (1980). Play, problem-solving and creativity. In K. H. Rubin (Ed.), *New directions for child development: Children's play* (pp. 49–68). San Francisco: Jossey-Bass.

Van Zee, N. (1976). Responses of kindergarten children to musical stimuli and terminology. *Journal of Research in Music Education, 24*(1), 14–21.

Wang, C. C. (1984). Effects of some aspects of rhythm on tempo perception. *Journal of Research in Music Education, 32,* 169–175.

Wang, C. C., & Salzberg, R. S. (1984). Discrimination of modulated music tempo by string students. *Journal of Research in Music Education, 31,* 49–55.

Wassum, S. (1980). Elementary school children's concept of tonality. *Journal of Research in Music Education, 28*(1), 18–33.

Webster, P. (1992). Research on creative thinking in music: The assessment literature. In R. Colwell (Ed.), *Handbook of research on music teaching and learning* (pp. 255–280). New York: Schirmer.

Webster, P. R., & Schlentrich, K. (1982). Discrimination of pitch direction by pre-school children with verbal and nonverbal tasks. *Journal of Research in Music Education, 30*(3), 151–161.

Wendrich, K. A. (1981). *Pitch imitation in infancy and early childhood: Observations and implications.* Unpublished doctoral dissertation, University of Connecticut, Storrs.

Yarbrough, C. (1987). The effect of musical excerpts on tempo discriminations and preferences of musicians and non-musicians. In C. K. Madsen & C. A. Prickett (Eds.), *Applications of research in music behavior* (pp. 175–189). Tuscaloosa: University of Alabama.

Young, L. (1982). *An investigation of young children's music concept development using non-verbal and manipulative techniques.* Unpublished doctoral dissertation, Ohio State University, Columbus.

Zimmerman, M. P. (1971). *Musical characteristics of children.* Washington, DC: Music Educators National Conference.

CHAPTER 9

# Art for Young Children

## CAROL SEEFELDT

ART AND young children are a natural combination. Uninhibited, anxious to explore their environment, experiment with materials, understand their world, and communicate ideas and feelings, children find creating art an intriguing and gratifying experience. Given the slightest opportunity, children the world over create drawings, sculptures, and paintings with assurance and interest (Thompson, 1995). Whether in the high Andean Mountains, in the jungles of the Amazon, or on the sidewalks of New York City, children leave their mark by drawing in the sand or mud, or on the sidewalk with sticks, stones, or any other tool they can find.

Responding to children's natural interest in creating art, early childhood educators have historically given the visual arts an honored place in the curriculum. Perhaps the long tradition began in the Frobelian kindergarten, where children wove placemats, punched designs in paper, or folded paper to create ornate shapes.

The early nursery schools treasured children's art as well, but the artwork they advocated differed greatly from the rigid Gifts and Occupations Froebel had prescribed. Rose Alschuler, Harriet Johnson, and other leaders of the nursery school movement during the early 1900s encouraged the use of raw materials—clay, paints, and crayons—as a means of fostering children's freedom of expression, and thus promoting their total development (Beatty, 1995).

Guided by Lowenfeld's *Creative and Mental Growth* (1947) and Read's (1947) *Education Through Art,* the visual arts were prevalent in schools for young children during the 1940s and 1950s. During the 1960s, spurred by the ideas and research of Gardner and the staff of Project Zero (1989), as well as by the concern for fostering children's creative thought and expression, the visual arts retained an honored place in the curriculum.

More recently, during the 1980s and 1990s, the role of the arts in the elementary and secondary curriculum, however, has been questioned. The push for accountability, higher standards, and mastery of basic skills became paramount. Because of pressure to foster achievement of isolated academic skills, the role of all the arts, not just the visual, in schools was challenged. Nevertheless, despite the push for earlier academic skill development, art continued its centrality in programs for young children in child care, preschools, and kindergartens, and in most primary grade classrooms.

Wanting to provide the optimum learning environment for children, meet individual needs, and foster symbolic and creative thinking, teachers today believe the visual arts are critical not only to children's development but also to the development of an integrated, meaningful early childhood curriculum (Kindler & Darras, 1994; Thompson, 1995). This chapter offers teachers theory and research to support the inclusion of art in the curriculum. Beginning with an overview and critique of the theories of children's art, the chapter concludes with implications for teaching art.

## THEORIES OF ART

Theories have been advanced to explain the art of young children. Among these are the developmental, cognitive, psychoanalytic, and perceptual theories. Each of these theories has influenced the teaching of art to children, and each is useful in explaining the nature of children's art.

### Developmental Theories

As early as 1885, Ebenezer Cooke drew attention to the successive stages of development found in children's drawings and advanced the theory that children drew in accordance with their general development. Since that time, others have documented that children's artwork follows a general pattern of development (Hong-Ik, 1997). Children in schooled societies and cultures the world over appear to progress through the following stages in the production of art:

1. The use of circular, ovoid, and sticklike representations of people and things during the early preschool years

2. The creation and representation of people and things by around age 4 or 5
3. The creation and repetition of basic representational formulas, including representations of space and motion, during the primary grades
4. The development of an increasing degree of visual correspondence during the elementary grades
5. The reproductiion of the shape, color, and spatial location of objects during the upper elementary grades
6. The development of a type of realism in adolescence

Lowenfeld (1947) codified this description of children's developing artistic skills by delineating the following stages:

1. *Scribbling* (ages 2–4). The first stage of self-expression
2. *Preschematic* (ages 4–7). The first representational attempts
3. *Schematic* (ages 7–9). Achievement of a form concept
4. *Gang* (ages 9–11). The dawning of realism
5. *Reasoning* (ages 11–13). Pseudo-realistic stage

Lowenfeld (1947) described these stages as the unfolding of a genetic program. Each of the stages was believed to be a part of the natural and normal aspects of human growth and development. Children, he claimed, must pass through one stage before they can achieve another. Changes in children's total development—that is, their affective, intellectual, social, and physical growth and development—are reflected in their art. No external teaching could assist a child in moving from one stage to another.

More recently, Wolfe and Perry (1989) refined the idea of development stages of art. They believed it was possible, beginning with the first attempts at drawing, between 12 and 14 months of age, to identify the advent of a series of distinct systems. Each system is characterized by different rules about the kinds of information to be recorded and the most powerful or satisfying ways to make those records. These stages are not viewed as a progression toward realism, however, but rather as drawing systems with distinct motives and purposes. These distinct drawing systems are outlined as follows:

1. *Object-based representation* (12–14 months). Children treat art and art materials as they treat other objects: they use them as objects, not tools.
2. *Gestural representations* (14–24 months). Children focus on the representation of motions and movements.

3. *Point-plot representations* (24–35 months). Children attempt to give meaning to their graphic expressions. The scribble can be named.
4. *Visual-spatial information systems* (3–5 years). The use of relative size and shapes to depict a geometric reality begins to appear.
5. *Rule-given visual spatial systems* (5–7 years). A schematic and highly conventional attempt to give geometric reality dominates children's drawing efforts.

Just as many endorse developmental theories of art, others find the theories lacking. On the grounds that developmental theories do not account for the role of culture, instruction, or how individual differences affect children's artistic development, the validity of maturational theories have been challenged. Research does suggest that there are differences in the way children progress through stages of art based on their culture. The indigenous art of a society and having the opportunity to draw or attend preschool (Martlew & Connolly, 1996), as well as other cultural factors, have been found to affect children's developing artistic abilities.

Preferences for representing the human form have been found to vary by culture. An example is the "Islamic torso" found in children's drawings throughout the Middle East (Martlew & Connolly, 1996). Further, children living in cultures with little interest in art or opportunity to draw produce simple, more basic forms than do children in more artistically sophisticated societies (Goodenough & Harris, 1963).

Nor do developmental theories account for the role of instruction on the development of art. Vygotsky (1986) pointed out that what children can do when left alone, working without assistance, does not indicate what they could do if they were given the proper guidance and support. Research suggests that very limited adult assistance can affect the level of children's art (Mathews, 1997).

The role of individual differences in the production of art has led to questioning developmental theories. Praisner (1984) questioned the maturational theories of art. He studied the childhood drawings of Toulouse-Lautrec, Picasso, and Klee and concluded that these childhood drawings were more adultlike and significantly advanced as compared to the usual drawings of young children. Winner (1996) studied the artwork of children with a wide range of physical and mental disabilities. She concluded that the art of children with disabilities was unrelated to, or independent of, their cognitive ability as measured by tests of verbal or general intelligence.

Accompanying the recognition of the role that culture, instruction, and individual differences play in children's art is a general rejection of developmental theories of human growth and learning:

> Views of human development have changed profoundly. . . . We have, instead, begun to understand that what we once thought were ordered sequences or steps are better understood as additions to a growing repertoire. (Wolf, 1998, p. xi)

## Cognitive Theories

Cognitive theories are, in part, developmental. The theories accept the idea that children's art develops along predictable, predetermined maturational lines. The explanation for this development, however, is that children's drawings mirror their cognitive growth and development, not their general maturation. "To little children, drawing is a language—a form of cognitive expression—and its purpose is not primarily esthetic" (Goodenough, 1926, p. 14). Thus Goodenough and others who advocated the cognitive theory of art believed that explanations of children's art must go beyond simply attributing artistic development to maturation. The more valid explanation is that children's art is representative of general cognitive, or concept, development, not simple maturational development.

Representation gradually becomes not only imagery, but rather images that inhere within certain relationships, including spatial ones, which are increasingly understood and reproduced in children's expressions. The inaccuracies that occur in children's art are believed to be caused by the fact that children neglect spatial relationships of proportion, distance, orientation, and perspective; this neglect results in failure to synthesize image elements.

Goodenough (1926) believed that children's ability to form concepts is an intellectual ability, requiring children to recognize similarities and differences among a group of objects or ideas. If children can make these distinctions and are able to recognize instances of a class when they confront it, they have attained a concept of that class (Goodenough & Harris, 1963a). By analyzing the amount of detail and realism that appear in children's drawings, then, it would be possible to obtain an index of a child's intellectual maturity by asking the child to draw a picture of a man and evaluating that drawing according to a set of specified criteria.

The *Goodenough Harris Draw-A-Person Test* (1963b) does just that. The fact that children's scores on the test correlate highly with their scores on standardized tests of achievement—such as the Wechsler Intelligence Scale for Children and the Stanford-Binet (U.S. National Center for

Health Statistics, 1970), and other measures of children's mental abilities—gives support not only to the test but also to the idea that children's
drawings represent the level of their concept formation; that is, children
draw what they know.

Piagetian theories added credence to the idea that children's drawings are reflective of their cognitive growth. Piaget and Inhelder (1955)
suggested that children, in order to draw or produce art, must first be able
to evoke what is absent or past, in order to think about it. This evocation
requires symbolization to represent what is not present in the here-and-
now world of the child.

Howard Gardner (1982) and Mansilla and Gardner (1997), by linking creativity, symbol development, and drawing with cognitive or mental development in the theory of multiple intelligences, also supported
cognitive theories of art. In Gardner's view, artistic activities are cognitive
through and through, for our symbol systems use drawing, writing, and
gesture and are basic vehicles of understanding the world, without which
the mind hardly exists, at least in the human sense. Others also point out
that the ability to represent things that are not present in the here-and-
now world is a form of language (Dyson, 1990; Eisner, 1997). Gardner's
work with Project Zero led to the conclusion that the extent to which
children fail to attend to repleteness, expression, and composition supports the idea that artworks are functioning for children as nonaesthetic
cognitive symbols such as maps or graphs (Gardner, 1987).

Just as maturation theories of children's art have been challenged, so
have cognitive theories. Basically, these challenges arise from the same
concerns about the role of experience and culture that have been used to
challenge developmental theories of art. Cross-cultural studies of Japanese and American children's drawings, as well as those of Native American children, seem to cast doubt on the validity of attributing children's
drawings to their level of cognitive growth. In each of these three cultures, Wilson and Wilson (1989) found that the cultural values of imitation and copying, as well as the use of paint brushes to write with, greatly
influenced children's developing artistic abilities.

Regardless, educators who reject developmental theories of art because of the passive role assigned to the teacher find cognitive theories a
comfortable alternative. As Vygotsky (1986) pointed out, the richer the
experience and the more fluent the instruction, the greater the possibility
of extending children's existing knowledge, skills, and abilities.

## Psychoanalytic Theories

Children do not draw what they know; rather they draw what they feel.
Art comes from "deep down inside" a child (Cole, 1966). Firmly based on

the concept of an unconscious—a type of mental activity that people are not even aware of—this theory of child art postulates a relationship between children's psychological development and their art. Children's art products are believed to reflect their emotions and to be expressions of deep, unconscious feelings instead of reflections of their conscious knowledge, general development, or concept formation.

According to psychoanalytic theories of art, children draw themselves as large circles with sticks that represent arms and legs not because they are unaware of shoulders, necks, or stomachs, but because the circle represents a force within the child as a symbol for the womb, breast, or some other emotionally potent object. The progression from a circle to realistic representation is explained as a growth process. As children grow, their conscious thoughts suppress the powerful force of the unconscious and they are able to draw and paint more realistically.

Historically, psychoanalytic thought greatly influenced the nursery school curriculum. Well before Alschuler and Hattwick (1947) analyzed children's paintings and reached the conclusion that children's painting styles were correlated with their personality traits, Freudian theories of infant sexuality and concepts of psychosexual development led to the use of fingerpaints, clay, wide brushes, and flowing easel paints. These free-flowing materials, it was postulated, would give children a healthy way with which to express hidden sexual urges and feelings. Small crayons, pencils, and fine paint brushes were seen as too restrictive.

Over the course of time, Freudian theories were questioned and the idea that children drew what they felt fell out of favor in the early childhood community. The theories, however, are still prevalent in the area of art therapy. Allowing children to fully and freely explore a variety of materials—such as clay, paints, and other materials believed to be freeing—has been found to help ease children's separation anxiety (Muri, 1996); circumvent problems before being treated in pediatric hospitals (Prager, 1995); and offer at-risk children a safe way to express their feelings (Essex, 1996).

## Perceptual Theories

To those endorsing perceptual theories of art, children draw what they see, not what they feel or know (Arnheim, 1974). Gestalt psychology maintains that children do not see objects as the sum of observed parts; rather they see perceptual wholes or total images structured in an active process. The brain acts on the basis of retinal impressions. For the Gestaltists, perception is an active process. The brain acts on incoming visual perceptions according to laws of perception. Arnheim (1974) expressed it this way:

The perceiver works on his sensations; he makes something with the sensory excitations focused in his eyes and transmitted to his brain. It is a mistake to believe that human perception is completely like the action of a camera . . . our brains organize and restructure the electrochemical impulses received from our eyes. (p. 128)

Thus children draw a person as a head (the circle) with arms attached not because this is the only thing they know about people, but because this is all that is seen as necessary to represent a human being. Children know that arms come from the trunk of their body, not their head, and the circles children draw to represent the human body are not simply heads without trunks—rather they are undifferentiated head-trunk units.

June McFee advanced perceptual theories of art in her book *Preparation for Art* (1972). She based her theory on concepts from perceptual theory as well as behavioral theories. She claimed that art is based on several factors, not just one. The readiness of the child, the psychological environment in which children work, children's ability to handle information, and their delineation skills all affect the level of their artwork.

## IMPLICATIONS FOR TEACHING

Implications for teaching art to young children stem directly from the different theoretical explanations of children's art. Theories are not the only belief systems guiding art education for young children, however. Societal forces and values and our increasing technology have also affected the art education.

### Theories and Direct Action

There is major conflict among early childhood art educators (McWhinnie, 1992) as to whether art is a form of self-expression (the psychoanalytic approach); a form of language or symbol system (cognitive theories); or a perceptual phenomenon (perceptual theories). Nevertheless teachers use theories to guide them as they select (1) artistic materials; (2) art content; and (3) teaching strategies.

**Selection and Use of Art Materials.** Today, developmental and psychoanalytic theories continue to influence art curriculum in schools for young children. Using Bredekamp and Copple's (1996) *Developmentally Appropriate Practice in Early Childhood Programs Serving Children Birth Through Age 8* (second edition) as a reference and the national standards for arts education (Consortium of National Arts Education Associations [CNAEA], 1994), which state that "students in the earlier grades should engage in developmentally appropriate learning experiences" (p. 21), many teachers endorse psychoanalytic and maturational theories of art. Believing that art is an activity of self-expression that cannot be taught and that this self expression develops according to a maturational plan, they refuse to apply any form of external standard, whether of technique or form. Doing so, they believe, would immediately induce inhibitions and frustrate children's artistic development.

There are problems with this "hands-off" approach. Because teachers may view their role as passive, they too often become the providers of materials and builders of an environment in which children are expected to explore, experiment, and express themselves fully. Following children's development, and believing children need to express their emotions freely, they offer children large paper in great amounts and large markers, paint brushes, and paint. Knowing these very young children cannot control their scribbling, they do not confine children to the boundaries of the paper.

To keep children interested as they grow, teachers continually search for new and more interesting materials for children to draw or paint with. Thus teachers have children drawing in shaving cream, rolling marbles through paint, or trying to paint with sticks.

Further, it is clear that it is not enough to simply make materials available. Kindler (1995) found that many children did not take advantage of materials, and when they did so they used the materials in random ways, without thought or care. Even when children actually used the materials, they did so without attempting to create images or to communicate ideas or feelings (Baker, 1994; Zurmuehlem, 1990).

Then, too, children continually presented with new media are never able to gain control over, or develop skill in, the use of any one medium and may not be able to acquire the skills and techniques necessary to actually use these materials to create art. The stunning artwork of children in Reggio Emilia, Italy, and Far Eastern cultures might be attributed to the fact that art materials there are carefully introduced to children. When social knowledge about how to use materials, such as using slip to join two pieces of clay, is necessary to its use, children are given direction in how to use the technique. They are also given time to experience and explore the same material over and over. By doing so they gain control over the media, learn what can result from the interaction of hand and eye with the material, and then use it to express ideas, concepts, experiences, or emotions (see Chapter 12, this volume; Seefeldt, 1995; Thompson, 1995).

Art materials have also been found to either hinder or foster children's production of art. Offering 5-year-olds fine (one-quarter to one-half inch wide) paint brushes instead of the traditional inch or wider brushes enabled children to incorporate significantly more detail in their easel paintings (Seefeldt, 1979). Salome (1967) explored children's use of pencils and crayons and found that although there were no significant differences in the amount of details in their drawings, children tended to fill more space when using crayons than markers.

**Selection of Art Content.** When materials are the focus of art, teachers may not think setting goals or objectives is necessary. One researcher found that teachers, when asked about their goals, were unable to do so, but talked instead about art in general (Brittain, 1979). On the other hand, teachers who believe, as Goodenough (1926) did, that drawing is a language and thus a form of cognitive expression, see goal setting and planning for art as a part of their role. Believing in a more active role for the teacher, they (1) establish goals and objectives, (2) plan to motivate and instruct children, and (3) foster children's reflection on and appreciation for art.

Goals for art can stem from a number of sources. The national standards for arts education (CNAEA, 1994) is one source of goals. The standards organize goals around content and achievement, stating that children should

- Understand and apply media, techniques, and processes
- Use knowledge of structures and functions
- Choose and evaluate a range of subject matter, symbols, and ideas
- Understand the visual arts in relation to history and cultures
- Reflect upon and assess the characteristics and merits of their work and the work of others.
- Make connections between visual arts and other disciplines

These goals would be applied in light of consideration of children's maturational learning levels. An understanding of children's thought processes permits teachers to select achievable goals and plan for interaction between children and themselves.

Children's growing awareness of the link between art and their ideas, a developmental milestone, "requires also recognition and response from teachers and peers" (Thompson, 1995, p. 92). Thompson pointed out that only 30% of 4-year-olds appeared to know what they were going to draw before they put crayon to paper, while 80% of 5-year-old children begin to draw with an intention firmly in mind. Thus, by 5 years of age, teachers can ask children to discuss their plans and ideas for an art project, as well as to monitor their actions in achieving these goals.

**Teaching Strategies.** Believing art is an expression of ideas, thinking, or emotions, teachers plan for motivational experiences and other teaching strategies. Motivational experiences can be artistic, intellectual, or imaginative (Seefeldt, 1995). Artistic motivation could stem from the materials or the artwork of children or of others. Mixing paints, making clay, and watching tempera paints flowing together serve as a form of motivation. The artwork of others—illustrators of children's favorite authors, or looking at and reflecting on art prints—might serve to motivate children. By age 5 or 6, children can begin to think about works of art from the artist's point of view, speculate on the artist's intentions, and measure an artist's success against their own response. Children use this knowledge in many ways; for example, they may borrow an artist's theme or methodology (Thompson, 1995).

Imagination, which empowers humans to create and to engage in works of art (Greene, 1997), is another motivational tool. Egan (1997) claimed that imagination and fantasy stories, which "most powerfully engage children" (p. 346), are other sources of motivation for art. He suggested that teachers read fantasy stories to children and provide appropriate props with which children can reenact the stories in their play. Then teachers can provide art materials that would enable children to represent either the fantasy stories, or their own fantasies, in their artwork.

If one endorses the cognitive theories of art, then the most potent form of motivation is experiential. The idea is that creating art involves taking an experience and creating it anew and in a form for others to take information from. Eisner (1994, 1997) describes an experience as a transaction between individual and environment. This transaction involves sensory, first-hand interaction with both the environment and others; is continuous; and includes language and the opportunity for reflection (Dewey, 1938).

An example of how experiences lead to art productions is found in *The Amusement Park for Birds* (1990), a video of children's experiences building an amusement park for birds in Reggio Emilia. Children decided to create an amusement park for the birds they observed in the open space in back of their center. Creating this amusement park involved recalling their visits to an amusement park and finding out that water and fountains were attractive to birds. After discussions and study, the children produced drawings of various types of water wheels and fountains they imagined the birds would find attractive. Language was used; teachers offered instruction in the use of paints, paper, and clay. Not only did children have repeated encounters with visiting and observing fountains and water wheels, but they had repeated encounters with art materials, processes, and techniques that allowed them to give form to what they had seen and learned.

When experiential learning is at the heart of the early childhood curriculum, there is a role for teachers. Teachers in Reggio Emilia interacted with children, discussing plans for their art products, describing the work, as well as asking questions and challenging children to higher levels of production. Talking about art is a necessary component of a true experience. Still, Engle (1996) cautioned that visual works do not always have to be interpreted through verbal discussion. She suggested that teachers can look and talk about what the product is made of, what they see (lines, shapes, colors, and so forth), what it represents, how it is organized, what it is about, and where the ideas came from—but only when done so with sensitivity.

More direct teaching strategies have been advocated by those endorsing perceptual theories of art. These typically involve focusing children's attention on the details and the nature of things in their environment (Haanstra, 1996; McFee, 1972). The goal is to improve children's visual discrimination and enable children to fully perceive their environment. Generally, research suggests that visual training does help children to see more details and significant relationships as they respond to their environment, both visually and cognitively (McFee, 1972). Haanstra (1996), in a meta-analysis of art education research literature, concluded that art education is more effective in producing results when it focuses on aesthetic perception than when it focuses on visual-spatial abilities.

This training need not be extensive. Richards (1988) gave students in the United States and Jamaica perceptual training that appeared to have an effect on children's production of art in both countries; and Mathews (1997) demonstrated that something as minor as showing children a sphere, an elongated ovoid, and a straight-sided ovoid, and focusing their attention on the differences in the three shapes, increased 4- and 5-year-olds' ability to accurately draw these shapes.

Smith and the Drawing Study Group (1998) believe that asking children to observe and to focus their attention on the object or things they are drawing "concretizes strategies children have been using unconsciously and furthers their understanding that this kind of responsive drawing is not a matter of talent, but a matter of hard work and thinking" (p. 11).

More direct teaching strategies have been advanced by Betty Edwards, author of the best-selling *Drawing on the Right Side of the Brain*

(1978), who convinced millions of people that anyone, at any age, could learn to draw if given the proper instruction. Mona Brookes (1988, 1989) also emphasized the idea that all children, at any age, could be taught to draw by being taught to copy. Wilson and Wilson (1985), based on a study of drawings by Egyptian children, concluded that children learn to draw by copying, but not as in the case of Monart Schools, by copying the drawings of an adult artist or master. They copy the drawings of other children.

There seems to be no doubt that direct instructional strategies can, in fact, produce results. The question remains, however, as to the efficacy and efficiency of any of the teaching strategies. Too many of the strategies seem to be designed to answer what Piaget and Inhelder (1969) once termed "the American question," that is, "How can you advance children through the stages of art more quickly?" One may ask whether or not it is efficient, or even ethical, to teach children skills, techniques, or responses to the visual arts that will occur naturally, as children grow and mature.

## Societal Forces and Values and Technology

Societal forces have led to questioning the role of the visual arts in curricula for young children. Pressure to account for children's learning, increase standardized test scores, and ensure that all children are learning has led to decreasing emphasis on the visual arts. Many who do not understand or accept the centrality of art in schools for young children continue to view the visual arts as a frill, not worthy of children's time in a school setting.

Educators, however, can challenge these views. Making and studying art contributes to integrating the curriculum by emphasizing unique and alternative modes of thinking and acting that are intrinsic to art (Anderson, 1981; Cohen & Hoot, 1997; Egan, 1997). Kay (1992) argued that arts education should be basic because of its contributions to children's intelligence. She outlined three phases of research concerning spatial ability and theories of perception, highlighting the role between art education and general education.

Educators also see a role for art as an integrator of the curriculum. Art can be combined with children's language learning. Because art helps children differentiate between shapes, it has been related to reading readiness skills. Mills (1973) found that children receiving 10 art lessons achieved significantly higher reading readiness scores on the Metropolitan Reading Readiness Test than those without the instruction.

Teachers can easily incorporate art into children's language learning.

Teachers can ask children to incorporate drawing into their written journals (Fahey, 1996; Manning & Manning, 1996) and can use children's
literature to extend and inspire children's thinking, which in turn could
enhance their art. Others have found that infusing art into the curriculum
provides a necessary image for children to write with clarity and purpose,
and leads to improved learning. The *Learning to Read Through the Arts* project, which consisted of three programs for children at least 2 years below
reading level, reported significantly reading gains, as well as increased
enthusiasm for school (Mills, 1973).

Art is also helpful in mathematical learning. In a study of Japanese
culture, Senger (1997) incorporated concepts of geometry and patterns
as children learned to make origami. Forseth (1980) demonstrated how
experiences with art could positively affect children's attitudes toward
mathematics, as well as toward achievement gains.

Today's technology, and the omnipresent computer in classrooms for
even the youngest children, is another way art is integrated into the total
curriculum. Through use of clip art software, word processing, graphics,
and color, the computer allows children to combine the symbol systems
of drawing, talking, writing, and symbol weaving (Blackstock & Miller,
1992). Gouzouasis (1994) described the effectiveness of a multimedia
project with children ages 8 to 10 years old. The program, composed of
both acoustic and visual elements, linked the arts with computer literacy
and the existing curriculum.

Regardless, making art and learning about art are basic for young
children. Children need art in the curriculum for art's sake (Balke, 1997).
The value of art lies in the contributions it makes to individuals' experience with and understanding of their world. No other reason is necessary
to justify the inclusion of art in curriculum for young children. How else
would children learn about color, form, line, shape, and texture if it were
not through their experiences with learning to see their environment
with all its richness and complexity, and then learning how to represent
their environment and experiences through art?

## REFERENCES

Alschuler, R., & Hattwick, L. B. (1947). *Painting and personality: A study of young
    children.* Chicago: University of Chicago Press.
*The amusement park for birds.* (1990). Amherst, MA: Performantics Press.
Anderson, T. (1981). Wholes and holes: Art's role in holistic education. *Art Educa-
    tion, 34*(6), 36–39.
Arnheim, R. (1974). *Art and visual perception.* Berkeley: University of California
    Press.

Baker, D. W. (1994). Toward a sensible education: Inquiring into the role of the visual arts in early childhood education. *Visual Arts Research, 20*(2), 92–104.

Balke, E. (1997). Play and the arts: The importance of the unimportant. *Childhood Education,73,* 355–360.

Beatty, B. (1995). *Preschool education in America.* New Haven: Yale University Press.

Blackstock, J., & Miller, L. (1992). The impact of new information technology on young children's symbol-weaving efforts. *Computers and Education, 18,* 209–221.

Bredekamp, S., & Copple, C. (1996). *Developmentally appropriate practice in early childhood programs serving children birth through age 8* (2nd ed.). Washington, DC: National Association for the Education of Young Children.

Brittain, W. L. (1979). *Creativity, art and the young child.* New York: Macmillan.

Brookes, M. (1988). *Drawing with children.* Los Angeles: Tarcher.

Brookes, M. (April, 1989). *Nondrawing with young children.* Remarks at the National Art Education Association Super Session, Washington, DC.

Cohen, M. D., & Hoot, J. L. (1997). Educating through the arts: An introduction. *Childhood Education, 73,* 338–340.

Cole, N. (1966). *Art from deep down inside.* New York: John Day.

Consortium of National Arts Education Associations (CNAEA). (1994). *Dance, music, theatre, visual arts: What every young American should know and be able to do in the arts.* Reston, VA: Author.

Dewey, J. (1938). *Experience and education.* New York: Macmillan.

Dyson, A. (1990). Symbol makers, symbol weavers: How children link play, pictures and print. *Young Children, 45*(2), 50–57.

Edwards, B. (1978). *Drawing on the right side of the brain.* Los Angeles: Tarcher.

Egan, K. (1997). The arts as the basics of education. *Childhood Education, 73,* 346–349.

Eisner, E. (1994). *Cognition and curriculum reconsidered* (2nd ed.). New York: Teachers College Press.

Eisner, E. (1997). Cognition and representation: A way to pursue the American dream? *Phi Delta Kappan, 78,* 348–354.

Engle, B. S. (1996). Learning to look: Appreciating child art. *Young Children, 51*(3), 74–79.

Essex, M. (1996). In the service of children: Art and expressive therapies in public school. *Journal of American Art Therapy, 13*(3), 181–190.

Fahey, P. (1996). Magic eyes: First grade children's sketchbooks. *Visual Arts Research, 22*(1), 34–43.

Forseth, S. D. (1980). Art activities, attitudes, and achievement in elementary mathematics. *Studies in Art Education, 21,* 22–27.

Gardner, H. (1982). *Art, mind, and brain.* New York: Basic Books.

Gardner, H. (1989). Zero-based arts education: An introduction to ARTS PROPEL. *Studies in Art Education, 30*(2), 71–83.

Gardner, H., & Winner, E. (1983). First intimations of artistry. In A. Sarno (Ed.), *U-shaped behavioral growth* (pp. 34–46). New York: Academic Press.

Goodenough, F. L. (1926). *Children's drawings as measures of intellectual maturity.* New York: Harcourt Brace.

Goodenough, F. L., & Harris, D. (1963a). *Children's drawings as measures of intellectual maturity.* New York: Harcourt Brace.

Goodenough, F. L., & Harris, D. (1963b). *The Goodenough-Harris Draw-a-Person Test.* New York: Harcourt Brace.

Gouzouasis, P. (1994). Multimedia constructions of children: An exploratory study. *Journal of Computing in Early Childhood Education, 5*(3–4), 273–384.

Greene, M. (1997). Metaphors and multiples: Representation, the arts, and history. *Phi Delta Kappan,78,* 387–394.

Haanstra, F. (1996). Effects of art education on visual-spatial ability and aesthetic perception: A quantitative review. *Studies in Art Education, 37,* 197–209.

Hong-Ik. (1997). Children's drawings of model houses: A developmental study. *Visual Arts Research, 23*(1), 62–72.

Kay, S. (1992). Cognitive theory: An element of design for arts education. *Design for Arts Education, 92*(2), 10–20.

Kindler, A., & Darras, B. (1994). Artistic development in context: Emergence and development of pictorial imagery in the early childhood years. *Visual Arts Research, 20*(2), 1–13.

Lowenfeld, V. (1947). *Creative and mental growth.* New York: Macmillan.

Manning, M., & Manning, G. (1996). Arts in reading and writing. *Teaching Pre K–8, 26*(6), 90–91.

Mansilla, V. B., & Gardner, H. (1997). Of kinds of disciplines and kinds of understanding. *Phi Delta Kappan, 78,* 381–387.

Martlew, M., & Connolly, K. J. (1996). Human figure drawings by schooled and unschooled children in Papua New Guinea. *Child Development, 67,* 2743–2764.

Mathews, J. (1997). Manderian for two objects are not the same. *Visual Arts Research, 23*(1), 73–96.

McFee, J. K. (1972). *Preparation for art* (2nd ed.). Belmont, CA: Wadsworth.

McWhinnie, J. (1992). Art in early childhood education. In C. Seefeldt (Ed.), *The early childhood curriculum: A review of current research* (2nd ed., pp. 264–286). New York: Teachers College Press.

Mills, J. C. (1973). The effect of art instruction on a reading development test: An experimental study with rural Appalachian children. *Studies in Art Education, 14,* 62–64.

Muri, S. (1996). Mommy don't go bye bye: How art activities can ease separation anxiety. *Early Childhood News, 8*(1), 31–32.

Piaget, J., & Inhelder, B. (1955). *The child's conception of* reality. London: Routledge & Kegan Paul.

Piaget, J., & Inhelder, B. (1969). *The psychology of the child.* New York: Basic Books.

Prager, A. (1995). Pediatric art therapy: Strategies and applications. *Journal of American Art Therapy, 12*(1), 32–38.

Praisner, D. (1984). Artist's drawings. *Studies in Art Education, 22*(2), 34–43.

Read, H. (1947). *Education through art.* New York: Pantheon.

Richards, A. G. (1988). Perceptual training in drawing among students from two countries. *Studies in Art Education, 29,* 302–308.

Salome, R. A. (1967). A comparative analysis of kindergarten children's drawings in crayon and colored pencil. *Studies in Art Education, 72,* 25–27.

Seefeldt, C. (1979). The effects of a program designed to increase young children's perception of texture. *Studies in Art Education, 20,* 40–44.

Seefeldt, C. (1995). Art: A serious work. *Young Children, 50*(3), 39–45.

Senger, E. S. (1997) *To make a portrait of a lion.* Commune di Reggio Emilia, Centro Documentazione Ricurca Educativa Nidi e Scuole dell'Infanzia. Available through Baji Rankin, 346 Washington St., Cambridge, MA 02139.

Smith, N., & the Drawing Study Group. (1998). *Observation drawing with children: A framework for teachers.* New York: Teachers College Press.

Thompson, C. M. (1995). Transforming curriculum in the visual arts. In S. Bredekamp & T. Rosegrant (Eds.), *Reaching potentials: Transforming early childhood curriculum and assessment* (Vol. 2, pp. 81–96). Washington, DC: National Association for the Education of Young Children.

U.S. National Center for Health Statistics. (1970). *Intellectual maturity of children as measured by the Goodenough-Harris Draw-a-Man test* (PHS Publications no. 100, Series 11, No. 105). Rockville, MD: Author.

Vygotsky, L. (1986). *Thought and language.* Cambridge, MA: MIT Press.

Wilson, M., & Wilson, B. (1985). A view of imagery sources in drawings. In A. Hardimon & R. Zernich (Eds.), *Foundation for curriculum development in art education* (pp. 45–47). Boston: Davis.

Wilson, M., & Wilson, B. (1989). A tale of four cultures. In R. Hurwitz & J. McCleary (Eds.), *Art and education international* (pp. 134–147). University Park: Penn State University.

Winner, E. (1996). What drawings by atypical populations can tell us. *Visual Arts Research, 22*(2), 90–95.

Wolf, D. (1998). Foreword. In N. Smith & the Drawing Study Group, *Observation drawing with children* (p. xi). New York: Teachers College Press.

Wolfe, D., & Perry, M. D. (1989). From endpoints to repertories. *Journal of Aesthetic Education, 22,* 17–34.

Zurmuehlen, M. (1960). *Studio art: Praxis, symbol, presence.* Reston, VA: National Art Education Association.

CHAPTER 10

# The Multicultural Worlds of Childhood in Postmodern America

## LOURDES DIAZ SOTO

True peace is not merely the absence of tension; it is the presence of justice.
— Martin Luther King, Jr., Letter from a Birmingham Jail

IN THE "MULTICULTURAL worlds of childhood," in postmodern America, a landscape is emerging that includes both challenges and opportunity for the early childhood curriculum. The challenges are an integral part of the historical and contemporary context of our nation. The opportunity is heralded by the voices of children, families, early childhood advocates, critical researchers, and decades of multicultural wisdom keepers.

How is it possible for young children to begin to make sense of the contemporary multicultural worlds of childhood that include *Mother Goose, Mighty Morphin Power Rangers,* martial arts video games, Barbie dolls, the dismantling of affirmative action, and the bombing in Oklahoma City? How do the research literature and contemporary events in our nation help to inform the field of early childhood education?

Madhu (pseudonym), a student of color in one of our graduate seminars, relayed a scenario that reminded us of just how crucial it is for early childhood educators to critically analyze issues of race, power, equity, social justice, socioeconomic class, and gender. Madhu is a mature graduate student and loving mother who volunteers at a local day care center. She described how White children in the center have rejected her attempts to nurture them. "Don't touch me!" "Get away from me!" She has interpreted these incidents as relating to her skin color, since one child rubbed and tried to "clean his skin" after he fell and she tried to comfort him. For Madhu, these experiences have been reminiscent of the caste system in India, where the untouchables have been regarded as unclean. The research and this recent incident show how at an early age young children attain ethnocentric tendencies. The early childhood curriculum can provide an optimal space capable of affecting young children's daily lived realities.

In this chapter I explore the complexity of the historical context of multicultural America and the possibility of an early childhood critical multicultural curriculum with *border crossings.* Salient multicultural theoretical paradigms capable of informing the field of early childhood education are included in this discussion, as well as a brief review of how selected early childhood education literature is organized around issues of multiculturalism.

## THE HISTORICAL CONTEXT

*How does America's historical context relate to multiculturalism and the early childhood education curriculum?* Our nation has a sad history of intolerance and oppression, as exemplified by the Massachusetts Colony's anti-Quaker provisions; the removal of the Cherokees from Georgia, later known as the Trail of Tears; the U.S. Constitution's definition of a slave as the equivalent to three-fifths of a free man; violence in Philadelphia, the city of "brotherly love," against Catholics, Irish, and African Americans; the Chinese exclusion laws in California that were not repealed until 1952; the Japanese internment camps; the Indian wars; the myth of a Jewish conspiracy and continued anti-Semitism; the lynching and killing of Tejanos; the refusal of the Three Rivers community to bury Felix Longoria, a Tejano killed in the line of duty; the Ku Klux Klan's (KKK) reign of terror; a former grand dragon of the KKK, David Duke, running for the presidency of the United States; and the fact that today gays and lesbians are the most frequent target of hate crimes (Carnes, 1995).

In spite of progress with civil rights, the Southern Poverty Law Center documents how skinhead, Ku Klux Klan, and neo-Nazi organizations are an integral part of our nation, with more than 300 hate groups scattered throughout America actively recruiting members. Between 1990 and 1993 alone there were 108 bias-motivated murders, thousands of assaults, cross-burnings, and acts of violence and intimidation. In addition, Jim Carnes (1995) found that in a 1992 survey of high school students, 30% said they would participate in racist incidents and 17% said they would silently support them. To Carnes, "These numbers suggest that we still have much to learn from the bitter harvests of our past— that our democracy is still a work in progress" (p. 128).

In the United States today, powerful voices of an increasingly mean-spirited political agenda disregard the needs of young children. When early childhood educators view, examine, and critique how issues of power are affecting their lives and children's lives, they will also see the need to map an early childhood utopian dream in solidarity. As Maxine Greene (1996) notes:

> Perhaps we might begin by releasing our imaginations and summoning up the traditions of freedom in which most of us were reared. We might try to make audible again the recurrent calls for justice and equality. (p. 28)

The Children's Defense Fund (1996) shows that 15.3 million children live in poverty. Our youngest children comprise the poorest children (one out of every four children younger than 6 years old), while the richest one-fifth of American families received 11 times as much income as the poorest one-fifth. This constitutes the widest economic gap in our nation since 1947. The child poverty rates in the United States are the highest among 18 industrialized countries.

Poor children, bilingual children, immigrant children, and women are caught in our nation's politically conservative net: California continues to approve mean-spirited propositions (Proposition 186, Proposition 209); presidential candidates openly support English-only measures; a Texas judge seriously considers taking a child away from a native-Spanish-language-speaking mother; conservative radio talk-show host Rush Limbaugh continues his relentless attacks on women, calling us "femme-Nazis" while denigrating and objectifying people of color. All of these attacks continue until our lives are ridiculed, dehumanized, and devalued. As Henry Giroux (1995) maintains, our nation is experiencing a popular construction of a "national identity that is read as white, heterosexual, middle class, and allegedly threatened by contamination from cultural, linguistic, racial, and sexual differences" (p. 48).

Many of our young children growing up at the gate of the new millennium find themselves immersed in an education that may appear far removed from their daily realities. In *Savage Inequalities,* Jonathan Kozol (1991), for example, relates:

> Nearly 1,000 infants die within these very poor Chicago neighborhoods each year. An additional 3,000 infants are delivered brain damaged or with other forms of neurological impairment. But entering a kindergarten classroom

this autumn morning, one would have no sense that anything was wrong. . . .

In a somewhat mechanical way, the teacher lifts a picture book of *Mother Goose* and flips the pages as the children sit before her. . . . Mary is white. Old Mother Hubbard is white. Jack is white. Jill is white. Little Jack Horner is white. Mother Goose is white. Only Mother Hubbard's dog is black. "Baa, baa, black sheep," the teacher read, "have you any wool?" the children answer: "Yessir, yessir, three bags full. One for my master. . ."

The master is white. The sheep are black. (pp. 43–45)

How do young children make sense of the education provided by professionals in schools, by families at home, and by their communities? The intersections and multiple complexities among issues of race, poverty, gender, and religion are depicted in James McBride's (1996) *The Color of Water.* This oral history depicts a black child growing up with 11 black siblings and a white Jewish mother, the daughter of an Orthodox Jewish rabbi. James tried to make sense of his "multicultural worlds of childhood" and asked his mother:

"Does he [God] like black people or white people better?" "He loves all people. He's a spirit," she responded. "What color is God's spirit?" he asked. "It doesn't have a color," she said. "God is the color of water. Water doesn't have a color." (p. 51)

In James McBride's home, "the question of race was like the power of the moon" (p. 94).

## MULTICULTURAL THEORETICAL PARADIGMS

*What are salient examples of multicultural theoretical paradigms capable of informing the field of early childhood education?* Theories in multicultural education and about multiculturalism emanate from a variety of fields and perspectives. John Ogbu (1982, 1987, 1988), for example, pursues an anthropological perspective and reflects proponents of the research theory that views society as organized into systems that privilege the dominant group. This research examines relationships among institutions and schools that create distinctions among dominant and "minority" groups leading to social inequality. Ogbu describes voluntary, involuntary, and caste-like minority groups and sees the need for reform at a variety of levels, including the school and the community.

Paulo Freire's (1985, 1970/1996) work explains why the "banking concept" of education is erroneous. Such a mechanistic model of repetition and memorization needs to be replaced with a problem-posing concept whereby learners are viewed within a humanistic curriculum. He describes "cultural invasion" where "invaders penetrate the cultural context of another group, in disrespect of the latter's potentialities; they impose their own view of the world upon those they invade and inhibit the creativity of the invaded by curbing their expression" (1996, p. 133). His reflections are crucial to our understanding of how power affects the lives of young children in postmodern America.

Jim Cummins' (1996) extensive research with linguistically and culturally diverse learners has helped us to gain insights into young children's educational needs. The "threshold hypothesis," for example, helps early childhood educators understand that there may be levels of proficiency children must attain in order to reap the benefits of bilingualism and biliteracy. The issue of power is highlighted by Cummins, who distinguishes between "collaborative" and "coercive" power, where the latter is imposed to the detriment of a subordinate group while the former is generated in interpersonal and intergroup relations.

Christine Sleeter and Carl Grant (1988) describe various approaches available in multicultural education, including their own choice that integrates issues of race, class, and gender. The five approaches described by Sleeter and Grant include: (1) teaching the exceptional and culturally different; (2) human relations approach; (3) ethnic studies, women's studies, labor studies; (4) multicultural education approach; and (5) education that is multicultural and social-reconstructionist.

Education that is multicultural and social-reconstructionist extends the multicultural curriculum "into the realm of social action and focuses at least as much on challenging existing social stratification as on celebrating human diversity and equal opportunity" (p. 28). An education that is multicultural and social-reconstructionist has been recommended in the past decade by early childhood educators for, among others, day-care settings (Swadener, 1988), infant and toddler settings (Whaley & Swadener, 1990), and teacher education (Soto & Richardson, 1995).

The stages of ethnicity theory developed by James Banks (1993) relay a paradigm focusing on cultural and racial choices. This theory emphasizes differences and has the potential for assisting with interpretations of racial attitudes and self-perceptions. The stages assume a hierarchical progression from a place of negative beliefs and stereotypes to a place of positive identification of skills and knowledge. Banks lists the following stages: (1) cultural psychological captivity, (2) cultural encapsulation stage, (3) cultural identity clarification, (4) biculturalism, (5) multiculturalism and reflective nationalism, and (6) globalism and global competency. Banks draws connections between the research depicting the origins of racial attitudes and his theory.

Joe Kincheloe and Shirley Steinberg (1998), influenced by McLaren and Morris's (1997) work, describe five typologies of multiculturalism, including "critical multiculturalism." This critical analysis emphasizes the importance of power as an integral part of multiculturalism and examines the meaning of multiculturalism:

> Multiculturalism means everything yet at the same time nothing . . . While we cannot be sure of what individuals are suggesting when they employ the term multiculturalism, we can reasonably guess that they are alluding to at least one of the following issues: race, socio-economic class, gender, language, culture, sexual preference, or disability. . . . In public conversation, multiculturalism is a term used as a code word for race. (p. 1)

The five types of multiculturalism described by Kincheloe and Steinberg include the following:

1. Conservative multiculturalism/monoculturalism is the belief in the superiority of Western traditions and a form of neocolonialism that embraces white male supremacy and blames anyone falling outside the "boundaries of the white, male, middle/upper-middle class" (p. 3).
2. Liberal multiculturalism embraces the notion of color-blindness and the idea that we should work toward a community where there is one race—the human race. Proponents of liberal multiculturalism believe we share a natural equality and common humanity, yet this exclusive concern for sameness neglects the power exerted by forces that undermine the democratic process.
3. Pluralistic multiculturalism, unlike the liberal focus on sameness, focuses on differences. In pluralistic multiculturalism learners are expected to develop "multicultural literacy," diversity is valued, and there is less emphasis on assimilation. Pluralistic multiculturalism has obtained intellectual respectability yet leaves issues of inequity intact.
4. Left essentialist multiculturalism includes an analysis of how essentialism (belief in unchanging properties) within multiculturalism subverts differences within categories such as race and gender. The left essentialist multiculturalism disregards the idea that identity formation is a dynamic process that is socially constructed, shifting, and unstable.
5. Critical multiculturalism is influenced by the critical theorists who focused on power and domination at the Frankfurt School of Social Re-

search. Critical theorists promote self-reflection and consciousness about the etiology of political opinions, gender roles, racial images, social class, and beliefs. Critical multiculturalists strive for egalitarianism, work in solidarity toward the elimination of human suffering, expose the hidden "curriculum" that oppresses many and privileges few, and seek diversity "that understands the power of difference when it is conceptualized within a larger concern with social justice" (p. 34).

In *Bilingual Education: A Dialogue with the Bakhtin Circle,* Marcia Moraes (1996) proposes "dialogic-critical pedagogy" as a means of moving the oppressed and the oppressors toward emancipatory democracy:

> We need to construct a dialogic-critical pedagogy that takes as its founding objective a living dialogue between oppressed and oppressors from which both groups can understand the social constraints. . . . It is within such a dialogic-critical pedagogy that we can think about individual emancipation and also about collective transformation. (p. 113)

Moraes, like Giroux (1986), relies on the theoretical frameworks of the Bakhtin circle and Paulo Freire. Giroux in his analysis notes how the dominant educational discourses, namely liberal and conservative, "fail to analyze how the school as an agent of social and cultural control is mediated and contested by those whose interest it does not serve" (p. 57).

Each of the theories and typologies offers opportunities for the early childhood education curriculum. Freire's (1985; 1970/1996) work, for example, highlights the process of cultural invasion and the need for a problem-posing project. Jim Cummins' (1996) work helps us to further analyze issues of power and to value children's home languages and home cultures. Sleeter and Grant's (1988) work moves the practitioner beyond rhetoric to a place of social action. Banks' (1993) work is helpful by drawing connections between the research depicting the origins of racial attitudes and how young children begin to make sense of their world. Kincheloe and Steinberg's (1998) work provides information about both the complexities and the possibilities present in the field of multiculturalism. Moraes' (1996) work can challenge the field to initiate new directions for dialogue "from the margins and from the center," leading to the emancipatory place envisioned by Martin Luther King, Jr., and referred to by Giroux (1986) as the "politics of human dignity."

## MULTICULTURAL RESEARCH AREAS

*How is the early childhood education literature related to issues of multicultur-
alism?* The research initiated over half a century ago examining racial and
ethnic attitudes of young children has consistently shown that young
children not only are aware of racial and ethnic differences but also have
also internalized the views of their society (Banks, 1993). The pioneering
research of the 1920s and 1930s indicated that racial attitudes are initiated during the earliest years of a child's life. In this sense it has taken a
whole "oppressive village" to systematically educate young children to
internalize the emotional components of racism. At the same time, these
research projects help make the case that early childhood education is
truly a window of opportunity for multicultural education.

Banks in his review of racial and ethnic attitudes and their modification found that preschool and kindergarten African American children
often make out-group preferences while most White children make own-
group racial preferences. This research shows that young White children
hold ethnocentric attitudes and express negative attitudes toward other
racial and ethnic groups beginning at age 4. The intervention studies
Banks reviewed show that the research on children is much more hopeful
than the intervention research on adults. Since the evidence indicates
that it is increasingly difficult to influence the attitudes of children as they
grow older, clearly "early childhood educators have the best opportunity
to positively influence the racial and ethnic attitudes of children" (p. 244).

Just as the theories in the field of multicultural education have been
informed by a variety of disciplines, so has the literature examining multiculturalism and young children. The paradigms viewing young children
and multiculturalism are multiple and complex and have overlapping
spheres. For the purposes of this discussion, however, I will identify five
areas of research (and literature): (1) child development paradigms;
(2) qualitative interpretive research paradigms; (3) bilingual/bicultural
research; (4) advocacy research and literature; and (5) reconceptualizing
models.

### Child Development Paradigms

Chud development paradigms have a longstanding tradition in early
childhood education, based largely on the field of psychology and child
development. Most of the published research in the scholarly journals in
the field of early childhood education falls into these paradigms with
largely quantifiable, predetermined hypotheses and discrete point data.

Readers interested in these paradigms are referred to the "Special issue on minority children" of *Child Development* (1990, vol. 61, no. 2). This special issue views developmental outcomes, identity processes, school achievement, child-rearing practices, and the psychosocial experiences of "disadvantaged minority mothers." McLoyd (1990) points to the "gap" in our knowledge and to the need for diverse scholars and additional research funds.

Genishi and Fassler note the need for early childhood programs that are both multicultural and developmentally appropriate, as well as the need to take into account the nature of the learner (see Chapter 3, this volume). Since in this approach the teacher's expertise is valued, it stands to reason that we need to critically examine how we think about teacher education in the field and the existing knowledge that informs the field.

The contributions to the field by the child development paradigms are abundant; but as Block (1992) points out, the century-long domination of the psychological and child development perspective in the field has meant a lack of recognition or acceptance of alternative theoretical and methodological perspectives.

> The terms "critical theory," "interpretivist or symbolic research", or "postmodern" are rarely heard in seminar rooms, publications, or conferences focusing on early childhood education. . . . The few scholars who identify with both these perspectives *and* early childhood education have called for and created their own forums for discussion of these issues. (p. 3)

The child development paradigms include writings viewing developmentally appropriate practice (Bredekamp & Copple, 1997) and the Piagetian stages of children's growth and development (Piaget, 1970, 1977). Much of this literature has been "taken-for-granted" knowledge that is rarely critiqued, and only recently have issues of language and culture been integrated as a part of what Michael Apple refers to as the "politics of cultural incorporation," where dominance is maintained with a process of compromise and "mentioning" (discussed in Lubeck, 1994). (For a critical analysis of developmentally appropriate practices, see Jipson [1991] and Lubeck [1994].)

At the 1996 annual conference of the National Association of Education for Young Children (NAEYC), Piaget's decades of research were celebrated upon the hundredth anniversary of his birth. In conjunction, the National Association of Early Childhood Teacher Educators engaged a panel on discussions of the constructivist paradigms. In response, in a multicultural critique of the Piagetian and post-Piagetian constructivist paradigms, I challenged the field to move beyond the scientific and biologically derived origins of the Piagetian perspective toward a "critical constructivist paradigm" that examines issues of power and pursues a utopian early childhood dream of equity and social justice (Soto, 1997a).

In spite of Piaget's remarkable research for over half a century, the genetic epistemology of these writings is evidenced by the language included in the descriptions of "the individual," "the organism," "the assimilation," and "the biological." Piaget's early work showed his biologist's credentials as he demonstrated a fascination for *limnaea stagnalis* (snails), which helps to explain his interpretation of the mechanism of "equilibration."

Although Piaget did not completely overlook social elements, recent research has helped us to gain additional understandings about children's cognitive development (Fosnot, 1996; Lambert et al., 1995; Perret-Clermont, Perret, & Bell, 1991; Resnick, Levine, & Teasley, 1991; Wertsch, 1991). The work conducted by Perret-Clermot observed children to progress from one Piagetian stage to another in a very short time (5 to 10 minutes). Contemporary biologists also note that the biological and the social are not separate but complementary (Lewontin, Rose, & Kamin, 1984). Recent research (Cobb, Yackel, & Wood, 1992) is demonstrating that we cannot understand cognition without observing the interaction within a context, within a culture. Yet as Kincheloe and Steinberg (1996) note in their theory of postformalism: "Developmental psychological principles have become so much a part of teacher education programs that it is hard to see where questions about them might arise" (p. 171).

Vygotsky's emphasis on the sociohistorical aspect of knowledge is an important contribution to this knowledge base. Vygotsky, like Piaget, believed in the idea that learning is developmental but distinguished between "spontaneous" (pseudo, naturally occurring) and "scientific" (structured learning activity) concepts. His now-famous ideas include, among others, the "zone of proximal development," the formation of inner speech, and dialogue. Bruner extended Vygotsky's work with the notion of "scaffolding." Although not all constructivists agree with these theories, the work of Piaget, Vygotsky, and others helps to form the basis for constructivism. Newly evolving terminology is evident and includes a distinction among the "cognitive constructivism" and the "social constructivism."

## Qualitative Interpretive Research Paradigms

Qualitative interpretive research paradigms have been influenced not only by anthropology but also by linguistics and philosophy. Selected examples regarding issues of multiculturalism include the Hawaiian KEEP

Project (Au & Jordan, 1981); the Warm Springs Indian reservation study viewing communication patterns in the classroom and the community (Philips, 1983); in-depth descriptions of family literacy and young children growing up in the inner city (Taylor & Dorsey-Gaines, 1988); Heath's (1983) "ways with words" study in the Carolina Piedmont detailing two children's learning communities; Swadener's (1988) ethnographic case study; Delpit's (1995) description of cultural conflicts in the classroom for African American children, often viewed as "other people's children"; and Wilcox's (1982) view of socioeconomic class differences. These researchers have noted differential treatment of young children and the schools' role in cultural transmission.

Wilcox (1982), for example, notes the differential treatment young children receive merely for having been born into a particular neighborhood and a particular socioeconomic class. In her study, she found:

> The pattern of differences . . . [is] directly in conflict with the promise of equal opportunity offered by the educational system in the United States. At the tender age of six, these children have done practically nothing as individuals to account for the kind of differential treatment they are receiving, except to have been born by chance into one neighborhood and social class background or another. (p. 295)

Swadener's (1988) earlier work called for an education that is multicultural in early childhood settings. This ethnographic case study conducted in two day-care programs helped Swadener to conclude that "interactions with racially and culturally diverse peers and teachers remains one of the best early childhood strategies for creating education that is multicultural" (p. 26).

Lisa Delpit (1995) has observed how our society maintains stereotypes, portrays young Black children negatively, and values the worldviews of those in privileged positions. Delpit underscores the combination of power and "otherness" by stating:

> We must all find some way to come to terms with these two issues (power and "otherness"). When we teach across the boundaries of race, class, or gender—indeed when we teach at all—we must recognize and overcome the power differential, the stereotypes, and the other barriers, which prevent us from seeing each other. . . . Until we can see the world as others see it, all the educational reforms in the world will come to naught. (p. 134)

Walsh, Tobin, and Graue (1993), in their extensive review of qualitative research in early childhood education, point to the importance of interpretive research in the field, since it holds the potential for collaborative, negotiated relationships among players and the opportunity to give voice to children and practitioners who "historically have been silenced and isolated" (p. 473).

## Bilingual/Bicultural Research

Bilingual/bicultural research has helped early childhood educators to value young children's home language and home culture. Researchers have shown that a strong home-language base facilitates not only second-language learning but also young children's emotional and academic well-being (Hakuta, 1986; Krashen, 1988; Soto, 1993, 1997c; Wong Fillmore, 1991). It is helpful to organize the bilingual education research studies into eras: (1) the bilingual "handicap" era; (2) the positive-findings era; (3) the era of newly evolving paradigms; and (4) the era with a futuristic vision that critically analyzes issues of power.

First, the bilingual "handicap" era denotes findings in keeping with the notion that bilingualism was synonymous with deficiency. The initial research is responsible for creating what Cummins (1989) refers to as the myth of the bilingual handicap. Hakuta (1986) notes that it is important to view this early literature in light of the historical context. Unfortunately, the research era of the 1920s through the early 1960s continues to drive existing programs, in spite of additional contemporary research.

Studies in the positive-findings era showed that children raised bilingually were more attentive to semantic relationships, showed superiority in awareness of linguistic rules and structures, outperformed monolinguals on a variety of measures of metalinguistic awareness, demonstrated divergent thinking and creativity, showed positive effects of bilingualism on a variety of cognitive performance measures such as concept formation, indicated positive effects on Piagetian conservation and field independence, demonstrated an ability to monitor cognitive performance, showed significant gains in cognitive measures including the Raven Progressive Matrices, and demonstrated that learning concepts in the native language will transfer and enhance second-language learning (Bain, 1974; Bain & Yu, 1980; Ben-Zeev, 1977; Cummins & Gulutsan, 1974; Cummins, 1978; Cummins, 1979; S. Duncan & DeAvila, 1979; Hakuta & Diaz, 1985; Ianco-Worrall, 1972; Liedtke & Nelson, 1968; Torrance, Wu, Gowan, & Alliotti, 1970).

The era of newly evolving paradigms has relied, to a greater extent, on qualitative methods and initiated ways of viewing issues of language and culture as related domains. Findings from this era have helped us to understand the effects of teacher assumptions about children's English-language proficiency on the quality of instruction (Moll & Diaz, 1987);

the importance of the distinction between social language skills and the more complex academic skills (Cummins, 1989); why the loss of the primary language can be costly to children, families, and society as a whole (Wong Fillmore, 1991); the long-term benefits of bilingual education programs on children's attitudes (Collier, 1989, 1992); and the need to incorporate "funds of knowledge" in the bilingual education classroom (Moll, 1995).

The field will continue to build on this knowledge base and evolve, explore, and experiment with research methods, theoretical frameworks, and alternate paradigms (Soto, 1992a, 1992b). Researchers are seeing the need for social science research to redirect itself from deficient stereotypical paradigms to exploratory and creative paradigms capable of meeting the needs of teachers, learners, and families. The research studies conducted by Ada (1986), Cummins (1996), and Soto (1997c), among others, can be viewed as initiating an era that includes a futuristic vision by critically analyzing issues of power in bilingual education. A critical bicultural pedagogy "holds the possibility for a discourse of hope in light of the tensions, conflicts, and contradictions that students must face in the process of their bicultural development" (Darder, 1991, p. 96). These researchers can envision an education that is built on a theory of cultural democracy and acknowledges issues of power.

## Advocacy Research and Literature

Advocacy research and literature include multiple voices in the field and voices speaking on behalf of young children. These writings include research evidence (e.g., California Tomorrow on behalf of immigrant children), curricular literature (e.g., anti-bias, tolerance), demographic data (e.g., Children's Defense Fund, 1996), advocacy literature, and selected children's literature. Jonathan Kozol's (1991, 1995) work, for example, has served as a powerful ally in the advocacy literature. His willingness to portray the daily lived realities of children whose lives are disregarded continues to influence the "conscience" of Americans.

California Tomorrow's work, which originated on behalf of immigrant children, has evolved as a voice for California's young children. The report *Affirming Children's Roots* (Chang, 1993) features racially, culturally, and linguistically diverse child-care centers. This field research project targeted 450 child care centers in California. Included in these findings is the fact that children of color are significantly less likely to be cared for by teachers of their same racial background than White children. The researchers provide recommendations for further research, state agencies, the federal government, national early childhood professional organizations, resource and referral networks, training institutions, and private foundations.

In a subsequent study conducted by California Tomorrow (Chang, Muchelroy, Puledo-Tobiassen, Dowell, & Olsen Edwards, 1996), 300 child-care providers, trainers, and parents were interviewed, leading to principles based on their observations and their collaborations with participants. The five principles identified can be implemented in early childhood settings to prepare young children to "thrive in a multicultural world":

1. Combat racism and foster positive racial identity in young children.
2. Build on the cultures of families and promote respect and cross-cultural understanding among children.
3. Preserve family languages and encourage all children to learn a second language.
4. Work in partnership with families to respond to issues of race, language, and culture.
5. Engage in dialogue and reflection about race, language, and culture on an ongoing basis.

These researchers also see the need to broaden the research in early childhood education, since child development theory is built on the research conducted on White middle-class American children. New (1992, as cited in Chang) noted that only 9.3% of the research in the field of child development is devoted to non-Whites.

Marian Wright Edelman (Children's Defense Fund, 1996) has been an advocate and a powerful voice for young children via multiple publications and lobbying activities for more than two decades. The CDF yearly reports and the accompanying advocacy literature are valuable not only for early childhood professionals but also for parents and policy-making agencies. As we examine the daily realities children face in our nation, it will be important to reflect on Sharon Lynn Kagan's (1996) notion that professionals in our field need to stop viewing advocacy as leftist behavior.

Louise Derman-Sparks's (1989) *Anti-Bias Curriculum* has helped to inform early childhood educators for almost a decade. This guide includes resources, developmental guidelines, and ideas of empowerment based on Freire's "practice of freedom": "the means by which men and women deal critically and creatively with reality and discover how to participate in the transformation of the world" (cited in Derman-Sparks, 1989, p. ix).

## Reconceptualizing Models

The dialogue initiated by Shirley Kessler and Beth Blue Swadener (1992) helps the field to examine ways of reconceptualizing the early childhood curriculum. Scholars from the reconceptualizing model include William Ayers, Marianne Block, Janice Hale, Jan Jipson, Nancy King, Shirley Kessler, Sally Lubeck, Janet Miller, Valerie Polakow, Lourdes Diaz Soto, Beth Blue Swadener, and many others. The scholars representing this paradigm realize how the field has been influenced by science, psychology, and child development theory. These early childhood educators envision alternative perspectives in both theory and practice; are willing to ask the difficult questions that have not previously been addressed; integrate multiple voices, especially the voices that have so often been disregarded; and draw from both the critical and feminist theories. They believe:

> If knowledge is power . . . , the nature of knowledge, as well as the practices that are valued or privileged in the early childhood curriculum, must be examined within a number of larger contexts as well as from multiple perspectives. In order to reconceptualize . . . we will need to become better listeners, . . . honor the voices, and . . . learn how to make the "familiar strange" and many of our prized assumptions problematic. (Kessler & Swadener, p. 293)

Scholars ascribing to the critical postmodern perspective are also helping to influence early childhood curriculum by integrating knowledge from critical constructivism, multiculturalism, Freire's (1970/1996) work, and feminist ways of knowing, and by examining issues of power, especially as these relate to popular culture. In *Kinderculture,* for example, Steinberg and Kincheloe (1997) expose the corporate construction of childhood in America. This volume examines early childhood taken-for-granted activities in the postmodern world of Disney movies, interactive video games, children's television viewing, eating at McDonald's, Barbie dolls, and dolls from the American Girl Collection.

In the chapter examining the *Mighty Morphin Power Rangers* (MMPR), McLaren and Morris (1997) point out that younger viewers have come to consider MMPR as a favorite and have made it the most highly rated children's television program. MMPR captures 99% of the 2– to 11–year-old viewers. This is an alarming statistic, especially when we learn what Peter McLaren heard during a telephone interview with a representative of the program. When McLaren asked

> if half-Korean and half-American meant Adam was Korean and possibly African, she said, No–he's American. Ask[ing] if Adam could be Korean and

perhaps Latino, I was given the same response. Apparently if you are Korean you are not American and if you are half-American that excludes you from being either African or Latino. American means one thing: being white. (p. 121)

The examination of how corporate America views children is important to our discussion of the early childhood curriculum since so many companies are invading children's lives at home and at school. Carpenter, Huston, and Spera (1989) found that children devoted more time to television than to any other activity except sleep, so it is crucial for the adults in children's lives to continue to critically analyze this situation. Is the consumer mentality with its preoccupation for material objects, neglect of humanistic caring perspectives, emphasis on psychological manipulation, and disregard for the environment benefiting children?

## ADVOCATING FOR EQUITY AND SOCIAL JUSTICE

*How can the field move toward a place of equity and social justice in the multicultural worlds of childhood?* Gaining insights from research, theories, and children's daily lived realities can guide the field to critically examine long-held practices and find a place of equity and social justice. Giroux (1992) uses the term *border crossings* when emphasizing the importance of solidarity among critical theorists, feminists, multiculturalists, and antiracist theorists. In curriculum theory, Slattery (1995) maintains, *crossing the border* "necessitates a commitment to postmodern democratic reform where subject-area disciplinary boundaries are traversed" (p. 31). Children, families, critical multiculturalists, early childhood advocates, proponents of dialogic-critical pedagogy, and keepers of traditional multicultural wisdom can help the nation to heal its historical past and alter its mean-spirited present. Only by maintaining solidarity will the field impact the complex daily realities young children and their families are facing. Only when the field moves beyond the rhetoric, beyond the fashion shows (Soto, 1997b), and beyond the genetically driven scientific epistemologies (Soto, 1997c) will the humanization and the liberation of child-care teachers, children, and families begin to evolve.

Cummins (1994, 1996) has shown how coercive power imposes oppression, abuse, inequity, and totalitarianism, and violates human rights and freedoms; while collaborative power affords democratic expression, human rights, and freedom. Our discussions can be strengthened by including notions of dialogic-critical pedagogy, critical multiculturalism, feminist ways of knowing, and reconceptualizing paradigms. The national rhetoric about young children and families has taken a mean-spirited tone, making it crucial for multiple voices to address reform. The need for collaborative power models that include teachers, students, and families is also underscored by Darder (1991): Schools "must work in collaboration with bicultural educators, students, parents, and their communities. Anything short of this effort suggests an educational process that is in danger of oppressing and disempowering students of color" (p. 121).

Are there explanations for the etiology of ethnocentrism, hate, and racism? Daniel Jonah Goldhagen (1997) indicates in his recent research that Hitler's willing executioners were ordinary people, ordinary Germans:

> My explanation—which is new to the scholarly literature on the perpetrators—is that the perpetrators, "ordinary Germans," were animated by anti-Semitism, by a particular type of anti-Semitism that led them to conclude that the Jews ought to die. . . . . The perpetrators having consulted their own convictions and morality and having judged the mass annihilation of Jews to be right, did not want to say "no." (p. 14)

The life of Janusz Korczak of Poland (Brendtro, Brokenleg, & Van Bockern, 1990) was also impacted by the Holocaust. Korczak was a writer, teacher, and the director of a school and orphanage for Jewish children of the street. His school was moved to the Warsaw Ghetto when the Nazis occupied Poland. He chose to remain with his 200 children, and when it became evident that he and his children would be sent to a death camp, "he prepared them for what was to come." They prepared a play based on Rabindrinath Tagore's *Post Office,* a story about a dying Hindu boy. The day the soldiers arrived they were dressed in their best and marched behind the biggest boy, who led them carrying a green flag. This children's parade made its way to the chlorinated boxcars and ultimately the gas chambers of Treblinka.

There are no buildings in the place where Korczak and his children met their death, only trees, grass, and a circle of stones. The only individual name on any one stone reads "Janusz and children," along with names of the cities and countries of the victims. A manuscript entitled *Ghetto Diary* was recovered by Korczak's friends from behind a brick wall in the children's home. He summarized the meaning of his life by stating, "I exist not to be loved and admired, but to love and to act."

There is no way of knowing all the challenges future generations will face, but we do have evidence that will guide us as we prepare our children for a life beyond the new millennium. At a time when so many of us are concerned for our youth (e.g., violence, drugs, proliferation of hate groups and paramilitary groups), it seems crucial to learn collaboratively and in solidarity to critically analyze the oppressive elements in our lives within a dialogic-critical pedagogy as *border crossers* willing to gain wisdom from multiple groups and multiple ways of knowing.

A recent visit to New Mexico reminded me how little we have valued Native American traditions, for example. Members of the Cochiti family I met there have clear memories about the Carlisle Indian Industrial School in Pennsylvania, founded in 1879 by Captain Richard H. Pratt, whose motto was: "Kill the Indian and save the man." The process initiated by the "Carlisle School" included the loss of language, the loss of culture, the loss of family connections, and the loss of identity. This deliberate process of cultural invasion also led to cultural and linguistic genocide. The Cochiti families described how family members who returned home found it difficult to cope with and relate to their families and traditions.

Some Native American traditions offer the potential to ameliorate the many concerns Western/competitive, consumer-driven child-rearing practices have produced. Some traditional Native American wisdom may hold possibilities for the field. This is not intended to privilege Native American traditions over other diverse groups but merely to share the multitude of possibilities available as we begin to explore decades of child-rearing practices in multiculturalism in our *border crossing* journey. George Bluebird, a Lakota Sioux artist (in Brentro et al., 1990), portrays a Native American child-rearing philosophy by depicting a person standing in a circle surrounded by four directions. This Circle of Courage depicts four themes: belonging, mastery, independence, and generosity. The authors maintain that the Circle of Courage is not only a cultural belonging for Native Americans but also a cultural birthright for all children.

Selected Native American children's literature provides a rich possibility for viewing child-rearing practices that include attributes from the Circle of Courage. In *Shaman's Circle* (Wood & Howell, 1996), for example, life is depicted as a series of circles where harmony, continuity, the bonds with nature, and the need for personal meaning are evident. Excerpts from this book afford the opportunity for reflection for both children and adults:

> From my grandmother I learned courage, the kind needed to fight for what I believe in. From my grandfather I learned patience, the winter he went hungry so that our family could eat. . . . I was given the opportunity to exchange self importance for wisdom. (p. 33)

Rainbows and their colors are important to the Navajo traditional culture, since rainbows are viewed as blessings. In *Rainbow at Night: The World in Words and Pictures by Navajo Children* (Hucko, 1996), the reader will find Navajo children's ideas about art and culture. The author notes that this book "is guided by the idea that if we all learn a little bit about each other's culture and ways of living, and treat each other with respect, then the world can be a better place" (p. 1). Next to the illustrations and children's photographs, the author suggests questions and activities that children and adults can share. The illustration "A Sunrise Girl," by Stephanie, for example, shows how the Navajo traditional culture can envision that every part of nature is related the way families are related. In the "Three Punk Birds," by Katherine, the importance of wild animals as a part of the natural world is depicted. In Melissa's illustration "Navajo Indians," we see what can happen when the connection between people and nature is broken, while Vanessa in "Weird Rug" shows the challenges children face as a part of the dilemma between modern life and traditional life.

In *The Magic of Spider Woman* (L. Duncan & Begay, 1996), a story is told about a legendary being who taught the Navajo how to weave blankets in order to survive the winters. This teaching tale depicts a most basic value—our need for a well-balanced life. How many of us would be leading healthier and happier lives if our early childhood curriculum had included this concept? The legendary figure reminds us that, "It is good to take pride in our work but we must not allow that pride to become master of our spirits" (p. 36).

There are many Native American stories that are considered sacred since they are a part of religious traditions to which the people who tell them belong. Sometimes Coyote plays a role in the religious stories, but at other times the coyote stories are told for entertainment. The Coyote stories do not belong to any single tribe and can be found throughout the people of the U.S. West. The stories can change from tribe to tribe, from storyteller to storyteller, so that each story may have multiple versions based on the storytellers' imagination and the inspiration of the old stories.

*Coyote Goes Walking* (Pohrt, 1995) is an example of this genre, in which Coyote has obtained a prominent role as a mythical figure in the oral tradition that stretches back to prehistory and continues among contemporary families. *Coyote and the Winnowing Birds* (Sekaquaptewa & Pepper, 1994), which is illustrated by Hopi children, is a story that helps to address issues of home language and culture with a notable lesson, "always be happy with yourself just the way you are" (p. 62). This story may stimulate interest in bilingualism and may help to integrate issues of identity and belonging.

A spirit of mutual caring is a key to eliminating many of the complex problems our children face as we try hard to reach a place that is humanizing and liberating, and as we begin to abandon bureaucratic educational notions and mythic quantifiable scientific paradigms. A successful community incorporates collaborative power models with shared beliefs, values, and ceremonies. In solidarity we can mend the circle of courage and sow the seeds of encouragement. It seems more important than ever that we collectively arm ourselves with wisdom as early childhood *border crossers*. Native American traditions, and other traditions, can help us to examine our legacy for future generations. Not only have genetic, scientific, developmentalist epistemologies disregarded issues of power and traditional multicultural wisdom, but we have allowed them to rule our lives. Smith (1995) notes that it is "a signal feature of our century's close that we recognize that this turn to science was mistaken. Not entirely mistaken. . . . What was mistaken was to expect science to answer ultimate questions, for its method doesn't connect with them" (p. 10). Smith adds that "modern science . . . must be reassessed in light of the changing times and the continuing struggle for social justice. But if we single out [the scientists'] conclusions about reality and how life should be lived, they begin to look like the winnowed wisdom of the human race" (p. 246). As early childhood educators the "winnowed wisdom of the human race" has certainly impacted our profession, but we need not lose hope. As professionals who have for so long imagined a utopian world of equity, we can join in solidarity the many voices, the like-minded voices, the disregarded voices willing to critically examine, dialogue, border cross, and advocate on behalf of young children.

## REFERENCES

Ada, A. F. (1986). Creative education for bilingual teachers. *Harvard Educational Review, 56*, 386–394.

Au, K., & Jordan, C. (1981). Teaching reading to Hawaiian children. Finding culturally appropriate solutions. In H. Trueba & G. Guthrie (Eds.), *Culture and the bilingual classroom: Studies in classroom ethnography.* Cambridge, MA: Newbury House.

Bain, B. (1974). Bilingualism and cognition: Toward a general theory. In S. Carey (Ed.), *Bilingualism, biculturalism, and education.* Edmonton: University of Alberta.

Bain, B., & Yu, A. (1980). Cognitive consequences of raising children bilingually: One parent one language. *Canadian Journal of Psychology, 34,* 304–313.

Banks, J. (1993). Multicultural education for young children: Racial and ethnic attitudes and their modification. In B. Spodek (Ed.), *Handbook of research on education of young children* (pp. 236–250). New York: Macmillan.

Ben-Zeev, S. (1977). The influence of bilingualism on cognitive strategy and cognitive development. *Child Development, 48,* 1009–1018.

Block, M. (1992). Critical perspectives on the historical relationship between child development and early childhood education research. In S. Kessler & B. Swadener (Eds.), *Reconceptualizing the early childhood curriculum: Beginning the dialogue* (pp. 3–20). New York: Teachers College Press.

Bredekamp, S., & Copple, C. (Eds.). (1997). *Developmentally appropriate practice in early childhood programs.* Washington, DC: National Association for the Education of Young Children.

Brendtro, L., Brokenleg, M., & Van Bockern, S. (1990). *Reclaiming youth at risk: Our hope for the future.* Bloomington, IN: National Educational Service.

Carnes, J. (1995). *Us and them. A history of intolerance in America.* Montgomery, AL: Southern Poverty Law Center.

Carpenter, C., Huston, A., & Spera, L. (1989). Children's use of time in their everyday activities during middle childhood. In M. Bloch & A. Pellegrini, *The ecological context of children's play* (pp. 165–190). Norwood, NJ: Ablex.

Chang, H. (1993). *Affirming children's roots: Cultural and linguistic diversity in early care and education.* San Francisco: California Tomorrow.

Chang, H., Muchelroy, A., Pulido-Tobiassen, D., Dowell, C., & Olsen Edwards, J. (1996). *Looking in, looking out: Redefining child care and early education in a diverse society.* San Francisco: California Tomorrow.

Children's Defense Fund. (1996). *The state of America's children: Yearbook 1996.* Washington, DC: Author.

Cobb, P., Yackel, E., & Wood, T. (1992). Interaction and learning in mathematics classroom situations. *Educational Studies in Mathematics, 23,* 99–122.

Collier, V. (1989). How long?: A synthesis of research on academic achievement in a second language. *TESOL Quarterly, 23*(3), 509–531.

Collier, V. (1992). A synthesis of studies examining long-term language minority student data on academic achievement. *Bilingual Research Journal, 16*(1&2), 187–212.

Cummins, J. (1978). Bilingualism and the development of metalinguistic awareness. *Journal of Cross-Cultural Psychology, 9*(2), 131–149.

Cummins, J. (1979). Linguistic interdependence and the educational development of bilingual children. *Review of Educational Research, 49*(2), 222–251.

Cummins, J. (1984). *Bilingualism and special education: Issues in assessment and pedagogy.* Clevedon, UK: Multilingual Matters.

Cummins, J. (1989). *Empowering minority students.* Sacramento: California Association for Bilingual Education.

Cummins, J. (1994, April). Keynote speech at the annual meeting of the National Association for Bilingual Education, Los Angeles.

Cummins, J. (1996). *Negotiating identities: Education for empowerment in a diverse society.* Ontario, Canada: California Association for Bilingual Education.

Cummins, J., & Gulutson, M. (1974). Some effects of bilingualism on cognitive functioning. In S. Carey (Ed.), *Bilingualism, biculturalism* (pp. 35–43). Edmonton: University of Alberta.

Darder, A. (1991). *Culture and power in the classroom.* Westport, CT: Bergin & Garvey.

Delpit, L. (1995). *Other people's children.* New York: New Press.

Derman-Sparks, L. (1989). *Anti-bias curriculum: Tools for empowering young children.* Washington, DC: National Association for the Education of Young Children.

Duncan, L., & Begay, S. (1996). *The magic of Spider Woman.* New York: Scholastic.

Duncan, S., & DeAvila, E. (1979). Bilingualism and cognition. Some recent findings. *NABE Journal, 4,* 15–50.

Fosnot, C. T. (1996). *Constructivism: Theory, perspectives and practice.* New York: Teachers College Press.

Freire, P. (1985). *The politics of education: Culture, power, and liberation.* South Hadley, MA: Bergin & Garvey.

Freire, P. (1996). *Pedagogy of the oppressed.* New York: Continuum. (Original work published 1970).

Giroux, H. (1986). Radical pedagogy and the politics of student voice. *Interchange, 17*(1), 48–69.

Giroux, H. (1992). *Border crossings: Cultural workers and the politics of education.* New York: Routledge.

Giroux, H. (1995). National identity and the politics of multiculturalism. *College Literature, 22*(2), 42–57.

Goldhagen, D. J. (1997). *Hitler's willing executioners: Ordinary Germans and the Holocaust.* New York: Vintage.

Greene, M. (1996). In search of a critical pedagogy. In P. Leistyna, A. Woodrum, & S. Sherblom (Eds.), *Breaking free: The transformative power of critical pedagogy.* Cambridge, MA: Harvard Educational Review. (Reprint No. 27, 13–30)

Hakuta, K. (1986). *Mirror of language: The debate of bilingualism.* New York: Basic Books.

Hakuta, K., & Diaz, R. (1985). The relationship between degree of bilingualism and cognitive ability. In K. E. Nelson (Ed.), *Children's language* (pp. 319–344). Hillsdale, NJ: Erlbaum.

Heath, S. B. (1983). *Ways with words: Language, life, and work in communities and classrooms.* Cambridge, MA: Cambridge University Press.

Hucko, B. (1996). *A rainbow at night: The world in words and pictures by Navajo children.* San Francisco: Chronicle.

Ianco-Worral, A. (1972). Bilingualism and cognitive development. *Child Development, 43,* 1390–1400.

Jipson, J. (1991). Developmentally appropriate practice: Culture, curriculum, connections. *Early Education and Development 2*(2), 120–136.

Kagan, S. L. (1996). The new advocacy in early childhood education. In K. M.

Paciorek & J. H. Munro (Eds.), *Sources: Notable selections in early childhood education* (pp. 366–370). Guilford, CT: Dushkin.

Kessler, S., & Swadener, B. (1992). *Reconceptualizing the early childhood curriculum: Beginning the dialogue.* New York: Teachers College Press.

Kincheloe, J., & Steinberg, S. (1996). A tentative description of post-formal thinking: The critical confrontation with cognitive theory. In P. Leistyna, A. Woodrum, & S. Sherblom (Eds.), Breaking free: The transformative power of critical pedagogy. *Harvard Educational Review,* Reprint No. 27, 167–195.

Kincheloe, J., & Steinberg, S. (1998). *Changing multiculturalism.* London: Open University Press.

King, M. L. (1963). Letter from a Birmingham jail. In *A. J. Muste Memorial Institute essay series.* New York: A. J. Muste Memorial Institute.

Kozol, J. (1991). *Savage inequalities.* New York: Crown.

Kozol, J. (1995). *Amazing grace.* New York: Crown.

Krashen, S. (1988). *On course.* Sacramento: California Association for Bilingual Education.

Lambert, L., Walker, D., Zimmerman, D., Cooper, J., Lambert, D., Gardner, M., & Slack, P. J. F. (1995). *The constructivist leader.* New York: Teachers College Press.

Liedtke, W., & Nelson, L. (1968). Concept formation in bilingualism. *Journal of Educational Research* (Alberta), *14,* 225–232.

Lewontin, R., Rose, S., & Kamin, L. (1984). *Not in our genes.* New York: Pantheon.

Lubeck, S. (1994). The politics of developmentally appropriate practice. In B. Mallory & R. New (Eds.), *Diversity and developmentally appropriate practices* (pp. 17–43). New York: Teachers College Press.

McBride, J. (1996). *The color of water: A Black man's tribute to his White mother.* New York: Riverhead Books.

McLaren, P., & Morris, J. (1997). Mighty Morphin Power Rangers: The aesthetics of phallo-militaristic justice. In S. Steinberg & J. Kincheloe (Eds.), *Kinderculture: The corporate construction of childhood* (pp. 115–126). Boulder, CO: Westview.

McLoyd, V. (1990). Minority children: Introduction to the Special Issue. *Child Development, 61*(2), 263–266.

Moll, L. (1995). Bilingual classroom studies and community analysis. In O. Garcia & C. Baker (Eds.), *Policy and practice in bilingual education* (pp. 273–279). Clevedon, UK: Multilingual Matters.

Moll, L., & Diaz, S. (1985). Change as a goal of educational research. *Anthropology and Education Quarterly, 18,* 300–311.

Moraes, M. (1996). *Bilingual education: A dialogue with the Bakhtin circle.* Albany: State University of New York Press.

Ogbu, J. (1982). Cultural discontinuities and schooling. *Anthropology and Education Quarterly, 13*(4), 290–307.

Ogbu, J. (1987). Variability in minority school performance: A problem in search of an explanation. *Anthropology and Education Quarterly, 18,* 312–334.

Ogbu, J. (1988). Class stratification, racial stratification and schooling. In L. Weis (Ed.), *Class, race, and gender in American education* (pp. 163–182). Albany: State University of New York Press.

Peal, E., & Lambert, W. (1962). The relation of bilingualism to intelligence. *Psychological Monographs: General and Applied, 76* (27, whole no. 546), 1–23.

Perret-Clermont, A., Perret, J., & Bell, N. (1991). The social construction of meaning and cognitive activity in elementary school children. In L. Resnick, J. Levine, & S. Teasley (Eds.), *Perspectives on socially shared cognition* (pp. 40–47). Washington, DC: American Psychological Association.

Philips, S. (1983). *The invisible culture.* New York: Longman.

Piaget, J. (1970). *Structuralism.* New York: Basic Books.

Piaget, J. (1977). *Equilibration of cognitive structures.* New York: Viking.

Pohrt, T. (1995). *Coyote goes walking.* New York: Farrar Straus Giroux.

Resnick, L., Levine, J., & Teasley, S. (1991). (Eds.). *Perspectives on socially shared cognition.* Washington, DC: American Psychological Association.

Sekaquaptewa, E., & Pepper, B. (1994). *Coyote and the winnowing birds. IISAW NIQW TSAAYANTOTAQAM TSIROOT.* Santa Fe, NM: Clear Light.

Slattery, P. (1995). *Curriculum development in the postmodern era.* New York: Garland.

Sleeter, C., & Grant, C. (1988). *Making choices for multicultural education: Five approaches to race, class, and gender.* New York: Macmillan.

Smith, H. (1995). *World's religions: A guide to our wisdom traditions.* New York: Harper.

Soto, L. D. (1992a). Alternate paradigms in bilingual education research. In R. Padilla & A. Benavides (Eds.), *Critical perspectives on bilingual education research* (pp. 93–109). Tempe, AZ: Bilingual Press/Editorial Bilingue.

Soto, L. D. (1992b). Success stories. In C. Grant (Ed.), *Research and multicultural education* (pp. 153–164). London: Falmer.

Soto, L. D. (1993). Native language for school success. *Bilingual Research Journal, 17* (1&2), 83–97.

Soto, L. D. (1997a). Boricuas in America. *The Review of Education/Pedagogy/ Cultural Studies, 19*(3), 349–365.

Soto, L. D. (1997b). Constructivist theory in the age of Newt Gingrich: The post-formal concern with power. *Journal of Early Childhood Teacher Education, 3*(1), 43–56.

Soto, L. D. (1997c). *Language, culture and power.* Albany: State University of New York Press.

Soto, L. D., & Richardson, T. (1995). In R. J. Martin (Ed.), *Practicing what we teach: Confronting diversity in teacher education* (pp. 203–217). Albany: State University of New York Press.

Steinberg, S., & Kincheloe, J. (Eds.). (1997). *Kinderculture: The corporate construction of childhood.* Boulder, CO: Westview.

Swadener, E. B. (1988). Implementation of education that is multicultural in early childhood settings: A case study of two day-care programs. *Urban Review, 20*(1), 8–27.

Taylor, D., & Dorsey-Gaines, C. (1988). *Growing up literate.* Portsmouth, NH: Heinemann.

Torrance, E., Wu, J., Gowan, J. C., & Alliotti, N. (1970). Creating functioning of monolingual and bilingual children in Singapore. *Journal of Educational Psychology, 61,* 72–75.

Vygotsky, L. S. (1981). The genesis of high mental functions. In J. V. Wertsch

(Ed.), *The concept of activity in Soviet psychology* (pp. 105–134). New York: Sharpe.

Walsh, D., Tobin, J., & Graue, M. E. (1993). The interpretive voice: Qualitative research in early childhood education. In B. Spodek (Ed.), *Handbook of research on education of young children* (pp. 464–476). New York: Macmillan.

Wertsch, J. (1991). A sociocultural approach to socially shared cognition. In L. Resnick, J. Levine, & S. Teasley (Eds.), *Perspectives on socially shared cognition.* Washington, DC: American Psychological Association.

Whaley, K., & Swadener, E. B. (1990, Summer). Multicultural education in infant and toddler settings. *Childhood Education,* pp. 238–240.

Wilcox, K. (1982). Differential socialization in the classroom: Implications for equal opportunity. In G. Spindler (Ed.), *Doing the ethnography of schooling* (pp. 269–309). Prospect Heights, IL: Waveland.

Wong Fillmore, L. (1991). When learning a second language means losing the first. *Early Childhood Research Quarterly, 6,* 323–346.

Wood, N., & Howell, F. (1996). *Shaman's circle.* New York: Delacorte.

CHAPTER 11

# Curricular Considerations for Young Children in Inclusive Settings

## JOAN LIEBER, ILENE SCHWARTZ, SUSAN SANDALL, EVA HORN, AND RUTH ASHWORTH WOLERY

EARLY CHILDHOOD special education (ECSE) is a relatively new field. Thirty years ago, teachers, psychologists, speech pathologists, and other professionals were developing the first ECSE programs and attempting to answer the big question—Is early intervention for children with disabilities effective? That question has been answered with a resounding yes (see Guralnick [1997] for a thorough review of the early intervention efficacy literature), and now those in the field of ECSE are struggling with questions about the relative effectiveness of different types of early intervention services and how to provide children and their families with services that facilitate optimal development in inclusive settings.

The purpose of this chapter is to provide a brief history of ECSE; to describe the recent changes in how special education services are delivered to young children with disabilities; to highlight challenges for professionals in inclusive programs; to outline some of the similarities and differences in how curriculum is viewed in ECSE and early childhood education (ECE); and, finally, to review the current state of curricular practices in ECSE and describe how these practices can be used by professionals in ECE.

## A BRIEF HISTORY OF EARLY CHILDHOOD SPECIAL EDUCATION

Early childhood special education is linked historically with special education, early childhood education, and compensatory education (Peterson, 1987). Each of these fields made unique contributions to professional practice and societal attitudes that paved the way for the rapid growth of the field of ECSE. ECSE also has historical ties with disciplines outside of education. The work of professionals in the fields of nursing, developmental psychology, speech pathology, and rehabilitation has a direct influence on the educational services that young children with disabilities and their families currently receive.

ECSE services are also strongly influenced by, and to some extent defined by, legislation. Perhaps the most important piece of legislation for ECSE is PL 99-457, passed in 1986. This legislation, a reauthorization of PL 94-142, the Education of All Handicapped Children Act (now called the Individuals with Disabilities Education Act [IDEA]), mandated a free, appropriate public education for all 3- to 5-year-old children with disabilities and extended discretionary services for infants and toddlers with disabilities. As a result, education and related services for young children with disabilities have been provided by every state and territory in the United States since the 1990–1991 school year. Some of the primary components of IDEA that govern services for young children with disabilities include

- Zero reject
- Individualized and appropriate education
- Nondiscriminatory testing, classification, and placement
- Least restrictive environment
- Rights to procedural due process
- Shared decision making (Bailey & Wolery, 1992)

The least restrictive environment provision of the law has had the most influence on where special education services are provided for young children with disabilities. This provision stipulates that, whenever possible, early intervention services are to be provided in "natural environments, including the home, and community settings in which children without disabilities participate" (IDEA, 1991, Sec. 672).

## EVOLUTION OF PRESCHOOL SERVICE DELIVERY

Prior to the passage of PL 99–457, if children with disabilities below the age of 5 were served at all, those services were primarily delivered in segregated programs. Young children were taught by special education teachers, their assistants, and related services personnel.

During the recent past attempts were made to provide joint programs for children with and without disabilities. A number of programs were developed and funded through model demonstration monies provided by the U.S. Department of Education. Examples include the Community Integration Project (Bruder, 1993) and Project BLEND (Brown, Horne, Heiser, & Odom, 1996), in which toddlers and preschool children with disabilities are served in community early childhood programs. In addition, inclusive services are provided in some university-based child-care programs (Buyusse & Bailey, 1993) and in Head Start programs whose policies, since 1972, mandate that 10% of the children enrolled in each program have disabilities.

The landscape continues to change as more children with disabilities are served alongside their typically developing peers. In a nationwide survey of early education and child-care programs, Wolery and his colleagues (1993a, 1993b) found that children with disabilities were included in more than 70% of the responding programs. They reported that that number represented a doubling of children enrolled since 1986. In a less heartening finding, however, McDonnell, Brownell, and Wolery (1997) recently surveyed 276 preschool teachers working in programs accredited by the National Association for the Education of Young Children (NAEYC). In these high-quality programs, over 40% of the teachers reported that their programs did not include children with disabilities. Further, the majority of children who were included had speech/language problems or other mild disabilities. Fewer than one-third of the teachers had ever taught children with more severe disabilities.

Currently, services to young children with disabilities are provided in community-based child-care centers, Head Start programs, and public school programs (Odom et al., 1997). As shown in Table 11.1, within these settings, professionals offer individualized services to children in a variety of ways (Odom et al., 1997; Thompson, Wickham, Wegner, & Ault, 1996).

Each approach benefits from collaboration among ECSE and ECE staff; however, the team teaching and itinerant services: consultation approaches require extensive collaboration to be successful.

## CHALLENGES FACING PROFESSIONALS
## IN INCLUSIVE PROGRAMS

The proliferation of inclusive programs presents challenges to the adults who teach in them. Training programs that prepare early education

**Table 11.1.** Approaches to the Provision of Special Education Services for Young Children with Disabilities in Inclusive Settings

| Type of Approach | Staff Members Who Provide Special Education Services |
| --- | --- |
| Team Teaching | Special educator and early education teacher |
| Itinerant Services: Consultation | Early education teacher with consultation provided by special educator |
| Itinerant Services: Direct | Special educator and/or related services personnel |
| Integrated Activities Approach | Special educator |
| Reverse Mainstreaming | Special educator |
| Early Childhood Model | Early education teacher who has little contact with special educator |
| Inclusion Facilitator | Paraprofessional with consultation provided by special educator |

teachers, in either general or special education, focus primarily on working with children. Although there is usually a secondary focus on families and paraprofessionals, few teacher preparation programs address how to collaborate effectively or how to share status and responsibility with other adults.

Nevertheless, to meet the needs of young children with disabilities, ECSE and ECE teachers must work together and collaborate. One factor that leads to effective collaboration is good communication (Donegan, Ostrosky, & Fowler, 1996; Lieber, Beckman, et al., 1997; Peck, Furman, & Helmstetter, 1993), which may be a particular issue in programs where adults are not together throughout the day, as they are in team-teaching classrooms. Strategies that facilitate communication include finding informal times to communicate (Lieber, Beckman, et al., 1997) as well as arranging formal meeting or planning times (Friend & Cook, 1996). Communication is also facilitated by stability in working relationships when staff turnover is limited (Donegan et al., 1996; Lieber, Beckman, et al., 1997).

Rainforth and England (1997) note that collaborative efforts are successful to the extent that collaborators hold collective values, including parity, shared responsibility, and shared goals. Parity may be difficult to achieve with the changing nature of roles in inclusive programs. Some staff members interviewed by Lieber, Beckman, and colleagues (1997) were unclear about what their roles were in team teaching and in itinerant models. Peck and colleagues (1993) reported similar concerns for related service providers who felt their roles had become obscure. Teachers interviewed by Thompson and her colleagues (1996) suggested that a solution to the confusion was for staff members to be flexible and inventive.

Parity is strengthened among staff members when they share responsibility for children with and without disabilities. Lieber, Beckman, and colleagues (1997) found that shared ownership was more easily achieved in team-teaching programs. In contrast, in some itinerant models or in models using an inclusion facilitator, children with disabilities were seen as the responsibility of the special educator. That attitude was not inevitable, however. Thompson and colleagues (1996) found that a collaborative attitude was enhanced to the degree that the early childhood program staff felt "empowered as principal players on the team, valued rather than judged, and supported rather than intruded upon" (p. 46).

## UNIQUE NEEDS OF YOUNG CHILDREN WITH DISABILITIES

The final challenge to collaboration that Rainforth and England (1997) identified—having shared goals—may be particularly difficult for ECE and ECSE professionals to achieve. Although the fields of ECSE and ECE share many goals, professionals in inclusive programs must be responsive to the unique needs of children with disabilities and the special concerns faced by their families.

One of the primary goals of ECSE is the amelioration of handicapping conditions and the prevention of secondary disabilities (Allen & Schwartz, 1996; Hanson & Lynch, 1995). This goal may require that families and early interventionists take a more directive approach than is used in most ECE programs. Another important goal of ECSE is to support the needs of families who have children with disabilities (Bailey & Wolery, 1992; Hanson & Lynch, 1995). This goal requires that practitioners work in partnership with families to identify their concerns, priorities, and needs as well as plan interventions that are effective in addressing them. This intervention plan must be specified and agreed to by the family and the service providers in the form of the Individualized Education Plan (IEP).

These differences, or perceived differences, in goals for ECE and ECSE programs are accentuated by different meanings attributed to the same words. Examples that we have experienced and others have written about include the terms *individualized, teaching or instruction,* and *child-directed* (e.g., Johnson & Johnson, 1992; Wolery & Bredekamp, 1994). On one occasion, when an ECSE teacher told an ECE teacher that a child had *individualized* goals that needed to be addressed in the context of ongoing activities in the classroom, the teacher responded, "But I don't have time to do any *one-to-one instruction* with him." Other ECE teachers told us that they see their role as presenting materials/activities to children and supporting their engagement, not *teaching or instructing*. In this view, teaching is linked to the terms *teacher-controlled* or *teacher-directed*. Yet many naturalistic approaches to instruction, described later in this chapter, emphasize the critical importance of capitalizing on child-initated activities, providing choices to children and following their lead, as part of the teaching or instructional process.

A second issue that may result in philosophical barriers is the meaning that we attribute to the use of terms by others. For example, the issue of *teacher-directed* versus *child-initiated* is often portrayed as a simple dichotomy. In this view, ECE teachers are viewed as erring on the side of withholding teacher involvement and possibly missing opportunties to challenge and support children's learning. On the other hand, ECSE teachers are seen as so quick to intervene that they intrude when less directive strategies, such as supporting play and peer interactions, may be effective.

In spite of these semantic challenges, there is an increasing convergence in ECE and ECSE toward a compatible philsophy of instruction. Both fields have been strongly influenced by social-constructivist theorists who believe that learning builds on a child's prior knowledge and experience, and occurs when children are full participants in learning activities. In addition, those theorists suggest that teachers provide the learning opportunities and mediate knowledge acquisition by bridging what a child knows with what the child needs to know at precisely the point when and where knowledge is created. Further, many current special education approaches are designed to fit into the routines and activities in early education settings. In the remainder of this chapter we review what we know about the convergence of ECE and ECSE curricular approaches in inclusive settings for young children.

## OUR DEFINITION OF *CURRICULUM*

According to Wolery and Sainato (1993), curriculum has three elements: (1) the content that can be taught, (2) the methods used to determine what content to teach each child, and (3) the methods used to ensure that the identified content for each child is acquired and used. This definition represents the view of the Division for Early Childhood, the primary professional group in ECSE. It is very similar to the joint definition from the National Association for the Education of Young Children (NAEYC) and the National Association of Early Childhood Specialists in State Departments of Education (NAECS/SDE), which states:

> A curriculum is an organized framework that delineates the content that children are to learn, the processes through which children achieve curricular goals, what teachers do to help children achieve these goals, and the context in which teaching and learning occur. (1991, p. 21)

Thus both definitions include the content, or what is to be taught and learned, and the methods, or how children are to acquire and use this content. We assume that, for the most part, the content (curricular goals) of early childhood is similar for children with and without disabilities. This shared curriculum includes such goals as becoming a more confident learner, learning to interact positively with peers, learning to respect others, learning to communicate effectively, acquiring and using problem-solving skills, enhancing gross motor skills, and so forth.

In addition to these shared curricular goals, children who receive special education also have personalized goals and objectives based on their unique needs. These appear on the child's IEP, a written document that must include the child's present levels of performance, annual goals and short-term instructional objectives, a statement of services needed, dates for initiation and expected duration of services, justification for the placement, and identification of individuals responsible for implementation. It is the responsibility of the team to ensure that services and interventions are implemented, and that information is collected to document progress toward achievement of the child's goals and objectives.

Unfortunately, the IEP is sometimes viewed as a separate curriculum for the child, one that may appear unrelated to the goals and objectives for all children in the classroom. Sometimes this view is reinforced by the way the IEP is developed and written (Goodman & Bond, 1993). That is, sometimes narrow, measurable, but insignificant objectives appear rather than objectives that are more functional, generalizable (i.e., able to be used in a variety of settings), and important. Objectives that meet the latter standards are more apt to be valued behaviors or skills in a child's natural environment.

Thus the IEP represents a child's unique needs and objectives and the methods and approaches that may be used to address those needs and objectives. It should not supplant the classroom curriculum or restrict the child's participation in classroom activities. The teacher's task is to build the curriculum around the needs, interests, experiences, and current knowledge of all children in the program as well as to address the unique needs of children with disabilities.

We now turn our attention to curricular approaches that help young children with disabilities achieve the goals and objectives specified on their IEPs, while at the same time supporting their meaningful participation in activities with their peers.

## CURRICULAR APPROACHES IN EARLY CHILDHOOD SPECIAL EDUCATION

Our experience has shown us that including children with disabilities as full, participating members of a classroom community is not an easy process. Bricker (1995) suggests that children's involvement in programs can happen in one of two ways. The first is an "add-on" approach in which a child with disabilities is granted access into an inclusive classroom but is not functionally a member. In this approach, a child with disabilities might sit with the group during circle time, but few attempts are made to make the activity meaningful for the child. In the second approach, which Bricker labels "integrated," children with disabilities are involved and included in all activities to the extent they can participate.

### Existing Early Childhood Curricula

One method for providing meaningful inclusion for young children with disabilities is to use a curriculum that ensures participation of all children. The Montessori, High/Scope, and Creative Curriculum are examples of curricula that promote inclusion for preschoolers with disabilities (Thompson et al., 1996). The authors identified attributes of those curricula that make them promising for use in inclusive programs, including encouraging child initiation and choice, establishing a predictable environment, and providing ample materials for use by children with a wide range of developmental levels.

An early study of the use of the High/Scope curriculum in integrated settings (Ipsa & Matz, 1978) showed that children with disabilities made gains in their cognitive development and that they interacted successfully with other children. There have been few additional studies, however, in which researchers have investigated outcomes for children with disabilities using these well-known ECE curricula.

### Naturalistic Approaches to Instruction

As noted elsewhere in this chapter, including young children with disabilities as full, participating members of a classroom community presents challenges to personnel and curriculum. In an attempt to address some of these challenges, as well as improve outcomes for children with special needs, researchers and practitioners in ECSE have embraced the use of naturalistic teaching approaches.

This approach to teaching attempts to "integrate the theories of Vygotsky, Piaget, and Dewey while using learning principles espoused by behavior analysts" (Bruder, 1997, p. 530). Known by names such as incidental teaching, milieu teaching, and activity-based instruction, naturalistic approaches share several characteristics:

1. Teaching occurs in the natural environment.
2. Individual teaching interactions are typically very brief and distributed or spaced over a period of hours or days.
3. Instructional interactions are typically child-initiated.
4. Instruction uses natural consequences (objects and events are highly salient and desired by the child) (Noonan & McCormick, 1993, pp. 238–239).

The popularity of naturalistic instruction has resulted in a drastic change in services for young children with disabilities. Whereas even 10 years ago, young children with disabilities were likely to be found sitting at desks, participating in individual or small-group teacher-led instruction, currently they spend more time in child-directed, teacher-supported activities, using materials that are typical of ECE programs and participating in activities with their peers.

Although naturalistic instruction is an excellent strategy for facilitating the successful inclusion of children with disabilities into early childhood education programs, it presents a number of challenges to researchers, practitioners, and consumers in ECSE. First, practitioners who received training in a more prescriptive approach to ECSE may understand effective instructional practices but be less prepared to plan interesting early childhood activities that are engaging and provide multiple opportunties to practice the target objectives. This can be especially challenging in classrooms that include children with a wide range of abilities, interests, play skills, and objectives that must be addressed.

Second, it is much more difficult to document the amount of instruction children are receiving and their concomitant progress using a naturalistic approach. Practitioners need to develop data collection systems that are accurate and sustainable, and use the data from these systems to inform team members about child progress and to make data-based decisions about intervention. Accountability is an essential component of ECSE (Carta, Schwartz, Atwater, & McConnell, 1991); however, traditional data collection systems may not be practical when using a naturalistic approach.

Finally, when using a naturalistic approach to intervention, simply providing access to the activity is not sufficient for many children with disabilities to learn their targeted objectives. Children with disabilities need support, scaffolding, and in some cases deliberate teaching to acquire and generalize new skills (Wolery, Strain, & Bailey, 1992). Researchers, practitioners, and consumers need to work together to define what specialized instruction looks like in the context of naturalistic approaches and how this type of instruction is best delivered. Guidance is needed about what skills are best suited to this approach and how additional support can be provided for children who are not making adequate progress with this type of intervention. Researchers have started to address this question and other issues of effectiveness. For example, one important consideration in adopting a curriculum that relies on naturalistic approaches is to determine if it indeed leads to children's skill acquisition, as Bricker (1995) suggested. A further consideration is practitioners' willingness to use naturalistic approaches. In the following section we review literature that addresses these issues.

**Do Children with Disabilities Learn When Naturalistic Approaches Are Used?** There is an extensive literature on the use of naturalistic approaches to promote skill acquisition in children with disabilities. Probably the earliest use of this approach, called "incidental teaching" by Hart and Risley (1968, 1975), was developed for use with children with delayed language production who came from families with low incomes. Incidental teaching was characterized by an unstructured activity, such as free-play or snack; an initiation or request (verbal or nonverbal) on the part of the child, which sets the occasion for language learning; and a response from an attentive adult. Hart and Risley found that children who participated in incidental teaching interchanges generally increased their production of the targeted language forms.

The incidental teaching approach was refined, extended, and experimentally validated in numerous studies by Kaiser, Warren, and their colleagues who developed milieu teaching procedures (Warren & Kaiser, 1988). Milieu teaching relies on following the child's interests and embedding the "teaching episode" into ongoing interactions between the teacher and the child (Kaiser, Yoder, & Keetz, 1992, p. 9). Evidence indicates that this approach results in improvement of children's use of language during conversation.

Other naturalistic approaches have been applied to objectives in areas other than language development. Venn and colleagues (1993) used progressive time delay to teach children with autism to imitate their peers during art activities in an inclusive preschool. Using this technique, teachers gave a child with autism a direction to imitate one of his peers, then immediately assisted the child with the imitation. As the intervention proceeded and the target child was successful, the length of time between the teacher's direction and her assistance was lengthened. Using this approach, Venn and her colleagues were successful in teaching imitation to the three participants. Generalization to activities other than art was measured, but only when the teacher directed the children to imitate their peers; spontaneous imitation was not measured.

Grisham-Brown and Hemmeter (1997) used additional approaches to teach skill acquisition in typical classroom activities in integrated preschool programs. In addition to using time delay, they used other response-prompting procedures, such as the system of least prompts, simultaneous prompting, and most to least prompts (see Wolery & Wilbers [1994] for a description of these approaches). In their first study, four children with severe disabilities (i.e., multiple disabilities and deafness/blindness) were taught IEP objectives by classroom assistants during a variety of classroom routines and activities. In their second study, two children with developmental delays acquired their objectives during similar activities. Overall, five of the six children were successful in acquiring some of their objectives; there was some evidence that children maintained their performance over time; and the two children in the second study demonstrated two of their objectives in a novel setting.

Garfinkle and Schwartz (1997a, 1997b) conducted a series of studies to examine the effectiveness of embedding deliberate teaching into small-group activities in integrated preschool classrooms. The participants were children with autism and related disabilities whose objectives included imitation and use of an alternative communication system (picture exchange system [PECS]) with their peers. These skills were taught in the context of typical small-group activities (e.g., making books about a classroom theme, playing with modeling clay) in groups that included children with and without disabilities. In both studies children learned the targeted behavior during the small-group activity and demonstrated generalized use of the skill during a free-choice time later in the day. Additionally, the participants demonstrated increases in the quantity and quality of peer interaction during both the small-group activity and free-choice time.

Fox and Hanline (1993) incorporated additional naturalistic approaches into their intervention. In their first study, fine-motor and language objectives were taught to a child with Down syndrome who attended a university child-care center. The intervention occurred during free-choice time after the target child selected the area in which he wanted to play. The interventionist initiated a series of steps: first, modeling or commenting about a peer who was performing the targeted behavior; followed by asking, directing, and physically prompting the child to demonstrate the behavior. After 30 sessions, the child demonstrated each of the targeted behaviors and subsequently maintained them. Fox and Hanline extended this investigation with a second child who had developmental delays and also attended a child-care program. Results indicated that he acquired and maintained his objectives over time and that he generalized his objectives to a new activity.

Based on the limited evidence from the studies described above, we can have some confidence that children with disabilities can acquire new skills in the context of typical activities in inclusive preschool classrooms. However, there are characteristics of these studies that suggest further investigations are needed. For example, participants in Venn and colleagues' (1993) study were children with autism who attended a model program in which the ratio of children with disabilities to children without disabilities was higher than in typical child-care programs. Further, the staff-to-student ratio was higher than in many early childhood settings. Fox and Hanline (1993) conducted their studies in a child-care setting with larger group sizes; however, it was connected with a university, and the intervention was conducted by a practicum student. Thus, despite some evidence that children learn using naturalistic approaches, we are left asking what training and resources are required to make these interventions feasible and sustainable for teachers in typical early childhood programs.

**Are Naturalistic Approaches Feasible and Sustainable?** Mudd and Wolery (1987) provided an early response to this question when they successfully taught four Head Start teachers to use the incidental teaching strategy developed by Hart and Risley (1968). In a brief inservice workshop, teachers learned to use free-play as the setting to increase children's use of requests for particular toys. All four teachers were effective in implementing the components of incidental teaching. Two of the teachers required only the group-presented inservice; two teachers increased their use of the strategy when they received oral and written feedback as well. Although Mudd and Wolery demonstrated that Head Start teachers could acquire this effective teaching strategy, their study was not designed to measure whether the teachers used incidental teaching during additional classroom activities.

In another investigation, Venn and Wolery (1992) taught staff members in an infant-care program that included children with disabilities to engage in interactions with the children during the caregiving routine of diapering. The training for these paraprofessionals was more intensive than the training offered to the Head Start teachers. Training was provided individually and included direct instruction, demonstration and practice, and coaching in specific behaviors. Staff members increased the number of interactive games (such as peek-a-boo) that they played with the children during diapering; however, they did not generalize this behavior to another routine—feeding.

In both investigations by Wolery and his colleagues, the researchers selected the teaching strategies used to improve the children's skills. Peck, Killen, and Baumgart (1989), however, used a different approach. They assumed that teachers would be more likely to implement an intervention if they were actively involved in designing the intervention and if it was compatible with the current classroom routine. In an inventive approach, Peck and colleagues videotaped three community child-care teachers interacting with three children with disabilities during selected routines and classroom activities. The researchers met later with the teachers and asked how they might incorporate the children's IEP objectives into the activities. The role of the researcher during the discussion was to facilitate idea generation, rank ideas, and provide positive feedback. Peck and colleagues found that this nondirective consultation increased the targeted teacher behavior, and two of the three teachers generalized their behavior to another activity.

In an attempt to make their intervention easier to implement and more likely to be carried out in typical early childhood programs, Peck and colleagues taught a special education staff member to provide the consultation and eliminated the videotaping. This refined intervention was successful as well. The two teachers increased their rate of providing IEP-targeted instruction to two children in an inclusive day-care facility; however, as Peck and colleagues note, the quality of the teachers' instruction was not measured.

Thus we are beginning to generate evidence that teachers can implement naturalistic approaches to instruction and that children can learn the targeted skills. In addition to the above approaches, which have been systematically studied in controlled investigations, both ECE and ECSE practitioners have developed a number of strategies that teachers and teams can use to modify or adapt activities, materials, and routines to facilitate the meaningful participation of children with disabilities in inclusive classrooms and to meet children's individual goals and objectives. Often the needed modifications are already in the teacher's repertoire, while other modifications are more specialized. In the following sections, we describe some of these modifications, beginning with those that are easier to implement.

## CURRICULAR PRACTICES FOR INCLUSIVE
## EARLY CHILDHOOD EDUCATION

### Curriculum Modifications

Wolery and his colleagues (1994) surveyed general early educators to obtain their perceptions of the ease with which activities and areas could be adapted to accommodate children with disabilities. Building on this study, Sandall, Chou, and Joseph (1997) conducted focus groups in five states with more than 100 participants, including teachers, therapists, and directors/supervisors. They asked questions related to the modifications used in early childhood settings that allow incorporation of children's IEP objectives into ongoing classroom activities and routines. These modifications are described below.

**Environmental Support.** Teachers can alter the physical space or offer particular materials that promote engagement and learning. Socially, teachers can ensure that the child has models, is in proximity to peers, and has access to consistent, responsive adults who join the child's play and help extend it. Modifications to the temporal environment include adjusting the length of activities or the sequence of activities, and carefully planning for transitions (such as altering the signal to change activities or using picture schedules).

**Adaptation of Materials.** Sometimes it is helpful or necessary to modify materials so that the child can participate as independently as possible. Examples include stabilizing materials (with tape, Velcro, or clamps), enlarging materials (with foam or commercial devices), and clarifying boundaries (with tape, trays, or cardboard box lids). The response itself can be modified or changed if the child's disability limits participation. For example, a nonverbal child might participate in singing by using gestures, pictures, or props; a child with physical disabilities might participate in a cutting activity by describing each of the steps to a peer buddy as they do the project together.

**Simplification of Activities.** Another strategy that is appropriate for some children is to simplify a complicated or complex activity or routine by breaking it into smaller parts or by reducing the number of steps involved. The aim is not just to make the activity easier but rather to simplify the activity so that the child's attempts are effective enough to encourage continued participation. For example, in one classroom the usual routine for handwashing required using the soap dispenser on the wall of the bathroom. One child found this step too difficult and always stopped at this point. The complexity was modified by attaching a plastic soap dispenser to the counter with a suction cup, thereby eliminating the difficult steps of reaching across the sink and using an upward hand motion.

**Use of Children's Preferences.** If the child is not taking advantage of the available opportunities, a modification is to identify and use the child's preferences. For example, particular materials, activities, or individuals might entice the child to a learning center or activity. The expectation is that the child will then participate and learn.

**Adult Support.** There are a variety of ways that the adult can intervene to support the child's learning. Examples include providing a model, providing a prompt, giving specific feedback, and giving hand-over-hand assistance. Once again, the aim is not simply to make the activity easier or to complete the activity for the child but to provide enough support so that the child's attempts are effective and the child continues to participate and learn.

**Peer Support.** Peers can be very effective in helping children learn important objectives. Children can be paired with a peer who can engage them in the learning activity or demonstrate how to participate. Peers can also be taught to model a specific behavior, provide prompts, and give positive feedback.

**Special Equipment.** Special or adaptive equipment or devices can allow children to participate or increase children's level of participation. For example, some children use adaptive chairs or standers. Such equipment means that the child does not have to expend energy sitting or standing and can use that energy to play. Some children use augmentative communication devices or systems such as sign language, picture symbols, or computers. Teachers need to learn and use the child's communication system and incorporate it in classroom activities and routines.

## Embedded Learning Opportunities

We have developed another teaching strategy that might be useful for teachers in inclusive classrooms. Drawn from activity-based intervention techniques developed by Bricker and Cripe (1992), it is based on the following premise: Although many ECE programs offer learning opportunities across the day, children with disabilities may need guidance and support in order to recognize and learn from those opportunities. Ideally, teachers identify the opportunities most salient to the individualized learning objectives for each child and embed short systematic instructional interactions into the existing routines and activities. In this manner, the child's IEP objectives can be addressed in the context of the classroom curriculum.

We have conducted several studies of the embedded learning opportunities (ELO) strategy and found that in all cases children made gains on their target behaviors when the teachers implemented the strategy. With support and guidance, all the teachers were able to identify learning opportunities, create additional opportunities, and establish systematic instructional interactions within ongoing routines and activities. We found, however, that the maintenance of and generalized use of the ELO strategy by the teachers seemed dependent on both the nature of the target objective and on how instruction was delivered in the classroom. For example, an IEP objective such as "pouring with minimal spillage" was easier to embed and support in a natural activity flow than increasing verbal responsiveness in a large-group choral responding activity. We also found that teachers' beliefs about their role in supporting children's learning needed to be addressed prior to implementation. The ELO strategy does require intervening with the child, potentially disrupting the child's current focus, and providing instruction matched to the child's current proficiency with the skill. For some teachers the intervention conflicted with their beliefs about teaching roles (Lieber, Capell, et al., 1998). Some prior discussions to resolve this conflict must occur to insure "buy-in" by the teachers and thus maintenance and generalized use.

## Specialized Instruction

Modifying activities, routines, and materials and embedding planned learning opportunities are appropriate and sufficient to meet the needs of some young children with disabilities. Sometimes, however, more specialized instruction may be required. For example, some children with physical or sensory impairments may need to learn to use a wheelchair or Braille. Other children may not learn well from trial and error, and others may not generalize without systematic instruction. Consequently, there are times when specialized, deliberate teaching is needed. These situations call for time and resources whether the child's learning setting is inclusive or segregated. This situation may also call for more systematic data collection to monitor the effectiveness and efficiency of the instruction.

## WHERE DO WE GO FROM HERE?

As we review the research and state of the practice in ECSE curricula, one of the first questions that emerges is, What are the child outcomes we are trying to achieve? Although the process of education that occurs for most young children with disabilities has changed dramatically in the past 10 years, the way we talk about the outcomes of these changes has not. Our conceptualization of valued child outcomes has remained focused on discrete skills and domains, while our talk about intervention includes ideas about integrated curriculum, functional outcomes, and holistic child development. As a field we need to change the way we discuss child outcomes to be more congruent with current practices in ECSE classrooms. In many cases there is not a good match between the way we envision outcomes, write objectives, and deliver services, and the actual way in which the child uses these targeted skills to have an impact on his or her life. This lack of correspondence between goals and intervention is often most apparent in inclusive early childhood programs.

Some researchers have started to redefine outcomes so that a better fit exists between inclusive programs and what we know about child development. It is important to note, however, that in this attempt to more accurately define what is happening for children in inclusive classrooms, there is not an attempt to deemphasize the importance of skill building in traditional domains. Rather, there is an emphasis on acknowledging other skills that are also being acquired, as well as attempting to put the skills from traditional domains into the context of the social ecology of the classroom. For example, Billingsley, Gallucci, Peck, Schwartz, and Staub (1996) described an outcome framework for students involved in inclusive education. This framework was developed based on a sample of 35 children with moderate and severe disabilities who were involved in inclusive education. At the beginning of the study, the children ranged in age from 3 to 12 years old. The children were followed for 4 years; and extensive classroom observations, teacher interviews, and parent interviews were conducted for all participants. As a result, Billingsley and colleagues propose an outcome framework consisting of three interrelated domains of outcomes: membership (i.e., interactions with groups in the classroom, school, and outside of school), relationships (i.e., peer relationships), and development (i.e., more traditional ECSE skills, such as communication, motor skills, and self-care skills). These domains are firmly embedded in the classroom community, and skills within the domains are acquired through participation in valued roles, routines, and activities in the classroom. To achieve skills in this type of outcome framework, the child must participate in a meaningful way in the planned activities and opportunities for specialized instruction in the early childhood program. Along with reconceptualizing child outcomes, a challenge for the field of ECSE is how to facilitate, support, and maintain the meaningful participation of children with disabilities in activities in inclusive ECE programs.

In this chapter we have provided an overview of the basic principles that influence the development and implementation of curricula in ECSE. Some early childhood educators may wonder how this chapter applies to them or even why it was included in this volume. We suggest that information pertaining to planning and implementing effective educational programs for young children with special needs is essential for all people working with young children. Early childhood educators face a number of challenges in their everyday practice. Foremost among these challenges is providing high-quality services for children who have a wide range of risk factors, including poverty, prenatal exposure to alcohol and other drugs, cultural/linguistic differences, as well as identified disabilities. The information presented in this chapter can be beneficial in planning high-quality educational programs for all young children, not just those with identified disabilities.

In addition, it is important to note that in our current political context, it is increasingly important for professionals in ECE to have knowledge and understanding about young children with disabilities. Inclusion of children with disabilities in community-based early childhood programs is becoming more commonplace. Parents of children with disabilities have made clear that inclusion is here to stay, and the courts have been clear that inclusion is a right, not a privilege (*Oberti* v. *Borough of Clementon School District,* 1993). The challenge facing early childhood educators, therefore, is how to make inclusion successful for all involved— the children, their families, and the professionals. In this chapter we provide some suggestions for developing strategies to support children and adults in inclusive early childhood programs. It is our hope that these strategies can be combined with existing practices in the field to create ECE programs that are truly appropriate for all children.

**Acknowledgment.** The writing of this chapter was supported through a grant (H024K40004) from the U.S. Department of Education.

## REFERENCES

Allen, K. E., & Schwartz, I. S. (1996). *The exceptional child: Inclusion in early childhood education* (3rd ed.). Albany, NY: Delmar.

Bailey, D. B., & Wolery, M. (1992). *Teaching infants and preschoolers with disabilities* (2nd ed.). New York: Merrill.

Billingley, F., Gallucci, C., Peck, C. A, Schwartz, I. S., & Staub, D. (1996). But those kids can't even do math: An alternative conceptualization of outcomes for inclusive education. *Special Education Leadership Review, 3*(1), 43–55.

Bricker, D. D. (1995). The challenge of inclusion. *Journal of Early Intervention, 19*(3), 179–194.

Bricker, D., & Cripe, J. J. W. (1992). *An activity-based approach to early intervention.* Baltimore: Brookes.

Brown, W. H., Horn, E., Heiser, J. G., & Odom, S. L. (in press). Project BLEND: An inclusive model of early childhood services. *Journal of Early Intervention, 20*(4), 364–375.

Bruder, M. B. (1993). The provision of early intervention and early childhood special education within community early childhood programs: Characteristics of effective service delivery. *Topics in Early Childhood Special Education, 13*(1), 19–37.

Bruder, M. B. (1997). The effectiveness of specific educational/developmental curricula for children with established disabilities. In M. Guralnick (Ed.), *The effectiveness of early intervention* (pp. 523–548). Baltimore: Brookes.

Buysse, V., & Bailey, D. B. (1993). Behavioral and developmental outcomes in young children with disabilities in integrated and segregated settings: A review of comparative studies. *Journal of Special Education, 26,* 434–461.

Carta, J. J., Schwartz, I. S., Atwater, J. B., & McConnell, S. R. (1991). Developmentally appropriate practice: Appraising its usefulness for young children with disabilities. *Topics in Early Childhood Special Education, 11*(1), 1–20.

Donegan, M. M., Ostrosky, M. M., & Fowler, S. A. (1996). Children enrolled in multiple programs: Characteristics, supports, and barriers to teacher communication. *Journal of Early Intervention, 20*(2), 95–106.

Education of the Handicapped Act Amendments of 1986, PL 99–457, 20 U.S.C. 1400 *et seq.*

Fox, L., & Hanline, M. F. (1993). A preliminary evaluation of learning within developmentally appropriate early childhood settings. *Topics in Early Childhood Special Education, 13*(3), 308–327.

Friend, M., & Cook, L. (1996). *Interactions: Collaboration skills for school professionals* (2nd ed.). White Plains, NY: Longman.

Garfinkle, A., & Schwartz, I. S. (1997a, May). *Observational learning in an integrated preschool: Effects on peer imitation and social interaction.* Paper presented at the Association for Behavior Analysis conference, Chicago.

Garfinkle, A., & Schwartz, I. S. (1997b). PECS *with peers: Increasing social interactions in an integrated preschool classroom.* Manuscript submitted for publication.

Goodman, J. F., & Bond, L. (1993). The individualized education program: A retrospective critique. *Journal of Special Education, 26*(4), 408–422.

Grisham-Brown, J., & Hemmeter, M. L. (1997, December). *Effectiveness of embedded skill instruction on skill acquisition, maintenance and generalization.* Paper presented at the Division for Early Childhood Conference, Phoenix.

Guralnick, M. J. (1997). *The effectiveness of early intervention.* Baltimore: Brookes.

Hanson, M. J., & Lynch, E. W. (1995). *Early intervention.* Austin, TX: Pro-Ed.

Hart, B., & Risley, T. R. (1968). Establishing the use of descriptive adjectives in the spontaneous speech of disadvantaged preschool children. *Journal of Applied Behavior Analysis, 1,* 109–120.

Hart, B., & Risley, T. R. (1975). Incidental teaching of language in the preschool. *Journal of Applied Behavior Analysis, 8,* 411–420.

Individuals with Disabilities Education Act (IDEA) of 1991, PL 101–476, 20 U.S.C. 1400 *et seq.*

Ipsa, J., & Matz, R. D. (1978). Integrating handicapped preschool children within a cognitively oriented program. In M. J. Guralnick (Ed.), *Early intervention and the integration of handicapped and nonhandicapped children.* Baltimore: University Park Press.

Johnson, J. E., & Johnson, K. M. (1992). Clarifying the developmental perspective in response to Carta, Schwartz, Atwater, and McConnell. *Topics in Early Childhood Special Education, 12,* 439–57.

Kaiser, A., Yoder, P., & Keetz, A. (1992). Evaluating milieu teaching. In S. F. Warren & J. Reichle (Eds.), *Causes and effects in communication and language intervention* (Vol. 1, pp. 9–47). Baltimore: Brookes.

Lieber, J., Beckman, P. J., Hanson, M. J., Janko, S., Marquart, J. M., Horn, E., & Odom, S. L. (1997). The impact of changing roles on relationships between professionals in inclusive programs for young children. *Early Education and Development, 8,* 67–82.

Lieber, J., Capell, K., Sandall, S. R., Wolfberg, P., Horn, E., & Beckman, P. J. (1998). Inclusive preschool programs: Teachers' beliefs and practices. *Early Childhood Research Quarterly, 13*(1), 87–105.

McDonnell, A. P., Brownell, K., & Wolery, M. (1997). Teaching experience and specialist support: A survey of preschool teachers employed in programs accredited by NAEYC. *Topics in Early Childhood Special Education, 17,* 263–285.

Mudd, J. M., & Wolery, M. (1987). Training Head Start teachers to use incidental teaching. *Journal of Early Intervention, 11*(2), 124–133.

National Association for the Education of Young Children and the National Association of Early Childhood Specialists in State Departments of Education. (1991). Guidelines for appropriate curriculum content and assessment in programs serving children ages 3 through 8. *Young Children, 46*(3), 21–38.

Noonan, M. J., & McCormick, L. (1993). *Early intervention in natural environments: Methods and procedures.* Pacific Grove, CA: Brooks/Cole.

*Oberti* v. *Borough of Clementon School District.* WL 178480 (3rd Cir. N.J. 1993).

Odom, S., Horn, E., Marquart, J., Hanson, M., Wolfberg, P., Beckman, P. J., Lieber, J., Li, S., Schwartz, I. S., Janko, S., & Sandall, S. (1997). On the definition(s) of inclusion: Organizational context and service delivery models. Manuscript submitted for publication.

Peck, C. A., Furman, G. C., & Helmstetter, E. (1993). Integrated early childhood programs: Research on the implementation of change in organizational contexts. In C. A. Peck, S. L. Odom, & D. D. Bricker (Eds.), *Integrating young children with disabilities into community programs* (pp. 187–205). Baltimore: Brookes.

Peck, C. A., Killen, C. C., & Baumgart, D. (1989). Increasing implementation of special education instruction in mainstream preschools: Direct and generalized effects of nondirective consultation. *Journal of Applied Behavior Analysis, 22,* 197–210.

Peterson, N. L. (1987). *Early intervention for handicapped and at-risk children.* Denver: Love.

Rainforth, B., & England, J. (1997). Collaborations for inclusion. *Education and Treatment of Children, 20*(1), 85–104.

Sandall, S. R., Chou, H., & Joseph, G. (1997). [Curriculum modifications in inclusive preschool classrooms]: Unpublished raw data.

Thompson, B., Wickham, D., Wegner, J., & Ault, M. (1996). All children should know joy. In D. H. Lehr & F. Brown (Eds.), *People with disabilities who challenge the system* (pp. 23–56). Baltimore: Brookes.

Venn, M. L., & Wolery, M. (1992). Increasing day-care staff members' interactions during caregiving routines. *Journal of Early Intervention, 16*(4), 304–319.

Venn, M. L., Wolery, M., Werts, M. G., Morris, A., DeCesare, L. D., & Cuffs, M. S. (1993). Embedding instruction in art activities to teach preschoolers with disabilities to imitate their peers. *Early Childhood Research Quarterly, 8,* 277–294.

Warren, S. F., & Kaiser, A. P. (1988) Research in early language intervention. In S. L. Odom & M. B. Karnes (Eds.), *Early intervention for infants and children with handicaps: An empirical base* (pp. 89–108). Baltimore: Brookes.

Wolery, M., & Bredekamp, S. (1994). Developmentally appropriate practices and young children with disabilities: Contextual issues in the discussion. *Journal of Early Intervention, 18*(4), 331–341.

Wolery, M., Holcombe, A., Venn, M. L., Brookfield, J., Huffman, K., Schroeder, C., Martin, C. G., & Fleming, L. A. (1993a). Mainstreaming in early childhood programs: Current status and relevant issues. *Young Children, 49,* 78–84.

Wolery, M., Holcombe-Ligon, A., Brookfield, J., Huffman, K., Schroeder, C., Martin, C. G., Venn, M. L., & Fleming, L. A. (1993b). The extent and nature of preschool mainstreaming: A survey of general early educators. *Journal of Special Education, 27,* 222–234.

Wolery, M., & Sainato, D. (1993). General curriculum and intervention strategies. In S. L. Odom & M. McLean (Eds.), *DEC recommended practices: Indicators of quality in programs for infants and young children with special needs and their families* (pp. 50–60). Reston, VA: DEC.

Wolery, M., Schroeder, C., Martin, C. G., Venn, M. L., Holcombe, A., Brookfield, J., Huffman, K., & Fleming, L. A. (1994). Classroom activities and areas: Regularity of use and perceptions of adaptability by general early educators. *Early Education and Development, 5*(3), 181–194.

Wolery, M., Strain, P. S., & Bailey, D. B. (1992). Reaching potentials of children with special needs. In S. Bredekamp & T. Rosegrant (Eds.), *Reading potentials: Appropriate curriculum and assessment for young children* (pp. 92–111). Washington, DC: National Association for the Education of Young Children.

Wolery, M., & Wilbers, J. S. (1994). *Including children with special needs in early childhood programs.* Washington, DC: National Association for the Education of Young Children.

CHAPTER 12

# An Integrated Early Childhood Curriculum: Moving from the *What* and the *How* to the *Why*

## REBECCA S. NEW

THE PERIOD of early childhood is a time of precious opportunity and vulnerability. As knowledge of young children's potentials has become more widely shared, discussions of the early childhood curriculum have become increasingly contested. Usually considered a pedagogical plan, the term *curriculum* is linked with decisions regarding educational content and, often, with related instructional strategies. And yet a curriculum for young children embodies much more than the *what* and the *how* of children's learning experiences in early childhood settings. What children learn depends on how we regard them and what we hope for them. How children learn also reflects our ideas about children's rights and capacities as individuals and members of social groups. How *well* children learn depends to a large degree on our ability to keep our knowledge about them and our hopes for them clear and in the forefront of our deliberations. As children of all ages spend an increasing number of hours away from their homes and families, discussions of curriculum turn into discussions about children's lives. This chapter examines the relationship among the *what,* the *how,* and the *why* of an integrated curriculum designed for young children in a rapidly changing and challenging society.

For early childhood educators, mention of an integrated curriculum typically invokes consideration of the interface between "the whole child" and what I will refer to here as "the whole story"—that is, the nesting of discrete educational goals and objectives within conceptually and experientially rich learning opportunities that are deemed socially relevant and responsive to children's developmental characteristics. This interpretation was apparent in discussions of progressive education beginning in the seventeenth century (Bagley, 1941), was revisited in reforms proposed by Rousseau, and remains central to contemporary interpretations of high-quality, developmentally appropriate early childhood programs (Brede-kamp & Rosegrant, 1992, 1995; New, 1992). The adjective *integrated* is consistently cited as a descriptor of curricular activities deemed develop-mentally appropriate for the diverse needs, interests, and abilities of most classrooms of children (Hart, Burts, & Charlesworth, 1997). The *integra-tion* of content and method is considered virtually indispensable to curric-ulum planning that claims to respond to children's individual patterns of development (Krogh, 1997). And yet, in spite of the strong association between these two indicators of quality early childhood programs, the claim is also made that "developmentally appropriate practice is *not* a cur-riculum" (Brekedamp & Rosegrant, 1992; Vander Wilt & Monroe, 1998).

In contrast to these views, an underlying premise of this chapter is that contemporary interpretations of both an integrated curriculum and developmentally appropriate practices are inextricably linked. Each of these descriptors of early childhood programs reflects judgments about the nature of learning and development and the purposes of education. These judgments, in turn, influence the content, processes, and outcomes of children's learning. Building on this premise, the primary goal of the chapter is to propose an expanded interpretation of an integrated curricu-lum that is sufficiently dynamic to meet the responsibility inherent in teaching young children who will live most of their lives in a world adults can barely imagine.

In the following pages we revisit the two-pronged definition of an integrated curriculum, expanding on common understandings of "the whole child" and "the whole story" in a way that links them both to their cultural and ideological underpinnings. Following a necessarily brief overview of current understandings of young children as learners in par-ticular sociocultural contexts, the second part of the chapter turns to a consideration of essential qualities of an early childhood curriculum as it might reflect this knowledge. This discussion expands on the definition of an integrated curriculum by advocating for the inclusion of families and community members in the determination of curriculum goals and strategies. The chapter concludes with a call for a new version of an integrated curriculum that is both *contagious and courageous*—one that acknowledges the abilities, interests, and rights of young children; the values, beliefs, and goals of families and community members; and the responsibilities of educators in a pluralistic democratic society.

## MULTIPLE IMAGES OF "THE WHOLE CHILD"

Images of children have varied throughout history, across cultures, and within academic disciplines, in each case reflecting ideological presumptions and human experiences (Hwang, Lamb, & Sigel, 1996). Current theories of children's learning and development, influenced by a consortium of studies from the fields of anthropology, sociology, cultural psychology, and comparative child development, increasingly embrace this situated view of the child. The image of the child that has gained predominance in the Western developmental literature over the past decade is a far cry from the generic one described in previous years and is, rather, one of a child-developing-in-context (Rogoff, 1990). This image conveys increased understandings of children's competencies as learners who both influence and are influenced by the larger social and physical environment. Cumulatively, this body of research has contributed to an improved understanding of development as both an interpretive and collective process in which children actively participate in a social world full of culturally defined meaning and significance (Corsaro & Miller, 1992). This holistic and dynamic conception of development has also widened the observational lens through which children must be studied. Of particular importance in more fully comprehending "the whole child" is recognition of the child's membership in the multiple sociocultural contexts represented by the family, the community, and the larger society—each with its own set of interdependent characteristics.

### How Do Children Learn?

Cultural practices in homes, schools, and neighborhoods serve as contexts for children's development (Goodnow, Miller, & Kessel, 1995); they also provide opportunities and content for children's learning. Research in these and other situated settings has contributed to an increasingly sophisticated understanding of the sociocultural dynamics in children's learning and development (E. Forman, Minick, & Stone, 1993). The work of Jean Piaget, once associated with an almost exclusive emphasis on individual cognitive processes, is now aligned (e.g., DeVries, 1997) with Vygotskian perspectives (Bruner, 1996; Rogoff, 1990) in attesting to the power if not the primacy of social and cultural processes. For many in the field of cognitive psychology, "the important question to be asked is not whether the cognizing individual or the culture should be given priority in an analysis of learning, but what the interplay between them is" (Fosnot, 1996, p. 23). While much remains to be understood regarding this process, decades of brain research support the significant role of the environment in children's development by revealing the neurological flexibility of the young child in adapting to early experiences in ways that set the stage for subsequent learning (Newberger, 1997).

A recent interpretation of knowledge construction is that learning takes place through the child's active participation in, or *apprenticeship* to, the routines, rituals, and possibilities that are characteristic of these situated contexts—helping to set the table, celebrating a birthday, or writing a letter on a computer. In this perspective, learning and development proceed hand in hand and are "embedded in the context of social relationships" (Rogoff, 1990, p. 8). Through the process of *guided participation,* children's participation in social experiences and other normative activities is facilitated by others with more knowledge and expertise. What begin as shared understandings eventually become internalized knowledge, skills, and dispositions. While the concepts of apprenticeship and guided participation emphasize "the importance of tacit and routine arrangements of children's activities and their participation in skilled cultural activities *that are not conceived as instructional*" (Rogoff, 1990, p. 8; emphasis added), adults also create occasions and establish learning goals and expectations for children that correspond to the sociocultural tools and practices valued by the larger society.

## Changing Concepts of Competence

Cross-cultural studies support the premise of cultural diversity in adult beliefs regarding children's needs and abilities as well as the educational experiences deemed appropriate for optimal development. These studies have also contributed to a growing appreciation of children's remarkable capacity to learn what is expected of them, especially when that learning corresponds to deeply held values associated with the larger sociocultural context. Numerous studies of parental behavior in diverse cultures have revealed cultural practices that elicit, if not require, behavior in young children that is inconsistent with dominant American expectations and is sometimes contrary to standard recommendations for optimal health and early development (Harkness & Super, 1996).

Other insights into young children's early learning capabilities come from nations that have long acknowledged a societal responsibility for young children through the near-universal provision of preschool and kindergarten education. As a result of formal and informal observations in such cultures, we now understand that some American perceptions of children's early capabilities may be just that—perceptions. Elsewhere—for example, in Japan—it is not regarded as unusual for 4-year-old children to develop the patience to complete complex origami patterns

(Tobin, Wu, & Davidson, 1989), nor for 6-year-olds to be expected to assume the responsibility of classroom management (Lewis, 1995). Children from Reggio Emilia, Italy, demonstrate what would have previously (e.g., Goodenough, 1926) been regarded as precocious competencies if not advanced intellect in their work with clay and other graphic representational media (New, 1994). In each case, most young children learn the skills, understandings, and attitudes that are valued by their families, schools, and communities. Learning goals that appear inappropriate from one perspective are regarded as natural and/or desirable from another (New, 1997). Research on early intervention in other nations (Woodhead, 1996) confirms the premise of purposeful diversity in children's early childhood experiences, with distinct perceptions of optimal learning and development identified in diverse sociocultural contexts.

Cross-cultural studies are not the only source of challenges to prevailing beliefs and norms regarding children's learning potentials. Recent research conducted in the United States also suggests that young children have social and intellectual capabilities previously unrecognized. For example, the work of Corsaro and others has established the power of children's distinct peer culture (Corsaro, 1985; Corsaro & Eder, 1990) at the classroom level. This work has had a profound influence on our understanding of the richness of children's play as a context for children's development and as a source for adult intervention regarding children's social relations. More recent ethnographic classroom studies reveal distinct, stable, and enduring friendship groups of children as young as 2 years of age—each with its own locally constructed peer culture patterns—leading researchers to express the need for a multifaceted definition of social competence that varies across perspectives and across contexts (Fernie, Kantor, & Whaley, 1995; Kantor, Elgas, & Fernie, 1993). Young children not only engage in social practices that were previously assumed limited to older children; they also make judgments about their own behavior in ways that reflect a social conscience and an emotional awareness of the needs of others (Berman, 1997). There is little argument now among researchers of children's social competencies that preschoolers have the capacity to distinguish between hypothetical and actual transgressions (Smetana, Schlagman, & Adams, 1993); they have also been observed to adopt "justice and care orientations" to what might be regarded as moral dilemmas (Cassidy, Chu, & Dahlsgaard, 1997).

Research over the past decade has also contributed substantially to an increased appreciation of children's cognitive competencies and intellectual potentials, thanks to increasingly sophisticated brain research and more comprehensive research hypotheses. For example, we now have evidence of the emergence of core domains of thought that influence children's reasoning about physical, psychological, and biological phenomena (Wellman & Inagaki, 1997). Documentation of children's sophisticated exploration of scientific concepts in Reggio Emilia is joined by other research documenting young children's abilities to actively engage in hypothesis generating and problem solving (G. Forman & Fyfe, 1998). Such research challenges previously held beliefs about the primacy of children's play as opposed to purposeful work as a means of promoting symbolic and representational thinking (New, 1998b); it has also led to a reassessment of previously held beliefs regarding developmental constraints on young children's abilities to comprehend and learn from the use of abstract concepts (Metz, 1995).

This enhanced view of children's learning potentials is not limited to typically developing children. Studies of young children with developmental disabilities conducted over the past decade have resulted in remarkably different views of such children's social competence and intellectual potentials, especially when they have the opportunity to learn with their typically developing peers (Mallory, 1998). High-quality inclusive and heterogeneous classrooms at the preschool and primary levels have created new contexts for children's development that have proved beneficial to diverse populations of young children, including those with cognitive and sensory impairments as well as emotional or behavioral disabilities (Falvey, 1995; Wolery & Wilbers, 1994). Collectively, the past decade of theoretical advances and empirical research on young children challenges previous beliefs of limitations assigned to the egocentric, preoperational, and/or "disabled" child.

And yet recognition of the young child's readiness to learn also includes, by definition, a vulnerability to early experiences, including both their presence and their absence. While some variation in children's learning and development is the result of purposeful choices made by parents and teachers as individuals and as members of diverse communities and cultures, other differences result from lack of opportunity or understanding. Within the United States, research has consistently demonstrated inequities in children's learning as a function of gender, cultural, and linguistic factors, as well as developmental characteristics. Such categorical variation in children's learning often reflects our society's continuing inequitable distribution of economic resources, and prejudicial and categorical school policies and programs; some differences in learning outcomes also result from a noncritical acceptance of expected variation in children's learning (New, in press). While contemporary educators continue to promote the democratic notion that diversity ought to be perceived as an asset rather than a liability (Mallory & New, 1994a), different perceptions of children often come complete with diverse sets of adult expectations of and provisions for children's learning and development (New & Mallory, 1996). Thus discussions of "the whole child" must include *not only* an acknowledgment of the prevailing images of children within particular sociocultural contexts, *but also* the extent to which such contextualized images unfairly influence children's educational opportunities.

## AN INTEGRATED CURRICULUM AND DEVELOPMENTALLY APPROPRIATE PRACTICES: CHOICE TIME FOR THE GROWN-UPS

Much has been written about the implications of a transactional and contextualized theory of learning and development for educators of young children (Berk & Winsler, 1995), including those with special needs (Mallory & New, 1994b) and cultural and linguistic differences (Tharp & Gallimore, 1991). Without pretending to do justice to these and other more extensive reviews, principles of instruction that are consistent with this work may be summarized as follows:

- Children derive multiple benefits from opportunities to learn from and with one another.
- Motivation is higher when learning is personally meaningful and maximally challenging.
- Diverse populations of learners can contribute to the learning opportunities for both the more and the less capable among them.
- Children's play, problem-solving activities, and short- and long-term projects are effective means by which children can explore and represent their understandings of the larger social and physical environment.
- Children's learning can also be promoted through a variety of instructional strategies, assuming shared learning goals and reciprocal relationships.

These theoretically derived principles are consistent with many features typically ascribed to an integrated curriculum (New, 1992), which many continue to view as a methodological "answer to achieving coverage of the curriculum while also promoting meaningfulness" (Bredekamp, 1997, p. xvi). And yet the stance taken in this chapter is that discussions of an early childhood curriculum must move beyond those practical boundaries. Such an emphasis on the *how* of an early childhood curriculum begs the issue of both *content* and *intent,* each of which are central to decisions associated with the lives of young children.

What do we want for young children? In a previous review on this topic, I joined others in the field in advocating for an approach to early education "where the child rather than the subject is the unit of concern and measure" (New, 1992, p. 287). If, indeed, an early childhood education provides children with an opportunity to acquire skills and understandings that are "congruent with the requirements of the culture" (Bruner & Haste, 1987, p. 1), then a curriculum focus that is primarily child-centered is insufficient. Rather, an adequate response to the above question requires an inquiry into the needs, rights, and potentials of *children-in-context,* that is, as present and future citizens of a pluralistic democratic society. The integrated curriculum envisioned in this chapter emphasizes the necessity of making explicit connections between learning experiences in an educational environment and children's whole lives, including their experiences both inside and *outside* the classroom. In the process, this approach to curriculum has the potential to integrate adults and children, institutions and communities, and knowledge as well as dreams. What follows are four broadly defined qualities that might characterize an integrated curriculum that seriously acknowledges its responsibility to young children who are growing up in our pluralistic democratic society.

## Inclusive of All Children and Connected to Their Lives

Contemporary theories of learning and instruction join the writings of John Dewey (1902, 1916, 1938) in emphasizing the importance of connecting curriculum content with the larger context in which the child lives. Current research supports this philosophical and theoretical premise, making clear that when children's learning in school is linked to their lives outside the classroom, their interests are multiplied and they often seek additional opportunities to pursue related activities. Research on children's emergent literacy, for example, reveals the value of "connected texts"—material that is related to something outside the pages of the book (Snow, Barnes, Chandler, Goodman, & Hemphill, 1991). The quality of "connectedness" as a condition of an integrated curriculum means more, however, than in Florida studying orange groves and in Vermont, apple orchards. It also requires explicit acknowledgment of the diversity of the population in our pluralistic democratic society. Such an interpretation of curriculum regards the inclusion of children with cultural or developmental differences as an ethical imperative as well as a pedagogical strategy (Mallory & New, 1994a; New, 1998a).

The qualities of inclusion and connectedness entail more than accepting and embracing difference; they also require effective pedagogical responses to those differences. This approach to an integrated curriculum therefore requires teachers to actively pay attention to differences in children's lives and lifestyles as a means of creating an inclusive classroom culture that is "spacious enough to incorporate what children construct together" (Genishi, Dyson, & Fassler, 1994, p. 265). Perhaps the biggest challenge in promoting competence in the skills and knowledge deemed critical by the larger culture for diverse populations of young children is to make sure that knowledge promoted by the school environment is perceived as useful to the children, not only in their everyday lives but also as a means of helping them in the future to gain access to opportunities and resources otherwise unavailable (Delpit, 1995). For children attempting to bridge two worlds, the role of the teacher is to encourage them to explore and express their own specialized knowledge (Phillips, 1994), even as they learn to value and develop diverse forms and sources of competence.

Such an interpretation of curriculum embraces the classroom environment as a place in which children can find traces of their past experiences as well as their current interests, plans, and activities. Such an environment would look less like a catalogue display of high-quality classroom furniture and more like a composite of elements drawn from the local culture or cultures. Such an environment, like those of Reggio Emilia's municipal preschools, has the ability to serve as both an educational and caring space that includes spaces for children's work-in-progress and for family members to enter into and feel welcome. This interpretation of an integrated curriculum emphasizes the need for connections and continuity among the children, their activities, and the multiple (home and school) contexts of their learning and development.

## Challenging to Children and Adults

The American "obsession with self esteem" (Beane, 1991) has somehow been interpreted to mean that children should be given more opportunities to succeed than to fail and that perhaps it would be in their best interests if we don't ask too much of them. And yet, such a "culture of indulgence" (Damon, 1995) does little to contribute to children's education or to their sense of themselves as learners. It also does little to capitalize on the vast learning potentials of children described previously. An integrated curriculum that respects children's capacities and motivation to learn will be characterized by short- and long-term projects that *matter*—they don't just go on for no particular reason. Single-subject classroom activities will be selected that stretch children's imaginations and problem-solving capacities even as the problems themselves invite children to work hard together to find solutions. Such a curriculum entails a more sophisticated understanding of mastery motivation than has previously dominated the field, with recognition of both the social and intellectual properties of the problem or task that are essential to evoking the "I think I can!" response in young children (Hauser-Cram, 1998).

This interpretation of curriculum places a heavy emphasis on the role of teachers, who have the responsibility of helping children negotiate their learning goals and processes (G. Forman & Fyfe, 1998). This interpretation also requires that teachers provide children with multiple opportunities to learn from one another, to revisit their understandings, and to reflect critically on their own and each other's ideas. To insure that children are challenged may also require that teachers learn about subject matter of which they may have little prior knowledge or experience. Early childhood educators who often admit their reticence to incorporating science and technology into their curriculum will have to become more willing to expand upon their own incomplete understandings of these and other unfamiliar domains (New, 1998b).

This interpretation of a *challenging* integrated curriculum also requires that teachers see themselves as students of children's learning and development. Only then can teachers develop a curriculum that builds upon current understandings even as it facilitates new avenues of inquiry. This kind of knowledge about young children cannot be found in teachers' manuals, but, rather, comes from the hard work of daily observations, record keeping, and critical reflection (Drummond, 1994). The successful application of such knowledge in the form of curriculum goals and strategies requires teachers to develop an educational philosophy as well as a teaching repertoire that is responsive to the diverse learning styles and experiences of all of the children in their care.

Even as teachers develop new understandings of children's diverse needs, interests, and capabilities, they must also learn how to question their own beliefs about children, especially when those beliefs create obstacles to children's learning. The role that teachers assign themselves with respect to children's learning of subjects like mathematics is highly influenced by their beliefs about how children learn (Fennema, Franke, Carpenter, & Carey, 1993). Early childhood educators frequently share the view that such domains are best pursued by children through play and other child-initiated activities, eliminating the necessity for purposeful teacher involvement. Similarly, teacher interpretations of the significance of differences between children directly influence curriculum goals and strategies. Such beliefs support practices that include lesser expectations for girls to acquire computer skills or for special needs children to have academic goals on their Individualized Education Plans (IEPs) or for

Head Start children to engage in practices that promote emergent literacies. Such uncritical perceptions of children's learning potentials lead to an implicit *acceptance* of disappointments in educational outcomes and mitigates the advantages otherwise associated with inclusive and heterogeneous classrooms. Such "deference to difference" (New, 1998a) also denies children the right to acquire essential skills and knowledge valued by the larger society.

## Communal and Collaborative

In a presidential address to the Society for Research on Child Development, Robert Emde (1994) noted that "a sense of individuality, as well as a sense of communalism, is vital for functioning in a democratic society" (p. 724). Perhaps the most essential quality of an integrated curriculum is its communal and collaborative nature. An integrated curriculum such as that envisioned in this chapter can play a major role in contributing to the making of a classroom community for young children. Such a curriculum also has the potential to promote a coming together of parents and teachers, the school and the larger community based on the nurturing of collaborative and reciprocal relationships.

The concept of a classroom as a community relies heavily on children's developing abilities to move beyond a dependency on adults in their environment to establish interdependent relationships with one another. The value of children's social relations to their cognitive development and academic achievement has been well-acknowledged (e.g., Levine, 1993; New, 1992). Early childhood educators also now have access to a wealth of knowledge regarding the risks and the potentials of children's social relationships as they contribute to individual identities and a sense of belonging. Research on peer cultures (Kantor et al., 1993) and children's understandings of difference (Ramsey, 1998) as well as classroom narratives such as those by Vivian Paley (e.g., Paley, 1995) have established issues of inclusion, exclusion, and peer status as common themes in children's classroom lives. Although there was some question, a decade ago, about the risks associated with children's peer status (Parker & Asher, 1987), more recent research literature makes painfully clear the negative consequences to children who are consistently denied meaningful and respectful relationships with other children (Pianta & Walsh, 1996). Concurrently, a growing body of research supports a move away from trying to teach unsuccessful children how to be successful and, rather, to helping *all* children learn to be more adaptable in social interactions, to read social cues, and to access the necessary cultural knowledge of specific groups (Dyson, 1993). The teacher's role in such social negotiations is multiple and complex. Sometimes the teacher's contribution can be as simple as the provision of a "marker of affiliation" that allows others to perceive the excluded child as a new member of the group (Kantor et al., 1993). A more challenging interpretation of the teacher's role entails a change in attitude regarding children's conflicts, which might better be viewed as occasions for negotiation rather than prevention. While little research has actually been conducted on children's conflicts, much less on the role of adult involvement, teacher assistance in establishing intersubjectivity as a means of conflict resolution has both theoretical and empirical support (Goncu & Cannella, 1996). Long-term projects such as those that characterize classroom work in Reggio Emilia also serve as vehicles through which children develop conflict negotiation skills (New, 1998b).

Establishing communities of young children is not an easy task, given the emphasis on strong teacher-child relationships and conflict-free classrooms that characterize the U.S early childhood tradition (Tobin, Wu, & Davidson, 1989). And yet, the goal of developing collaborative relationships with adults is likely a far more problematic and challenging one for most early childhood educators. While few question the benefits of parent involvement in children's early education (Hoover-Dempsey & Sandler, 1995), the type of home–school relationship envisioned in this integrated curriculum goes beyond that typically associated with high-quality early childhood programs. This new version of parent involvement is manifest in ongoing discussions and negotiations regarding the real life of schools, including the nature and the content of the curriculum itself. *What do we want for our children? What do we know about them that will help us all to better teach them? How can teachers and parents support each other's roles in the children's development?* Responses to these questions reflect cultural values, social norms, and educational goals and, as such, require the full participation of all of those who care about and are involved in the lives of the children and the future of the community. And yet both parents and teachers cite numerous obstacles to effective partnerships, including different interpretations of parental versus professional expertise and a lack of administrative support for true parental engagement within the cultural context of schools. These concerns are exacerbated in settings characterized by ethnic, socioeconomic, and political differences regarding the aims and characteristics of high-quality early childhood programs. The importance of developing trust in such relationships is especially critical, and yet, as numerous parents and teachers acknowledge, it doesn't come easy (Drummond, 1994).

Perhaps the greatest obstacle to effective home–school relationships is teacher hesitation to invite controversy into discussions of the early childhood curriculum, especially when the contributions are from groups already suspected of having alternative perspectives on how best to care for and educate young children (King, 1998). And yet this type of discussion is essential to a curriculum that embraces the democratic principle of open participation in the negotiation of issues of public concern. This interpretation requires acknowledgment of the minimal role some adults play in children's early educational experiences. While the research literature continues to grow on the critical importance, for example, of male involvement in children's development (Lamb, 1997), men's presence is rare in early childhood programs (Levine, 1993). The feminization of the field of early childhood reflects more than the low status associated with child care; it also reflects age-old biases about men's abilities to respond to the particular needs of young children (Silin, 1995). The determination of educational goals and strategies within a pluralistic democracy requires just such an inclusive community of adults.

This version of an integrated curriculum envisions teachers in extensive networks of relationships outside those associated with children in the classroom, where issues of rights and responsibilities may well continue to be highly contested. This community of learners must also include other teachers, caregivers, and administrators. And yet one of the greatest obstacles to a more effective and equitable system of early childhood education (Kagan & Cohen, 1997) and the type of integrated curriculum envisioned in this chapter is the field's highly segregated nature. Only occasionally, for example, are infant–toddler caregivers routinely invited to share their observations of and concerns for young children with the preschool teachers in a community. Likewise, preschool and Head Start teachers are often disregarded by kindergarten teachers and frequently play little or no role in the transition process, much less the identification of appropriate curriculum goals and strategies. The contentious debates between kindergarten teachers and those responsible for the primary grades are almost a tradition in the field. This lack of collaboration within and between programs contributes to discontinuous experiences for young children and their families; it also makes it unlikely that substantive discussions can take place regarding the purposes and processes of high-quality early education. A truly integrated curriculum will actively develop, maintain, and utilize linkages between multiple programs that serve young children and their families.

Reggio Emilia's philosophy of education embraces the notion that schooling is a system of relations (Edwards, Gandini, & Forman, 1998), with the quality of the program for children inextricably linked to the quality of the relationships among and between the adults. The three decades of work in that Italian community provide ample evidence that,

when adults work together to identify the skills, knowledge, and dispositions that they believe will best serve young children in their current and
future lives, they contribute to the curriculum's developmental appropriateness even as they become a more collaborative and integrated community of adults (New, 1997). Other contemporary curriculum frameworks
such as an emergent curriculum (Jones & Nimmo, 1994) also acknowledge the challenges and the rewards of working toward successful adult
relationships on behalf of young children.

## Courageous

The previously discussed qualities of an integrated curriculum—being
inclusive and connected, challenging to young and old alike, communal
and collaborative—all contribute to a curriculum's capacity to be contagious, that is, generative in the spreading of ideas and relationships. And
yet these qualities are insufficient to enable a curriculum for young children to respond to the anticipated skills, attitudes, and knowledges essential for life in the twenty-first century. New interpretations of an early
childhood curriculum must go beyond that of "curriculum is what happens" (Dittman, 1974) to envisioning an early childhood curriculum that
represents *how things ought to be.* Such a curriculum requires that teachers promote educational goals and utilize educational strategies that acknowledge children's past, respond to their present, and hold promise for
their future. This interpretation of an early childhood curriculum requires
tremendous courage on the part of educators.

   This approach to an early childhood curriculum places explicit emphasis on the need for professional integrity, in which teaching and moral
perception go hand in hand. As teachers help children solve social and
intellectual problems, as they respond to children's creative and emotional responses to classroom events, as they plan and implement projects
that represent multiple learning opportunities for diverse learners, they
are teaching young children powerful lessons in what knowledge is important, what behaviors are valued, and what sorts of relationships are
essential to a safe and inclusive learning community. When adults are
viewed as "recognizing and responding thoughtfully to the needs, interests, beliefs, values, and behavior of others" (Simpson & Garrison, 1996,
p. 252), they serve as important models for children's own developing
sense of what is right and wrong. A "curriculum" from this perspective
includes not only what is being taught, but how and to what end.

   This interpretation of curriculum necessitates a recognition that virtually *all* pedagogical decisions carry moral weight, including those
required when teachers must balance their concern for accurate subject-

matter knowledge with concern for the students, including but not limited to their processes of learning. The courage associated with teacher decision-making is acknowledged in contemporary research on teachers' struggles over how to convey content knowledge—for example, in mathematics or social studies—while simultaneously respecting students' own thinking (Ball & Wilson, 1996). Courageous teachers are often asking of themselves, "When does it matter enough to set things straight?" Sometimes the right thing to do is to wait and see, giving primacy to children's rights to develop conceptual understandings through their involvement and participation in the problem-solving activity. In this sense, assessment strategies become a part of the curriculum, with their potential to serve as means of identifying learning possibilities rather than learning deficiencies (Drummond, 1994). Authentic forms of assessment, in turn, can be linked to subsequent curriculum plans and activities.

Teachers also require a certain amount of courage to directly intervene, especially when that intervention goes against the grain of traditional interpretations of developmentally appropriate practices. Vivian Paley (1994) describes her personal difficulties in taking on the sacred territory of children's free play by declaring, "You can't say you can't play." Acknowledging her own responsibility as an adult in a setting that was rife with rejection and ridicule, Paley drew upon her own ethics as well as her belief in young children's capacities to develop empathic relations to insist that they play in a manner that conveyed a respect for one another as human beings (Paley, 1994). In addition to helping children learn how to avoid rejecting one another, teachers must also help children understand rejection by adults. Lisa Delpitt (1995) and others have noted the critical need to teach children about adult prejudices so that they will better understand the need to learn new ways of talking and behaving as strategies for successful participation in diverse settings. Such a curriculum is more honest and helpful than one that simplistically teaches children "everyone is the same on the inside." It also requires a considerable amount of courage on the part of the teacher.

For a curriculum that integrates not only bodies of knowledge but also the consumers of such knowledge, perhaps the most difficult thing that teachers must learn to do is to *go public* with their understandings of and hopes for children. This form of advocacy requires that teachers become more skilled at observing and recording children's learning and more willing to share their findings with others, each of whom is likely to have his or her own set of opinions and understandings. The work of educators in Reggio Emilia has served as a catalyst for teachers to utilize various documentation strategies as a means of conveying their changing images of children to others. In spite of the growing popularity of this observational strategy, U.S. teachers are often hesitant to display their observations of young children, explaining that they are "afraid that parents will see their mistakes" (Gorham & Nason, 1997, p. 23). Teacher avoidance of conflicts with parents and administrators, especially regarding known controversial topics, is understandable. And yet teacher advocacy for children in general and a classroom of children in particular is an essential component of the process of establishing fair, feasible, and relevant educational goals for diverse populations of young children. This process also requires that teachers learn how to listen to what others are observing and hoping for, and assume a negotiating role regarding the potentials and significance of children's learning. Through their work with parents and other educators, teachers can learn how to recognize and articulate their own prejudices and priorities; see the results of their own efforts as learners; and become more capable advocates for children.

## CONCLUSION

The influence of cultural values, beliefs, and goals on children's development is now well established. Research in the United States and in other cultural contexts makes clear that children learn a great deal from the adults who care for them, not only as a result of direct instruction and other planned learning opportunities, but through the rites, rituals, and routines that are a part of daily living. Put another way, the manner in which young children are cared for and the social relationships they develop with adults and other children in early educational settings profoundly influence their developmental progress as well as the lessons they learn along the way. These experiences and their associated relationships, in turn, are informed by a larger set of values and beliefs associated with the surrounding sociocultural context. Such an interpretation of cultural practices as contexts for development not only makes culture come alive; it also challenges the very notion of a distinction between concepts of curriculum and developmentally appropriate practices.

This interpretation of culture practices also challenges the notion of culture as the status quo. Adults are not necessarily bound to the historic presumptions associated with diverse cultures but, rather, draw on selected traditions as they make choices about children's present lives and future opportunities. Throughout the history of early childhood education in the United States, parents and teachers have debated the *what* and the *how* of children's early experiences as these choices corresponded to changing conditions within the larger sociocultural context. Froebel's Gifts and Occupations, Montessori's daily living, Dewey's practical experiences—each of these approaches to early education included new and different interpretations of what children need most as determined by the risks and potentials found in the larger society.

Today, the major discussion in the field of early education continues to revolve around the question of what constitutes an appropriate curriculum for young children. A decade ago, the controversy centered on the competing advantages of an academic curriculum versus a more child-centered approach and teacher-directed versus child-initiated instruction. Professional responses to this debate were articulated in the first guidelines for developmentally appropriate practices (DAP; Bredekamp, 1987). By the middle of the decade, the DAP guidelines themselves were the source of controversy as a result of the "one size fits all" interpretation and the inadequate attention to diverse perspectives (Mallory & New, 1994a). The recently revised guidelines address many of the earlier criticisms (Bredekamp & Copple, 1997), and yet the controversy continues as parents, teachers, administrators, advocates, and other interested citizens vie for position in determining essential features of an early childhood curriculum.

And so, we close the twentieth century with many of the same questions that faced adults one hundred years ago. *What should children learn and how ought they best learn it?* Most would agree that schools should teach children how to do things that our culture values—that is, to read, to compute mathematical problems, to communicate effectively. And yet such a response in a pluralistic society such as the United States is much less simple than it might appear. What do we mean, after all, by the phrase "communicate effectively"? That all children should learn Spanish? Sign language? Computer skills? Discussions about curriculum (content *and* method) lack integrity if the discussants cannot also respond to these two related questions: *Who says so, and why?* The version of an integrated curriculum described in this chapter acknowledges the current controversies associated with such choices as listed. It also respects the critical need to justify decisions associated with educational imperatives. Indeed, this version of an early childhood curriculum includes, by definition, the need for adults to struggle aloud and together with such decisions, knowing that their choices create as well as preclude opportunities for children's current learning and future lives. Such a requirement not only makes adults more directly aware of their responsibilities for their own and each other's children; it also requires that adults learn how to work together on their behalf.

This version of an integrated curriculum expects that children can benefit from working hard at learning together and that they deserve help in understanding what to *do* with what they know. Children living in a democratic society need to be provided with ample occasion *and need* to use their new skills and understandings to make a difference in their own circumstances or those of a friend or someone in the larger community. Such an educational aim requires a sense of self as a competent individual; it also requires a sense of membership in a group as a way to give meaning to a developing sense of responsibility. As children learn how to participate in a community of learners (that, in this version of an integrated curriculum, includes their parents as well as their teachers), they contribute to the quality of that community. They learn good citizenship by being treated and expected to act as citizens—with shared and individual rights, needs, and competencies. This integration of academic content with social cause is distinct from most multidisciplinary interpretations of a curriculum in which discrete skills and disciplinary knowledge remain central in the minds of the adults (Beane, 1997). Rather, this version of an integrated curriculum represents a convergence of forces and includes the context as part of the content and integrates the learners, the learning environment, and the learning process as a part of "the whole story." Such a curriculum reflects

- A belief in children's rights to learn about what is of interest to them in a manner that insures that they will also develop those skills and understandings that are critical to their participation in the larger society
- An acknowledgment of adult responsibility (parents *and* teachers) to negotiate for educational goals and strategies that reflect common ground among diverse points of view
- A respect for teachers' capacities to use what they are learning about children and what they believe in as catalysts for public conversations about the purposes of an early childhood education

As parents and teachers pool their respective observations and opinions to construct new understandings about children's needs, interests, and potentials, adult understandings of children's lives then become both the sources and the recipients of educational decisions. From this perspective, educational goals and teaching practices can do much more than reflect the broader culture (Bruner, 1996); they have the potential to contribute to the education of a new culture. Such an integrated curriculum is worthy of imposing on young children.

## REFERENCES

Bagley, W. C. (1941). The case for essentials in education. *Today's Education. Journal of the National Education Association, 30*(7), 201–202. Reproduced in G. Hass (Ed.), 1983, *Curriculum planning: A new approach* (4th ed., pp. 21–23). Boston: Allyn & Bacon.

Ball, D. L., & Wilson, S. M. (1996). Integrity in teaching: Recognizing the fusion of the moral and intellectual. *American Educational Research Journal, 33*(1), 155–192.

Beane, J. A. (1991). Enhancing children's self-esteem: Illusion and possibility. *Early Education and Development, 2*(2), 153–160.

Beane, J. A. (1997). *Curriculum integration: Designing the core of democratic education.* New York: Teachers College Press.

Berk, L., & Winsler, A. (1995). *Scaffolding children's learning: Vygotsky and early childhood education.* Washington, DC: National Association for the Education of Young Children.

Berman, S. (1997). *Children's social consciousness and the development of social responsibility.* Albany: State University of New York Press.

Bredekamp, S. (Ed.). (1987). *Developmentally appropriate practice in early childhood programs serving children from birth through age 8.* Washington, DC: National Association for the Education of Young Children.

Bredekamp, S. (1997). Introduction. In C. H. Hart, D.C. Burts, & R. Charlesworth (Eds.), *Integrated curriculum and developmentally appropriate practice.* Albany: State University of New York Press.

Bredekamp, S., & Copple, C. (Eds.) (1997). *Developmentally appropriate practice in early childhood programs* (rev. ed.). Washington, DC: National Association for the Education of Young Children.

Bredekamp, S., & Rosegrant, T. (1992). *Reaching potentials* (Vol. 1). Washington, DC: National Association for the Education of Young Children.

Bredekamp, S., & Rosegrant, T. (1995). *Reaching potentials: Transforming early childhood curriculum and assessment* (Vol. 2). Washington, DC: National Association for the Education of Young Children.

Bruner, J. (1996). *The culture of education.* Cambridge, MA: Harvard University Press.

Bruner, J., & Haste, H. (Eds.) (1987). *Making sense: The child's construction of the world.* New York: Methuen.

Cassidy, K. W., Chu, J. Y., & Dahlsgaard, K. K. (1997). Preschoolers' ability to adopt justice and care orientations to moral dilemmas. *Early Education & Development, 8*(4), 419–434.

Corsaro, W. A. (1985). *Friendship and peer culture in the early years.* Norwood, NJ: Ablex.

Corsaro, W. A., & Eder, D. (1990). Children's peer cultures. *Annual Review of Sociology, 16,* 197–220.

Corsaro, W. A., & Miller, P. J. (Eds.) (1992). *Interpretive approaches to children's socialization* (New Directions for Child Development No. 58). San Francisco: Jossey-Bass.

Damon, W. (1995). *Greater expectations: Overcoming the culture of indulgence in our homes and schools*. New York: Free Press.

Delpit, L. D. (1995). *Other people's children: Cultural conflict in the classroom*. New York: New Press.

DeVries, R. (1997). Piaget's social theory. *Educational Researcher, 26*(2), 4–17.

Dewey, J. (1902). *The child and the curriculum*. Chicago: University of Chicago Press.

Dewey, J. (1916). *Democracy and education*. New York: Macmillan.

Dewey, J. (1938). *Experience and education*. New York: Macmillan.

Dittman, L. (1974). *Curriculum is what happens*. Washington, DC: National Association for the Education of Young Children.

Drummond, M. (1994). *Learning to see: Assessment through observation*. York, ME: Stenhouse.

Dyson, A. (1993). A sociocultural perspective on symbolic development in primary grade classrooms. In C. Daiute (Ed.), *The development of literacy through social interaction* (New Directions for Child Development No. 61, pp. 25–40). San Francisco: Jossey-Bass.

Edwards, C., Gandini, L., & Forman, G. (Eds.). (1998). *The hundred languages of children: The Reggio Emilia approach to early childhood education* (2nd ed.). Norwood, NJ: Ablex.

Emde, R. 1994. Individuality, context, and the search for meaning. *Child Development, 65*(3), 719–737.

Falvey, M. A. (1995). *Inclusive and heterogeneous schooling: Assessment, curriculum, and instruction*. Baltimore: Brookes.

Fennema, E., Franke, M. L., Carpenter, T. P., & Carey, D. A. (1993). Using children's mathematical knowledge in instruction. *American Educational Research Journal, 30*(3), 555–583.

Fernie, D., Kantor, R., & Whaley, K. (1995). Learning from classroom ethnographies: Same places, different times. In A. Hatch (Ed.), *Qualitative research in early childhood settings* (pp. 155–172). Westport, CT: Praeger.

Forman, E., Minick, N., & Stone, C. A. (1993). *Contexts for learning: Sociocultural dynamics in children's development*. New York: Oxford University Press.

Forman, G., & Fyfe, B. (1998). Design, documentation and discourse: A theory of negotiated learning. In C. Edwards, L. Gandini, & G. Forman (Eds.), *The hundred languages of children: The Reggio Emilia approach* (2nd ed.). Norwood, NJ: Ablex.

Fosnot, C. (Ed.). (1996). *Constructivism: Theory, perspectives, and practice*. New York: Teachers College Press.

Genishi, C., Dyson, A., & Fassler, R. (1994). Language and diversity in early childhood: Whose voices are appropriate? In B. Mallory & R. New (Eds.), *Diversity and developmentally appropriate practices: Challenges for early childhood education* (pp. 250–268). New York: Teachers College Press.

Goncu, A., & Cannella, V. (1996). The role of teacher assistance in children's construction of intersubjectivity during conflict resolution. In M. Killen (Ed.), *Children's autonomy, social competence, and interactions with adults and other children: Exploring connections and consequences* (New Directions for Child Development No. 73, pp. 57–70). San Francisco: Jossey-Bass.

Goodenough, F. L. (1926). *Children's drawings as a measure of intellectual maturity.* New York: Harcourt Brace Jovanovich.

Goodnow, J. J., Miller, P. J., & Kessel, F. (Eds.) (1995). *Cultural practices as contexts for development. New Directions for Child Development, no.* 67. San Francisco: Jossey-Bass.

Gorham, P. J., & Nason, P. N. (1997). Why make teachers' work more visible to parents? *Young Children, 52*(5), 22–26.

Harkness, S., & Super, C. (Eds.). (1996). *Parents' cultural belief systems: Their origins, expressions, and consequences.* New York: Guilford.

Hart, C. H., Burts, D. C., & Charlesworth, R. (Eds.). (1997). *Integrated curriculum and developmentally appropriate practice.* Albany: State University of New York Press.

Hauser-Cram, P. (1998). I think I can, I think I can: Understanding and encouraging mastery motivation in young children. *Young Children, 53*(4), 67–71.

Hoover-Dempsey, K. V., & Sandler, H. W. (1995). Parental involvement in children's education: Why does it make a difference? *Teachers College Record, 97*(2), 310–331.

Hwang, C. P., Lamb, M. E., & Sigel, I. E. (1996). *Images of childhood.* Mahwah, NJ: Erlbaum.

Jones, E., & Nimmo, J. (1994). *Emergent curriculum.* Washington, DC: National Association for the Education of Young Children.

Kagan, S. L., & Cohen, N. (1997). *Not by chance: Creating an early care and education system for America's children* (Abridged Report: The Quality 2000 Initiative). New Haven, CT: The Bush Center in Child Development and Social Policy.

Kantor, R., Elgas, P., & Fernie, D. (1993). Cultural knowledge and social competence within a preschool peer culture group. *Early Childhood Research Quarterly, 8*(2), 125–147.

King, J. R. (1998). *Uncommon caring: Learning from men who teach young children.* New York: Teachers College Press.

Krogh, S. L. (1997). How children develop and why it matters: The foundation for the developmentally appropriate integrated early childhood curriculum. In C. H. Hart, D.C. Burts, & R. Charlesworth (Eds.), *Integrated curriculum and developmentally appropriate practice* (pp. 29–48). Albany: State University of New York Press.

Lamb, M. E. (1997). *The role of the father in child development* (3rd ed.). Hillsdale, NJ: Erlbaum.

Levine, J. A. (1993). Involving fathers in Head Start: A framework for public policy and program development. *Families in Society, 74*(1), 4–19.

Lewis, C. C. (1995). *Educating hearts and minds: Reflections on Japanese preschool and elementary education.* New York: Cambridge University Press.

Mallory, B. (1998). Educating young children with developmental differences: Principles of inclusive practice. In C. Seefeldt & A. Galper (Eds.), *Continuing issues in early childhood education* (2nd ed., pp. 213–237). Columbus, OH: Merrill/Prentice Hall.

Mallory, B., & New, R. (1994a). *Diversity and developmentally appropriate practices: Challenges for early childhood education.* New York: Teachers College Press.

Mallory, B., & New, R. (1994b). Social constructivist theory and principles of inclusion: Challenges for early childhood special education. *The Journal of Special Education, 28*(3), 322–337.

Metz, K. (1995). Reassessment of developmental constraints on children's science instruction. *Review of Educational Research, 65*(2), 93–127.

New, R. (1992). An integrated early childhood curriculum. In C. Seefeldt (Ed.), *The early childhood curriculum: A review of current research* (pp. 286–322). New York: Teachers College Press.

New, R. (1994). Culture, child development, and developmentally appropriate practices: An expanded role of teachers as collaborative researchers. In B. Mallory & R. New (Eds.), *Diversity and developmentally appropriate practices: Challenges for early childhood education* (pp. 65–83). New York: Teachers College Press.

New, R. (1997). Reggio Emilia's commitment to children and community: Reconceptualization of quality and DAP. *Canadian Children, 1,* 7–12.

New, R. (1998a). Diversity and early childhood education: Making room for everyone. In C. Seefeld & A. Galper (Eds.), *Continuing issues in early childhoood education* (2nd ed., pp. 238–267). Columbus, OH: Merrill/Prentice Hall.

New, R. (1998b). Theory and praxis in Reggio Emilia: They know what they are doing, and why. In C. Edwards, L. Gandini, & G. Forman (Eds.), *The hundred languages of children: The Reggio Emilia approach to early childhood education* (2nd ed., pp. 261–284). Norwood, NJ: Ablex.

New, R. (in press). Playing fair and square: Issues in preschool science, math, and technology. In *Dialogue on early childhood science, mathematics, and technology education.* Washington, DC: American Association for the Advancement of Science.

New, R., & Mallory, B. (1996). The paradox of diversity in early care and education. In E. J. Erwin (Ed.), *Putting children first: Visions for a brighter future for young children and their families* (pp. 143–167). Baltimore, MD: Brookes.

Newberger, J. (1997). New brain development research—A wonderful window of opportunity to build public support for early childhood education! *Young Children, 52*(4), 4–9.

Paley, V. (1994). *You can't say you can't play.* Cambridge, MA: Harvard University Press.

Paley, V. (1995). *Kwanzaa and me: A teacher's story.* Cambridge, MA: Harvard University Press.

Parker, J., & Asher, S. (1987). Peer relations and later personal adjustment: Are low-accepted children at risk? *Psychological Bulletin, 102*(3), 357–389.

Phillips, C. (1994). The movement of African-American children through sociocultural contexts: A case of conflict resolution. In B. Mallory & R. New (Eds.), *Diversity and developmentally appropriate practices: Challenge for early childhood education* (pp. 137–154). New York: Teachers College Press.

Pianta, R. C., & Walsh, D. J. (1996). *High-risk children in schools: Constructing sustaining relationships.* New York: Routledge.

Ramsey, P. (1998). *Teaching and learning in a diverse world: Multicultural education for young children* (2nd ed.). New York: Teachers College Press.

Rogoff, B. (1990). *Apprenticeship in thinking: Cognitive development in social context.* New York: Oxford University Press.

Silin, J. G. (1995). *Sex, death, and the education of children: Our passion for ignorance in the age of AIDS.* New York: Teachers College Press.

Simpson, P. J., & Garrison, J. (1996). Teaching and moral perception. *Teachers College Record, 97*(2), 252–278.

Smetana, J. G., Schlagman, N., & Adams, P. W. (1993). Preschool children's judgments about hypothetical and actual trangressions. *Child Development, 64,* 202–214.

Snow, C., Barnes, W., Chandler, J., Goodman, I., & Hemphill, L. (1991). *Unfulfilled expectations: Home and school influences on literacy.* Cambridge, MA: Harvard University Press.

Tharp, R., & Gallimore, R. (1988). *Rousing minds to life: Teaching, learning, and schooling in social context.* New York: Cambridge University Press.

Tobin, J., Wu, D., & Davidson, D. (1989). *Preschool in three cultures: Japan, China, and the U.S.* New Haven, CT: Yale University Press.

Vander Wilt, J. L., & Monroe, V. (1998). Successfully moving toward developmentally appropriate practice: It takes time and effort! *Young Children, 53*(4), 17–24.

Wellman, H. M., & Inagaki, K. (Eds.). (1997). *The emergence of core domains of thought: Children's reasoning about physical, psychological, and biological phenomena* (New Directions for Child Development No. 75). San Francisco: Jossey-Bass.

Wolery, M., & Wilbers, J. S. (Eds.). (1994). *Including children with special needs in early childhood programs.* (Research Monograph, Vol. 6). Washington, DC: National Association for the Education of Young Children.

Woodhead, M. (1996). In search of the rainbow: Pathways to quality in large-scale programmes for young disadvantaged children. *Early Childhood Development: Practice and Reflections* (10). The Hague, Netherlands: Bernard van Leer Foundation.

# About the Editor and the Contributors

**Carol Seefeldt** has been a Professor of Human Development at the Institute for Child Study, University of Maryland, for the past 28 years. She received the Distinguished Scholar–Teacher Award from the University of Maryland. Among the 20 books she has published are *Social Studies for the Preschool–Primary Child, Early Childhood Education: An Introduction,* and *Continuing Issues in Early Childhood Education.* Professor Seefeldt's research has revolved around intergenerational attitudes. Currently she is principal investigator of one of the 31 Head Start–Public School Transition Demonstrations, and her current research focuses on belief systems of former Head Start children, their parents, and their teachers.

---

**Patricia F. Campbell** is an Associate Professor of Mathematics Education in the Department of Curriculum and Instruction at the University of Maryland, College Park. She teaches both graduate and undergraduate courses in mathematics education. Currently, she is the principal investigator of a National Science Foundation–funded project addressing mathematics teaching and learning across kindergarten through fifth grade in Baltimore, Maryland. The project supports systemic reform in mathematics addressing curriculum, instruction, professional development, administrative support, and parent involvement.

**Rebekah Z. Fassler** is Assistant Professor of Early Childhood Education at St. John's University in New York City. She received her Ed.D. from Teachers College, Columbia University. A main focus in her research has been oral communication and emergent literacy in early childhood classrooms in which children have a wide variety of linguistic backgrounds.

**George E. Forman** is Professor of Education at the University of Massachusetts, Amherst. His research and writing cover early cognitive development, drawing to learn, constructivism in early education, exhibit design for children's museums, digital technology for children, and the analysis of the Reggio Emilia principles of teaching young children. He is the author of *The Child's Construction of Knowledge, Constructivist Play, Action, and Thought,* and *Constructivism in the Computer Age.*

**Doris Pronin Fromberg** is Professor of Education and Director, Early Childhood Teacher Education, Hofstra University. She has served as a teacher and administrator in public and private schools, as well as director of Teacher Corps projects. She is a past president of the National Association of Early Childhood Teacher Educators and chair of the Special Interest Group on Early Education and Child Development of the American Educational Research Association, through which she advocates for high-quality services for young children, with meaningful teacher and administrator certification. Among her publications are *The Full-Day Kindergarten: Planning and Practicing a Dynamic Themes Curriculum, Play from Birth to Twelve and Beyond* (co-edited with D. M. Bergen), and the *Encyclopedia of Early Childhood Education* (co-edited with L. R. Williams).

**Linda B. Gambrell** is Professor of Education in the College of Education at the University of Maryland, where she teaches graduate and undergraduate courses and conducts research. She has been an elementary classroom teacher and reading specialist in schools in Prince George's County, Maryland. She is the co-author of six books on reading instruction, including *Reading Comprehension in the Elementary School,* and numerous articles published in the *Journal of Educational Research.* Her primary interests are in the areas of reading comprehension strategy instruction, literacy motivation, and the role of discussion in teaching and learning. From 1992 to 1995 she served as an elected member of the Board of Directors of the International Reading Association. Her most recent publication is *Lively Discussions: Fostering Reading Engagement.* She received the International Reading Association's Outstanding Teacher Education in Reading award in 1998.

**Celia Genishi** is Professor of Education in the Program in Early Childhood Education and was Chair of the Department of Curriculum and Teaching at Teachers College, Columbia University. She is a former secondary school Spanish and preschool teacher and now teaches courses related to early childhood education and qualitative research methods. She is co-author of *Language Assessment in the Early Years, Ways of Assessing Children and Curriculum,* and *The Need for Story: Cultural Diversity in Classroom and Community.* Her research interests include collaborative research with teachers on alternative assessment, childhood bilingualism, and language use in classrooms.

**Eva Horn** is Assistant Professor of Special Education at Peabody College of Vanderbilt University. She also serves as chair of the Program in Early Childhood Special Education and as a Kennedy Center Scientist at Peabody. She has 10 years of teaching experience with young children with multiple and severe disabilities. She served as a Project Coordinator for the Peabody Integration Project for Children with dual sensory impairments, as a Principal Investigator researching motor skills development of young children with cerebral palsy, and as Co-Director of an early childhood special education model demonstration project. Currently she is an investigator at the Early Childhood Research Institute on Inclusion, University of Washington.

**Richard K. Jantz** is Professor of Education at the University of Maryland, College Park. He has been a member of the faculty for the past 25 years. His scholarly interests include the teaching and learning of concepts related to elementary school social studies and the preparation of elementary school teachers. He has published several chapters on teaching elementary school and early childhood social studies, as well as articles in journals such as *Theory and Research in Social Education, Social Education, The Social Studies, International Journal for the Social Studies,* and *Elementary School Journal.*

**Christopher E. Landry** has a strong interest in the application of learning theory to the design of interactive museum exhibits for children. A veteran of both children's museums and history museums, he has developed a wide variety of educational exhibits and programs in the arts and sciences. He currently serves as Executive Director of Historic Deerfield, Inc.

**Joan Lieber** is Associate Professor of Special Education at the University of Maryland. She taught in public school, elementary and preschool classrooms for 8 years. Her research focuses on how differences in the environments available to children with disabilities affect their participation and their social competence. She is also interested in facilitating relationships among adults who work together in inclusive preschool programs. She is an investigator at the Early Childhood Research Institute on Inclusion, University of Washington, and Co-Director of an inservice project to facilitate teachers' collaboration skills funded by the U.S. Department of Education.

**Susan Anders Mazzoni** is a doctoral fellow in the Department of Curriculum and Instruction at the University of Maryland, College Park, where she is studying reading education. She is also a research assistant at the University and teaches undergraduate reading methods. She has co-authored chapters in books on reading and reading methodology and published articles in *The Reading Teacher.* Ms. Mazzoni has taught in Baltimore County and Baltimore City schools since 1988. She is a member of the International Reading Association and Phi Delta Kappa. Her research interests are in the areas of reading motivation, discussion, and comprehension strategies.

**Marie McCarthy** is Associate Professor in the School of Music at the University of Maryland, College Park, where she teaches courses on elementary and middle school general music, music cultures in classrooms, and music learning theory and research. Her research interests include music as a cultural expression with implications for music teaching and learning, the influence of sociocultural factors on the historical development of music education internationally, the philosophy of multiculturalism, and gender issues in music education. Her publications have appeared in the *Journal of Research in Music Education, The Bulletin of Historical Research in Music Education, Irish Musical Studies,* and the *International Journal of Music Education,* and she has written *Passing It On: Music in Irish Culture.* She is active as a clinician and conducts teacher inservice workshops on world music and dance in the general music curriculum.

**Rebecca S. New** is Associate Professor of Early Childhood Education at the University of New Hampshire, where she teaches graduate and undergraduate courses. She has been conducting cross-cultural research on child-rearing practices in Italy for the past 15 years. As a part of her research she has studied children and early childhood education in the city of Reggio Emilia.

**Susan Sandall** is the Research Coordinator for the Early Childhood Research Institute on Inclusion at the University of Washington. Her initial work was as a teacher at the Center on Human Development Preschool at the University of Oregon. While in graduate school, she coordinated the program for infants with disabilities and their families at the Experimental Education Unit. As a faculty member at the University of Colorado at Denver and the University of Delaware, she coordinated personnel preparation efforts in early intervention and early childhood special education.

**Ilene Schwartz** is Associate Professor in the College of Education at the University of Washington and works closely with the inclusive preschool programs at the Experimental Education Unit. Her research focuses on autism, communication skills, and children's social relationships, and the implementation of systematic instruction in acceptable and sustainable ways in inclusive classrooms. She is an investigator with the Early Childhood Research Institute on Inclusion at the University of Washington, and the principal investigator on a model demonstration project examining school-based services for children with autism. She is the co-author of *The Exceptional Child: Inclusion in Early Childhood Education.*

**Lourdes Diaz Soto,** Associate Professor at the University of Pennsylvania, is Coordinator of Bilingual/Multicultural Programs. She has taught diverse early childhood, elementary, secondary, and university students since 1970. She has authored numerous research articles, received a Spencer Grant, and is the author of *Language, Culture and Power: Bilingual Families and the Struggle for Quality Education.* Her most recent work has examined issues of equity and social justice. She serves on the Professional Development Panel, chairs the Bilingual Caucus, and is past president of the Pennsylvania Association for Bilingual Education and past chair of the Early Childhood Special Interest Group of the National Association for Bilingual Education.

**Cherie K. Stellaccio** has performed extensively for the Maryland State Arts Council's Artists-in-Education program and is the recipient of several awards for her performances of American folk and contemporary music. Ms. Stellaccio serves as adjunct lecturer in music education for the University of Maryland and teaches courses in music education, theory, and voice at Anne Arundel Community College. Her research interests center on multicultural curriculum development in general music education and assessment in music/movement education. Her publications have appeared in *Teaching Music, China Music,* and other professional journals. She is an active clinician and consultant for the Peabody Outreach Program of Johns Hopkins University and a music curriculum consultant to preschools and day-care centers.

**Leslie R. Williams,** Professor of Early Childhood Education at Teachers College, Columbia University, is a curriculum developer and teacher educator who focuses on the collaborative refinement of practice with experienced teachers. Her special interests include multicultural education and the history, philosophy, and theoretical foundations of the early childhood field. She is co-editor of the *Encyclopedia of Early Childhood Education* and co-author of two texts on multicultural early childhood curriculum, as well as the author of articles on early childhood education in both practitioner and research journals.

**Ruth Ashworth Wolery** is Research Coordinator at the University of North Carolina at Chapel Hill. She received her Ph.D. in Learning Disabilities from the University of Pittsburgh. She was a first-grade and special education teacher for 14 years. Her current research interests are literacy development in young children with disabilities and staff development.

# Index